THE DEVELOPMENT OF COMMUNICATION

From Social Interaction to Language

David J. Messer
University of Hertfordshire, UK

JOHN WILEY & SONS

Chichester · New York · Brisbane · Toronto · Singapore

Copyright © 1994 by John Wiley & Sons Ltd,
Baffins Lane, Chichester,
West Sussex PO19 1UD, England

Telephone National (01243) 779777
International (+44) 1243 779777

First published in paperback April 1995

Other Wiley Editorial Offices

John Wiley & Sons, Inc., 605 Third Avenue,
New York, NY 10158-0012, USA

Jacaranda Wiley Ltd, 33 Park Road, Milton,
Queensland 4064, Australia

John Wiley & Sons (Canada) Ltd, 22 Worcester Road,
Rexdale, Ontario M9W 1L1, Canada

John Wiley & Sons (SEA) Pte Ltd, 37 Jalan Pemimpin #05-04,
Block B, Union Industrial Building, Singapore 2057

British Library Cataloguing in Publication Data

A catalogue record for this book is available from the British Library

ISBN 0-471-94076-3
ISBN 0-471-95838 (pbk)

Typeset in 10/12pt Palatino from editor's disks by Production Technology Department,
John Wiley & Sons Ltd, Chichester
Printed and bound in Great Britain by Biddles Ltd, Guildford, Surrey

THE
DEVELOPMENT OF
COMMUNICATION

For my Father
in memory of my Mother

CONTENTS

PREFACE

This book concerns the development of communication from birth to about 3 years. In some cases this age span has been extended to include relevant and interesting material. The chapters follow a rough chronological order, but because there are different approaches to language acquisition it has been necessary sometimes to break this order and instead supply cross-references to other material.

The aim of the book is to give an idea of the different traditions and areas of study which impinge on the development of communication. This topic is of concern to many disciplines, including psychology, linguistics, education, and philosophy. In turn all these disciplines provide important perspectives and explanations about this process. The study of communication and in particular language continues to be a field where there are vigorous debates about nature/nurture, learning/cognition, modular/general abilities, and rule-based/connectionist views. As a result, the study of the development of communication and language is now an enormous enterprise, and there is a very real danger that investigators who take one approach will lose sight of the work in related and relevant areas. Thus, another aim of this book is to provide a meeting point for different perspectives so that a more holistic view of development can be obtained. One emphasis in the book is the importance of social processes in the development of communication; this reflects my personal interests and reflects my belief that the contribution of this area is still sadly neglected.

The book starts with considering aspects of early communication that are present in the first days and weeks of life. This provides a starting point to think about the process of communication. Chapter 2 builds on this with an outline of different theoretical positions espoused by important figures in this field. These theories provide a context for the later chapters, but the theories are not of a type that permits a simple test to prove or disprove them. The third chapter continues the examination of early communication in the first half year of life. This discusses the types of social interaction that occur, and the way that social interaction is organised.

Chapter 4 marks the beginning of the explicit consideration of speech processes. This chapter provides answers to the question of how children identify the referent of adult speech, an important process in the acquisition of words; and also examines the features of interaction which are associated with the acquisition of larger vocabularies by children in the second year of life. Chapter 5 returns to younger infants to review the development of vocal abilities and this leads on to a consideration of the production of the first words. However, being able to use words is not simply a matter of vocal development and the learning of associations between words and referents, it also involves concepts and category formation dealt with in Chapter 6, together with the understanding of meaning in Chapter 7. Issues related to the use of one-word speech are also considered in Chapter 7. The theme of lexical development is continued in Chapter 8 where there is a review of ideas about pre-school children having constraints and assumptions which will help them acquire words on the basis of a brief example.

A change in emphasis occurs in Chapter 9. Up to this point the main interest has been in the development of pre-linguistic communication. This chapter begins with a discussion of definitions of language, followed by an examination of the first multi-word utterances in children, and then a discussion of ape "language". The next two chapters examine linguistic perspectives about language acquisition, outlining Chomsky's theories and then reviewing research relevant to his work. An alternative perspective from cognitive science is discussed in Chapter 13. Chapter 14 initially deals with a practical issue, the effect of the modifications of adults' speech on language acquisition, although it becomes apparent that this practical issue has an important theoretical dimension.

The last two chapters draw on all the previous material to examine the development of communication in children with disabilities. Chapter 15 reviews the acquisition of language in children who experience sensory deprivation, isolation, deafness and blindness. These studies are important because of the practical information that is obtained and they are also theoretically important in telling us what is possible when only certain sorts of information are available from the environment. Similarly, studies of children with learning disabilities such as autism, Down's syndrome and William's syndrome are of practical and theoretical significance. The development of communication of these children is examined in the last chapter.

This book deals with many of the important issues in the understanding of early communicative development. I hope you have a good read of a very interesting subject.

ACKNOWLEDGEMENTS

Although the section is short the gratitude is large. First and foremost is the gratitude to my family, who have had to deal with absences at early morning and at weekends, together with computers on holiday (and the very occasional bad temper as deadlines loomed and were missed). Unfortunately writing about development means missing development.

I have also very much appreciated the time given by colleagues who provided criticism and advice. The comments of Martyn Barrett, John Clibbens, Paul Coates, Julie Dockrell, Alison Green, Pat Hasan, Rita Jordan, Eeva Leinonen, Sarah Libby, Jean Mandler, Lesley Messer, Lynne Murray, Alan Slater and Pam Smith have been invaluable. A special acknowledgement is due to Glyn Collis for previous collaborations which have provided the basis for material in the early chapters. I have also appreciated the comments of various tutorial groups at the University of Hertfordshire on drafts of the chapters. Special thanks also go to Jean Thomas for her unstinting work to make order out of the chaos of my references, and to Noel Lawler for recovering files when I most needed them. I would also like to thank Michael Coombs for initiating this enterprise and Wendy Hudlass for her patience and support.

1

THE BEGINNINGS OF SOCIAL BEHAVIOUR AND COMMUNICATION

The most important development in the growth of human communication is the ability to use language. For parents and researchers the way children start to use speech is still a mystery and a source of fascination. For parents, the use of the first words is usually marked with excitement and interest. For researchers, the fact that there is a change from a newborn to a talking child in two years continues to be a source of wonder and perplexity.

During the first months of a child's life, the lack of speech does not of course prevent social interaction and communication from occurring between infants and adults. It is also apparent that this social interaction and communication is rather special and different from that occurring at older ages. During the first three or four months, social interaction typically occurs without objects or external events serving as a topic or focus of the interaction. The most obvious questions about this early social behaviour are: what contributions do infants make to it? and how is it related to later communicative development? This chapter examines the way very young infants are specially adapted to interact and communicate with adults. In order to provide some structure to the discussion I will distinguish different forms of social and communicative preparedness.

At the most simple level, infants may be orientated only to people and give more attention to people than to other things. If this were the case, newborns would have a predisposition to attend to people and social activities, but would not have the capacity to do much more than appear interested in what people do. The issue of an orientation to people is considered in the first section of this chapter.

A second question is whether infants are more receptive to special people, such as parents, and are able to distinguish them from other adults. If this were the case, newborns would be able to identify those adults who are likely to be the primary source of social and communicative experiences. In this way, they would be in a better position to develop a special relationship with these adults, and to develop a shared understanding of communication. The second section addresses this question.

A further dimension of preparedness is not just attending to people but also having a set of behaviours which adults regard as social. If this were the case then adults would be more likely to become involved in social activities with their baby. An outline of such behaviours is given in the third section.

How do these forms of preparedness relate to the development of communication? If infants pay special attention to people and if they are able to produce social behaviours, then they start off in life with a basic repertoire that will aid the growth of communicative abilities. The benefits of such a repertoire should not be underestimated. Being orientated to people means that infants can observe and gain information from them. This orientation also signals a readiness to engage in social interaction, an invitation that is often responded to by adults. Equally importantly the production of socially appropriate behaviours by infants, such as smiling, will help to initiate and maintain social interaction by making it rewarding to adults. The possession of this basic repertoire enables infants to be involved in social interaction, and in this way they can acquire further communicative and social skills that are appropriate to their culture.

Before considering the question of the ways infants are adapted to communicate with people, it is worth putting this question in a broader context of one of the longest running debates in the study of human behaviour. This is the debate between nativists and empiricists, or as it is often termed, between nature and nurture. The basic question is whether human attributes are a product of the genetic make up of an individual (nativist and nature) or are acquired through experience (empiricist and nurture). In terms of the development of communication this question concerns whether newborns have capacities which help them to take part in social interaction (nativist), or whether such abilities are absent and need to be acquired (empiricist).

This general debate occurred in the eighteenth century, with an empiricist position being espoused by Locke, and a nativist position by Rousseau. In the last 50 years the pendulum of opinion has swung from one direction to the other. The reaction against introspection by the behaviourists led to an emphasis in the 1930s, 1940s and 1950s on knowledge being acquired by learning. Such an approach emphasised the role of experience. However, a further reaction against this occurred in the late 1950s and early 1960s in a number of areas. One of the most influential positions was in linguistics with Chomsky's attack on Skinner's use of learning as a way of accounting for the acquisition of language, and Chomsky's argument that there must be an innate capacity for this process. This wish to demonstrate the sophisticated (and possibly innate) capacities of infants became something of a bandwagon during the 1960s and 1970s. Since then there has been less tendency for a prevailing orthodoxy, however, and as we will see in this chapter the issue of innate capacities still serves to motivate research and argument.

IS THERE AN ORIENTATION TO PEOPLE?

If infants came into the world without an orientation to people then they would be unable to make any fundamental distinction between inanimate and social phenomena. If this were the case then newborn babies might not find adults any more interesting than a mobile placed above their crib. Treating humans and inanimate objects in a similar way would have disastrous results, as social interaction might be inappropriately directed at inanimate objects. Another serious consequence would be the difficulty of identifying appropriate entities that would provide a model for learning about social interaction. In fact a whole array of research of the last 30 years points to babies having a special orientation to people. This research has concerned people's voices, their faces, their odour, and their movement.

Are Infants Interested in Human Speech?

The hearing of newborn infants is not quite as sensitive as that of adults. Infants appear to find the human voice particularly salient (Aslin, 1987). In general, babies prefer higher pitched to lower pitched sounds, that is they prefer higher musical notes to the lower ones (Kessen, Haith & Salapatek, 1970), and they prefer sounds which contain a number of musical notes to those with single notes (Eisenberg, 1976).

Adults' speech to infants is usually different from speech among adults, it has a higher pitch, greater range of pitch, and is simpler in meaning (see Chapter 14 for a fuller discussion). The modified speech is often termed A–C speech (adult to child speech, it is also called motherese and adultese). It would appear that soon after birth infants have a preference for A–C speech over the type of speech that occurs between adults (Cooper & Aslin, 1990).

What are the characteristics of A–C speech that make it attractive? Fernald & Kuhl (1987) compared A–C speech and adult conversation in terms of fundamental frequency (this can be thought of as the general pitch of the sound), amplitude (i.e. loudness), and duration of sounds. The speech was transformed by computer analysis so that adult conversations and A–C speech only differed in one or two relevant dimensions (e.g. fundamental frequency or duration). Infants preferred to listen to the fundamental frequency of A–C speech, but showed no preference for the other dimensions. As these infants were studied at 4 months it is difficult to know whether the preference is a result of experience, or is an innate preference.

Infants have another surprising capacity. By one month, infants are able to distinguish between different speech phonemes (Eimas, Siqueland, Jusczyk & Vigorito, 1971). A phoneme is the smallest unit of sound that can be identified in a language. Acoustically the difference between a "p" sound as in "pa", and "b" as in "ba" is small, but the difference is significant for the understanding of words. For "b" sounds the vocal chords vibrate at the time the lips begin to open, in the case of the "p" the vocal chords vibrate after the lips open. This delay is usually referred to as the VOT (voice onset time). Sounds with a VOT of less than 25 milliseconds tend to be heard as a "p", and over 25 milliseconds tend to be heard as a "b".

What is interesting is that although speech sounds are on an acoustic continuum, adults tend to categorise sounds and do not detect differences within a category. As a result, we hear a difference between "p" and "b", but are much less aware of differences between "b"s with different VOTs. Without this capacity it would be difficult to differentiate similar sounds which are said by different people on different occasions.

In the experiment by Eimas et al., infants responded not according to the size of the acoustic difference in VOT between "p" and "b", but according to whether the sounds were at different sides of the +25 millisecond boundary in adult auditory perception. Thus, two sounds which were 10 milliseconds apart but were on the same side of the +25 millisecond boundary would be treated as similar, but sounds which differed by the same amount and crossed the boundary would be treated as different. This suggests that infants, like adults, categorise the sounds of speech.

An initial reaction to these findings was that infants may be tuned in to the sound structure of speech. However, it has been found that this phenomenon is not a uniquely human capacity, since chinchillas (Kuhl & Miller, 1975) and macaque monkeys respond in a similar way (Kuhl, 1981). Another interesting twist to this story is that although Spanish and Kikuyu adults cannot make certain phonemic distinctions their infants can. In both cases the children appear to lose the capacity to make a distinction between "b" and "p" during development (Lasky, Syrdal-Lasky & Klein, 1975; Streeter, 1976). Related research on Japanese infants has indicated that the ability to make certain phonemic distinctions is lost by 12 months.

These investigations raise questions about evolutionary adaptation. Have infants become adapted to the phonemic structure of language, or has speech become adapted to the auditory capacities of infants? The fact that chinchillas and macaques make similar responses to phonemic distinctions as humans suggests that speech may have become adapted to infants' auditory capacities.

The Attractiveness of Faces

Faces attract the interest of infants. Newborns can focus best on stimuli about 1 metre from their faces, and as Stern (1977) has suggested, this may direct their attention to those adults who come close to them. There is plenty of evidence that the human face contains many of the perceptual qualities that infants find attractive. These include: movement (Carpenter, 1974), the three-dimensional rather than two-dimensional nature of the stimuli (Fantz, 1966), contrast between light and dark (Slater, Cooper, Rose & Morison, 1989), a preference for curved rather than straight lines (Fantz & Miranda, 1975), and a preference for symmetry around a vertical axis rather than a horizontal axis (Bornstein & Krinsky, 1985).

There has been a long-standing debate about whether the general visual properties of faces make them interesting to infants, or whether the interest is due to the specific arrangement of features. A recent re-examination of this question has been made by Kleiner (1987). She argues that infants simply prefer stimuli with high *amplitude*, they do not have a special preference for faces. Amplitude can be thought of as being related to the energy a stimulus produces, a stimulus with high contrast (a large difference between the brightest and darkest parts) has high amplitude. As we will see, Johnson and Morton (1991) disagree with this position and suggest there are complex developments which govern infants' interest in faces.

Faces are not special

Kleiner's investigations involved comparing infant interest in a diagrammatic face with other stimuli that either had the amplitude of the face or had the same pattern of visual features. To make these comparisons computer programs transformed the stimuli A and B in Figure 1.1 to give the stimuli C and D which contain characteristics of the diagrammatic face and of the squares.

Figure 1.1 The stimuli used in Kleiner's study of visual preference (reproduced with permission from K. A. Kleiner (1987) Amplitude and phase spectra as indices of infants' pattern preferences. *Infant Behavior and Development, 10*)

Stimulus D has the amplitude of the face and the pattern arrangement (termed phase structure) of the squares. If the only influence on infant interest is amplitude then stimulus D should be treated by infants as being equivalent to the diagrammatic face (A): both contain the same amplitude. However, if infants respond to visual pattern then stimulus D should be less attractive than the diagrammatic face, this is because only the face has the preferred visual pattern.

Thus, by comparing infant preference for stimuli A and D competing predictions about the reason for the attractiveness of faces can be tested. In this case the findings supported the prediction that the pattern arrangement influences infant preference. Other predictions can be derived on a similar basis. For example, those involving stimulus C are made on the basis that this stimulus has the amplitude of the squares and the pattern arrangement of the face. The complete set of predictions that Kleiner derived for amplitude hypothesis was $A>B$, $C<D$, $B=C$, $D=A$, $A>C$, and $B<D$.

In Kleiner's study infants who were less than 3 days old were simultaneously presented with pairs of stimuli, and the time they looked at each one was recorded. This type of task is usually referred to as a *preferential looking task*. Analysis of the data revealed that all the predictions were supported except the one that has been mentioned. On the basis of the general trend of findings Kleiner concluded that amplitude provides a better predictor of preference than face-like appearance.

Using the same paradigm, 2-month-old infants have been found to have a preference for diagrammatic faces over patterns with the same amplitude (Kleiner & Banks, 1987). A similar development has been reported by Dannemiller and Stephens (1988). They found that at 6 weeks infants did not show preference for any of the stimuli, but at 12 weeks stimulus A was preferred to B and D (see Figure 1.2). These stimuli were created to ensure that they contained the same amount of white and dark areas. It is likely that these changes are a result of the infants' contact with adults, or because of maturation of the visual system.

An alternative view: faces are special

The opposite view to that of Kleiner, is that faces are attractive because of their special arrangement of features. There are findings that support this viewpoint. Newborn babies, less than an hour old, have been found to prefer to *follow* two-dimensional schematic face patterns more than control patterns. The control patterns consisted of a random arrangement of the facial elements (Goren, Sarty & Wu, 1975; Dziurawiec & Ellis, 1986; see Figure 1.3 for an example of the stimuli). In these studies the degree of head

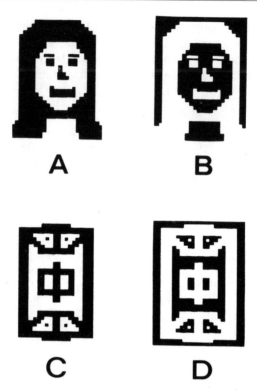

Figure 1.2 The stimuli used in Dannemiller and Stephens' study of infant and visual preferences (reproduced with permission from J. L. Dannemiller & B. R. Stephens (1988) A critical test of infant pattern preference models. *Child Development*, **59**, 212; © 1988 Society for Research in Child Development)

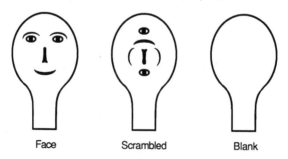

Figure 1.3 The type of stimuli used in Goren, Sarty and Wu's (1975) study of visual tracking (reproduced with permission from M. H. Johnson & J. Morton (1991) *Biology and Cognitive Development: The Case of Face Recognition*. Oxford: Blackwell)

turning the infant made to a slowly moving schematic face was recorded, and this was used to provide an indication of visual preference (the more the head turned the more the infant was assumed to be attracted to the stimulus).

Thus, investigations by Kleiner using the visual preference paradigm have found that infants usually respond to amplitude rather than the configuration of facial stimuli. In contrast, investigations using the visual following paradigm have revealed a preference for faces over comparable stimuli.

An explanation of the attractiveness of faces

Some resolution between the conflicting findings and interpretations comes from a model developed by Johnson and Morton (1991). They have argued that very young infants' reaction to faces can be explained by the presence of two features, termed *conspec* and *conlern*, which play a part in directing the infants' visual system.

Conspec is believed to contain information about the characteristics of human faces, and this is innate information available at birth. The information is in a primitive form so that infants will treat schematic faces in a similar manner to real ones. Johnson and Morton suppose that when infants identify a stimulus with the correct schematic characteristics they will follow it when it moves. From this they predict that newborn infants should be attracted to human faces, rather than other comparable stimuli. Support for this prediction comes, as we have seen, from Goren, Sarty and Wu (1975), Dziurawiec and Ellis (1986), and from Johnson and Morton's replication of these studies. Other research by Johnson and Morton suggests that this pattern of following continues until about 4 weeks, thereafter no significant preference is shown for a schematic face when a *visual tracking task* is used (see Figure 1.4; note at 8 weeks a preference was found for static faces over other comparable stimuli by Kleiner & Banks, 1987).

Because Johnson and Morton regard the attractiveness of faces as being due to the presence of special features, they take issue with the claim that stimulus amplitude can account for infants' response to faces (e.g. Kleiner's work). Johnson and Morton argue that the one failure in Kleiner's predictions indicates that infants are not responding to stimuli solely on the basis of amplitude (she found a diagrammatic face was preferred to a transformed stimulus of the same amplitude). Johnson and Morton also cite the findings from the visual following studies as support for their model (Goren, Sarty & Wu, 1975; Dziurawiec & Ellis, 1986; Johnson & Morton, 1991). In these studies, it may be recalled, schematic faces were more attractive than control stimuli containing a rearrangement of the facial elements (the amplitude of these two types of stimuli should be about equal).

Figure 1.4   The testing of infant visual tracking (reproduced with permission from M. H. Johnson & J. Morton (1991) *Biology and Cognitive Development: The Case of Face Recognition*. Oxford: Blackwell. Copyright ©1991 Priscilla Barrett)

However, Johnson and Morton have some difficulties in explaining one of their own findings. They report that newborns prefer a chequer board pattern (i.e. a high amplitude stimulus) to a schematic human face. A finding which Kleiner might have liked to report because it indicates the importance of stimulus amplitude! This leads Johnson and Morton to suggest that stimulus amplitude provides a good predictor of infants' preference for non-face-like stimuli, but when the amplitudes of two stimuli are similar (or mildly different), the one with the features of a face will be more attractive. In other words faces may be special, but are not always more attractive than other stimuli.

The development of conspec and conlern

As we have seen, Johnson and Morton suppose that the function of conspec is to direct infants' attention to faces. They believe that this allows a device called *conlern* to acquire information about the visual characteristics of frequently seen faces. Thus, conspec allows infants to identify human faces and attend to them, and conlern acquires information about particular faces so that they can be recognised. In this way conlern may later help to establish contact and initiate interaction with individuals who are going to be important to infants.

Another issue that Johnson and Morton address is the question of when a preference for faces begins. The findings from studies using the visual following paradigm suggest that newborns have a preference for faces. In contrast, when using the *visual preference* paradigm, schematic faces are only found to be more attractive than scrambled faces after about 2 months (Maurer & Barrera, 1981; Kleiner & Banks, 1987; Dannemiller & Stephens, 1988; Johnson & Morton, 1991).

Johnson and Morton suggest that the two methodologies are assessing different psychophysiological processes. They believe that the tracking task involves a subcortical, automatic, following response which is mediated by conspec and is present at birth. Later on, at about 2 months, they suppose that the cortically mediated conlern process becomes operational. This enables infants to respond to show a choice to diagrammatic faces in the visual preference tasks.

Unfortunately for these proposals there is evidence that visual preferences occur before conlern is supposed to be operational, and this disagrees with Johnson and Morton's predictions. Kleiner found visual preferences in neonates without using a visual tracking paradigm. In addition, as we will see later, infants have been found to show a preference for their mother's rather than a stranger's face within a few hours of birth (Bushnell, Sai & Mullin, 1989). Another problem is that the experimental evidence for conlern existing in human infants mostly rests on extrapolation from work with hen chicks, rather than clear experimental evidence showing the way infant preference emerges for certain adult faces.

I have paid some attention to the issue of whether infants have a special interest in human faces. It would seem that both amplitude and pattern arrangements are important in influencing infant visual attention. The issue is a complex one, and the answers that we have so far contain more uncertainties than we might wish. However, I hope that by going into these studies in some detail it is possible to convey some of the problems of conducting work with infants, and to highlight the ways in which issues change as more complex processes are uncovered in attempting to answer the original question.

Are Infants Interested in the Movement of Adults?

Not only do infants prefer human speech and faces, but they also seem to prefer to watch the types of movements made by humans. A record was made of light points which were attached to the joints of people. This record of moving lights was then transformed by a computer to give a pattern of movement that would not be possible for humans; for example, joints were made to move in the wrong way. Infants of 3 months preferred to look at the lights from a person walking rather than the computer-generated displays (Bertenthal, Proffitt, Spetner & Thomas, 1985). In addition, it is reported that an upside down figure is not distinguished from a similar figure with random movements (Bertenthal & Proffitt, 1986).

Butterworth (1990) has argued that these findings are congruent with a theory that supposes that infants perceive many aspects of their world as a unified coherent source, the individual elements are not perceived in isolation, but are linked and related.

Summary

The findings from these studies suggest that by at least 3–4 months infants have a well established preference for people over other equivalent stimuli. In addition, there is reasonably good evidence that a preference for faces and for A–C speech is present in newborn infants. These abilities have important consequences for social interaction and the development of communication.

IS THERE AN ORIENTATION TO SPECIAL PEOPLE?

Very young infants have a preference for people over comparable stimuli, do they have a preference for certain people over others? Do they prefer their mothers (and perhaps fathers) to other people? Such a preference, as I have already argued, would ensure that infants are orientated to those adults who are most likely to socially interact and communicate with them. This should assist the development of social and communicative abilities since infants would be able to identify those adults with whom they come into regular contact. As a result infants could more easily develop a shared repertoire of communicative activities and a shared knowledge about the world.

A Preference for the Mother's Voice?

The inability of newborns to make precise movements makes it difficult to study their reactions to sounds, or to allow them to identify the sort of sounds they prefer. One ability that newborns have which is relatively well advanced is their ability to suck and control the rate of sucking. It has been known for some time that babies will alter their rate of sucking when doing so will switch on a sound. Using this technique it has been found that day-old infants will alter their sucking so that they can hear their mother's rather than a stranger's voice reading a story (DeCasper & Fifer, 1980). Similar findings have been reported for a nursery rhyme which was sung before birth (Panneton & DeCasper, 1986) and a story that had been read prenatally (DeCasper & Spence, 1986). Even more remarkably, newborns will prefer to listen to speech sounds which are transformed to make them more similar to the way sounds would be perceived inside the womb, rather than speech spoken in the normal manner (Fifer & Moon, 1989). Thus, newborns seem to prefer to listen to sounds they have heard before—they have even shown a preference for the theme tune of the popular TV soap "Neighbours" (Hepper, 1991), presumably because they have heard it countless times while in the womb. As a result of this preference for the familiar, infants will be more interested in their mother's voice than other similar sounds.

A Preference for Mother's Face?

Not only do newborn infants make a special response to their mother's voice, but more remarkably they also seem to prefer their mother's face to that of another female (Field, Cohen, Garcia & Greenberg, 1984; Bushnell, Sai & Mullin, 1989). Bushnell, Sai and Mullin have reported that newborns looked longer at their mother than at a stranger, even when a control was used for olfactory cues and for mothers attracting their infants' attention. Walton, Bower and Bower (1992) report that slightly older infants, aged 12–36 hours, will suck more to see their mother's face presented on a video screen than for a stranger's face.

To explain their findings Bushnell, Sai and Mullin suggest that infants may very quickly acquire the ability to identify their mothers on the basis of non-visual prenatal experiences, such as hearing the voice of the mother while being inside the womb, and gaining olfactory cues from amniotic fluids. This identification can then provide a basis for the rapid learning of the visual features of their mothers.

It is worth noting that these findings pose a problem for Johnson and Morton's model of the way infants' preference for faces develops. If new-borns can recognise their mothers' faces in the first few days of life then either there must be a very rapid shift from conspec to conlern, which makes for difficulties in other parts of their model, or the hypothesis about conlern is incorrect, since it is supposed to make its appearance from about 2 months of age.

Studies of older infants have sometimes failed to find a preference for the mother's rather than a stranger's face. These studies have typically used photographs rather than an actual face, and this may account for a poorer ability at older ages. One month olds have not been found to look longer at photographs of their mother's face than that of a stranger (Melhuish, 1982). Other experiments using photographs have found a preference for the mother's face at 5 weeks, but this preference seems to be based on differences in the outer shape of the face rather than its internal configuration (Bushnell, 1982). Such a finding is not that surprising as infants who are less than a month old tend to look at the edges of shapes. At about 8 weeks infants begin to look more at the internal features of a stimulus (Maurer & Salapatek, 1976), and even by 5 weeks infants pay special attention to the eyes (Haith, Bergman & Moore, 1977). As a result one would expect a better discrimination of faces, a greater awareness of the content of any facial communication, and the establishment of social contact with another person.

A Preference for Mother's Odour?

It is apparent that sound and sight are important bases for identifying special people. Humans usually pay much less attention to odour but even so it would appear that infants are able to make use of this cue. A widely quoted study by MacFarlane (1975) found that infants older than 6 days reliably turned towards a pad which had been in contact with their mother's breast, rather than a breast pad from another mother.

The precise mechanism which causes this effect is not yet clear. However, there is evidence that infants respond (and possibly prefer) odours with which they are familiar. For example, one study exposed infants to the smell of cherry or of ginger in the first day of life, and then tested for preference on the next day. The findings indicated that female infants turned reliably to the odour to which they had been exposed while the responses of males were inconsistent (Balogh & Porter, 1986). Similarly, it has been found that 2-week-old breast-fed babies turned towards pads which contained the underarm odour of their own mother rather than that of another mother. Bottle-fed infants are not in such close contact with their mother, and these infants do not distinguish the underarm odour of their mother from that of a stranger. Furthermore, breast-fed infants do not reliably distinguish between the odour from their father and that from an unrelated male (Cernoch & Porter, 1985). All this supports the idea that close familiarity with an odour will lead to preference for that odour.

Summary

What is fascinating from all of these three areas of research is that exposure of the infant to a particular person prior to birth, or shortly after birth, seems to lead to preference for the sight, sound and smell of that person. The person most associated with these sounds, sights and smells is, of course, likely to be the infant's mother. Thus, it is clear that very early in life infants develop preferences for specific people. What is less clear is whether we should consider this to be a truly social capacity, or a result of familiarity.

It is also worth remembering that these preferences are not so powerful that newborns' behaviour is different with their mother in comparison to other adults. Nor do these preferences appear to be so powerful that they determine later relationships. Adoption within the first few months of life appears to cause minimal disruption to the infant (Yarrow, 1964), so these preferences may be useful tuning, but not be so powerful as to cause problems if someone other than the mother takes on the caregiving role.

THE SOCIAL REPERTOIRE OF INFANTS

In the first few months after birth, infants have neither the physical capacities (nor the cognitive capacities) to survive by themselves. Instead they have a repertoire of activities and capacities which enable them to survive in a social environment. For example, crying and smiling are two obvious and powerful forms of infant signalling; another potentially important capacity is the imitation of social behaviour.

Before discussing these three capacities it is worth noting that other actions which at first sight may not seem to be intrinsically communicative in nature, may nonetheless have important social implications. For example, although sucking may be primarily an act of feeding, it inevitably brings people into contact with the baby. It has even been suggested by Kaye (1977) that the structure of infant feeding, with a burst of sucks and then a pause, provides a structure for social interaction and interventions from the mother.

Crying

Adults find the cries of infants disturbing (Frodi, 1985) and they are likely to respond by picking up the infant and trying to remove the causes of the distress. As a result, crying can serve to initiate social interaction between adult and infant. Crying is a useful signal to alert parents to distress and discomfort, or when infants are overexcited and need to be calmer. It is also worth remembering that its power can have unfortunate consequences as unceasing crying is often reported as a precipitating factor in child abuse.

There is evidence that different sources of distress—pain, hunger, tiredness, etc.—elicit perceptually different types of cry (Wasz-Hockert, Lind, Vuorenkoski, Partanen & Valanne, 1968). Furthermore, it would appear that adults can distinguish between different types of cry: basic cry, angry cry, and pain cry. However, it is less clear whether adults can reliably distinguish cries according to the circumstances which elicited them. An experiment by Sherman (1927) investigated this issue. Infants 3–7 days old were subjected to the following: a 15 minute delay in feeding, being dropped 30–60 cm towards a table, being held down for 5 seconds, or having a needle stuck in his/her face four times. A variety of listeners could not distinguish between the cries produced by these experiences. Needless to say it is doubtful whether this study would pass present day ethical guidelines! Taken together, these two sets of findings suggest there is a need to find out more about the relationship between causes of different crying patterns, and the ability to distinguish between them.

There have been few investigations of young infants' non-cry vocalisations. An investigation by Papousek (1989) revealed that crying and some discomfort sounds of 2-month-old infants are reliably identified by adults, while others such as joy are less consistently identified.

Smiling

Like crying, smiling is a powerful signal. Infant smiles are useful indicators of pleasure for adults, and adults will work very hard at social activities to obtain a smile. Smiles can be seen in newborn infants but there usually is no clear external cause of such smiles. From about 2–3 months infants are likely to smile in response to various stimuli, especially those associated with humans. For example, they will smile when presented with the schematic characteristics of the human face. This responsiveness increases until about 4 months and then declines. At an early age a simple configuration of eye dots will elicit smiling, but as infants mature the more similar a stimulus is to the human face the more likely it is to cause a smile (Ahrens, 1954). By about 3 months infants are beginning to smile more at familiar than at unfamiliar people (Camras, Malatesta & Izard, 1991). Exposure to the smiling of other people does not seem to be necessary for the development of smiling as children who are blind start to smile at the same age as children with sight (Freeman, 1974). However, the development of smiling may be influenced by the overall maturation of the child and the availability of appropriate social experience. Studies of infants in institutions, which provided less stimulation than at home, found that the infants in institutions started smiling about a month later than those at home (Ambrose, 1961).

Infants also exhibit a variety of facial expressions which adults may interpret as expressive. A detailed analysis of the expressions of very young infants by Oster (1978) revealed a complexity that is done scant justice with descriptions such as "smiling" or "angry" face. Facial expressions which correspond to shock, distress, disgust, and simple smiling can be observed in newborns (Izard & Malatesta, 1987). By 3–4 months facial expressions corresponding to anger, surprise and sadness can be identified. What is unknown is the emotional basis of these very early facial expressions, and the relationship they have with adult emotions. However, at least by 2 months infants will reliably produce an expression in certain circumstances, such as distress when being inoculated (Izard, Hembree & Huebner, 1987).

Imitation

One surprising ability that has been reported in newborns is the ability to imitate actions of others, even when they cannot see their own action, as in the case of tongue protrusion and mouth opening. The findings from Meltzoff and Moore's experiments (1977, 1983a) challenged Piaget's observation and theory that imitation of new actions only occurs towards the end of the first year. Meltzoff and Moore suggested that imitation is possible because newborn infants can translate what they see into actions.

A study by Jacobson (1979) replicated the findings, but discovered that tongue protrusion and hand opening were elicited not only by the appropriate modelling behaviour of an adult, but also by moving a pen backwards and forwards, or a ring up and down. Jacobson interpreted her findings as indicating that infants' imitation is caused by a releasing mechanism which can be triggered by general classes of activities and is not the copying of specific behaviours. A similar type of finding is that infant imitation is more likely when they are exposed to moving facial expressions rather than static ones (Vinter, 1986). In older infants of 6 weeks Meltzoff and Moore (1992) report imitation of static facial expressions (mouth openings and tongue protrusion), and higher rates of imitation of static than of moving facial expressions. This may be partly due to improved perceptual abilities.

The infants' ability to imitate may cease within several weeks of birth. Abravanel and Sigafoos (1984) examined the occurrence of imitation between

4 and 21 weeks. They only found evidence of the partial imitation of tongue protrusion at 4–6 weeks. Abravanel and Sigafoos suggest that imitation may occur in the first few weeks after birth; the ability then declines only to re-emerge towards the end of the first year. However, more recently, Meltzoff and Moore (1992) have reported that the imitation of facial expressions continues until 3 months of age, thus reopening debate about this issue.

The claim that newborns can imitate has been disputed by a number of investigators. Hayes and Watson (1981) and Koepke, Hamm and Legerstee (1983) failed to replicate Meltzoff and Moore's findings. McKenzie and Over (1983a) reported that student judges were unable to reliably discriminate the effects of different models, and no significant difference was found in the frequency of imitative acts according to which model was presented.

Meltzoff and Moore (1983b) replied to these criticisms by suggesting: that the replications sometimes used video recordings which do not provide sufficient detail of the gestures to be imitated; that movements may have been too fast and have provided insufficient response time. These counter-criticisms have produced a rebuttal by McKenzie and Over (1983b).

Despite these disputes there has been a growing acceptance of the accuracy of the findings, and there have been fewer publications of "failure to replicate". More recently, Meltzoff and Gopnik (1993) have taken discussion further, putting forward the idea that imitation occurs because infants recognise that adults are like them and because infants recognise that they themselves can perform the same motor actions as adults. As a consequence, the infant's reaction to an adult is "here is something like me" (p. 336). Furthermore, Meltzoff and Gopnik suggest that the "like me" identification is based on infants being able to monitor their own body movements and being able to detect equivalent movements in others. This is seen as a cross-modal matching between their own movements that they detect by proprioception, and the movements of others which are identified through vision. Another important aspect of the "like me" process is that adults imitate the actions of infants, thus infants see their actions reflected back in the actions of others.

As imitation has been reported soon after birth Gopnik and Meltzoff (1986) suggest that the infant perception of adults being like themselves must occur at the same age. In addition, Meltzoff and Gopnik (1993) make the claim that infants have an innate assumption that the behaviour of an adult is related to the adult's mental state. They believe that this provides a basis for the development of theory of mind, the understanding that others have different mental states from oneself (see Chapter 14). Another related proposal is that the imitation of facial expressions may lead to the perception of the emotions that such expressions convey (there is some evidence for this in adults, Ekman, Levenson & Friesen, 1983; Zajonc, Murphy & Inglehart 1989). Thus, it is suggested that the infant's imitation of an adult's facial expressions may lead to the perception and therefore understanding of the adult's emotion.

These ideas have many attractions as they help to explain the feeling of interacting with a communicating partner that most parents report about their young babies. However, there are issues that need to be addressed: why do infants regard adults as "like me" when there are differences in size, precision of movement and so on? How far can the "like me" response be extended—to primates? to mammals? to vertebrates?—and how do blind children and children with cerebral palsy establish a "like me" response? All these questions pose problems for the ideas put forward by Meltzoff and Gopnik and it will be interesting to see their answers to these and similar questions.

Another fascinating feature of early imitation is that it appears to involve the processing of several sources of information. It has been discovered that adults' perception of speech sounds is influenced by both the sound and the mouth movement that accompanies the sound. If adults hear a speech sound whilst watching a mouth making a movement for another sound, then their perception will be distorted by the movement they see; they will give an inaccurate description of the sound they have heard (McGurk & MacDonald, 1976). Legerstee (1990) reports that imitations of sounds are more likely when there is a match between sound and mouth movements, than when there is a mismatch.

THE PARENTS' RECOGNITION OF THEIR INFANT

Not only do very young infants prefer stimuli associated with their mother, but parents can identify the stimuli associated with their baby (usually it has been the mother who has been tested). I know of no studies which have attempted to test how soon a mother can visually identify her baby from a set of others—presumably it is assumed that this learning occurs very rapidly. Tests have been made of mothers' ability to identify their babies' cries; this ability appears to be present as soon as 3 days after birth. Mothers also appear to be more likely to wake to the sounds of their own baby's crying than that of others.

One of the first studies which examined mothers' ability to identify the odour of their baby was conducted by Schaal, Montagner, Hertling, Bolzoni, Moyse and Quichon (1980). By the third day after birth mothers were better than would be expected by chance at identifying the cotton shirt worn by their infant, from two others worn by other infants. A later study has found this effect occurs as early as 6 hours after birth (Russell, Mendelson & Peeke, 1983).

It would seem that mothers are not alone in having the ability to discriminate the odour of their infants; fathers, grandparents and aunts also seem to have this ability (Porter & Moore, 1981). Interestingly, in these tests, mothers and fathers commented they recognised the infant's odour because it was similar to that of their spouse or elder child. This explanation seems to be correct. When unrelated adults were asked identify a match between the odour of a mother and baby, they were able to do this (Porter, Cernoch & Balogh, 1985). Porter, Balogh and Makin (1988) suggest that the available evidence points to humans having an "olfactory signature" which is genetically influenced, that is, individuals who are genetically related will have similar olfactory signatures. In this way those with a biological relationship can be identified from an early age and such processes may well facilitate social interaction between parents and infants, although at this time there is no evidence to support such a speculation.

It is also worth remembering that claims have been made that contact immediately after birth may help mothers to "bond" to their infant, and may influence the communication and interaction a mother has with her infant. However, there is considerable debate about what this process involves, the circumstances in which these effects occur and the mechanism by which they occur (Sluckin, Herbert & Sluckin, 1983).

SUMMARY

This chapter describes some of the remarkable infant capacities which result in their paying attention to people, showing a preference for special individuals, and being able to produce powerful signals. In terms of the nature–nurture debate it is not clear what is the precise origin of these abilities. The interest in faces may involve some process like conspec, which has an innate template which enables face-like stimuli to be identified. However, the work on preference for speech and sound suggests that we cannot conclude that just because an ability is present soon after birth it is innate. The findings from a number of studies have revealed that prenatal learning takes place, with the result that newborns show an early preference for the sound of their mothers' voices and sometimes to the theme tune to "Neighbours". It is worth bearing this general point in mind, that very early abilities can be learnt and are not necessarily innate. It is also worth remembering the corollary, that capacities that emerge later in life can be under genetic control, as in the case of puberty and perhaps language development.

All these infant capacities have consequences for the development of communication. The preference for people means that infants are socially responsive. They look at you when you approach them, they attend to your actions. Imagine what it would be like if a baby showed little or no interest in adults. Not only are infants interested in people in general, but from very soon after birth they have a preference for the sight, sound and smell of their mothers. As a result they pay more attention to the person who is likely to be their closest social partner. The interest in people is not a passive process. Infants are able to produce powerful social signals, such as smiling and crying, so that their responses affect other people. All these aspects of the infants' repertoire enable social interaction to begin at birth and the development of further communicative abilities can take place through the experience of such activities.

2

THEORIES ABOUT THE DEVELOPMENT OF COMMUNICATION

This chapter considers theories about the way that infants develop communicative abilities, and the origin of these abilities. This provides a change of emphasis from the previous chapter which was concerned with the description of early infant capacities. It also provides a link between Chapter 1 and Chapter 3. Chapter 3 examines the organisation of early social interaction, and evaluates the findings relevant to theories about the development of communication.

The effort to explain the dramatic changes in communicative and social abilities as infancy progresses has given rise to a number of contrasting theoretical positions. To outline the different positions in this debate the views of a few authorities are summarised and discussed. These cover a wide range, from claims that infants are endowed with quite sophisticated social capacities, to claims that social and non-social abilities are similar. In some theories great emphasis is given to maturation, while in others social experience is seen as crucial.

These theoretical positions provide important reference points for any discussion of the development of communication. Without these reference points it is easy to become lost among the different views and the different interpretations that are given to findings. This is not to say that each position has an inflexible orthodoxy. Often, views are expressed about development which combine elements from different theories. However, by having an idea of these reference points it is easier to locate new or related views about development, and easier to ask questions about what are the implicit assumptions about a particular position. Furthermore, each theoretical position provides an important perspective about development, and an important insight into the way that children's communication may develop. I will argue that a problem with many of the theories is that they take a limited view about the processes that contribute to the development of communication.

WHAT IS COMMUNICATION?

Before one can sensibly discuss the development of communication it is of course necessary to consider what we mean by the term. Rather than strive for a new definition I will outline the dimensions that need to be considered in such discussions. The issue is rather complicated, but the main lines of argument should become apparent. An essential feature of most definitions of communication is that it involves the transfer of information by non-verbal or verbal means. However, having said this, the issue quickly becomes much more complicated.

Important dimensions of this debate are whether or not the communication is transmitted intentionally, accurately received, or perceived as intentional/unintentional (see Figure 2.1 for an outline of the structure of the following discussion). An example of intentional communication would be when a child is told the name of an object: "This is a doll", or told to do something: "*Be* Quiet" or when a younger child makes pleading noises because it wants a forbidden object. Some people would restrict the definition of communication to circumstances such as these.

However, it is important to remember that not everyone would consider that communication has to involve an intention. The transfer of information can occur without intention. A traffic signal communicates information, but has no intentions. Body movements may provide information that someone is nervous in an interview, but there is no intention to communicate

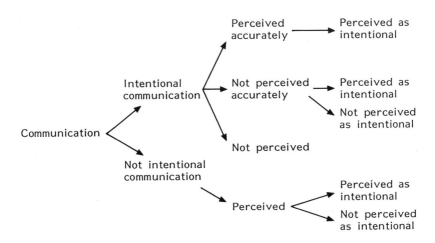

Figure 2.1   A diagram of the process of communication

this information. In the same way newborn babies may not intend to communicate when they cry, but they do provide information about discomfort to the parents. Thus, an important aspect of the definition of communication is whether or not it is necessary to include the idea of intentionality.

If intentions are regarded as a necessary part of the definition of communication then there is a problem of how to identify intentional communication. It is relatively easy to infer intentions, but it is much more difficult to clearly establish that they occur and what they are. For example, most people (but not all) would agree that a newborn baby does not cry for attention or to get an adult to comfort it. Most people also would agree that by 12 months infants will cry to obtain attention and to summon the presence of an adult. The difficulty for the scientific observer is that there are no consistently clear objective signs available to identify when this transition has taken place; the change is an internal one involving the way infants think about their world. Perhaps the most useful move in this direction has been the suggestion that intentionality should be associated with a persistence to reach an objective despite difficulties (Bruner, 1981).

Unfortunately, like the difficulties of identifying intention, there are similar problems in knowing whether or not information has been received, and whether or not it has been received accurately. This dimension makes up the third column from the left in Figure 2.1. At the most simple level one could say that if information is received (irrespective of whether or not it is intentional) then communication has occurred. Not everyone would accept this very general definition. In particular, discussion often occurs about whether or not the information has to be received accurately (e.g. the baby's cry might be thought of as due to tiredness, when it is caused by hunger). As can be seen in Figure 2.1 the message can be perceived accurately, or inaccurately, or fail to be detected.

Another dimension of this complicated picture is whether or not the receiver of information believes the message to be intentional. This is not always regarded as important in definitions of communication. However, it is often commented on in discussions of adult–infant communication. In particular, the possibility of adults treating unintentional infant communication as if it were intentional figures prominently in discussions about a social basis for the development of communication (e.g. Lock, 1978).

This information processing approach to communication has been questioned by Fogel (1993). He believes that it is a mistake to see social interaction as a set of discrete responses to discrete previous events. Instead he suggests that there is a process of *co-regulation* where there is a continuous adaptation to both the present and anticipated behaviour of the other person. Such behaviour can be seen when mother and infant continuously adapt and change their positions when exchanging an object. Fogel also emphasises the way that social interaction is only partly planned and is an open process which is subject to modification and adaptation in the light of joint processes. These criticisms need to be borne in mind in any discussion of communication. However, it is unclear how far this approach can be developed to provide a method for the systematic study of communication. Rather, it may be necessary to apply different methods and models depending on the type of communication that is being studied and the questions that are being asked.

This discussion of communication has shown that there are a number of ways of defining the process. I am less concerned about which configuration is called communication; what is more significant is to recognise that there are important distinctions between these configurations. I would also argue that although these distinctions need to be constantly borne in mind when considering communication, in practice it is often very difficult to identify which of the configurations describes a particular set of behaviours. As we will see in the discussion of the views of different theorists, different assumptions are made about parts of this process, for example when intentionality begins, and different assumptions are made about the definition of communication.

PIAGET AND PIAGETIAN APPROACHES

For Piaget there is little that is special about social cognition, and there are no cognitive structures serving specifically communicative or linguistic functions. Hence, social and communicative developments are believed to come about as a result of developments in general cognitive capacity. In addition, cognitive structures are believed to be *constructed* as a consequence of action and interaction with the world. Thus, the child's understanding of the world is not the result either of innate abilities or of experience alone, but the result of infants applying a set of general cognitive processes to their experiences of the world. In this connection, Piaget emphasises the importance of infants physically acting on the world.

Piagetian theory has been used to account for links between cognitive abilities and communication. One link that has attracted interest is the possibility that general cognitive developments towards the end of the first year may be associated with developments in the use of intentional communication. Piaget has suggested that at about this time infants start to be able to use new ways to solve problems, and to be able to go beyond the immediate problem to find solutions in the broader context of their activities. This is termed the development of means-ends abilities.

Bates, Camaioni and Volterra (1975) used this and other aspects of Piaget's theory to help account for the development of communication in a small sample of Italian children. They considered that before about 8 months children do not recognise that their actions can have a communicative effect on others. As a result, if a child wanted a toy it would struggle to obtain it, but would not look to an adult for help. At about 8–9 months they found that the emergence of means-ends abilities was associated with a change in the pattern of communication. Infants started to enlist help from adults when solving problems. For example, the infants would now look at the adults when they were trying to obtain a toy. In a similar way, infants would start to use objects as a way of obtaining adult attention. In other words, general cognitive developments seemed to be associated with the development of communicative capacities (see also Chapter 16).

Another feature of Piaget's theory is that he supposed that the general capacity to manipulate symbols is necessary for word use, and partly for this reason he regarded the ability to handle abstract concepts as being fundamental to the development of language. In their study of Italian children, Bates, Camaioni and Volterra reported that infants started to use words when they were showing evidence of symbolic use in other activities, for example, pretending to drink from a cup. However, they also found that words were slowly introduced into interaction. There was not a clear cognitive revolution, with words suddenly being used extensively, rather the process was much more gradual.

There have been numerous criticisms of Piaget's ideas. One particularly salient issue for communication is the idea that abilities develop as a result of children's actions, and the feedback from these actions. However, infants with motor disabilities can develop an understanding of space and locations (Lewis, 1987), and children with disorders of the speech apparatus can develop language (Bishop, 1988). Both these sets of findings seriously question Piaget's emphasis about the importance, for development, of acting on the world. The individuals in both examples can develop an understanding of space and of language, despite having severe limitations on their ability to act on the world.

Piaget's ideas have had a great impact on our thinking about cognitive development. Issues that he raised are still the subject of debate and research. However, his impact on our thinking about communicative development has been more limited. For some investigators his work has provided a position to attack because it gives an asocial account of development. For other investigators, as we will see later, it has provided a starting point for examining the ways in which cognition and communication are linked.

VYGOTSKY

The theories of Vygotsky and of Piaget have often been contrasted. Piaget has been characterised as supposing that cognitive advances provide the basis for development, whereas Vygotsky has been characterised as supposing that social interaction and culture provide the basis for development. A widely quoted aspect of Vygotsky's theory is that understanding has to occur in a social context *before* it can be incorporated into a person's cognitive structures. This gives prominence to the role of social behaviour in developing skills. A particularly important aspect of Vygotsky's ideas is the distinction between children's skills that can be performed independently of others, and other unconsolidated abilities that are in a *zone of proximal development*. The abilities in the zone of proximal development can only be performed with the support and assistance of more competent individuals. Vygotsky believed that such support and assistance results in increasing competence so that eventually children can accomplish a task without the support of others.

Because of this theoretical position, Vygotsky's ideas have provided a focus for accounts of development which emphasise the importance of social processes. In particular, his work has been extended to help explain the transition between social interaction, intentional communication, and language acquisition (Clark, 1978; Lock, 1978, 1980). According to this perspective, initially, infant actions do not involve any intent to communicate with others. However, certain actions can be interpreted by adults as being intentional. These actions may be an involuntary response (e.g. crying), or be a more or less random activity (e.g. lifting up both arms), or be an action carried out for some purpose (e.g. reaching for an object). During social interaction it is supposed that adults will respond to these types of actions *as if* they are intentional communications. The result is that infants come to recognise that their actions can influence others and that they have communicative powers. For example, infants may reach for toys in an attempt to obtain them, even though they are too far away. After a while they find that adults pick up the toy and give it to them. In this way social responses will transform the communicative power of infant actions. Infants will start to discover that they can influence adults and that they have social powers of communication.

A similar process is supposed to occur in the development of speech. The initial impetus comes from adults indicating objects and labelling them. Infants will imitate these words, but it is supposed that infants have little or no understanding about the meaning of the first words they imitate. Words start to take on a communicative purpose and meaning through the adults' social responses. In addition, adult–infant games may help in this process, often adults will ask infants to name objects ("what's this?"), or ask them to locate named objects ("where's the teddy?"). Both Lock and Clark have suggested that games like this could extend and improve children's use and understanding of words. As I have already commented (Messer, 1986) this description of the development of communication has many attractions. The mechanisms that are proposed to account for the transition to word use, however, seem unsatisfactory. There is little evidence that children typically produce their first words with no understanding of them. In addition, there are many sources of information which would allow children to comprehend words before being able to say them.

Thus, theories in the Vygotskian tradition propose that social communication develops out of interaction with adults. From this it is supposed that the adults' social responses to infant actions and words lead to the emergence of the intention to communicate, and to new methods of communication.

KAYE

The position adopted by Kaye (1982) is in many ways similar to that of Vygotsky. Kaye holds that social interaction is responsible for many of the cognitive developments of infancy. He accepts that infants have the inherent potential to develop the cognitive characteristics of the mature human, but he emphasises that the realisation of this potential depends on the special fit between adult and infant behaviour, a fit that is the product of evolutionary processes.

A longitudinal study by Kaye was originally expected to show that processes in early adult–infant interaction were related to later communicative abilities. For example, one might expect that the early emergence of pointing would be related to the early use of words, as both seem to involve similar processes. However, few relations were found between early interaction and later communication once the statistical analyses had taken account of continuing patterns of parental behaviour. This lack of predictability led Kaye to conclude that infants have little direct influence on the structure of early social interactions. He reasoned that young infants cannot be part of a *social system* because they have no experience or knowledge of the nature of social activities. In many ways this is an issue of definition; members of a social system need to have certain knowledge and experience, and according to Kaye's use of the terms infants cannot have this knowledge because they inevitably lack a history of social experiences.

A central question for Kaye concerned the way that communication can develop in an organism that lacks intentions to influence people. He rejects the hypothesis that infants engage in social relations only after certain cognitive skills have developed (a Piagetian position), and he also rejects the notion that infants are innately endowed with certain social skills (Trevarthen's position—see the next section). Instead, he suggests that infants develop social and cognitive skills during a process which he likens to an apprenticeship. An important concept here is the *parental framing of infant behaviour*. Framing refers to a process whereby adults provide support or context for an infant's activities, that is when infants lack a skill adults compensate for the absence.

Kaye identifies a sequence of social skills that parents are involved in developing. In the first 3 months, Kaye suggests that shared rhythms emerge as parents build a semblance of dialogue (e.g. vocal turn-taking) by fitting in with the temporal regularities in infants' behaviour. At this early stage, it is assumed that the parent is responsible for giving interaction an appearance of co-ordination and intentionality. Between 2 and 8 months, parents recognise intentions in their infant's behaviour and, by so doing, foster the emergence of *shared intentions*. For much of this time, it is adults who use their memory of past events to enhance social activities and thereby help to build up a repertoire of shared activities and knowledge. In time infants take on a role, so that *shared memories* emerge which provide a basis for the development of word use. Shared memory also makes possible the development of self-consciousness, an understanding of social roles, rules and conventions that characterise human social life. Kaye sees language and socialisation as being intimately related:

> "a little language changes the nature of thought a little, advances the socialisation process a little, which enables language to advance to a more sophisticated level, and so forth."
>
> (Kaye, 1982, p. 238)

One general difficulty with Kaye's account of development is that it ignores the possibility that non-social experience or maturation can lead to changes in functioning. Kaye provides a fascinating model of the way social interaction leads to cognitive development, but he does not establish that it does. In addition, Kaye's ideas may be too closely related to Western culture. Work by Schieffelin and Ochs (1983) suggests that other cultures do not provide the intense social interaction characteristic of our own (see Chapter 14). This detracts from Kaye's approach as a satisfactory explanation of the development of social and cognitive skills that are consistent across cultures, but his apprenticeship idea remains attractive as an explanation of the way people, objects and activities become significant to children within their cultural setting.

TREVARTHEN

Trevarthen has taken the position that children from an early age have the capacity for "intersubjectivity". He explains the idea as follows:

> "for infants to share mental control with other persons they must have two skills. First, they must be able to exhibit to others at least the rudiments of individual consciousness and intentionality. This attribute of acting as agents I call subjectivity. In order to communicate, infants must also be able to fit this subjective control to the *subjectivity* of others: they must also demonstrate *intersubjectivity*."
>
> (Trevarthen, 1979a, p. 322)

Trevarthen sees social and cognitive development as proceeding not through a relationship with a more competent adult, but as the maturation of innate capacities. He believes that infants interact with people in what he terms the communicative mode, and with objects in what he terms the praxic mode. Actions used in the communicative mode include hand movements which Trevarthen calls pre-gestures, and what he calls pre-speech mouth movements, the latter being sustained and active movements of the mouth and tongue which often occur when infants are interacting with people. Actions used in the praxic mode include behaviours such as reaching and grasping. The changes in social activities during infancy are believed to be a consequence of changes in the balance of control between these two modes of functioning.

The idea that neonates can, for communicative purposes, distinguish between inanimate and animate objects seems to be based on an assumption that something akin to direct perception of human movement is in operation (see Collis, 1981). Infants, according to Trevarthen (1977, 1979a) discriminate persons from objects not by obvious features such as facial expression, but by the rhythms of movement. The movement of people consists of surges and changes of direction; the movement of objects usually involves simple changes or the gradual diminution of movement as when a ball bounces. Furthermore, the movements of people correspond to the movements that infants can make, whereas this is not true for most objects.

Another important dimension of Trevarthen's work is his discussion of motivation and intention. Basic motivations are supposed to exist from a very early age. One primitive motive is to achieve interactive relationships with others. This of course will drive infant social behaviour. Trevarthen distinguishes between motives and intentions; for him, an intentional action is the result of a motive in particular circumstances. Thus, intentions, unlike motivations, have a specific goal. During development basic motivations may remain relatively stable, but intentions will show greater change as capacities increase. However, there is also the possibility that motivations will alter, and this will have important consequences for the organisation of behaviour.

Trevarthen has provided a developmental description to chart the growth of communication during infancy. He believes newborns have latent sociability and intentionality, and claims they play an active role in interaction, co-operating with the mother and anticipating her signals in situations such as feeding and holding (Trevarthen, 1979b). At this stage one of the strongest motives is to engage in social interaction. From about 2 months onwards, infants go through a phase he calls *Primary Intersubjectivity*. During this phase, gaze and facial expressions are selectively directed towards persons, as are the pre-gestures and pre-speech movements. There is a further claim that two subjectivities, the adult's and the infant's, are coupled in reciprocal and shared control of social interaction (hence intersubjectivity).

It is suggested that the onset of well-controlled reaching and grasping marks a change in motivation, and the praxic mode becomes prominent. As a result there is a cooling of interest in persons and an avid interest in objects and the inanimate environment. This phenomenon is described by many investigators when observing infants who are 4 months and older. During this period, adults often have to make use of the child's interest in objects as a vehicle for social interaction (Collis, 1977). Trevarthen (1979b) calls this phase the *epoch of games*.

A further developmental phase is ushered in when the two modes of functioning regain a new balance and become capable of integration, so that objects can be shared with people, usually at around 9 months. Trevarthen calls this phase *Secondary Intersubjectivity* (Trevarthen & Hubley, 1978). He concludes that the many new achievements of the 9 month old could not be mastered unless they were dependent on the maturation of an innate endowment for sociability. Such a theory allows little scope for the effect of divergent cultures in the early months as other people are seen to play a minor role in the development process. Indeed, psychological, as opposed to neurological processes, have a minimal role in development.

CHOMSKY

Chomsky's work is primarily concerned with language and language development, and his concern with infant development has been minimal. However, his views about the development of communication have had an enormous impact, and this is mainly because he clearly limits the influence of environmental and pre-linguistic experiences on the language acquisition process. Thus, his views about infants are important because he does not see the skills that are developed during this period as being of importance to language development. His views also are of interest because he sees language as being different from other forms of communication, an issue which is considered in more detail in Chapter 9.

A critical argument for Chomsky, and most linguists, is that the grammar of language makes it different from other forms of communication. All languages have a finite set of elements, but the grammar of a language allows these elements to be combined to make an infinite number of different messages. As Chomsky observed, much of the speech we say and hear consists of entirely new utterances, but there is no difficulty in producing these utterances, and there is no difficulty in understanding them. In addition, it is supposed that language is a unique form of communication because it involves structural-dependency of elements, for example, verbs usually agree with their related nouns (e.g. "the dog bites" vs "the dogs bite"). Behind these claims is the assumption that the way the linguistic elements are organised influences the message that is conveyed, and that certain forms of combination are regarded as inappropriate or incorrect. The same type of organisation is not believed to be present in other forms of communication. For example, in infants' pre-linguistic communication the order of the gestures does not usually affect the meaning of the message, but this is often crucial in English (i.e. "the man bites the dog" vs "the dog bites the man"), and there is no evidence of structural dependency in pre-linguistic communication.

Chomsky sees language as being possible because of the special capacities that humans have to process the speech they hear. He does not deny that some pre-verbal skills may be necessary for language, but in considering the language acquisition process these are regarded as of minor importance. Thus Chomsky, like Trevarthen, regards the maturation of biologically pre-programmed abilities as being the main cause of the change to linguistic communication.

SUMMARY

Each of these major theorists has given prominence to particular processes which contribute to development, whether maturational or experiential, social or non-social, but in each case there is a lack of attention to the other contributions, and an absence of integration. As a result one is left with a feeling that only part of the story has been told. We have seen that the approaches of Trevarthen and Kaye provide a stark contrast. Trevarthen emphasises maturational processes and hardly mentions the possibility that social interaction has implications for development. He explicitly dismisses not only learning theory-based environmental approaches but also constructivist approaches. On the other hand, Kaye scarcely mentions the implications of maturational changes for changes in psychological functioning. An embarrassment for Kaye's position is that it is very closely tied to child-rearing practices in modern Western culture. Cultures which do not provide the same level of intense social interactions would seem to require a different developmental route (Schieffelin & Ochs, 1983). Trevarthen's approach does not suffer from this drawback, but this is achieved by virtually ruling out social processes as having a role in infant development. Instead, the emphasis is on neurological development, which does not receive much attention from other theorists. In a similar manner Chomsky's emphasis on an innate endowment means that a minimal role is given to social interaction in the language acquisition process.

The views of Piaget and Vygotsky also provide a contrast. For Piaget the issue of the way that infants acquire social abilities is a minor one. Instead he concentrates on the way development occurs by virtue of children interacting with their environment and resolving conflicts between their model of the world and their experience of how the world behaves. Social cognition is seen as a simple extension of cognitive concerns to an animate environment. In contrast, Vygotsky and other theorists see the social events as fundamental to development: without social experiences significant advances would not occur.

It is also worthwhile highlighting the way that these theories deal with the development of intention. For Trevarthen, infants have an intention to communicate from birth or soon afterwards. Bates, Camaioni and Volterra (1975) use a Piagetian perspective when they suggest that the desire to affect others by communication is part of a general cognitive development. The Vygotskian account suggests that intention to communicate emerges because of adults' reactions to infant activities, which allows infants to discover their social powers, while Kaye sees intention in communication as being linked to an understanding and knowledge of a social system.

The ideas contained in these viewpoints are important and highlight different ways of thinking about the early development of social interaction and communication. I have emphasised differences, and in some cases fundamental differences exist between the positions. For example, it is interesting that these theories describe similar behaviour from very different viewpoints. The use of objects at 8–9 months is seen by Trevarthen as a product of the integration of the communicative and praxic modes; by

Bates, Camaioni and Volterra as a product of a change in means-ends understanding which enables infants to use objects to enlist adults' attention; by theorists in the Vygotskian tradition as an opportunity for infant activities to be transformed so that they have communicative intention; and by Kaye as part of the opportunity of infants to acquire knowledge from adults' assistance and support. However, there are some meeting points. Most theories give some acknowledgement to the active and investigative aspect of infant activities; infants are not seen as passive recipients of information from the world.

It is tempting to ask which of these theories is correct. There is not sufficient evidence totally to discredit any of the positions. Because the lack of a clear answer is frustrating, a more useful approach is to think of each theory as providing a set of hypotheses about the development of communication. Each gives insight into the processes that need to be thought about, and each raises further questions about the precise nature of the mechanism of development. We should also recognise that the development of communication is a complex business, and it is unlikely to be explained from only one of these perspectives.

This chapter has outlined various theories and views about the way that infants become social and develop the capacity to take part in social interaction. In the next chapter I will consider investigations about early social interaction to see how well these theories are supported. We will see that a major problem in these investigations has been in discovering a way to distinguish between social interaction and other behaviour.

3

TAKING PART IN SOCIAL INTERACTION

Infants come into the world with an orientation to people rather than objects, an orientation to mothers rather than unfamiliar adults, and they possess social behaviours which can influence adults (see Chapter 1). In other words they have *social capacities*. These social capacities are impressive, especially as they provide a basis for participating in social interaction. In this chapter I will argue that although infants have social capacities, the evidence that they have the capacity to take an *integrated* and *reciprocal* part in social interaction is much weaker (I will use integrated as referring to the use of appropriate behaviours at an appropriate time when interacting with another person, reciprocal as referring to the ability to take an equal part in interaction).

Why should we concern ourselves about whether infants take an integrated and reciprocal part in non-verbal social interaction? The most important reason is that communication invariably takes place in the context of social interaction. Social interaction involves many skills; some of these are not concerned with directly transmitting a message, but the skills are needed for communication to occur. When the normal process of social interaction breaks down it becomes more difficult to communicate; an example of this would be a group of people all talking at the same time. Thus, for infants to begin to communicate with adults, they not only need to know the appropriate gestures and words, but they also need to be able to place these gestures and words in a culturally appropriate sequence of activities.

A second, and related issue, is that the development of more advanced abilities inevitably requires simpler abilities to be in place, therefore it becomes important to discover which capacities for social interaction infants already possess, and which capacities need to develop. A better understanding of the process of early adult–infant social interaction should lead us to greater comprehension of the larger process of the development of communication.

Thirdly, an examination of the capacity of infants to take part in social interaction has implications for theories about social and communicative development. Some theories, like those of Trevarthen, predict that from an early age infants have a capacity to take an active role in the social process. Other theories, like those based on Vygotsky, predict that active involvement will occur at a later age.

WHAT IS SOCIAL INTERACTION?

So far I have avoided defining the term social interaction, and have avoided defining it in relation to communication. The two concepts are similar and overlapping. Schaffer (1984) considers that for interaction to occur "the separate activities of the participants must be co-ordinated in such a way as to form a unitary sequence" (p. 5). In other words social interaction involves participants altering their behaviour to adapt to the activities of a partner, and in doing this a coherent sequence of activities is created.

From this it follows that communication (the transmission of information) can occur without social interaction. An example would be sending a letter. Although no *behavioural* co-ordination is needed when sending a letter, the success of communication is the result of an established set of procedures. In the letter example these include the language used, knowing an address, the style of writing and so on. Thus, in some circumstances communication is possible without social interaction by relying on a set of conventions. The reverse case would be social interaction without any communication, but in such cases it is always possible to argue that the co-ordination of social interaction involves communication in that some information is exchanged between the participants.

It is also worth considering the way that the term *interaction* is employed. In everyday use the social activities of adults with infants are usually described as "interaction"; the term may even be used by people who do not believe that infants *co-ordinate* their behaviour with adults. The inconsistency of the latter position is illustrated by the example of a person talking to his pet goldfish. Social behaviours may be displayed by the person ("how are you today?, you don't look very hungry? oh yes, you would like some food?"), but because the goldfish does not co-ordinate its responses with that of the person we would not want to call this social interaction. In contrast, most people would want to describe the same behaviours with an infant as "social interaction", whatever their belief about the capacity of infants to co-ordinate their responses with adults.

Another example will serve to make the problem of definition even more complex. A computer program called Elisa was devised to model a therapist. The program was able to ask a person a series of written questions. After each reply the computer asked a further question which was related to the preceding reply. The computer program worked something like this:

Computer:	What is worrying you?
Person:	I am unhappy at work
Computer:	Why are you unhappy at work?
Person:	I do not like my boss
Computer:	Tell me about your boss

The program worked so well that it is reported that some people thought there actually was a therapist responding to the answers they typed into the computer. The computer program gave the appearance of co-ordination because it could turn statements into open-ended questions, and could provide reasonable probes when it was unable to make sense of the answers. As a result, the computer program simulated the activities of a social partner, by merely reacting to the response of a person. It is true that the sequences may not always have had coherence, but with more sophisticated programming this could be achieved. However, when people understand what is going on, not many would want to call this social interaction, despite the fact that some form of co-ordination is occurring.

These examples serve to highlight the problem of deciding what activities constitute social interaction. The examples show that social interaction involves the co-ordination of behaviour, but it would also seem that co-ordination can occur without there being social interaction (e.g. Elisa). What needs to be added to the process of co-ordination to make it one of interaction? Trevarthen's argument that there needs to be an element of intersubjectivity, an awareness of the other person as a person, is one with which many would agree. After all this is the issue which might be seen as dividing a machine from the social interaction of people and some animals. One way to investigate the question is to see whether infants co-ordinate their behaviour with people in a different way than with objects. Basic forms of co-ordination have already been considered in Chapter 1; in the first part of this chapter there is an examination of the *integration* of infant actions into the stream of social behaviours.

Another important feature of social interaction is that the activities of one individual are influenced by the characteristics of the partner. This only occurs to a very limited extent in the case of Elisa and in the case of letter writing. In contrast, during social interaction each participant needs to adapt their behaviour to that of the other. Thus, a relevant question to ask is whether infants' behaviour is altered by the characteristics of their partner. Do infants *modify* their behaviour because of the person with whom they are interacting? And do they *modify* their behaviour because of the social behaviour to which they are exposed? The second section of this chapter is concerned with this issue.

The third section examines the forms of *co-ordination* infants employ during social interaction. One dramatic claim that has been made is that babies move in synchrony with the speech sounds of adults. If this claim is true then infants would have a remarkable social capacity to co-ordinate their activities with those of another person. Another claim is that infants co-ordinate their gaze according to where the mother is gazing. A further example of co-ordination is vocal turn-taking, and a number of studies have examined infants' contribution to this process.

ARE INFANTS ATTUNED TO PEOPLE?

A Description of Early Social Interaction

Before going on to discuss the infants' part in the organisation of social interaction it is worth giving an overview of this activity. One of the most telling observations about early social interaction was made by Stern (1977) who described it as being highly abnormal in relation to typical adult–adult interaction. Stern pointed out that early social interaction breaks a number of the conventions governing the usual process of social exchanges. Adult–infant interactions involve closer proximity, more touching, a slower pace, and more gazing into each other's eyes—behaviours which usually only occur between adults who have a very intimate relationship. In addition, adult–infant interaction tends to involve exaggerated facial expression, more head movement, a modified language, and to be very repetitive. In fact the type of interaction we sometimes employ with foreigners.

The repetitive and structured nature of early interactions has been described by Stern (1977) using the diagram of maternal behaviour given in Figure 3.1. Each individual behaviour of the mother is termed a *phrase*: these can consist of a vocalisation, or a pattern of movement such as head looming. The phrases tend to be organised into *runs* which are sequences of behaviour which have some common unifying characteristic. The runs could be content runs which contain sequences of the same behaviour, or temporal runs which contain different behaviours which occur at a similar rate. Runs which have a similar pace and which have a similar focus are referred to as *episodes of maintained engagement*.

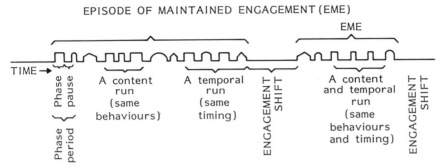

Figure 3.1 A schematic representation of different structures within a sequence of caregiver behaviours, represented here as ⊓⊓⌒ (reproduced with permission from D. N. Stern, B. Beebe, J. Jaffe & S. L. Bennett (1977) The infant's stimulus world during social interaction. In H. R. Schaffer (Ed.), *Studies in Mother–Infant Interaction*. London: Academic Press)

Another theme highlighted by Stern (1977), Brazelton, Koslowski and Main (1974) and Papousek and Papousek (1977) is the way that adults use interaction to ensure that infants are at an optimal level of arousal. Here the idea is that the pace and content of interaction will be altered to ensure that an infant does not become bored and inattentive, or become overaroused and start to turn away or even cry. If an infant starts to become bored, typically an adult will increase the intensity of behaviour and make the content more interesting; if the infant shows signs of overarousal the adult will slow the pace down and reduce the intensity. This provides a very useful model in thinking about early social interaction, but it is surprisingly difficult to confirm (Messer, 1993). The main problem is that the fine micro-analysis of every social behaviour is time-consuming, to which must be added the problems of assessing infant interest and arousal.

I have picked out some important features of early interaction. These do not of course give the full flavour of what occurs. To do this it is necessary either to have participated in such interactions, or to observe them. If you are not familiar with this type of interaction try to observe or take part in it, your insights might be just as important as the information obtained from reading a book!

Are Social Behaviours Directed at People but not Objects?

In Chapter 2 we considered Trevarthen's ideas about the development of social capacities. His ideas about intersubjectivity predict that infants are able to distinguish people from objects and can engage in reciprocal and integrated social behaviour. What evidence is there to support this type of claim? Some qualitative evidence was published in the 1970s which was claimed to show that babies responded to people in a different way from objects. For example, Trevarthen proposed that certain behaviours usually occurred in social situations (e.g. pre-speech behaviours involving tongue and mouth movements) while other behaviours occurred with objects (e.g. pre-reaching). For him the difference was so obvious that a formal test of the hypothesis was not needed. In a similar way, Richards (1974) proposed that babies used different behaviours when presented with people or things. He observed that the reaction to a thing involved looking with narrow eyes, a tense body posture, and arms and fingers directed to the object; in contrast the reaction to a person involved relaxed body posture, wider eyes, less focused attention, and more smiling. Similarly, Brazelton, Koslowski and Main (1974) commented that infant attention to people and objects was very different, and the difference in posture could be detected in any part of the infant's body.

Some support for these claims of a more quantitative nature comes from a study conducted by Frye, Rawling, Moore and Myers (1983). They found that parents and undergraduates could judge from video recordings whether 3–10-month-old infants were: (i) either alone with a moving object or with their mother; (ii) either with an active or passive partner; and (iii) whether the partner was either greeting them or withdrawing from interaction. Unfortunately for the confirmation of Trevarthen's ideas, the judges could not tell whether the 3-month-old babies were with an object or their mother, although this distinction was possible with 10 month olds.

Another study conducted by Sylvester-Bradley (1985) failed to find large differences in behaviour to objects and people. The object was a red wooden ball moved by the experimenter. Behaviour of 10-week-old infants in both sessions was coded. The sessions with the mother, in comparison to those with an object, had more mouth openings, more lowering of the eyebrows, and less turning away.

Although the findings are compatible with the idea of different behaviours occurring with people and objects, Sylvester-Bradley was reluctant to draw this conclusion. He gives three reasons for this reluctance. Firstly, the claim is usually made that infants will respond differently to people from objects, but observers in the Frye et al. (1983) study were unable to distinguish between sessions when infants were with their mother and when with an object; in addition their other findings could be interpreted as observers being able to distinguish between infant behaviour according to the *intensity* of interaction provided by their mother (i.e. distinguishing between alone or with a partner, active or passive, and greeting or withdrawing).

Secondly, in his experiment both pre-speech and pre-reaching behaviours occurred with objects and with people, but it was predicted that they should only occur with people. However, this may be an overstatement by Sylvester-Bradley of Trevarthen's position and this issue is further clouded by the fact that the red object was moved by a person rather than consisting of random machine movements. Thirdly, there were large individual variations in behaviours, with good consistency across sessions. This suggests that a more important dimension is the infant's sociability rather than the person–object distinction. The conclusion Sylvester-Bradley came to is that the behaviour patterns are the result of experience and are not due to innate capacities to distinguish and react to people and things.

The debate about infants' ability to understand that people are different from objects has received a new impetus from discussions about children's theory of other people's mental states (see Chapter 16). As we have seen in Chapter 1, Meltzoff and Gopnik (1993) proposed that infants are able to detect the equivalence between themselves and others because they notice similarity in body movements. This they believe is the basis for later more elaborate conceptions of people. Hobson (1991) has put forward a different theory which stresses that the perception of emotion provides the basis for infants to begin to identify people as different from other objects. He supposes that young infants directly perceive the emotional content of others' actions (i.e. they do not have to learn what a smile or an angry voice means) and also react to this emotional content. Hobson believes that the experience of social interaction enables infants to gradually differentiate the self from others and to understand that others have minds (Hobson, 1991). These two hypotheses are not necessarily incompatible, but seem to stress different aspects of the way an understanding of people may develop.

Leslie (1987) provides a very different perspective, and although there appears to be some agreement between Leslie (1987) and Hobson about the difficulty of inferring that people have mental states from sensory evidence alone, there is disagreement about the process which enables children to make this inference. Leslie's model suggests that children could not have the ability to understand the mental states of others until at least 18 to 24 months of age when an innate capacity to construct secondary representations emerges (i.e. symbolic play and pretence, see Chapter 16 for more details). Thus, Leslie claims that before 18 months the goal of communication is simply to change the behaviour of another person rather than their mental state.

It is likely that debate will continue about this issue. More sensitive methods of recording may establish a difference in behaviour to objects and to people. However, at the moment, we still lack conclusive evidence to support the argument that infants interact in a special way with people. In Chapter 1 we saw that infants appear to have the capacity to *distinguish* people from objects, but it would appear from the material reviewed in this section that infants are not able to use this discrimination to govern social interaction. In other words, it is possible for infants to make a distinction between people and objects, but it does not seem that this has a marked effect on their social interaction. Thus, infants may have a capacity for intersubjectivity, but this does not seem to be directly translated into the way they deal with people and objects.

Are Infants Tuned to the Rhythms of Speech?

One early and dramatic capacity attributed to infants was the ability to synchronise their movement with the speech they hear. If you watch a person's movements when talking it is noticeable that movements of the body (especially hands) are synchronised with the person's speech. The beginnings and ends of words often coincide with changes in direction of body movements, and emphasis in speech is often accompanied by more violent movements (just watch someone giving a speech). In addition, it seems likely that adult listeners adjust their movements to the rhythm of someone else's speech (Birdwhistle, 1970).

In the 1970s a claim was made by Condon and Sander (1974) that the initiation and changes in direction of infant movements were synchronised with the phonemic elements of adult speech. If infants possessed such a capacity then it would suggest that they can in some way "tune in" to the rhythm of speech. After all, to be able to move in time with speech involves, not simply responding to the sounds that are heard, but being able to predict when sounds begin and end. This latter capacity can be thought of as similar to dancing, with both partners moving in time to a common rhythm. To dance well entails predicting the rhythm, rather than respond-ing to the sounds when they occur; bruised feet are a product of not predicting the rhythm and/or not acting appropriately.

Although Condon and Sander (1974) described newborn infants as being able to move in time with adult speech, subsequent studies have failed to replicate these findings. This has led to the methods used by Condon and Sander being questioned (Dowd & Tronick, 1986; Pack, 1983; Rosenfield, 1981). One particular problem with Condon and Sander's methodology was that when they coded changes in movement they knew about any changes in the sound patterns. Consequently, we can have little confidence in the claim that very young infants can tune into the rhythms of speech.

Is Early Social Interaction Modified By Adult Behaviour?

Another way to examine infant sociability is to consider whether infants notice changes in the social behaviour of the adult. A number of studies have reported that infants will become distressed if mothers adopt a "still face" pose when they are asked by the experimenter to stop interacting (Tronick, Als & Brazelton, 1977). In a similar way some studies have asked non-depressed mothers to act as if they were depressed and found that the infants were distressed with the change in behaviour (Cohn & Tronick, 1983; Field, 1984). Unfortunately, such studies tell us that infants can detect a difference, but do not establish whether the detection is based on unusual *social* behaviour, or because infants merely notice a change in the perceptual stimuli and find it disturbing.

A more careful examination of this issue has been carried out by Murray and Trevarthen (1985). They compared infants' behaviour to their mothers in three circumstances: when interacting normally; an interruption, when the mother was interacting with a stranger; and when the mother presented a blank unresponsive face to her baby. The three infants in this study were between 6 and 12 weeks old. When the mother was interacting with a stranger, in comparison to the normal interaction, there were fewer tongue and mouth movements, as well as fewer smiles. The infants seemed to be less communicative but not distressed. The same comparison using the blank face condition, revealed fewer gazes at the mother, less eyebrow raising, less smiling, more frowning, and more grimacing. The infants seemed to be less communicative and more distressed.

The investigators interpreted these findings as showing that infants are sensitive to the communicative intent of the mother, so they are more upset in the unusual blank face condition. Certainly, the data support their interpretation, but the difficulty of making the interruption and blank face conditions equivalent leaves open the possibility that differences in the stimuli could account for the differences in behaviour (e.g. in the interrupt condition the mother turned away from the baby to talk to the stranger, in the blank face condition there were no vocalisations).

In a further study, Murray and Trevarthen (1985) manipulated social interaction by using a two-way video link. The interaction with the infant involved two conditions. One condition involved a real time presentation, the other a delay of 30 seconds. In the later condition the mother had been interacting with the infant in real time, and this was replayed to the infant. Thus, in one condition maternal social behaviour was keyed into infant behaviour, and in the other maternal social behaviour was not aligned with that of the infant. Four infants between 6 and 12 weeks old were studied.

In the delay condition the infants gazed less at the mother, exhibited fewer tongue movements, mouth movements, and positive eyebrow raises, together with more frowns, touching of clothes and grimaces. These findings clearly show that infants are sensitive to the contingencies of normal social interaction with their mother. The investigators also interpret their findings as showing that infants "possess a set of processes in which human stimuli are categorised in emotional and expressive terms. To this extent, the forms and communicative values of human emotions are innately formulated" (p. 194). While this conclusion may be accurate it goes beyond the data that were presented.

Maternal social behaviour is usually altered by post-natal depression. Mothers with depression typically show lower rates of social behaviour, more negative behaviour, and less willingness to engage in social activities (Cohn, Matias & Tronick, 1990; Murray & Stein, 1989). There also may be some depressed mothers who engage in a different pattern of interaction, who overstimulate their infants, and do not take account of their infant's behaviour and reactions.

What is the effect of maternal depression on the social behaviour of infants? Infants who have mothers who are depressed tend to show similar patterns of behaviour to the mothers; they seem depressed and withdrawn, have few instances of positive affect, and often look away from the mother (Cohn, Matias, Tronick, Connell & Lyon-Ruth, 1986; Cohn, Matias & Tronick, 1990). This pattern of interaction has also been found to occur when 3–6 month infants of depressed mothers interact with other adults (Field, Healy, Goldstein et al., 1988). The most obvious explanations of these patterns of infant social behaviour are that the lower levels of maternal stimulation fail to energise infant interaction, or that infants use their mother's behaviour as a model for their own interaction. In both cases the overall pattern of maternal behaviour appears to have an impact on infant social interaction. However, it is possible that some infants may be born with a predisposition for a subdued temperament and depressed style of social behaviour. It has been reported that infants of depressed mothers have lower activity levels and limited responsiveness to social stimulation shortly after birth (Field, 1985).

A further cause of differences in maternal social behaviour is cultural variation. A number of studies have found that social interaction differs with culture. For example Fogel, Toda and Kawai (1988) report that when 3-month-old infants are gazing at them, both American and Japanese mothers tend to use an expressive face, but that the American mothers will vocalise, while Japanese mothers will tend to be silent and to lean close to and touch their infants. In addition, there are differences in infant behaviour, such as American infants smiling more often, but for shorter durations than Japanese infants. Thus, different cultural experiences do seem to have an effect on the behaviours produced by infants. What is less clear is whether these constitute a different response to certain adult behaviours, and therefore a fairly simple adaptation (i.e. do American babies have more events to make them smile?), or are there substantially different patterns in the organisation of social interaction (i.e. is the sequence of events different in the two cultures?) so that the differences represent a sophisticated adaptation to adult social interaction.

Taken together all these findings suggest that changes in the pattern of adult social interaction are detected by infants. However, there is still much uncertainty about what constitutes the mechanism of these changes, and whether infants' social interaction changes in a mechanistic or more sophisticated way.

THE ORGANISATION OF ADULT–INFANT INTERACTION

Adult–Infant Gaze

An important dimension of social activity between infants and parents which has long been thought to have special significance is gaze (Robson, 1967). Robson reports that mothers feel that their baby knows them when he or she starts to gaze into their eyes. Gaze is a particularly important dimension of human social behaviour. Gaze at a person can be used to signify interest and attention to that person, gaze away from another can be used to signal a lack of interest and a wish to terminate interaction, while gaze at particular objects can indicate an interest which can become a topic of conversation.

The importance of gaze for early social interaction has graphically been described by Fraiberg (1977) in her work with children who are blind. In her early work Fraiberg noticed that she had difficulty relating to children who were blind. This was dramatically brought home to her when she visited one infant who was diagnosed as having a severe visual impairment. Despite the infant being neglected and living in squalid conditions, Fraiberg found she could relate to the child more easily than the other children she had been visiting. It was later found that the child did not have problems with his sight. Thinking about this experience Fraiberg came to the conclusion that the absence of mutual gaze (when both the adult and infant are looking into one another's eyes), and the lack of cues from the direction of eye gaze about the object of infant interest, made social interaction much more difficult. In particular, the lack of gaze at herself by children who were blind made it seem as if the children were not interested in her and were rebuffing her advances. This anecdote and the other work of Fraiberg indicates the significance of gaze for adult–infant interaction.

Several studies which have described the pattern of gazes between mothers and infants are discussed in the next two sections. An important question in these investigations has been concerned with whether infants make a contribution to the organisation of gaze interaction. Two ways of investigating this question will be described. The first examines whether infants alter their behaviour according to the gaze direction of the partner. The second takes this analysis further by examining whether gaze is different from that expected in a chance arrangement of this behaviour.

The influence of the direction of maternal gaze

In the early 1970s Stern and his colleagues conducted a number of observations of mother–infant gaze. The data analysis involved what is known as "dyadic state analysis" (mother–infant pairs were often described as dyads to emphasis the joint partnership between the two individuals). In this analysis mother–infant gaze was coded using the simplest set of possibilities: both individuals looking at each other, only the mother looking at the infant, only the infant looking at the mother, and neither looking at each other. This is shown diagrammatically in Figure 3.2, and these are called for convenience, *both, mother, infant,* and *neither.*

Coding behaviour in this way allows researchers to ask questions about the way that joint behaviour is organised, for example who usually finishes a joint gaze of "both", the mother or the infant? To answer questions like this it is necessary to do some further analysis. For example, we might have observed mother–infant gaze and obtained a sequence of dyadic states like that shown below:

Both, Infant, Neither, Mother, Mother, Both, Mother, Infant, Neither

How could we find out which behaviour usually follows another one? The simplest way is to make a transition table similar to the one shown in Figure 3.3. The next step would involve looking at each pair of gaze states in turn. The first pair would be both-to-infant, the second pair would be infant-to-neither, the third pair would be neither-to-mother and so on through the sequence.

As we look at each pair we would enter it into the table shown in Figure 3.3. The first pair both-to-infant would be entered with a tally mark in the cell labelled X. The second pair (infant-to-neither) would be entered with a tally mark in the cell labelled Y. If we went through the whole sequence

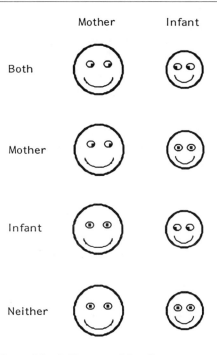

Figure 3.2 A diagram of dyadic gaze states

	Both	Infant	Mother	Neither
Both		X		
Mother				
Infant				Y
Neither				

Figure 3.3 An example of a transition table

in this way then we would end up with a transition table containing the frequencies of all the different pairs of behaviours.

Research workers who used tables like this quickly realised that it was more appropriate, when comparing different behaviours, to use transitional probabilities rather than the frequency of transitions. By using transitional probabilities it is possible to ask whether one transition is more likely to occur than another, irrespective of the overall frequency of the transitions.

Calculating a transition probability simply involves dividing each cell total by the row total, this gives the probability of one behaviour following another. If a sequence had a probability of 1 (i.e. 100%) this would mean that each time the first behaviour occurred, it was always followed by the second behaviour. As a probability gets closer to zero the less likely is the second member of a pair to follow the first.

Stern (1974) made these calculations and found that the sequence of dyadic mother–infant gaze states could be summarised as follows. When neither the mother nor the infant were gazing at each other, the mothers were more likely than the infant to initiate gaze at the partner. That is, there was a higher probability of neither-to-mother than neither-to-infant. The mothers held this gaze for a long time. Usually the infant would then gaze at the mother thereby bringing about a period of *Both* gaze.

Another pattern revealed by the analysis was that the infant would initiate gaze at the mother, and typically she would quickly respond to this gaze by looking at the infant. As a result both partners would be gazing at one another. Both these sequences suggest that mutual gaze was a highly likely outcome in the organisation of mother–infant gaze. Once mutual gaze was established, mothers maintained their gaze at infants, and infants alternated between gazes at the mothers and gazes away.

In addition, Stern carried out comparisons to see whether infant gaze was influenced by the mother's behaviour. The two changes of infant behaviour that can be examined are: beginning to look at the mother, and ending a look at the mother.

To illustrate the way analyses were conducted I will examine whether the probability of infant gazes at the mother is influenced by her behaviour. To answer this question it is necessary to compare two transitions, mother-to-both and neither-to-infant (see Figure 3.4). Both transitions contain the *same* change in infant gaze; in this case the change is from gazing elsewhere to gazing at the mother. In addition, the two transitions have a *different* form of maternal gaze. In one case the transition involves the mother continuing to gaze at the infant, and the other case involves the mother continuing to gaze elsewhere. Thus, both transitions have the same change in infant gaze, from gazing elsewhere to gazing at the mother, but the direction of maternal gaze is different.

The finding that there was a higher transitional probability in mother-to-both than in neither-to-infant suggests that infant social gaze is altered by the behaviour of the mother. In particular, infants appear to prefer to gaze at the mother when she is already looking at them, and this may mean that they are trying to establish mutual gaze. Stern also found that infants were

Mother to Both		
Mother Gazes at Infant	to	Mother Gazes at Infant
Infant Gazes Elsewhere	to	Infant Gazes at Mother
Neither to Infant		
Mother Gazes Elsewhere	to	Mother Gazes Elsewhere
Infant Gazes Elsewhere	to	Infant Gazes at Mother

Figure 3.4   A comparison of the transitions mother-to-both and neither-to-infant

less likely to end a gaze at the mother, when she was gazing at them rather than gazing elsewhere. In other words, both sets of analyses suggested that 3-month-old infants were taking account of their partner's behaviour when they were engaged in social activities. Using the same logic, analyses were conducted to examine the mothers' behaviour. A similar organisation was found in that mothers also, and less surprisingly, appeared to take account of infant behaviour in the organisation of their gaze.

The findings reported by Stern were important because they indicated that 3-month-old infants had the capacity to take an active part in social inter-action. It appeared that even very young infants would alter their gaze behaviour according to where the mother was gazing, and all this would be done quickly with fine integration between infant and maternal beha-viour. These are surprisingly advanced capacities for such young infants.

Comparing observed and chance arrangements of social gaze

Stern's findings were challenged by Hayes and Elliott (1979). They reported that the transitional probability of infants' social gaze was similar to the probabilities obtained from the same data when it was shuffled. The shuffling process is a way of rearranging the observed data to give a new record where there is no longer the same temporal link between the mothers' and infants' gazes. The best way to think of this process is to imagine two sets of cards. These would be laid out in two lines so that each card exactly matched the other. The two lines correspond to the behaviours of the mother and infant, and each card corresponds to a matched beha-viour. The next stage would be to take one line of cards, collect it together and shuffle it, and then relay the cards against the other line. The new arrangement of cards would contain the same number of elements, but the relationship between the two lines would be broken. We would expect a very different organisation of cards in the new line from the original.

The same logic underlies the shuffling of observations about maternal and infant gaze. By shuffling one set of behaviours it is possible to preserve the overall frequency and durations of behaviour, but to destroy the temporal relationship. Transitional probabilities can be calculated in the normal way from both observed and shuffled data.

Hayes and Elliott argued that if there is a close statistical similarity between the transitional probabilities from observed and shuffled data, then mother–infant gaze is essentially a chance arrangement of behaviour. Hayes and Elliott reported that the correlations between the transitional probabilities from the observed and the shuffled data were significant and highly positive. They concluded that there was no special organisation of social gaze.

However, there were a number of problems with Hayes and Elliott's study. The observation sessions were short (3 minutes) and occurred in a laboratory. In addition, the mothers looked at the infants for a very high proportion of the session (92%), this is higher than most other reports of gaze, and with such a high proportion it is not very surprising that there was little difference between the findings from the observed and shuffled data. If we return to the two sets of cards analogy this would be like 92% of the cards in one pack being the same, and so the same pattern is likely to occur in observed and shuffled data. A further issue is that the statistical analyses were limited to a calculation of correlations between the observed and random transitional probabilities. The finding of a significant positive correlation between two sets of numbers means that a high score on one set is matched by a high score on the other set. It does not tell us whether one set of scores is uniformly higher or lower than the other set. To do this a normal test of significance is needed.

These issues led Peter Vietze and myself to relook at some findings we had already published. In one study, we had followed Stern and used a similar analysis to him (Messer & Vietze, 1984). Our new method of analysis was to make a comparison between observed and shuffled data (Messer & Vietze, 1988). The most appropriate comparison seemed to be between transition *frequencies* which were separately calculated from the observed and shuffled records. In such an analysis there is no need for the method of analysis adopted by Stern.

High and significant correlations were found between the observed and the shuffled transitional frequencies, indicating that there was a high degree of similarity between the two sets of data. However, there were also some significant differences between the observed and the shuffled transitional frequencies. In some cases the observed frequencies occurred more often than those from the shuffled data, in some cases less.

Table 3.1 Findings of significant differences between observed and shuffled data

	Age in weeks		
	10	26	54
Beginning gazes at partner			
Mother to both (infant begins)	+ O > S	+ O > S	
Infant to both (mother begins)	+ O < S		+ O > S
Ending gazes at partner			
Both to mother (infant ends gaze)		− O > S	- O > S
Both to infant (mother ends gaze)	+ O < S		

+ significant difference which *increases* probability of mutual gaze
− significant difference which *reduces* probability of mutual gaze
O > S observed > shuffled
O < S observed < shuffled

Where there were significant differences, the actual numeric difference was small, but the difference occurred across most of the mother–infant pairs.

The transitions which were significantly different are shown in Table 3.1. Some of these differences suggested an organisation which would *increase* the probability of mutual gaze. These are indicated by the plus mark on the table. Other differences suggested an organisation which would reduce the probability of mutual gaze. These are indicated by a minus mark on the table. The presence of these transitions shows that, according to this set of analyses, social interaction was not uniformly organised towards maximising mutual gaze.

What conclusions can we draw from all this? The first implication is that mother–infant gaze interaction is not that different from what we would expect if there were a chance arrangement of behaviour. In other words the overall duration and frequency of gazes seem to be as important in determining the structure of interaction as the sensitivity of either partner to the behaviour of the other. Thus, the data do not give strong support to a position which claims that infants are taking an active part in social interaction. The findings do, however, give weak support to this position. Our finding that some transitions were significantly different from what would be expected from a random model suggests that there is some slight deviation. It is difficult to know whether this does indeed represent a true infant contribution to social interaction or whether some other artifact is producing a confound in the method of data analysis.

The Organisation of Adult–Child Vocalisation

The vocal interaction between infants and their mothers has also often been a focus of interest because of the possible relationship between turn-taking skills in pre-verbal social interaction and turn-taking during conversation. The idea of turn-taking implies that participants speak alternately rather than interrupting each other, and there is a similar topic or meaning in successive turns. Not surprisingly, alternation rather than meaning has been the focus of studies into pre-verbal interactions.

The assumption that mother–infant vocal interaction involves turn-taking was questioned by Stern, Jaffe, Beebe and Bennett (1975). They reported that simultaneous vocalising was a feature of a number of pairs in their sample of 3-month-old infants, and this occurred more often than would be expected by a simple probabilistic model. Stern et al. suggested that there are two distinct modes of social interaction, alternating and co-actional (simultaneous), and they proposed that co-actional vocalising was associated with moments of high arousal. Stern regarded such moments of what he termed "chorusing" as a positive aspect of interaction, with both infant and mother appearing to gain satisfaction from achieving synchrony of action. One can often see this when an adult and baby will make cooing sounds together. He even suggested that such chorusing may help to establish a bond between participants much like the singing at religious services, national songs, and even sports events. In relation to this Collis (1985) has argued that co-actional vocalising is most likely to occur when the meaning of the vocalisation is not particularly important, the alternating mode being used when adults act "as if" they are conveying meaning to the infant via speech.

Observations by Schaffer, Collis and Parsons (1977) on older children confirmed that overlaps were not necessarily a break down in turn-taking. However, Schaffer, Collis and Parsons identified a wider range of overlaps, ranging from the chorusing described by Stern, warning calls from the mother, and mothers trying to quieten down children who were fussing. Furthermore, in these infants, who were 12 months old, alternation rather than simultaneous vocalisations appeared to be the predominant pattern. A more recent study by Kato and Fernald (1993) has revealed cultural differences; Japanese mothers were quicker than American mothers in responding to infant vocalisations, responded more often, and there were more vocal overlaps.

The investigations of whether infants play a part in influencing the pattern of vocal interaction have followed a similar course to studies of mother–infant gaze. Trevarthen (1977) claims that very young infants play a role by following and influencing an interactive rhythm. This seems to suggest that infants synchronise their vocalisations with parental speech at a time scale of a fraction of a second. Such a process would require very precise rhythms with very brief cycle duration, for which there appears to be no good evidence (Collis, 1985). Arguments by Mayer and Tronick (1985) that very young infants have marked skills for regulating alternation do not seem to be supported by the data that the authors themselves present.

A study by Davis (1978) examined mother–infant vocalisations in 6–16 month olds. He compared the turn-taking pauses in observed and shuffled data. He found that the mother–infant speaker-switch pauses (the time from the end of the maternal vocalisation to the beginning of the infant vocalisation) were similar in the observed and shuffled data. In addition, these pauses tended to be longer and more variable than infant–mother pauses. This suggests that infant behaviour was not adapted to turn-taking, and was no different from that expected by a chance arrangement of vocalisations. In contrast infant–mother pauses were shorter in the observed than the shuffled data, suggesting mothers were responding to the infant quicker than might be expected by chance. A further analysis using a random-shuffling technique by Ellias, Hayes and Broerse (1986) also found evidence for maternal, but not infant, control of interpersonal vocal sequencing.

A valuable longitudinal study of the development of turn-taking has been conducted by Rutter and Durkin (1987). They conclude from an analysis of interruptions of children by mothers, and of mothers by children, that it is not until the third year that children begin to play a significant role in controlling interpersonal regularities in vocal behaviour. The implication is that, with younger children, it is the adult who adapts to the child's pattern of vocalising so that the interaction has an alternating pattern. Data on peer interaction (de Maio, 1982) seem to be consistent with this view.

It should be noted that claims about the presence of active control of vocal interactions by 9-month-old infants have been made by Jasnow and Feld-stein (1986) who see that there is a process of "mutual influence and interpersonal accommodation" (p. 754) on the length of pauses between different speakers' vocalisations. However, it is difficult to understand how this conclusion can be made without comparing the pattern of vocalisation with a random model or by using an experimental intervention.

Although infants may not be taking an active part in turn-taking it would appear that turn-taking by an adult alters infant behaviour. A comparison was made between sessions in which an experimenter spoke and produced social behaviours after each infant vocalisation (i.e. turn-taking), and sessions in which experimenters made comments irrespective of the in-fants' vocalisations (Bloom, Russell & Wassenberg, 1987). It was found that sessions with turn-taking contained more infant vocalisations which were vocalic (cooing sounds) than syllabic (sounds made with the mouth open and relaxed). In addition, infants in the turn-taking sessions made more pauses between vocalisations than infants in the control condition.

These findings suggest that infants may be adapting their behaviour during contingent social interaction in a way that gives adults a stronger feeling of conversation. Bloom, Russell and Wassenberg suggest this will encourage adults to take part in conversation-like exchanges. In addition, a pattern of interaction that provides contingent responses to infant actions could give them a sense of control, and an opportunity to acquire the skills needed for taking part in a dialogue. There is also evidence that infants may suppress their vocalising while another person is speaking, and be more likely to vocalise when an adult has finished speaking (Schaffer, 1984).

Together, these investigations suggest that at an early age turn-taking is not an invariant feature of interaction and chorusing is surprisingly common. When turn-taking occurs it would appear that this is achieved by mothers fitting their behaviour around that of the infant, rather than the infants organising their vocalisations in a non-random manner. There are some indications that infant behaviour is influenced by the vocalisations of others, but these reactions may not be of sufficient sophistication to enable infants to regulate their vocalisations in relation to those of others.

An Example of Fitting Different Social Behaviours Together

So far the discussion of social interaction has concentrated on the way a single dimension of behaviour is organised. This has been a feature of investigations which have examined longer time periods, or have wished to provide an in-depth study of one aspect of interaction. However, a number of investigations have studied the organisation of different types of behaviour during interaction.

A study of the way that gaze, facial expression, and vocalisations are organised was conducted by Kaye and Fogel (1980) with infants who were 6, 13 and 26 weeks old. Infants were found to cycle through periods of attention at and attention away from the mother. In a similar way, maternal facial expressions cycled through a period of activity and inactivity. By multiplying the two proportions of attention and activity it was possible to estimate the expected proportion of time that mothers' active facial expressions would co-occur with gazes at them by the infants. The observed amount of this behaviour was significantly greater than expected at all three ages.

This led Kaye and Fogel to ask whether behaviour was related to that of the partner. They found that mothers tended to use more touching and bouncing when the infants were not looking at them, presumably in an effort to regain infant attention. They also found that the infants, at 6 weeks, were more likely to *start* looking at the mother if her face was inactive rather than active. Infants were then more likely to *continue* to look at the mother if her facial expression was active rather than inactive. In other words, touching and bouncing may have been used to gain the infant's attention, and facial expression to maintain the attention.

At 6 weeks the rate of infant facial expressions and vocalising was similar whether or not the infant was looking at the mother. However, at 13 and 26 weeks there were more vocalisations and smiles when looking at the mother. Furthermore, these rates were even higher when the infants were attending to the mother and her facial expression was active.

Kaye and Fogel reported that the incidence of many infant behaviours was similar to what might have been expected from a random organisation. This led them to reject the claim that infants are being entrained to their mother's rhythms. Instead they suggest that the mother provides a "frame" or context which can alter infant behaviour, as in the case of maternal active facial expression appearing to reduce the likelihood that infants would look away. In other words, Kaye and Fogel suppose that the broad context of maternal behaviour will alter the likelihood of an infant behaviour, but that this is not the result of the fine tuning of infant responses to what the mother is doing.

Wider Issues: People, Interaction and Attachment

The first six months is a time when parents and infants can get to know one another, a time when children become accustomed to some of the aspects of their culture. In all cultures the tasks of feeding, cleaning, soothing, putting to sleep, and entertaining mean that the mother and a small number of other caregivers have to be in regular contact with the child. These caregiving functions are not purely mechanical; Kaye has described feeding as a process which involves social interaction and adaptation. Similarly, the task of soothing a disturbed or crying child is not a mechanical process, but one where the caretaker is investigating what has led to the disturbance, trying to remedy it, and using social behaviour to calm the infant. The helplessness of infants necessitates some form of contact with adults.

As we have seen, the first six months of life, in Western cultures, is a period where intimate social exchanges are occurring between infants and the adults with whom they come into regular contact. The focus of many of these exchanges is the participants themselves. These processes have an obvious relevance to the issue of the way that communication develops. They also have a wider relevance in terms of the relationships that infants develop. As has already been outlined, infants seem to have a special orientation to the sight, sound and smell of their mothers shortly after birth. In addition, the sort of social interaction that we see in the first six months of life can build on these capacities to promote what Field (1985) has termed an attunement between parent and infant. Social interaction provides a history of joint experiences and a developing knowledge of each other. It would be remarkable if this does not have some impact on the attachment of infants to their parents, or as attachment theorists might say on the working model an infant has of his or her world.

Interestingly, a classic study by Schaffer and Emerson (1964) found that infants form attachments, not necessarily to those who take care of their physical needs, but to those who interact with and are responsive to them. Other more recent research has suggested that maternal responsiveness and sensitivity to infants may lead to secure patterns of attachment (Ainsworth, Blehar, Waters & Wall, 1978; Grossman, Grossman, Spangler, Suess & Unzner, 1985; Isabella, Belsky & von Eye, 1989), but it should be noted that the methodology of some of these studies has been criticised (Campos, Barrett, Lamb et al., 1983), and not all studies find similar relationships (Miyake, Chen & Campos, 1985). What is also of interest is that the process of adapting to a new caregiver is much easier in the first six months of life than afterwards. Yarrow (1964) studied the reactions of infants of various ages to being adopted. He found that infants under 6 months of age were much less rejecting and more accepting of their new adoptive parents than older infants.

Thus, it is becoming increasingly accepted that social interaction has a part to play in the development of social relationships. There has also been some measure of acceptance that social interaction allows shared understanding of the world to develop between adults and infants. The part of this picture that often has been ignored is the way that social relationships, social interaction, and a shared view of the world are interrelated. Infants develop relationships with adults with whom they interact, and they develop a shared view of the world with these adults through a process of social interaction. As a result communication can develop more easily with a small number of adults to whom infants are attached, and with whom they have a history of shared experiences.

SUMMARY

Infants come into the world with an interest in the types of stimuli that people produce. This prepares them to take part in conversation-like social exchanges. However, recent analyses of movement, social gaze, and vocal turn-taking have suggested that during the first few months infants are not equipped to be full partners in these exchanges, but that in our culture at least, interaction is structured by the adult so that it appears to have the pattern of a social exchange and turn-taking. The findings indicate that infants are often put in the position of appearing to function as competent members of our culture before they actually achieve this. The result is that infants become enmeshed in social exchanges from an early age. This, of course, fits the Vygotskian view, in that such exchanges may provide a basis for the later development of communicative and cognitive capacities.

The studies reviewed also highlight the difficulty in answering the seemingly simple question "do infants take part in social interaction?" We have seen that infants can identify certain individuals with whom they interact, and do modify their own behaviour according to the behaviour of their partner. From the studies that have been reviewed it is uncertain whether infants have the capacity for intersubjectivity. Furthermore, it does not appear that infants take an integrated and reciprocal part in interaction involving gaze or vocalisations. All this may just allow us to consider that infants make a contribution to social interaction, but that it is not a particularly well organised one.

4

TAKING INTERACTION FURTHER

During the first few months social interaction provides a basis for infants to develop relationships (see previous chapter). Somewhere between 4 and 6 months infants' orientation to people seems to change. A colloquial expression for this is that "the baby has found her hands". I can remember, when one of my children was about 5 months old, that over the course of a week he suddenly had a fascination with moving his hands in front of his face. It was as if he had discovered that he was in control of his hands and was learning more about the new found ability. This phenomenon seems to be part of a more general process in which infants shift their attention from the behaviour of caregivers to the world around them. As a result, the focus of social interaction moves away from the participants themselves (and what they are doing) to objects and events connected with these objects. A number of the theories identified in Chapter 2 describe this change, each putting a slightly different interpretation on the process. It is also noticeable that another component of this general shift seems to be a change from exploring objects with the mouth to exploring objects with hands.

This chapter describes the way that from about 6 months, social interaction is taken further, to include a wider range of topics, and allows the growth of a shared view of objects and events. Both Newson (1989) and Trevarthen (1977) emphasised the importance of this process for the development of communication. Although infants are orientated to people from birth they have a lot to learn about their culture, they need to acquire from adults a shared perspective about what are appropriate routines, what are important objects, and what can and cannot be done; adults need to learn what interests infants, what calms them, and what activities they enjoy. Both adult and infant need to develop a shared perspective of the world and of each other's intentions if the rudiments of communication are to emerge. I will argue that this shared understanding is fundamental to the comprehension and production of words; this follows Nelson (1985) who sees the acquisition of a *shared meaning system* as the fundamental process in the development of the ability to communicate effectively.

The chapter begins with a consideration of the social activities which could help to make a link between a word and a referent. Three types of activity are considered: indication, joint activities, and established procedures. This leads on to an examination of the evidence for the effect of joint attention on speech development.

IDENTIFYING A REFERENT

To use words infants need to be able to make a connection between a word, an object or event, and a concept for that object or event. This crude portrayal of the issue is known as the reference triangle (see Figure 4.1), a term used by Ogden and Richards (1923). In many ways we can think of infants as being like visitors from another world, they have to work out the relation between what is being said and what they can perceive. A major problem in making the connections in the reference triangle is identifying the referent from the array of objects and events in the child's world. How can the child relate a particular word to a particular object—how do they know that "look at teddy" refers to a particular soft toy?

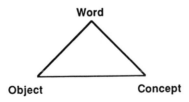

Figure 4.1 The reference triangle

The problem of relating words to referents has been a cause of concern to philosophers for centuries. For example, St Augustine is often seen as providing one of the earliest discussions of such developments. In his confessions he states that:

> "When they (my elders) named some object, and accordingly moved towards something, I saw this and I grasped that the thing was called by the sound they uttered when they meant to point it out. Their intention was shewn by their bodily movements, as it were the natural languages of all peoples: the expression of the face, the play of the eyes …Thus, I heard words repeatedly used in their proper places in

various sentences, I gradually learnt to understand what objects they signified; and after I had trained my mouth to form these signs, I used them to express my own desires."
(Augustine, *Confessions*, 1.8, translated in Wittgenstein, 1958)

Unfortunately, the *ostentive* view of reference, that words are learnt by the association of words and objects, fails to deal with the complexities of social interaction and the complexities of concept formation (see Chapters 5 and 6). However, it is still the case that there needs to be a variety of procedures that enable an adult and a child to attend to the same referent.

Following Adults' Pointing

A study in which I was involved (Murphy & Messer, 1977) investigated infants' ability to follow points. The infants were seated in high chairs next to their mothers, and there were three toys suspended on a wall in front of them (see Figure 4.2). Each mother was simply asked to draw her infant's attention to the toys. The mothers of 9-month-old infants invariably used conventional points. In pilot work we found that mothers of younger

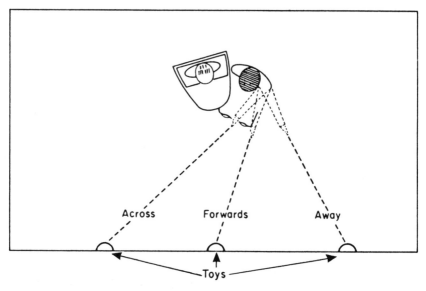

Figure 4.2 The three types of points that occurred during the observational sessions by Murphy and Messer (1977) (reproduced with permission from C. M. Murphy & D. J. Messer (1977) Mothers, infants and pointing: A study of a gesture. In H. R. Schaffer (Ed.), *Studies in Mother–Infant Interaction*. London: Academic Press)

infants tended to use other attention-getting devices in addition to pointing. They would click their fingers, wave their hand, or even in one case try to push the baby's head in the direction of the toy! This suggested that pointing to toys at a distance was not a usual activity with younger infants.

We found that 9-month-old infants could follow the forward points shown in Figure 4.2, which were directly in front of the pair. However, they usually could not follow points across their line of sight (see Figure 4.2). We supposed that in the case of maternal points to objects in front of the pair it was a relatively simple operation for infants to move from looking at the mother's hand to looking at the object. However, for points across their body, infants would have to extrapolate from the direction of the mother's arm to locate an object. Franco and Butterworth (1991a) have also suggested that young infants fail to utilise the geometric information inherent in a point.

In the same situation a group of 14-month-old infants were able to follow both the simple and more difficult points. A similar growth in ability has been observed by Lempers (1976) who found that most 9 and 10 month olds could follow points to objects which were near, but not to objects at a distance; by 12 months infants could follow points to distant objects.

Following Adults' Gaze and Head Turning

A more subtle form of joint attention occurs by following another person's direction of gaze. Scaife and Bruner (1975) conducted a study where an experimenter established eye contact with an infant before turning to face left or right. The findings suggested that following another's line of regard can occur by about 8 months (Collis, 1977). Similar studies have been conducted by Lempers (1976) and these suggest that infants of this age can follow head turning, but are unable to follow eye movements which are not accompanied by head turning.

A longitudinal investigation by Churcher and Scaife (1982) examined when infants began to follow head turning and pointing. The infants were first observed at 3 months. No target objects were used, rather the experimenter indicated an empty location. Most of the time the infants simply looked at the experimenter. By 40 weeks consistent following occurred in half the infants, suggesting that an ability to follow eye gaze emerges at about this age.

More recent studies by Butterworth and Grover (1988, 1989) have reported that at 6 months infants were able to follow an adult's gaze and head turning, but only when the target object was in their visual field and was readily distinguishable from the background. Further investigation of this ability by Butterworth and Jarrett (1991) has suggested that 6 month olds respond to the left or right direction of maternal looking rather than any precise locality. In contrast, 12-month-old infants are able to correctly locate one of two identical targets in their visual field, and therefore seem able to extrapolate from the direction of gaze of an adult to identify an object in their own visual field. These developments in the ability to infer direction of gaze seem to be similar to that present in the study of pointing that Cathy Murphy and I conducted. Butterworth and Jarrett (1991) found that by 18 months infants were able to go beyond their own visual field to locate objects (i.e. look behind themselves).

One reservation should be noted about these investigations of gaze. The investigations typically involve an adult first establishing eye contact with the infant and then turning their head and/or eyes in a particular direction. The adult and infant are usually seated facing each other. Thus, it is possible that in other circumstances, where the infant is less attentive of the mother, and has a less rich view of her head movements, then following would be less efficient.

Following the Infants' Lead: Pointing and Gaze

It is often assumed that adults direct infant interest but, however, infant behaviour can play an equally important role in the establishment of topics of mutual interest. The underestimation of infants' contribution is part of a perspective which regards children as less competent individuals who are recipients of adult wisdom. An important paper by Bell (1968) captured a mood which was moving away from unidirectional adult influences. Bell pointed out that infants also have effects on their parents, the direction of influence was not one way, and that often these influences had been ignored or underestimated.

Infants' direction of adult attention by pointing is an obvious example of their influence. Trevarthen (1977), and Fogel and Hannan (1985) have observed that infants a few months after birth employ manual activities which involve the extension of the index finger and curling of the others. Trevarthen (1977) sees these activities as reflecting a change in the level of communication itself. Fogel and Hannan report that this pointing is associated with mouth movements, and interpret it as being a reflection of emotional state rather than any desire to indicate something in the environment. There also is uncertainty about the relationship between this activity and later pointing.

It is generally accepted that the referential use of pointing only becomes an important activity for children older than 7 months (Murphy & Messer, 1977; Leung & Rheingold, 1981). There continues to be a debate about the way that pointing emerges. One suggestion is that it is the result of infants attempting to explore distant objects with their finger. For example, Vygotsky claimed that pointing originates from attempts to grasp a distant object, this action then becomes a social gesture through the response of adults (see Chapter 2). Some support for this account has been provided by Bower (1974) who has observed that early reaching is not followed by the infants being upset when they do not touch a distant object; from this he argues that these early reaches may in fact be a form of indication.

In contrast, Werner and Kaplan (1963) suggest that pointing originates independently from reaching because the activity is one of reference to an object or event. Franco and Butterworth (1991b) found that infants aged between 10 and 18 months (i.e. when pointing is already present), rarely reach for objects at a distance, will look at the mother after or during pointing, and make fewer points if their mother is not present. This led them to claim that pointing is the result of a referential function similar to that proposed by Werner and Kaplan. However, we should be careful about jumping to such conclusions without more information about the emergence of this capacity during the first year of life.

Children with autism have difficulties in their ability to communicate (see Chapter 16). Consequently, it is interesting that Baron-Cohen (1989a, 1993) has found that these children do not use or understand declarative pointing; this involves drawing attention to an object or event with eye contact being made between child and adult. However, children with autism will use and respond to points related to obtaining objects, and appear to use points in a solitary way when they do not look at adults to check their response. Thus, declarative pointing is implicated as an important process in the development of communicative abilities.

Adults very frequently respond to infant points. Murphy (1978) has reported that maternal naming of the appropriate object occurred more often than one would expect by chance when 14-month-old infants pointed at pictures during a book-reading session. The points of older children tended to be accompanied by mothers asking questions, a change which may reflect the mothers' sensitivity to the increasing verbal capacity of their children. Similarly, Masur (1982) has reported that infant points to distal objects were highly likely to be followed by the mother naming the object. Naming was more likely in these circumstances than after gestures which involved infants reaching for an object or showing an object to their mother. Such findings make it interesting that Baldwin and Markman (1989) found that naming plus pointing resulted in more attention to an object than pointing alone, and that this alteration in attention also occurred in a session afterwards when the adult was no longer pointing.

Co-ordination of attention is also achieved by adults following the direction an infant gazes. Collis (1977) has established that this occurs much more than would be expected by chance, and as a result the mother will often be looking at the same object as the infant. The mothers naturally enough then talk about the object of joint attention. Consequently, the careful timing of maternal behaviour appears to allow the infant to have the initiative in establishing subjects of shared visual interest. In a similar way, I have reported (Messer, 1978) that maternal speech often refers to objects that are being manipulated by the infant. As a result, maternal speech concerns objects which currently interest the child.

Joint Processes

So far the co-ordination of adult–infant interest has been described in terms of leading and following. We have seen that not only do adults follow the interest of infants, but also by the end of the first year infants are able to respond to adult gestures and interest. The end of the first year also sees the use of more complex processes. Interaction need not involve one individual directing the attention of the other by the use of explicit behaviours. Instead, it is possible to view the organisation of interaction as providing a structure which helps both participants locate a topic of shared interest. Children have a wider range of information about speech than is provided by ostentive activities such as pointing (Messer, 1983, 1986).

For example, it would appear that much of maternal speech consists of sequences of utterances which refer to the same object (Messer, 1980). We already know that many aspects of adult–infant social interaction involve some form of repetition. Speech is no exception to this; my transcriptions of mothers' speech to 11 month olds (and to 14 and 24 month olds) indicated that nearly 60% of maternal utterances involved the same referent as the previous utterance (e.g. "look at teddy", "isn't he nice", "make him walk"). I termed sequences of utterances which referred to the same object as "verbal episodes". The presence of verbal episodes means there is a high degree of redundancy about referents in speech to infants. A study of verbal episodes by Harris, Jones and Grant (1983) revealed that between 29 and 40 weeks there was a change in the reason for shifts in the topic of conversation. At the older age changes were more likely to be due to children's actions rather than their gaze.

The redundancy in maternal speech would be of very little use to pre-verbal children unless non-verbal information could be used to identify when a new referent is spoken about. For this reason I have been interested in detecting non-verbal cues which would help children to identify when a new topic of speech occurred, and my investigations identified three cues. The beginnings of verbal episodes were associated with infants or mothers having just manipulated a new object (nearly 70% of verbal episodes followed the manipulation of a new object). In addition, verbal episodes were more likely to follow a longer than normal pause between utterances. There was a pause of 2 to 3 seconds between maternal utterances in the same verbal episode, and an average pause of between 5 and 9 seconds (depending on age) between utterances which were in different verbal episodes. Thus, the structure and pace of speech could give infants a cue about a change of topic. I also found that the first utterance of an episode was more likely to contain the name of the referent. For children who have some command of words this could provide an important additional clue, as well as associating the word with the introduction of a new object. All this suggests that a complex arrangement of verbal and non-verbal behaviours marks out the topic of conversation between adults and infants. Thus, non-ostentive information is available to help children learn about new words that they hear.

Zukow (1990) has outlined an approach to viewing early social interaction which is based on the Gibsons' ideas about perception which are compatible with these observations (Gibson, 1979). Zuckow suggests that adults educate infant attention. They help to mark out what are important objects and events in terms of their cultural perspective. Adults also provide a context for their own utterances to aid interpretation. If they failed to do this they would not be able to make themselves understood during daily activities. In addition, Zukow argues that adults tend to repeat similar relations between utterances and context, so that infants experience similar formats (much as Bruner has suggested, see below). In these ways infants are able to understand speech within a cultural perspective.

However, it is also important to recognise that adult interaction may also be extending infant understanding beyond the here and now. Veneziano and Georgakopoulos (1993) have analysed the content of maternal speech to two French children in their second year of life. This analysis revealed that most adult speech was tied into current events, but also that about 40% of the adult utterances linked the current situation with some other past or future referent. These references increased with the age of the children.

Games and Procedures

Another aspect of social interaction which may help infants to begin to use words is behaviour rituals. Bruner (1975, 1983) has argued that taking part in the same activity over a number of months allows infants to understand the demands and the appropriate forms of communication that are required in the situation. For example, during book reading (Ninio & Bruner, 1978), maternal utterances appeared to occur in a specific order: a demand for attention—"look"; a question about the referent—"what's that?"; and a label—"it's a teddy".

Bruner suggests that the repeated exposure to rituals such as these enables children to come to understand their role in supplying conversation within an established format. The ritualised nature of these formats means that children have less difficulty in understanding the pragmatics of the situation—they already know how and when to respond. They can concentrate instead on working out the intricacies of the rules of language and how it maps onto the situation. In addition, such experiences are supposed to allow the infant to come to share with the adult a view of what is important, relevant, and of interest.

Joint Attention and Cognitive Development

The findings about joint attention have recently assumed significance in relation to discussions about the development of symbolic and metarepresentational abilities. Hobson (1993) has suggested that at about 8 months there is the beginning of "triadic relationships" which involve the infants themselves, another person, and a third entity. These relationships include following another's interest by using gaze or pointing, showing an object to another person, and social referencing (visually checking the response of another person to an event or thing). These behaviours, Hobson believes, indicate that infants are relating to another person's reactions to the world, a process that Trevarthen has described as secondary intersubjectivity (see Chapter 2). Hobson is not sure about the reason for the emergence of these abilities, but speculates they may be due to cognitive changes which involve the understanding of means-ends relations.

An interesting and crucial aspect of Hobson's argument is that these triadic relationships form the basis for the development of symbolic and metarepresentational abilities which allow children to distance themselves from reality. This is supposed to be achieved because infants start to notice that other people can have different reactions to the world than themselves, and in this way children discover that people can give different meanings to objects and events (the mother may find something funny which the child finds frightening). From these triadic relationships the child begins to understand that she can construct more than one representation of an entity. From this, Hobson suggests, it is a short step to have the capacity for symbolic play where children attribute new meanings to familiar objects.

The same set of phenomena has been interpreted in a different and more mechanistic way by Baron-Cohen (1993). He suggests that there is a cognitive module which involves an eye direction detector (EDD). Initially the module is attracted to eye-like stimuli and from this it starts to construct representations of the direction of another's eye gaze. These are dyadic representations which can specify where the self is gazing and where another (an agent) is gazing by the following notation [Agent–Eye Relation–Self], this means an infant registers that someone is looking at her.

Baron-Cohen believes that at about 6–9 months EDD builds representations of triadic relationships between self, agent, and a third entity. Consequently, the notation now contains an element that identifies when the agent and the infant are gazing at the same thing. Like Hobson, Baron-Cohen suggests that this triangular relationship allows infants to start to understand the mind of another by substituting "Eye" in the notation for states like interest, attention and so on. This process is carried further by EDD storing regularities about when eye gaze is associated with certain behaviours such as attending, wanting, referring, and acting upon. In this way EDD begins to identify mental states in other people.

Although Hobson and Baron-Cohen have very different orientations their explanations of the development of infants' understanding of other people are similar on many points. Particularly striking is the way that both investigators focus on triadic representations as providing the genesis of higher mental constructs. However, an important difference between them concerns the *way* their models are constructed. Hobson's is a descriptive account paying attention to the subtleties of social interaction. Baron-Cohen's account is in the cognitive tradition of providing a formal account of the development of an ability. This has the advantage of giving a clearer specification in terms of the operation of EDD. However, the cost of constructing this type of model is that the complexities of social behaviour are ignored in the drive to describe an autonomous system. For instance, Baron-Cohen states "once EDD can build dyadic representations, I propose that it develops further by building a new class of representations, called triadic representations". It is undoubtedly true that this statement captures part of the internal process that is occurring during early development. However, the statement glosses over the social processes *between* people which at the very least provide a context for the development of EDD, and must provide some type of input to the system. What is striking is that both these approaches maintain that the referential system is a crucial part of childhood development.

Summary

There is considerable evidence that, even before the onset of speech, adult–infant social interaction involves procedures which enable both participants to attend to and direct the attention of each other. These procedures are likely to be necessary before experience within a social setting can have an impact on the infant's cognitive skills, for without ways to regulate mutual attention, the task of acquiring knowledge and symbols becomes much more difficult. Because these skills are implicated in the acquisition of vocabulary, it is likely that they are the basis for further communicative and cognitive advances. These referential skills have recently received attention in relation to the part they play in the development of symbolic and representational capacities. Such theories serve to emphasise the crucial part these skills play in early development.

The use of all these methods of communication is likely to result in children not just being able to identify a referent, but also to develop further understanding of the objects and events which are important in their culture. It seems likely that children are not simply building a reference triangle, rather they are coming to understand their cultural environment, and as a result they start to share the adults' view of the world and their environment. When adults and children develop some type of shared understanding of their world, then indication and the establishment of topics can occur with much less effort and without the need for lengthy processes of indication. The shared understanding enables both partners to make reasonable guesses about the referent of conversation.

INTERACTION AND VOCABULARY GROWTH

Up to now arguments have been put forward that the structure of social interaction aids the acquisition of words by infants. What evidence do we have to support this argument? Findings from studies of twins, longitudinal studies, and experimental studies will be reviewed which all point to the importance of joint attention to language development.

Language Development in Twins

Studies in the 1930s suggested that the speech of twins was delayed in comparison to singletons (Day, 1932; Davis, 1937). Day reported a delay in the onset of speech, reduced vocabulary, and immature sentence construction. Day also observed that these problems decreased during the pre-school years. These findings have been broadly confirmed by more recent studies with it being found that the speech of twins has caught up with singletons by the school years, although there may be small deficiencies in some areas (Mogford, 1988). It should also be noted that being a twin does not inevitably result in delays. There are at least two studies in which there were no delays (Savic, 1980; McCormick & Dewart, 1986). In both these studies the parents had high levels of education and relatively advantaged social positions.

What are the explanations of this early delay in language? One is that the delay might be due to the greater sharing of biological resources during pregnancy or to complications during delivery. Lytton (1980) failed to find strong relationships between perinatal complications and language in a group of 2–3-year-old boy twins. Similarly, Mittler (1970) found only a few associations between pre- and perinatal characteristics with later language delay in twins. Another study by Record, McKeown and Edwards (1970) found no delay in the language and intellectual development of singletons whose twin sibling had died, thus suggesting that sharing a rearing environment, rather than sharing the womb, has a significant influence on development.

How might sharing a rearing environment cause an early delay in language? Two explanations have been put forward. One is that the close relationship between the twins reduces the need for verbal communication. The other is that adults have only finite resources of time and attention so that the division of these resources reduces opportunities for the child. What may be particularly important is that the adults will therefore be less able to relate their speech to topics in which each child has an interest.

Zazzo (1978) has identified language which may be the result of a close relationship between twins—a secret language in the sense that it is unintelligible to others. Zazzo suggests that these secret languages may impede the acquisition of the mother tongue. Surprisingly, Mittler reports that nearly half of his sample were reported to have a secret language. Thus, there is a possibility that the close relationship, and the presence of idiosyncratic methods of communication, may reduce the motivation for acquiring the mother tongue and may interfere with this process.

There is even stronger evidence for the delays also being caused by division of resources. Bornstein and Ruddy (1984) found no difference between twins and singletons at 4 months on the Bayley test or on habituation measures: i.e. both groups appeared to have similar cognitive abilities. However, mothers of twins encouraged infants to attend to their environment only half as much as singletons. At 12 months it was found that twins had on average half the vocabulary of singletons. For singletons the mothers who more frequently encouraged their 4-month-old infants to attend to the environment tended to have infants with larger vocabularies at 12 months (this was the most important behaviour of several that were measured, including the amount of speech). For twins there was no relation between these two sets of measures. Bornstein and Ruddy suggested that their findings indicate that maternal behaviour rather than initial abilities accounts for the early differences in language.

Tomasello, Mannle and Kruger (1986) have examined the speech of twins and singletons at a later age, between 15 and 21 months. The singletons were matched to the language level of the twins. The study showed that the mothers were as active with twins as singletons but that each twin received less joint attention to the same object or topic, and fewer maternal responses that extended the number of turns in conversation. These characteristics were found to be associated with poorer language development.

Thus, the evidence suggests that the difficulties that parents face in dividing resources between twins may lead to the delay in early speech. The studies also point to the possibility that joint attention to a topic may be important in developing shared understandings which form the basis for later language development. Furthermore, it should be recognised that not all twins have a delay in starting to use language and that in older children this delay is likely to disappear.

Reference to Objects—Longitudinal Studies

Non-experimental studies have suggested that mothers who provide a close link between speech and objects have children with larger vocabularies and more advanced speech. A study by Masur (1982) found that larger vocabularies were associated with mothers frequently naming objects at which their child pointed. Wells and Robinson (1982) commented that infants who received more speech about shared activities, and about topics that were identified by them, were more linguistically advanced at a later age. More recently Baumwell, Tamis-LeMonda, Kahana-Kalman and McClure (1993) have found that maternal verbal responsiveness to changes in 9-month-old infants' behaviour predicted comprehension at 13 months, even when a control was instituted for vocabulary size at 9 months. Furthermore, there are also studies which indicate that measures of maternal encouragement of attention with 4-month-old infants relate to vocabulary size at 12 months (Ruddy & Bornstein, 1982); and this might be explained by continuities in maternal interactional style.

Other investigations have also indicated the importance of reference to objects that are the focus of children's attention. Harris, Jones, Brookes and

Grant (1986) compared 2 year olds whose language was normal with those whose language was delayed. The comparison revealed that the mothers of the more advanced children spoke more about objects that were the current focus of interest, they referred less to objects which were not the focus of interest, and referred less to general features of the objects (e.g. interesting). A further investigation by Harris has suggested that the context of children's first word use corresponds to the most usual context in which the mother had previously used the word (Harris, 1993).

A longitudinal study by Tomasello and Todd (1983) examined social interaction at 12 months and children's vocabulary size at 18 months. Children who experienced longer episodes of joint attention had larger vocabularies at the later age. In addition, the frequency with which mothers directed infants' attention was negatively related to later vocabulary size.

These findings were replicated with 15 and 21 month olds by Tomasello and Farrar (1986). In this study a more detailed examination was made, and it was noted whether maternal utterances had these characteristics: following the child's interest; use of an accompanying non-verbal referential gesture; and the child focusing on the toy at the time of the reference. Mothers who produced more utterances with these three characteristics at 15 months had children with larger vocabularies at 21 months. The frequency of utterances which had none of these characteristics was related to having a smaller vocabulary at 21 months.

The benefits of following infant attention and not directing it are also reported by Akhtar, Dunham and Dunham (1991). Mothers who produced more commands directing their 13-month-old infants' attention in relation to an object the infant was already holding and/or looking at, had children with a larger vocabulary at 22 months.

These studies use a correlational approach and have found that vocabulary size is related to characteristics of maternal speech. These findings suggest, but do not establish, causal connections. Other explanations of the findings are possible, for example, maternal behaviour may reflect infant abilities rather than being a cause of the ability. Because of such difficulties of interpretation it is reassuring that experimental studies have examined similar issues.

Reference to Objects—Experimental Studies

Object words

A number of experimental investigations have shown that the learning of words becomes increasingly efficient with increasing age. Lloyd, Werker and Cohen (1993) assessed the ability of 8–14 month olds to associate novel words with novel pictures in a habituation paradigm, finding that the 14 month olds were much more efficient at this type of learning. Oviatt (1980) had a training session with a live rabbit and a live hamster. Each animal was labelled 24 times during a 3-minute session. Afterwards, half the 12–14 month olds looked at the animal when asked where it was, and 80% of 15–17 month olds were able to do this. Nelson and Bonvillian (1978) achieved a similar success in labelling objects for 16–17 month olds.

The sophisticated information processing abilities of even 16-month-old infants are shown in a study by Baldwin (1991). An experimenter labelled objects at which he was looking while the child was looking at another object, although the child could use peripheral vision to monitor the adult's activities. Children showed evidence of having acquired information about the appropriate words in a comprehension test. What is quite remarkable about these findings is that the infants did not simply assume that a word was paired with the object in which they were interested—this would have led to the learning of many incorrect associations. Instead, they appeared to use the experimenter's eye gaze as a clue about the appropriate referent. By 2 years children are even more sophisticated in their ability to work out the referent from the cues provided by the context, and they are able to associate a novel word with an object in the following situation. A person says they are looking for a thing which is referred to by a novel word. The person picks up a number of objects and eventually gives a pleased ex-pression when she picks up a particular toy; children treat that object as the referent of the novel word (Tomasello & Barton, in press; see Chapter 8 for a discussion of this and other studies).

An experimental study which examined the circumstances that promote word acquisition was conducted by Tomasello and Farrar (1986) with 17-month-old children. They used four training sessions of 15–20 minutes in which labelling occurred, either after the child had shown manipulative or visual interest in the target object, or when the child's interest was directed to a target object. Afterwards, a test of comprehension was con-ducted by asking children to identify a particular object from a group.

Names that had been used when following the child's interest were more likely to be comprehended than the names used in the more directive circumstances. From this it was suggested that not only is joint attention an important process in vocabulary development, but it is important for naming to *follow* the child's interest rather than for it to occur when the child's interest is being *directed*. An experimental study by Whitehurst and Valdez-Menchaca (1988) with 28–34 month olds obtained similar findings, that is, saying a word when a child was interested in an object was more effective in assisting acquisition than the incidental use of words.

Some caution still needs to be exercised before concluding that directiveness is an inappropriate strategy. For example, checks need to be made about the relation between attention to the referent and the timing of naming in both directing and following conditions. Thus, it may be premature to conclude that directing children's interests is a less effective method of vocabulary acquisition.

As children become older the close relation between words and ongoing activities appears to be a feature of less advanced conversations. A study by Cross (1977) with older children reports that a close relation between speech and ongoing activities was related to slower linguistic development. Similarly, Pappas-Jones and Adamson (1987) found that the referential use of words by mothers was related to smaller vocabulary size between 18 to 23 months, but asking questions about words was related to a larger vocabulary. Both studies suggest that with increasing age different sorts of relation between speech and environment are needed for the optimal development of language, and it seems likely that older children need conversations that provide opportunities to acquire more complex features of the linguistic system, such as past or future tenses and more complex constructions. This is sometimes known as the *fine tuning* hypothesis. It has also been found that social reinforcement assists the acquisition of foreign words by 2–3 year olds, again indicating the importance of the broader social context (Whitehurst, Fischel, Lonigan et al., 1988).

Action words

The acquisition of action words has been neglected in the research literature. An important paper by Tomasello and Kruger (1992) is likely to provide the foundation for research into the acquisition of these words. Action words (i.e. words which adults would consider as verbs), unlike object words, usually refer to short events which do not remain available to the child's senses (e.g. "the bricks fall down", "the bunny squeaks"). Tomasello and Kruger reason that pointing would be a difficult and inappropriate way to identify an activity. As a result, they suppose that acquisition might be assisted if an utterance containing an action word was produced before the activity; in this way the child could relate the word to the *impending* activity. Two other possible relations also were considered, action words related either to *ongoing* infant activities or to *completed* infant activities.

Observations were made of mother–infant interaction at 13 and at 18 months. This revealed that by far the most frequent relation, at both ages, between maternal verbs and infant actions was impending (these were 60% of all action word utterances). The least frequent relationship involved mothers using an action word when the activity was completed. Most of the impending utterances involved either a direct request for an infant action or the mother's anticipation of the infant's action.

The relationship between the three types of action word utterances at 13 months and the children's verb vocabulary at 18 months was assessed. The more frequent use of impending utterances during episodes of joint attention predicted a larger verb vocabulary at 18 months. The use of action words outside episodes of joint attention predicted smaller verb vocabularies at the later age. The other significant positive relation involved completed utterances about non-infant actions. A higher frequency of these during episodes of joint attention predicted a larger verb vocabulary at the older age.

This study was followed by an experimental training procedure to assess the effectiveness of the various strategies. The study revealed that impending action utterances were more likely to be associated with later production of the word, while both the impending and completed conditions were associated with comprehension of the word. The authors suggest that the problem with the ongoing condition is that it may overload the children's information processing capacity.

A study by Camarata and Leonard (1986) has found that object words are more accurately produced by young children than action words. Children of between 20 to 25 months were given training sessions where they were told the name of objects or actions in a conversational format where the word was linked to ongoing activities. They attributed their findings to the higher processing demands associated with action words. However, it should be noted that the work by Tomasello and Kruger casts doubt on the appropriateness of these comparisons; the production of verbs may have been impaired because they were said at the *same time* as the actions, rather than before the actions.

SUMMARY

The infants' home environment presents a rich source of non-verbal information that could help the understanding of speech. There are a variety of procedures which can be employed to make sure that both infant and adult are attending to the same entity. However, as I have tried to show in this chapter the identification of referents may be the result of the development of shared understanding. Adult and infant learn together what are the dimensions in the world which they regard as important and interesting. The understanding of the link between a word and a referent is the result of a shared history which allows infants to understand the intent of adult communication. In relation to this there is a growing body of evidence which indicates the importance of joint attention for the development of children's vocabulary (vocabulary size is a good predictor of later linguistic ability and of intelligence). Studies with blind children have also indicated the importance of shared attention and understanding (see Chapter 15). However, care is needed about assuming that these are universal patterns of behaviour. As will be discussed in Chapter 14 other cultures may not have the same set of close relations between speech and non-verbal activities. Furthermore, it should be remembered that the reference triangle is a gross simplification of the links between words and their referents. The development of children's concepts and the understanding of meaning is a complex process which is explained in a variety of ways, and this topic will be considered in Chapter 6. Chapter 5, the next chapter, considers the development of the capacity to produce vocalisations and words.

5

GETTING READY TO USE WORDS

Psychologists have often neglected the process of comprehension and vocal development in relation to language acquisition. Comprehension has been neglected because of the methodological problems surrounding such investigations and because it is easier to record what a child does than to infer what she understands. In the case of vocal development, models of language acquisition have often implicitly assumed that infants will effortlessly produce words when this skill is needed. I suspect that the neglect of vocal development partly stems from the problems of dealing with an already complex issue, and partly from the problems of understanding the linguistically-based literature about vocal development.

The initial section of this chapter considers children's ability to respond to and comprehend particular aspects of speech. This builds on the material which was presented in Chapter 1 about the general attractiveness of A–C speech. The second section provides an outline of vocal development and shows that there is a complex unfolding of innate capacities in relation to the speech models heard by infants. The last section of the chapter provides an outline of the way infants start to use words in a communicative manner.

NON-LINGUISTIC PATTERNS IN ADULT SPEECH AND INFANT RESPONSES

The first part of this section describes typical sound patterns in adult utterances to infants. We see that adults use similar ways of signalling the intent of speech across different cultures and languages. This leads on to an examination of the way infants respond to utterances with these special characteristics. Then theories about the way infants start to identify words in utterances are discussed. This is followed by a brief discussion of infants' ability to react to speech prior to language.

Adults' Speech to Infants

Before infants are able to speak or respond to individual words they can respond to the *suprasegmental* characteristics of speech (literally the characteristics of speech which continue across words and are present throughout an utterance). The term *prosodic* is also used in a similar way to refer to the sound patterns which cross segments.

Research by Fernald (1989) indicates that the prosodic characteristics of speech to children can provide useful cues about the intent of an utterance. Adult speech to children was electronically processed so that words were no longer recognisable, but the utterances retained their prosodic characteristics (i.e. the general pattern of sound which was not related to individual words). Adult judges were very accurate in identifying whether an utterance involved approval, a bid for attention, a prohibition, giving comfort, or a game. The judges were less accurate when attempting the same task using adult-to-adult speech (A–A speech).

There appear to be a number of distinct prosodic patterns in speech to infants. Stern, Spieker and MacKain (1982) observed that the use of rising pitch occurred when infants were inattentive and mothers wished to obtain their attention, and bell-shaped pitch contours (i.e. rising and then falling) were used when mothers appeared to want to maintain infant attention.

Further work in this area has been conducted by Papousek and her colleagues (Papousek, Papousek & Haekel, 1987) who claim that adults' speech to young infants contains a restricted number of melodic units. They classified the sound contours of utterances as: level, rising, falling, U-shaped, bell-shaped, or complex sinusoidal. Across three languages (American English, Mandarin and German), encouraging an infant turn was associated with a rising intonation, soothing with a falling intonation, rewarding a turn with a bell-shaped pattern (i.e. rising then falling; intonation refers to the pitch characteristics of a phrase which are associated with meaning). Papousek, Papousek and Haekel propose that these melodic units may constitute universal patterns of pre-linguistic communication. These melodic units are supposed to be used in consistent ways within a culture. In addition, they are supposed to be aligned with the perceptual preferences and abilities of infants. Mandarin Chinese is one of the languages in which differences of tone for the same sound can convey different meanings, and therefore such a system would be expected to place constraints on the use of tone in A–C speech (tone refers to the use of pitch on an individual word to give it different meanings). However, Papousek, Papousek and Symmes (1991) found that Chinese mothers use similar melodic contours to other mothers in nonsense expressions and they even violate the tone-rules of their language. Papousek and her colleagues see this as evidence for cross-linguistic universals which are used by parents when communicating with infants. The suprasegmental characteristics of speech to infants that have just been described appear to be present in many Western and non-Western countries (Garnica, 1977; Stern, Spieker, Barnett & MacKain, 1983; Fernald, Taeschner, Dunn et al., 1989; see also Chapter 1). Sometimes it has been suggested that the modifications represent universal adaptations. However, there are reports that in some cultures the modifications are not present. Their absence has been noted in the Kaluli of New Guinea (Schieffelin, 1979), in groups who speak Quiche-Mayan in Guatemala (Ratner & Pye, 1984), and in lower socio economic status (SES) blacks of the United States (Heath, 1983). To further complicate matters these studies have been criticised for either having a limited speech sample or for using only subjective assessments (Fernald, 1991).

Infant Reaction to Suprasegmental Characteristics of Adults' Speech

The suprasegmental characteristics that are present in A–C speech appear to have general effects on infant attention and arousal. Ryther-Duncan, Scheuneman, Bradley et al. (1993) found that 4-month-old infants were better at associative learning when they heard A–C speech in the background rather than A–A speech. Werker and McLeod (1989) have reported that at 4 months infants are more attentive and more sociable to video pictures of adults speaking A–C speech than to adults engaging in A–A speech. More specific analysis by Papousek, Bornstein, Nuzzo et al. (1990) has revealed that 4-month-old infants are more likely to look at a photograph of a face which was associated with approving sounds, and less likely to look at a face associated with disapproving sounds. Similarly, it would seem that by 5 months infants' facial reactions are more positive when they hear voices giving approval and more unhappy when the voices are scolding. This occurred with A–C speech, but not A–A speech.

Languages vary in their use of intonation, that is, the use of pitch to carry some form of meaning. For example, in Britain, questions are often spoken with a rising intonation, the pitch of the voice being raised towards the end of the utterance. In contrast, commands and statements are often spoken with a falling intonation. The possibility that infants may make sense of suprasegmental characteristics of adult speech before they understand words has been examined by Ryan (1978). She found that when a mother used rising intonation, 12-month-old infants were more likely to shift their attention from a toy that they were holding, to a toy held by the mother. Shifts in attention were not associated with other forms of intonation. Ryan suggested that rises tended to be used when mothers wanted to redirect their infants' attention, and falling intonation when a declarative utterance was used to refer to an object. Ryan speculated that the importance of these prosodic contours is that they allow both partners to understand when an utterance is non-referential and involves a shift in attention to something else.

Infant Identification of Salient Words in Adults' Speech

Infants appear to be provided with speech which helps them to understand the intent of an utterance. Another task for infants is to identify individual words in the speech they hear. Such a process is necessary before words can be produced.

What processes allow infants to locate salient words in the stream of speech that they hear? As adults, we hear spoken words as distinct auditory entities, separate from other words. The auditory characteristics of speech do not, however, show such a neat segmentation. When speaking there is a continuous production of sound, and silence between words is rare. We can recognise this problem when we have to detect the difference between "I scream" and "ice-cream" or to detect the word boundaries in an unfamiliar foreign language (Fernald, 1991b).

It has been argued by Gleitman and Wanner (1982) that infants will automatically segment speech into smaller elements (Ervin-Tripp, 1973). They suppose that infants do not have to acquire this ability, since it is part of the nervous system. Gleitman and Wanner (1982) argue that infants are predisposed to attend to stressed syllables, and by this means identify words. They base their argument on the fact that unstressed words appear to be absent from the vocabularies of young children who are starting to speak a variety of languages (e.g. words like, "a", "in", "you"). In addition, young children tend to produce the stressed parts of words, for example, they will say "raff" for giraffe, where the stressed rather than the unstressed syllable is produced.

Similarly, Peters (1983) believes that various cues will help infants to identify words. Her proposals have been influenced by Slobin's (1973) suggestions about the way infants process speech. Peters supposes that infants will first of all identify whole utterances by the silences before and after them, the suprasegmental contour, the melody of the utterance, and its rhythm. At the same time, infants begin to segment (i.e. split) an utterance into smaller units. This process is supposed to occur through infants identifying the following syllables from the rest: the first, the last, any stressed syllables, units at rhythmically salient places, and units at intonationally salient places.

There is also observational evidence that mothers stress or emphasise words in their speech to infants in ways that would help infants locate individual words which are semantically important. Stress or emphasis on words can make them more prominent than others. The perception of loudness is a complex process in adults involving amplitude, intensity, fundamental frequency, and duration. Little is known about the mechanism of this process in infants, although it is unlikely to be very different from that in adult perception.

A study that I carried out was designed to examine the amplitude of words in mothers' speech to 14-month-old infants (Messer, 1981). The word which had the highest acoustic amplitude in each maternal utterance was identified. Labels for objects were more likely than any other word class to be the loudest in an utterance. This could provide an important way for infants to identify labels in maternal speech. In addition, I found that labels tended to occur in the last position of the utterance, a position where they are more likely to be noticed and remembered. Furthermore, labels were more likely to be the loudest word in an utterance after there had been a change in topic of interaction. This also may help infants to relate the label to the referent.

These findings have been extended by Fernald and Mazzie (1991). They found that mothers consistently gave new words prominence when reading a story to their 14-month-old infants. A comparison of the mothers' speech to their infants with their speech to adults revealed that the new words in speech to infants were more likely to have a higher fundamental frequency, were more likely to be positioned at the end of utterances, and were more likely to be judged by students of linguistics to be given a greater stress. Thus, it would not only appear that there are a number of strategies which children can employ to identify individual words, but the speech to infants also provides a number of cues which would help the identification of important words.

Responding to Words

Before children produce their first words there is evidence that they react to some words used by adults (Benedict, 1979). One of the first responses to speech is infants stopping what they are doing and turning to the speaker when their name is called (Benedict, 1979). They may also stop what they are doing when adults use a loud and emphatic "No". These abilities are present before 9 months and even may be present several months earlier.

The exact status of this comprehension is uncertain. It has been argued by some (e.g. Bates, Bretherton & Snyder, 1988) that such responses reflect learning in a certain set of circumstances, and do not reflect adult-like comprehension of words. Particularly important has been the notion that these are limited responses which do not have the flexibility of true word comprehension (i.e. understanding that there are names for other people, and understanding that "no" can be disobeyed). According to a Piagetian perspective such responses to words might be seen as part of the association children have with a restricted set of circumstances; words do not have a symbolic function, rather they are part of the set of motor acts and sensations associated with the certain events (i.e. sensorimotor functioning). For instance, when infants say "bye-bye" it is always accompanied by the gesture of waving. More recent research by Harris, Barlow-Brown and Chasin (1993) has revealed that the understanding of object names (based on parental report together with experimental investigation) coincided with children starting to use gestural points, and they speculate that this may be the result of a change in cognitive abilities that allows both these capacities to develop at the same time.

Usually it has been assumed by parents and by investigators that children can comprehend more complex utterances than it is possible for them to speak (e.g. Huttenlocher, 1974). In other words they can understand multi-word utterances even though they are unable to produce them. It seems likely that the reason for this difference is the fewer cognitive demands involved in processing someone else's utterance compared to planning and producing one of your own (although there is some evidence that production may sometimes precede comprehension: McDonald & Lang, 1993).

Summary

Infants, in most cultures, are presented with speech which has the intent of the utterances clearly marked. By 12 months they are able to respond to these patterns in appropriate ways, by for example looking when there is rising intonation. There have been a number of suggestions about the way infants are able not only to respond to intonation, but also to identify individual words. Furthermore, in A–C speech individual, semantically important words seem to be marked out and this may aid acquisition and understanding. However, as yet we have few details about the way infants respond to and perhaps comprehend words before they can speak.

EARLY VOCAL DEVELOPMENT

The study of vocalisations involves two important areas of study, *phonetics* and *phonology*. The study of *phonetics* is concerned with the articulation necessary to produce sounds (the movements of the mouth, tongue, lips, etc.) and with describing the acoustic characteristics of sounds. The smallest unit of sound that can be identified is known as a *phone*. *Phonology* concerns the relation between sounds and meaning. The smallest unit of sound that conveys meaning in a word is known as a *phoneme*. There are differences between languages in the phonemes that are important to convey meaning. Thus, in some languages, a particular distinction between sounds can result in the production of different words, while in other languages the same two sounds can be accepted as variations that are used to produce the same word. For instance, the sounds "l" and "r" are distinguished in English, but not in Japanese, and as a result, Japanese have difficulty in distinguishing between English words which differ only in these sounds. In a single language, different versions of the same phoneme are produced by processes such as co-articulation, when the production of a sound is influenced by the preceding or subsequent sound in a word.

Infants' Production of Vocalisations

Because the motor movements employed to produce speech are so easy and automatic for adults, the production of speech appears deceptively simple. These movements are in fact intricate and carefully co-ordinated activities. Over the first year of life infants develop the capacity to produce more and more complex sounds, and the sounds they produce appear to be influenced by the types of sounds they hear.

Crying is the most prominent vocalisation for the first weeks after birth (see Chapter 1). At about 2–3 months, cooing and laughter appear as distinct vocalisations. Cooing involves the production of attractive vowel-like sounds and velar consonants (e.g. "g" and "c" type sounds). One proposal is that crying provides a basis for the development of vowel sounds. In the same way it has been suggested that the vegetative sounds involved in feeding and the clearing of the airways provide a template for the development of consonants (Stark, 1980, 1989). However, it is also possible that there is some discontinuity with earlier sounds (Oller, 1986). Indeed, more recent findings have led Stark (1989) to revise her earlier views and consider that there is some reorganisation of the production of sounds when cooing emerges. She also makes the interesting suggestion that the reorganisation could be related to the use of smiling and mutual eye gaze during social interaction.

Consonants appear after about 5 months. There is controversy about whether these sounds are already influenced by the language used in the home. Boysson-Bardies, Sargart and Durand (1984) report that both phoneticians and ordinary listeners could distinguish the sounds produced by 4-month-old infants according to whether their parents spoke Chinese, Arabic or French. Using human judges, rather than mechanical acoustic analysis, in such experiments has the advantage of fully utilising the appropriate human senses to make decisions about sounds. However, such judgements do not tell us which acoustic characteristics give rise to the differences in perception.

An analysis of acoustic characteristics by Thevenin, Eilers, Oller and Lavoir (1985) failed to detect phonological differences according to the home language group, and they suggest that the differences reported by Boysson-Bardies were due to intonation (the way the pitch of the voice varies), rather than phonology. Subsequent investigations have tended to support the claim that there are differences in the pre-speech vocalisations of infants which are related to the language used at home (e.g. Levitt & Utman, 1992). Of relevance to such findings is the suggestion by Papousek and Papousek (1989) that phonetic development will be influenced not simply by the exposure to speech, but also by the selective imitation of the more linguistically appropriate infant sounds by adults. In this way infants may be exposed to vocalisations which reflect back the phonological characteristics of their language.

It is also the case that the initial production of the sounds for words is constrained by the articulatory abilities of infants. Stampe (1969) identified phonological processes which children employ to allow them to substitute easier-to-produce sounds for more difficult-to-produce sounds (e.g. substitute "ting" for "sing"); perceptual processes may also play a part in this phenomenon (Smith, 1989). Similar processes have been observed in the production of American and British Sign Language where children adapt signs made by hands because of their difficulty in producing these movements (McIntire, 1977; Clibbens & Harris, 1993).

Babbling

Somewhere between 6 and 10 months infants start to babble. This often starts suddenly, rather than there being a gradual development of the behaviour. Canonical babbling, which usually emerges first, involves the production of a CV (consonant and then vowel) sound such as "ba". At the same time or shortly afterwards, infants produce reduplicated babbling in which there is a repetition of the CV structure (e.g. CVCV "baba").

Sometimes, as in the example of "baba", the sound is similar to a word; however, such sounds do not appear to be used systematically or to have symbolic content.

Petitto and Marenette (see Clibbens & Harris, 1993) observed deaf infants whose parents used sign language. The investigators report that 8–10 month olds produce "manual babbling" which is apparently meaningless but systematic hand gestures, and infer that this indicates children have innate, specific, abilities related to language acquisition which can be produced in various modalities (e.g. vocal or manual). However, Bates (1993) interprets such "babbling" as the result of the general capacity to imitate.

It has been supposed that variegated babbling, which does not involve repetition of elements, but involves a greater diversity of sounds, occurs later at 10–13 months (Oller, 1980; Stark, 1980). In some respects the variegated babbling can be thought of as bearing a closer resemblance to word production, with the use of sounds like "adega".

The supposition that babbling can simply be divided into stages has been challenged by Mitchell and Kent (1990) and by Blake and De Boysson-Bardies (1992). All suggest that the developmental progression is more complex than a stage model would suggest. However, there is agreement that there are different forms of babbling, but disagreement concerning the way they emerge.

The origins and significance of babbling

Questions about the origins of babbling have led to a number of studies being conducted on infants who are deaf. There has been an interest in determining whether babbling is a spontaneous activity under maturational control, as well as in whether hearing the vocalisations of others and oneself is necessary for its development. As might be expected from a complex issue such as this (there are problems in diagnosing hearing impairment and assessing the sounds that are produced), there are differences in findings between studies.

Studies prior to the 1980s indicated that vocal development was similar in children who could and could not hear (Lenneberg, 1967; Mavilya, 1972). However, subsequent studies have suggested that even by 6 weeks, infants who are deaf produce fewer vocalisations (Maskarinec, Cairns, Butterfield & Weamer, 1981), that there is a smaller range of vocalisations, and that the vocalisations decline in use with age (Stoel-Gammon & Otomo, 1986). In addition, reduplicated babbling is much less likely to occur with infants who are deaf, although there are some similarities in the vocalisations of infants who can hear and of those who are deaf (Oller, 1986). Furthermore, parents tend to ignore the vocalisations of children when they know that they are deaf, in marked contrast to their reactions to infants who can hear (Mogford & Gregory, 1982); such an absence of attention will influence interaction and possibly the development of vocal abilities.

There is still controversy over the importance of babbling for later sound production. Some have suggested that the absence of babbling will have adverse consequences for later speech production (Netsell, 1981; Locke, 1989). This debate has led to a small number of studies being conducted on infants who, because of a blockage to the upper respiratory tract, have had a tracheotomy performed on them. This surgical operation involves inserting a tube through the skin of the throat to allow breathing. In most cases the procedure prevents vocalisations as air does not pass over the vocal apparatus. When the illness is cured the operation can be reversed and this allows the child to produce sounds.

Locke (1989) has reported the case of a girl who was tracheotomised from 5 to 20 months, and found that she showed very poor articulation of sounds for the two months following the removal of the tube. Locke suggests that the failure to hear sounds produced by herself caused the delays in vocal development (of course it is also possible that the lack of practice in producing sounds could have caused these delays).

Other studies do not support Locke's interpretation. Lenneberg (1967) reported a case where there was a full range of sounds produced after tube removal at 14 months. Another case where the tracheotomy was administered at 2 months, with tube removal at 21 months, had a rapid development of sound production, but no babbling (Ross, 1982).

A large-scale study by Simon, Fowler and Handler (1983) provides a somewhat complex picture about the importance of babbling. The infants had tracheotomies at different ages and over different time periods. Many of the 77 children had mental disabilities. It was found that when tube removal occurred before children were expected to use single words, then they started to talk at an age appropriate for their cognitive ability. These children were not observed to babble. For children who had the tube removed when they might have been expected to be at a higher level of linguistic ability, there often were initial problems with the production of sounds. However, within six months of tube removal 8 out of 9 children reached an appropriate level of sound production. Thus, the majority of studies indicate that the lack of ability to babble does not appear to have long-term consequences for language development.

Summary

The picture that emerges from these studies and controversies is that the development of vocalisations is to some extent under maturational control. However, experience also plays a part in this process; infants need to be able to hear the sounds that they produce themselves in addition to the speech of others. The absence of a babbling stage does not preclude early speech development. When tracheotomies are reversed progress is usually made to appropriate levels in 6 to 12 months. Such findings suggest that pre-speech vocal production is not necessary for the later use of words, but may facilitate their development.

FROM SOUNDS TO WORDS

The Transition from Sounds to Words

Do infants use sound patterns to express communicative intent before they speak? There are a number of studies which report that prior to the use of words infants appear to produce particular sounds in certain contexts (e.g. Halliday, 1973). These findings have concerned the suprasegmental vocalisations in relation to curiosity, greetings, narratives, and being alone or with the mother.

A study of five Italian infants aged between 4 and 12 months by D'Ordrico and Franco (1991) provides a detailed description of the use of pre-speech vocalisations in relation to their context. The aim was to discover if certain sounds were used consistently by infants during the manipulation of toys. The findings indicate that suprasegmental characteristics of sounds were associated with certain contexts, but the type of association was not uniformly consistent across infants. In general there was a tendency for higher and rising pitch to be associated with occasions when the adult was holding a toy and the infant was looking alternately at toy and adult. During play with toys the infants tended to produce vocalisations with a lower pitch. The authors suggest that below about 9 months there is a lack of uniformity in the sounds produced in the same context. However, after this age there is much greater uniformity.

A similar study by Blake and De Boysson-Bardies (1992) examined the vowel and consonant-like characteristics of babbling in relation to the context. They could only reliably detect a match between vocalisations and context after 12 months. At this age, Flax, Lahey, Harris and Boothroyd (1991) report the use of rising contours in situations where infants could expect a response from adults, and this pattern was continued when the children produced words. The authors note some variability in use between children.

In the past it has been asserted that babbling and speech are different processes, not related to one another (e.g. Jakobson, 1968); a position which is being challenged by more recent investigations. Increasingly strong claims are being made that there is continuity between the sound production of babbling and the first words (Oller, Wieman, Doyle & Ross, 1976; Stoel-Gammon & Cooper, 1984; Vihman, Macken, Miller, Simmons & Miller, 1985; Blake & De Boysson-Bardies, 1992). Parts of this argument concern the drift of babbling towards the phonetic characteristics of the home language, and the way babbling continues even at ages when words are also produced.

Thus, pre-speech vocalisations of infants appear to share many of the phonetic characteristics of the first words. There seems to be continuity rather than discontinuity in the development of vocal abilities. Not only is there preparation for the use of words by the development of phonetic abilities, but before words are produced suprasegmental aspects of vocalisations are associated with particular circumstances.

Starting to Use Words

According to Bates, Bretherton and Snyder (1988) children will start to use words in the following manner. The first development is that children will start to consistently use their existing vocalisations, such as grunts or effortful noises, to make their intentions known to adults. Following this, children will progress to using arbitrary sounds to communicate specific messages; for example one Italian child used "nana" for requesting objects. Vocalisations similar to these have been described in a number of studies (see previous section) and are sometimes referred to as *phonologically consistent forms*.

Children will also employ adult words in a similar way, but often there seems to be only a distant relationship with the adult meaning for the word. A famous example of this is the production by one of Piaget's children of "panama" (grandfather), which was employed as a general request, irrespective of the presence or absence of the grandfather.

These early forms of communication are believed to give way to a more adult-like use of vocalisations. A convincing example from one child involves the use of the sound "bam". The first use of this sound was limited to games when an infant was knocking over a tower. A few weeks after this it had become a well used format.

> "Carlotta was seated among her toys momentarily silent and empty-handed. She looked up, said the word 'bam', and after a brief hesitation, turned to bang on her toy piano. Note that the sound had become in some sense decontextualized or 'unstuck' from the original 'bam' script ... the utterance 'bam' is now functioning as a kind of primitive verb ... it has been selected out and elevated to a different status from the other elements in the original routine—and as such it has begun to function as a *symbol*".
>
> (Bates, Bretherton and Snyder, 1988, pp. 171–172)

Bates and his colleagues also report that similar changes occurred for other sounds which became used in a wider set of circumstances and they believe that this might be the result of a general cognitive change.

Context-Bound and Context-Flexible Words

As we have just seen Bates, Bretherton and Snyder suggested that the first words are used in a context-bound way. Their use is limited to a specific set of circumstances. A number of investigators have observed a similar phenomenon, where the use of such words is highly restricted to the same object in the same context (Barrett, 1986; Bates, O'Connell & Shore, 1987; Bloom, 1973; Harris, 1992). However, not all early words are used in this way and children often use a word in a context-flexible way across a variety of situations.

One of the first systematic studies of this issue was conducted by Snyder, Bates and Bretherton (1981) who used maternal reports to examine two types of word use: context-bound and context-flexible. Context-bound use involves a limited set of circumstances (always with the same objects in the same situation), context-flexible use involves the word being employed in a variety of dissimilar circumstances. It was found that children who had a high proportion of context-flexible names in their vocabulary had larger vocabularies for production and comprehension. In addition, at 28 months these children had more advanced language.

Bates, O'Connell and Shore (1987) use these data as a basis to claim that the understanding of naming is signalled by the use of context-flexible words, and early understanding gives children a head start in the development of language. Thus, unlike some other investigators, Bates and his colleagues believe that the acquisition of "true" words can be considered to occur when words are used in a flexible manner.

Harris (Harris, Barrett, Jones & Brookes, 1988; Harris, 1993) provides further interesting findings about the initial use of these words. She reports that of the first ten words produced by a small group of children, just over half were context-bound. A context-bound word was considered to be one that was said in the same context three times, and these words were mainly what were termed nominals (words associated with an object). All children had both context-bound and -flexible words in their first ten-word vocabulary. The findings also revealed that words which were initially context-bound were relatively quickly used in a flexible manner. In a subsequent study it was found that there was considerable similarity in the use of context-bound and -flexible words in production and comprehension. Thus, a context-flexible word in production was also likely to be a context-flexible word in comprehension (based on maternal report together with systematic investigation).

The methodological problems of identifying context-bound and context-flexible words have been highlighted by Ninio (1993). She points out that the criteria for a word being classified as context-bound involve assumptions about identifying relevant criteria in the environment. When an infant word is classified as context-bound the experimenter is identifying some unchanging aspects of the context while ignoring other aspects that have changed (e.g. the clothes worn may be different, but this would be considered as irrelevant). Thus, Ninio seems to be arguing that to classify words in this way entails a set of assumptions about what aspects of the context should be considered as changing or stable. In these terms context-bound words will be difficult to identify. She also attacks the idea that context-bound words may lack communicative intent and she argues that if the words held no communicative intent there would be little reason to produce them.

Thus, the first words have some interesting characteristics. In general, a significant proportion of the words are used in a very restricted way and this may represent a different or more limited representation of the words (see Chapter 7). However, as Ninio has pointed out there are methodological problems in identifying context-bound words, and it is easy for an adult-centric view of their use to occur. Despite this objection, the classification scheme appears to capture an important characteristic of early word use.

SUMMARY

Adult speech to infants is marked with particularly clear patterns of intonation, and semantically important words are marked out. In this way children in many cultures are provided with non-linguistic sound patterns which will help them to understand the intent of the speaker and help them to identify the important words in an utterance. The speech input appears designed to assist language acquisition. During the first year infant vocalisations develop and become similar to the speech in their home. There seems to be a gradual growth in the abilities needed to produce the sounds necessary for the words of the mother-tongue. When word-like sounds first appear they are gradually introduced into a limited set of contexts. Starting to say words is a slow process, there is no dramatic change in behaviour, and as we will see in Chapter 7 the boundaries between what does and does not constitute a word are unclear.

6

THEORIES ABOUT WORDS AND CONCEPTS

It has been argued that infants can make use of information in their environment to help them identify a referent (Chapter 5). It should be emphasised that for infants to understand the meaning of words, identifying the referent has to be accompanied by complementary processes. This chapter discusses two of the most important of these processes, constructing *categories* and forming *concepts* in relation to infants below about 18 months.

A *category* consists of a set of entities which are similar. The traditional view has been that categorisation involves a set of definitions which allow category members to be identified. However, as we will see the process is more complicated than this. In speech the use of a category allows the referents of a word to be identified (e.g. the category of dog refers to a group which includes Great Danes and Pekineses). Thus, a category allows a group of entities to be identified and distinguished from other entities (e.g. distinguish birds from planes).

In discussions about words the term *concept* is often employed, and the term is used in slightly different ways by different authorities. I will start by using the term concept to refer to the representation of a group of entities which are considered to be similar, and will consider a concept as containing more information than is necessary to identify instances of a concept (i.e. more information than is needed for the categorisation process). For example, we have certain ideas about the characteristics that are necessary to identify the category dog: barking; having a tail that wags; having a certain anatomical structure, etc. However, our concept of dog can be considered to include additional information that is not necessary to identify dogs: the circumstances in which they wag their tails; the way they will run after balls; whether we like them; and so on. Thus, a concept contains idiosyncratic and general knowledge about an entity, whereas a category simply contains the information necessary to identify an entity as being a member of a class. It is worth emphasising that not everyone would agree with this use of the term concept, but this provides a useful starting definition.

Occasionally it has been supposed that categories and concepts can only occur in relation to words. I do not believe that this is the case since there seems sufficient evidence that animals have categories of entities to which they respond (e.g. food, predators, etc.), and very young infants can show categorisation in habituation tasks. It is more difficult to establish that animals have concepts associated with these categories, but it seems likely that the more intelligent animals have some knowledge of the attributes and qualities of certain categories (see Chapter 9 about the use of signs by apes).

At first sight, the construction of concepts and categories seems an obvious process; we simply identify how entities are similar and group entities which are similar together. For example, it has been argued that words are in some way associated with the objects themselves, ideas about objects or some internal image of the objects. In this way words would become associated with a thought or an idea in an infant's mind. Such theories can be traced back to Aristotle and Locke.

The problem with these views is that there is no explanation of the way that words can be used in circumstances different to the original pairing of word, object and thought; how do we explain that after a child associates the word "dog" with a particular animal she is able to generalise this relationship to other examples of dogs? As a result, the explanation of category and concept formation is moved elsewhere. Words are regarded as pictures or ideas, but we still do not have an explanation of the way that these pictures or ideas are formed, and there is no explanation of why a word is used to refer to this entity as opposed to another.

Recently there has been a tendency to extend the ideas of the Gibsons to account for concept formation. The Gibsons believe that the formation of concepts is a product of perceptual processes; there is a direct perception of the invariant characteristics of different objects in a category. Gibson (1979) states "the perceptual system simply extracts the invariants from the flowing array; it resonates to the invariant structure or is attuned to it". As I have just argued, such a view actually explains very little about the process of category or concept formation.

Thus, more careful thought reveals that this process of forming concepts is very complex. How does an infant manage to understand that dogs, which share many characteristics with cats, are indeed a different group of animals? Especially when infants have much less experience and knowledge about the world than adults. The difficulty of this process has been high-lighted by Murphy and Medin (1985) who have argued that the number of similarities and differences between any two entities could be infinite irrespective of whether or not the entities are considered to be in the same category. This is because by making comparisons at the level of fine detail, by establishing that both objects are not something (e.g. not lawnmowers or not furniture) or by establishing that both entities have certain common characteristics (e.g. over 1 gm in weight) one can quickly identify very many dimensions of difference and similarity. Various theories which attempt to deal with this issue will be discussed in this chapter.

Before going on to deal with these theories some other points of terminology need to be considered. The study of meaning is considered to be the domain of *semantics*. Ironically, meaning can be defined in a variety of ways. Meaning is usually understood to involve the communication of information and the inferring of a message from some event, behaviour or display. The way that words convey meaning has been the subject of philosophical discussion over the centuries, and is a topic considered in the next chapter. For our present purposes, the important point is that the domain of semantics is wider than that of concepts and categories. This is because semantics is concerned with the conventional interpretation of words and utterances.

It also is worth noting that the lexicons of languages differ in the categories that are used for words. A famous example is that there are many more words to describe snow in Eskimo languages than in English, and unsur-prisingly, finer distinctions are made by Eskimos in classifying and naming snow. Sometimes it has been proposed that the categories of words will influence thinking so that different language groups may think in different ways. This has become known as the Whorfian hypothesis after its influen-tial proponent.

THE SEMANTIC FEATURE HYPOTHESIS

The early 1970s saw an upsurge of interest in the relation between words, concepts and meaning in child language. At this time, Clark (1973) pro-posed the "semantic feature hypothesis". Her views corresponded to many characteristics of what has become known as the classic view about con-cepts. She suggested that the meanings of words are analysed into smaller elements termed semantic features (sometimes referred to as semantic markers or semantic components). For example, the meaning of "father" could be broken down to male, adult, and so on. In supposing this Clark was drawing on an important tradition which regarded the meaning of a word as being composed of identifiable component elements, and the sum of these elements would supply the meaning of the word. Clark also supposed that the semantic features are based on comparatively high level perceptual units which are common to all humans (e.g. has four legs, has fur). This assumption that all humans are born with all the elements of all concepts may appear surprising to some, but as we will see it is one which continues to attract interest and debate.

To identify the category of a word Clark hypothesised that children simply attach a single semantic feature to a word they hear, and that the semantic feature is usually perceptual in nature. An example she used may help to make the process clearer. Clark claimed that on hearing the word "dog" children would choose a semantic feature like "four-legged" as being the definition of the word dog. An important point about this claim is that the child would then treat "dog" as meaning "four-legged", and be unaware that the word has other additional meanings and restrictions.

This suggestion had the advantage of being able to account for a phenomenon known as overextension in children's speech. It often has been noted that children will apply a word to inappropriate referents (e.g. say "dog" when they are talking about a sheep), and when this occurs the use of the word appears to have some relationship to the appropriate referent. Such mistakes are predicted by the semantic feature theory. In our example of "dog", we would expect this word to be applied to a variety of four-legged animals including sheep, cows and cats, and in some cases children appear to do exactly this. In the same way the theory can account for underextension, that is when children restrict a word's use to a subset of the adult category (e.g. Dromi, 1987); here it can be supposed that the child has chosen a semantic feature which does not include all members of a category. Clark supposed that the convergence of child and adult meanings would occur by children observing adults using particular words and on this basis semantic features would be added (or removed) from a word's meaning. Subsequently, Chapman, Leonard and Mervis (1986) have found in an experimental study that adult correction and explanation were the most effective methods of correction.

The theory was also able to explain later confusions in children's speech. Children when learning contrasting words like more/less, high/low, in/on seem to know what the relevant dimension of the word is (quantity, height, position), but will usually acquire the positive expression before the negative one (i.e. high before low). The semantic feature hypothesis is able to account for this because it predicts that children first acquire what could be considered the more simple dimension (e.g. the positive dimension).

Clark's theory was soon criticised. One practical problem concerned the lack of specification of what constituted semantic features and how they could be identified. Another problem came from findings which indicated that overextensions are often the result of innovative use of a limited vocabulary (Huttenlocher, 1974). According to this argument, a child might know the difference between a dog and a cat. However, because she does not know the word "cat", she will use the word "dog" to refer to a cat. In using the word "dog" she is simply being creative with a very limited vocabulary. Huttenlocher found that although children would overextend a word, they could correctly identify the object when asked to point one out of a group of pictures. Similar findings have been reported by Fremgen and Fay (1980). A comprehensive criticism of the semantic feature theory, which deals with this and other issues, has been provided by Richards (1979).

A further criticism of Clark's theory, made by Nelson (1974), stems from the problem of how to explain the way infants identify a *class* of objects, and can thereby identify a semantic feature for a group of entities. This difficulty comes from the logical problems that we face in describing concept formation. An infant needs to have a concept to identify a semantic feature, and needs to identify a relevant semantic feature to form a concept. For example, Clark supposed that children are able to choose a semantic feature (e.g. four legs) that is a relevant characteristic of a group of entities (e.g. dogs). However, it is not enough to say that children simply see that dogs have "four legs" and so they assume that the word "dog" refers to all animals with four legs. Any theory has to explain why a child chooses to form a concept based on the characteristic of having four legs from all the perceptual possibilities that are available. Thus, there is a real problem of explaining how children break into what appears to be a circular process. Clark has ceased to defend her semantic feature theory, but it provides a very useful introduction to this area. As we will see in Chapter 8 she has developed a different theory concerned with the organisation of words and concepts in children's lexicons.

FUNCTIONAL CORE THEORY

An elegant solution to the problem of identifying concepts is that they are formed on the basis of functional relations. This proposal was made by Nelson (1974) and is known as the functional core theory (although as we will see the theory has a perceptual component). Nelson supposed that the development of a new concept begins with the first experience of a new object; this provides a set of relations which an object has with other entities (e.g. a ball may be thrown by the mother, by self, it may be positioned on a chair, etc.). Once a list of functions has been identified, then other objects which possess the same characteristics are categorised as belonging to the same concept. Further experience leads to a refinement of the functional core so that irrelevant dimensions are discarded. Nelson also supposed that as concepts are being formed there is a parallel process which identifies the perceptual characteristics of an object (e.g. balls are round, coloured, smooth, etc.). This enables children to identify new instances of a concept without having to see the functional use made of the object.

Nelson believed that before children acquire words they will already have formed concepts about the objects in their world. According to Nelson, words are acquired by children noticing that a word is consistently associated with a particular concept; they then assume that the word refers to their *existing* concept of that object, and the word would take on that meaning. Of course, in many instances the child's meaning and the adult meaning would not correspond, but with experience children's meanings would undergo modification.

Nelson (1974) criticised the semantic feature theory for not being able to deal with the way children break into the circular processes of needing to have a concept to identify relevant attributes, and needing to identify relevant attributes to form a concept. However, Nelson's theory can be criticised on the same grounds. Infants still have to categorise objects according to their functional similarity, and therefore still have to identify what are the similar features of different examples of the same function (Bowerman, 1978; i.e. chairs might be identified by the act of sitting, but there are many ways of positioning oneself on chairs: kneeling, lying, straddling and so on).

A more widespread criticism of Nelson's theory has been that overextensions are often on the basis of perceptual rather than functional characteristics (e.g. Bowerman, 1978). To my mind this represents a misreading of Nelson's position, as she postulates that during the formation of any concept there will be a parallel process which identifies the perceptual characteristics of the entity. A greater problem is that Bowerman reports that overextensions sometimes occur with little or no regard to the functional relationships between objects; her daughter was observed to use the word "moon" to refer to a ball of spinach, hangnails, magnetic capital letters and half a grapefruit. In addition, although Nelson predicted that names would first be used in a functional context, it was found that words were sometimes first said when an object was at a distance of at least a few feet from the child and did not appear to be involved in a functional relationship with the child. Thus, the functional theory provided an important focus for research, but it has been superseded by Nelson's more recent proposals and these are discussed later on in this chapter.

PROBLEMS WITH THE CLASSIC VIEW OF CONCEPTS

The semantic feature theory and other theories about the development of concepts were influenced by what has become known as the classic theory of concepts. The classic view is that a concept is a group of entities which have some common characteristic and differ from other groups of entities. Many people in the general population appear to believe that this is the way that concepts are defined (McNamara & Sternberg, 1983). This view has come under attack from a number of sources. As a result, theories about concept formation and meaning have started to be revised. Before considering these revisions it is important to consider the criticisms of the classic theory.

One source of criticism came from the work of Wittgenstein (1958). There has been increasing recognition of the importance of his argument that there is no defining feature (or set of features) which would allow us to identify all instances of a word. One of his much quoted examples is the problem of finding the defining features of "games"—given that there are ball games, team games, card games, solitary games, board games, and so on. Instead, Wittgenstein favoured the notion that the structure of a concept involves sets of overlapping relations or *family resemblances*. In these terms a concept could include a subgroup of items which have a common characteristic (e.g. solitary games), as well as other subgroups which have another set of characteristics (e.g. team games); there would, however, be some overlap in the characteristics possessed by these different sets. In the example of games the types of overlapping sets could be rules, a defined outcome, played for fun and so on. These ideas were developed by Putman (1962) who used the term *cluster concepts*.

The uncertainty involved in identifying the defining features of a word has also been commented on by Quine (Quine, 1960, 1969). Quine started with the assumption that the understanding of a word occurs in a behaviouristic fashion. In his example, the child (or translator) hears the word rabbit on a number of occasions and has to work out what these occasions have in common, and what stimulus is associated with the word. Quine argued that in such circumstances one can never be *certain* about the referent of a word. As a result, one could never be sure, simply on the basis of experience, whether the word "gavagai" in another language refers to a rabbit or part of a rabbit or some other aspect of rabbits. The problem is that there are many possible associations between the word and the object to which it refers. The way Quine resolved this dilemma was by supposing that "reference is nonsense except relative to a coordinate system" (1969, p. 48). By this he supposed that reference and meaning can only be precisely located in relation to the whole linguistic system, and by talking about language, not simply by noticing the relation between language and the world.

The "causal theory of reference" provided another part of the shift in focus from the classic view to an alternative notion. Donnellan (1972) suggested that "the referent must be historically, or, we might say causally connected to the speech act" (p. 377). Similar arguments were contained in Kripke's (1972) writings about the use of proper names. He observed that we know who a person is by two processes, a naming event and a causal chain which produces a link between the name and the entity to which reference is made. Thus, in Kripke's example, George Washington is known because of books and teachers who refer to him and discuss events in his life. The importance of this argument is that according to the classic view "George Washington" should be a set of semantic features. What is proposed instead is that George Washington is known because of the way he has been described and talked about and this establishes a transfer of knowledge from one person to another.

These ideas were also applied by Kripke and by Putman (1975) to other entities which have been termed "natural kind terms" (e.g. water, gold, an electron, lead, and dogs). In essence the argument is that we learn labels for things in our world by someone telling us what a word refers to, or by being shown typical examples of an entity to which a word refers. It is also supposed that *full* definitions of these terms are not usually known except by experts, for example most of us would not know the full biological definition of dog, and as a result we may be uncertain whether dingoes or wolves are technically dogs. Even so the causal chain would give us enough information so that we can talk about dogs without any difficulty. Putman (1975) has used such observations to argue for a "division of linguistic labour", in that certain members of the community are responsible for defining and identifying categories of objects. Another part of this theoretical position is that the defining characteristics of the concept may be changed as knowledge about the topic is developed. Thus, it is logically possible for new discoveries to lead to a change in the biological definition of dogs.

Another related issue is the way we identify new examples of a concept. It has been argued by Murphy and Medin (1985) that categorisation in some circumstances may not be a process of matching stimuli to some definition, but a complex process of inference. They cite the example of jumping into a swimming pool at a party which could be categorised as "drunkenness" or "bravery" depending on the circumstances. Thus, for some concepts (especially those that are represented by adjectives or adverbs) there is great difficulty in identifying any unique set of defining features.

Thus, the idea that concepts can be identified by a set of defining features no longer seems tenable. The work of Wittgenstein indicates that for some concepts there are no simple sets of defining features. As Quine has shown there is the initial problem of the word learner identifying the appropriate concept from the vast range of possibilities; Quine argues that reference can only be established in relation to a larger system of understanding. Furthermore, the causal theory of reference and ideas about natural kind terms indicate that there is ambiguity about these concepts and that such concepts do not consist of a set of descriptions.

PROTOTYPES

Accompanying the demise of the classic theory has been the increasing acceptance that prototypes might provide a way of explaining category formation. A prototype is a representation which captures many of the common features of a group. Work in the 1970s by Rosch (1973) suggested that prototypes are formed after experience with a number of examples of a concept, and there is some type of averaging process which results in a prototype being formed. A good exemplar of a prototype would have many of the typical characteristics of the concept, and few characteristics of other related concepts. A good exemplar, for North Americans, of the prototype for birds might be a robin, while a much less appropriate exemplar would be a penguin or an ostrich.

In discussing structure of prototypes, Rosch and Mervis (1975) followed Wittgenstein by using the notion of family resemblances to suggest that word meaning is not specifically tied to clear definitions. Instead the referents of a word may share some but not all of a set of common features. Thus, penguins have feathers and lay eggs, but unlike many birds they swim underwater and cannot fly.

In a series of studies, Rosch and Mervis studied people's opinions about different entities which can make up a category. They found that entities which possessed more features of a category were rated by people as being more typical of that category; so a robin would be considered to be a more typical bird than a penguin. In addition, typical members of a category were identified more quickly as a member of the category, so that a robin would be identified as a bird faster than a penguin would be identified as a bird.

There have been a number of ingenious experiments with pre-verbal infants which appear to show that they form prototypes. For example, Strauss (1979) presented different faces to infants. Then a new face was presented which had not been seen before, but the new face was an average of the previous examples. The new face was treated as more familiar (looked at less) than ones which the infant had seen before. Such a finding suggests that infants are forming a prototype from their experiences.

More remarkably, a similar process has been reported to occur with 3–4 month infants who see distortions of a particular shape made up of dots. A set of distortions were formed from a triangle, a square or a diamond (see Figure 6.1). Infants were shown a sequence of the distortions of one of the shapes, and then would be shown the relevant prototype and one of the other prototypes. The infants preferred to look at the unrelated shape, indicating that they had formed some representation of the prototype from the distortions (Bomba & Siqueland, 1983).

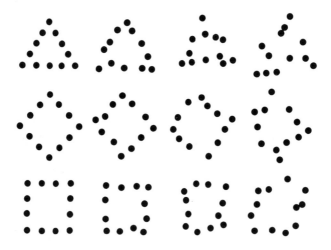

Figure 6.1 The stimuli (in the left-hand column) and the distortions used by Bomba and Siqueland (reproduced with permission from P. C. Bomba & E. R. Siqueland (1983) The nature and structure of infant form categories. *Journal of Experimental Child Psychology*, **35**, 295–328)

Another study that investigated this phenomenon was conducted by Younger and Cohen (1983). They showed 10-month-old infants pictures of make-believe animals and found evidence that by 10 months infants appear to react to entities in a way predicted by prototype theory (see Figure 6.2). In their study make-believe animals were made by using three different sets of attributes (e.g. club, web or hoof feet) for each of the regions of the animal's body (ears, body, legs, feet and tail). Thus, each region could have one of three different forms. Using certain combinations, two sets of four animals were made. Infants were habituated to these stimuli and then

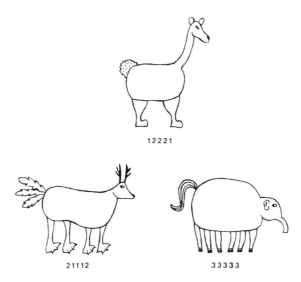

Figure 6.2 The stimuli used by Younger and Cohen (1983) (reproduced with permission from B. A. Younger & L. B. Cohen (1983) Infant perception of correlations among attributes. *Child Development*, **54**, 858–867 © 1983 Society for Research in Child Development)

shown one of three possibilities: (i) an animal which had characteristics in a similar combination to that seen before; (ii) an animal which had the characteristics seen before, but in a new combination or (iii) a completely new animal. Infants who were 10 months old treated the animal with a new combination of attributes in the same way as the completely new animal. This suggests that the infants were processing not just how many times they had seen certain forms, but also how often they saw those forms in certain combinations. Consequently, 10-month-old infants are not simply processing whether or not a feature is present, but are also attending to the relationship between the features. In relation to this, it is interesting that Rosch (1978) suggested that categories are formed from groups of entities which have a high degree of within-group similarity, and a low similarity with other entities.

Studies which have examined the choice of referents by children provide support for the prototype theory. When children are asked to pick out a referent from a range of similar objects they tend to choose an object which is central to the category, in other words something similar to a best exemplar (Fremgen & Fay, 1980). Furthermore, if choice continues to be made the selection of other objects seems to follow the gradient predicted by a prototype theory (Kuczaj, 1982), so that objects most unlike the prototype are selected last.

One of the first discussions about applying prototype theory to language acquisition was provided by Bowerman (1978). She drew attention to the possibility that children's concepts might be based on a prototype or best exemplar. However, she makes the important point that there may be not one but a number of methods of category formation occurring during early development. For example, she observed that children's use of words did not appear to correspond to a clear category as would be expected from the classic viewpoint. Instead she suggested that words were applied, much as Wittgenstein suggested, to groups of entities which shared some but not all the same characteristics (e.g. "kick" used to refer to a waving limb, a moth fluttering, the child rolling a bottle with her feet, and the child pushing her stomach against a mirror).

Various criticisms have been levelled at the prototype theory. One is that we need a consensus of what exactly is meant by a prototype as different investigators refer to the term in different ways (Barrett, in press). Another criticism has been made by Murphy and Medin (1985) who argue that the averaging process in prototype formation, sometimes termed detecting the correlational structure of an entity, has the same problems as the classic theory. It fails to explain how the similarities and differences are identified from the multitude of possibilities.

BARRETT'S THEORY OF EARLY WORD USAGE

Barrett (1986) provided a theory about the development of early word use which integrates a number of theoretical perspectives. A starting point for the theory is the observation that the initial word use of children is event-bound. One example of an *event-bound* utterance is provided by his son Adam who first produced "chuff-chuff" while pushing his toy train along the floor, but it was not used in any other circumstance. Barrett rejects the notion that these are "true" words as he believes they are "ritualised responses to the occurrence of particular events" (p. 42) in which the child is involved or is observing. However, he makes additional proposals about the semantic basis of this activity by suggesting that the event representation typically involves a person, an action, and an object. In the case of "chuff-chuff" this would be Adam + pushing + a train. There is the possibility that each slot could involve more than one similar entity. It is supposed that at first words will be associated with existing event representations that children already possess. This idea of event-bound words is similar to a proposal by Snyder, Bates and Bretherton (1981) that early words may be *context-bound* (see Chapter 7).

Barrett suggests that the next development is the use of some words (but not all) in more extended, but still limited circumstances. For example, a word might be produced if another person carried out the appropriate activity. In a similar way word use can become decontextualised, as when "duck" is first used to refer to hitting one of three specific toy ducks in a bath and then is extended to playing with the toys in other circumstances. A major change is believed to take place when the event representation is replaced by a prototypical exemplar, which involves identification of the perceptual and functional characteristics of the exemplar. As a result words are extended to entities which can be quite dissimilar to the original referent (real ducks, swans, geese, etc.), and in some cases are overextended (i.e. applied to inappropriate referents such as an aeroplane). Barrett suggests that some words may be acquired without going through an event-bound stage, but that this is only likely to occur after some progress has been made in concept development.

As new words enter a child's vocabulary these contrast with existing words which have been overextended. At the heart of the process of contrast is the assumption that two words cannot refer to the same thing, and if this occurs children will modify the categories of the words to eliminate the overlap. For instance, the use of "duck" became more restricted in scope with the entry of "geese" and "swan" into Adam's vocabulary. However, Barrett notes that restriction may occur without the presence of contrasting words, and may continue after the acquisition of contrasting words. In addition, he suggests that there are at least eight possible ways of starting to use words by making different entry points in his proposals. These caveats make theory testing difficult even if it represents the true state of affairs!

In a later development of his theory Barrett (in press) emphasises that there are two major routes for word acquisition. One route is for context-bound and social-pragmatic words ("no", "hi", "look"), and is similar to his previous description. The second route involves referential words for objects and actions. These words are believed to be associated with prototype concepts when they are first used. Initially, the words are closely restricted to the prototype, but gradually analysis of the properties of the prototype results in children applying the word to a wider group of referents and can result in overextension. The use of "duck" that has just been described is one example of this process. Although there are two major routes the model is made more complex by suggestions of different entry points for words in the developmental progression.

Thus, Barrett (in press) is supposing that the early use of words is restricted, but there are different reasons for this restriction. For some words restrictions are caused by the representation being event-bound, for other words the restrictions occur because of limited application of prototype concepts. Barrett believes that both these forms of representation can occur at the same age.

Barrett's model provides a very useful, detailed and complex description of early speech development. The problem with the model is testing its predictions, because of the uncertainty about what type of word is being used by children and the type of conceptual structure they are employing.

CONCEPTS, SCRIPTS AND SCHEMAS

Nelson has altered and developed her ideas about the early use of words. Her later perspective is that early word use is embedded in scripts and schemata (Nelson, 1985). This bears a number of similarities to Barrett's ideas that have just been discussed, but there are important differences in detail. Nelson argues that infants' initial knowledge about the world is not represented in terms of categories and attributes which involve a logical and mechanical process. Rather she believes that infants' knowledge is more likely to be represented in terms of relations, routines, and dynamic structures. She goes on to suggest that this knowledge of the world and knowledge of language develop as interlocking systems.

Nelson follows Rumelhart and Ortony (1977) in her identification of the properties of schemas. Their most important characteristic is that they concern knowledge rather than definitions. A schema involves variables which can be obligatory or optional (e.g. a living room schema involves four walls, a door and windows, options include a fireplace, a television and so on). These schemas may be embedded in other schemas (e.g. a living room schema may be embedded in a house schema).

Nelson goes on to identify *scripts* as a form of schema which concern a sequence of activities (Schank & Abelson, 1977). These scripts are very much like a written story and are the result of general knowledge about a situation. An example that is often employed is a restaurant script which provides details about what happens when you go to a restaurant. The script is organised into *scenes* which are coherent segments of a script (e.g. the scenes might be ordering the food, eating a course, paying for the meal, etc.). The script also has slots for the roles of different people in the script and rules about who can be placed in the slots (e.g. waiter, customer, manager). Nelson suggests that infants will have scripts for their activities, not in the sense of conscious representations, but in terms of knowledge which can involve the anticipation of events.

Nelson supposes that, at first, infants represent events as wholes which are not subdivided into parts, so that the use of the word "ball" implies throwing and is not separated from the event of throwing. Then children begin to break the wholes down so that there are separate concepts of objects, people and actions. These are identified in terms of their functional roles in the script. This process of separation is believed to be associated with the use of words to name objects, but at first the link between object, word, and concept may be somewhat fuzzy and inexact, so children's first words are not separated from the context associated with their use.

Nelson believes that at about 18 months there is a restructuring of cognition so that words begin to be employed as symbols. She suggests that this allows words to be associated with concepts. In her terms a concept is a single cognitive unit which can be used in thought processes, and it captures the essence of the word (e.g. dogginess). This allows communication to move away from shared contexts to be concerned with new or absent topics. Furthermore, she believes that such changes can partly account for the vocabulary burst which involves a dramatic increase in the vocabulary of some children at about this age.

An important aspect of Nelson's approach is that she proposes that "the study of language development in general and semantic development in particular is basically a problem in the acquisition of culture" (p. 250). She sees the problem for children as the need to achieve shared meanings by meshing their conceptual structure first with that of their family and then with the wider culture. Interestingly, the theory overcomes some of the difficulties in explaining the way children identify a category. This is achieved by supposing that children initially associate a word with a script, and what is important to remember is that certain scripts will be emphasised by adults when interacting with infants. However, there still remain problems of explaining the way in which children segment their experience into scripts, and the way that they identify similarities and differences between scripts which occur on different occasions. Another problem identified by Barrett (in press) is that the first words of some children are not context-bound, as predicted by her theory, and Barrett also argues that the acquisition process is much more variable than suggested by Nelson.

Theories about Concepts

An interesting and general proposal about the basis of category construction has been put forward by Murphy and Medin (1985). They argue that the coherence of categories comes from *theories* which are used to understand the relationship between entities. In their terms, a theory is "any of a host of mental 'explanations,' rather than a complete, organised, scientific account" (p. 290). Thus, a theory is any belief about the way the world is organised and the relationships among entities in the world. In making this proposal Murphy and Medin discard the notion that categories consist of a list of critical attributes. Instead they propose that decisions about category membership are based on a person's knowledge of the world (e.g. children often believe a whale is a fish because they know that whales live in water).

Some interesting phenomena lend support to Murphy and Medin's ideas. One finding is that people appear to be influenced by their existing theories when reporting which attributes can be assigned to a category: i.e. flightlessness might be reported as an attribute of penguins, but not of trout because flight is important to our theories about birds but not about fishes. Murphy and Medin also suggest that people are alerted to correlations among features because of their theory about the world (e.g. knowledge of the characteristics of fish and mammals might have made someone interested in whether whales breathe and the way they produce young). Furthermore, Madole, Oakes and Cohen (1993) report that in a study of object manipulation, 10 month olds distinguish objects on the basis of shape, but not function, whereas 14 month olds will distinguish on the basis of either form or function. Madole (1993) also reports that in an habituation task the presence of new functional parts was likely to result in an object being treated as novel. Both studies suggest that early in the second year infants are starting to process information about objects in more complex ways.

However, as Murphy and Medin themselves admit, the notion of theoretical coherence is of no more use than the notion of similarity as an explanation of why some entities are categorised together. The answer they give to this dilemma is that there is not a simple influence of theory construction leading to concepts. Rather they believe there is a bidirectional influence, with both theory and concepts living "in the same mental space, they therefore constrain each other both in content and representational structure".

Keil (1991) takes a similar view to Murphy and Medin in suggesting that beliefs and theories are important for the organisation of conceptual structure. Keil subscribes to the view that conceptual structure is the product of two different types of analyses, the criteria needed for categorisation and the theoretical basis of categorisation. Thus, he supposes that conceptual structure involves a network of atheoretical associative relations, and a set of explanatory causal beliefs. These two domains are supposed to be interrelated, and the relative importance of the two domains changes with development and with the entity being categorised. In this way Keil suggests that the two different sorts of categorisation identified in children's speech may be explained. One type is the global context-bound type of categorisation; this may be a result of the associative type of strategy. The other is the possibility that word meanings are only acquired in terms of a few features; this he suggests is a product of a more analytical process, where there is a belief about the features which help to identify a concept and such a process could lead to overgeneralisation.

A slightly different distinction has been made by Mandler (1993). She distinguishes between *perceptual* and *conceptual* categories. In her terms a perceptual category is the result of a low level and automatic process which is part of perception itself. For example, we can distinguish male faces from female faces, but it is not at all clear what the basis of this distinction is as there is no obvious set of invariant rules that can easily be specified. Furthermore, young infants are also able to make this discrimination (Fagan & Singer, 1979).

Mandler (1992) suggests that in the first months of life *perceptual* categories are formed and these are similar to prototypes. The development of *conceptual* categories begins with the active perceptual analysis of sensory information. This analysis involves the recoding of information. Mandler follows Lakoff (1987) and Talmy (1985) in supposing that image-schemas provide the basis for concepts. Image-schemas involve dimensions such as path, up-down, containment, force and so on. The use of such schemas may allow infants to make a conceptual distinction of animate from inanimate entities, for example by noticing that animals initiate the movement and move in certain paths. Mandler argues that conceptual schemas are formed early on in development as there is evidence for a complex understanding of the properties of objects by 3 months (Baillargeon, 1992), and for the memory of absent events by 9 months (Meltzoff, 1988). She also suggests that these image-schemas may later on map on to relevant words.

These suggestions are backed up with some fascinating studies. Mandler and McDonough (in press) used a task where 9 month olds were given a series of objects from the same category to play with, and then tested by presenting an object they had seen before and an object from a different category (Ruff, 1986). Their preference in terms of manipulation and exploration was recorded. Mandler reasoned that if the objects used in the test are perceptually similar then any difference in responding indicates that infants are making a distinction on the basis of their conceptual knowledge of the two groups (i.e. they understand that animals do different sorts of things than inanimate objects).

Using this methodology Mandler found that 9-month-old infants would make this distinction between, for instance, birds and planes, which look very similar, and she argues this is a conceptual distinction between animals and vehicles. However, the infants sometimes failed to make a distinction between items from the same global class (e.g. dogs and fish), even though they look very different. Mandler reasons that for this type of comparison infants could make a perceptual distinction, as infants can discriminate between similar shapes on habituation tasks. However, she also argues that they fail to show different amounts of manipulation because the infants have not yet developed different concepts for these items. Interestingly, the findings from 7 month olds were similar, but did not reach statistical significance.

These three sets of ideas have yet to be applied in detail to the early development of speech. Furthermore, there is obviously considerable difficulty in knowing how to investigate the theories of just-verbal children. This is a considerable challenge for the ingenuity of investigators. A common thread running through all these sets of ideas is that we may need to think about the construction of concepts and categories in new ways, to accept the possibility that there is not one unified monolithic process, and to think about there being different levels of processing in categorising the world.

SUMMARY

As we have seen, one problem for any explanation of concept formation is the fact that there are thousands of possible dimensions which can be used to compare the similarity and dissimilarity of any two entities. Undeniably this is logically true. However, this is unlikely to be true for infants since their knowledge of the world must of necessity be limited so that even if they wanted to, it is unlikely that they could utilise these thousands of dimensions for comparison purposes. In addition, it is clear that from birth infants can discriminate between stimuli. For example, they can distinguish their mother from other similar females, they can distinguish their mother's voice from that of others. Of course, the ability to discriminate does not necessarily mean that infants have a concept for the two groups of entities. However, it is not too far fetched to suppose that such abilities will lead on to the formation of concepts.

A related problem is the issue of intermediacy; how does a child know what aspect of the environment is referred to by a word? In the previous chapter and in other work (Messer, 1983) I have argued that the problem of intermediacy is minimised because parents and children develop a shared history of what is important, relevant and interesting. These claims can be related to Nelson's functional hypothesis which suggests that becoming familiar with objects helps children to form concepts for them. It can also be related to Nelson's later view that children are developing a shared meaning system, a system of meaning and knowledge which corresponds to that of the cultural group (Nelson, 1985, 1988). Not surprisingly, Nelson emphasises the importance of social interaction in the acquisition process. In relation to this she points out that the problem of intermediacy is minimised because adults tend to talk about those entities which children find interesting and for which children already have concepts. Such suggestions are not dissimilar from Quine's argument that understanding can only occur by locating meaning within an understanding of the world; here it is being proposed that meaning is established through the experience of joint endeavours.

The demise of the classic view of concepts has not been followed by the emergence of a generally agreed successor. It may well be that we will have to accept that concept formation is not a single logical process, as work by Barrett and others already suggests. Instead, the development of concepts could be a less predictable, less logical and more individual process. In particular, many different forms and sources of information may be utilised. All this implies that concept formation is a process not amenable to general theories which seek to explain all concept formation in terms of a limited set of operations.

There remain considerable gaps in our understanding of the cognitive processes that provide a basis for communication. This makes it all the more fascinating that young children make considerable advances from pre-verbal to verbal communication from 9 to 24 months. These changes are considered in the next chapter.

7

MEANING AND STARTING TO USE WORDS

The social context provides information about the referent of adult words (see Chapter 4). There are also important conceptual underpinnings of word acquisition and use (Chapter 6). This chapter concerns the period when children use single word speech. It begins with a section discussing theoretical issues associated with meaning and pragmatics. The second section considers meaning in relation to one word speech.

MEANING

Meaning is an important topic in any consideration of human communication. It involves questions about how we understand each other's speech from the speech itself and from other information. These are difficult but interesting questions which involve both psychology and philosophy. A lot of thought has gone into attempts to provide answers, but there still appears to be some way to go. Much has been written on this subject, and much of it is difficult to understand! In addition, some of the arguments run counter to common sense in that most of the time we understand one another's speech, and we do not fall into a morass of uncertainty about the truth, reference and meaning of every utterance we hear. This section is concerned with the way that meaning is conveyed by the use of words and with the problems of thinking about this process.

The study of *pragmatics* is concerned with the meaning of speech, the way that a speaker's utterances are understood by others and the way that speakers achieve various objectives by using utterances. The term meaning is often used in relation to communication, but it is a slippery word. It is used in various ways by various investigators.

A starting point for many discussions about meaning and pragmatics is a distinction made by Frege (1970) between reference and sense. An example which is often used to illustrate this distinction is the two utterances, "My daughter Kate" and "That dreadful child". These two utterances refer to the same entity, but they have very different senses. The crucial point is that these utterances express different thoughts, as sense refers to the way a speaker thinks about a referent. There can also be the same reference and similar sense as in "My beautiful daughter" and "My Kate is beautiful". Another pair of terms that are used during discussions about meaning are extension and intension. The term extension (Carnap, 1947) roughly corresponds to the category of a word (the entities to which a word can be applied), and intension corresponds to the characteristics and properties of the entities identified by a word (i.e. the general characteristics of dogs).

Unfortunately, the terms sense and reference are used in slightly different ways by other writers. Both Nelson (1985) and McShane (1990) follow Lyons (1977) in distinguishing between reference, denotation and sense. For these investigators *reference* involves the relation between what speakers say and the entities which are identified by a word. This level of analysis concerns what happens when speakers are using words in particular circumstances. *Denotation* concerns the way that a word identifies a group of similar entities that can all be referred to by the same word; this can be thought of as corresponding to the category of a word, and was the major concern of the last chapter. *Sense* concerns the way a word has relations with other words, for example, the relationship a word has to related superordinate expressions (i.e. the relation of the word "dog" to "animal").

Problems with the Classic View of Meaning

So far in this book it has been implicitly assumed that the meaning of communication can be inferred from the categories or the semantic features that underpin individual words. This was part of the assumption in the classic view of concepts and of meaning. As we have seen, support for the classic view of concepts has diminished. This was accompanied by doubts regarding the classic view about meaning and truth.

A problem with the classic view can be neatly summarised by the question "Do words mean or do people mean?" (Nelson, 1985, p. 8). This captures two features of the way meaning is inferred. It is clear that the meaning of words is partly influenced by their conceptual representation (i.e. words mean). It also clear that words can be used to mean different things from the conventional representation—with the use of sarcasm the meaning of a word is the opposite of the conventional one (i.e. people mean). Thus, new meanings can be generated by the use of words. This has been a basic criticism of the classic view of meaning. Understanding the communicative significance of words is not simply a process of identifying an entity to which the word refers. We are not just transferring an image of each word from one person to another when we are talking, we are using words in a much more complex way.

Another criticism of the classic view, which has already been mentioned, is that the meaning of speech cannot be separated from a person's understanding and view of the world. Quine has argued that no one meaning can be associated with a sentence, instead the meaning of a sentence has to be seen in relation to an understanding of the world, and cannot be separated from this general understanding. It is clear from numerous examples, that humans have a knowledge of the world that goes beyond the categories associated with individual words. Furthermore, this knowledge is used to help them understand speech. A classic example of this is that we know that two notices "We sell alligator shoes" and "We sell horseshoes" refer to very different forms of shoes; one made from alligators, and one made for horses. There is no apparent difference in the organisation of the words in the utterances, the difference in the meaning comes from our knowledge about the world. In other instances the meaning of an utterance can be very different according to the context in which it is said (e.g. sarcasm).

A further source of attack on the classic view came from arguments about whether statements can be considered true. Part of the "classic view" is that some statements are true because this is a matter of linguistic convention, e.g. the analytic statement "all bachelors are unmarried". The statement might be considered untrue if definitions of bachelor and marriage changed, but according to the classic view cannot be considered untrue by any process of investigation. In contrast, the synthetic statement "All bachelors have beards" is open to empirical investigation, and one can discover whether the statement is accurate.

An important attack on this position was made by Quine (1960, 1969) who argued that there is little or no distinction between questions of meaning and questions about the nature of the world. He argued that sentences only have meaning as part of a body of theory and knowledge about the world. Thus, Quine wishes to regard analytic sentences and synthetic sentences as similar. More recently, Davidson (1986) has taken Quine's views further to argue that there are no truths that cannot be questioned on the basis of evidence and science.

Harman (1971) in response to these problems has suggested that we should distinguish three levels of meaning: the meaning of thoughts, the meaning of messages in terms of their semantic constituents, and the meaning of speech acts given their contextual settings. In a somewhat similar way Nelson (1985) suggests that meaning should be distinguished from semantics. According to this argument the semantics of a word can be considered as corresponding to a dictionary-like definition of it. However, the meaning of a word will be derived, not just from the dictionary-like definition, but also from the context of its use. This argument can be applied, with even more force, to the meaning of an utterance which is not simply the sum of semantic features derived from the individual words of the utterance.

Theories which Go Beyond Words

Recognition of the problems in the classic view of meaning was accompanied by the development of alternative proposals. An influential departure from traditional theories was initiated by Grice (1957) who claimed that communication involves an attempt by a speaker to have an effect on a hearer through the hearer's recognition of the speaker's intention. In other words meaning was conveyed by the speaker attempting to transmit his or her intentions and the hearer attempting to discover the intentions. Surprisingly, this common sense notion had not attracted much academic interest until his paper appeared.

Another prominent figure in this field has been Strawson (1964) who has extended Grice's ideas; he suggested that for an utterance to have meaning, a speaker must intend:

1   to produce a response in an audience;
2   that the audience should recognise the speaker's intention;
3   that the audience's recognition of the speaker's intention should be part of the reason for their response.

Subsequent discussions have concerned the way that intentions are recognised.

The importance of these views is that they explicitly locate part of the meaning of utterances in a system which goes beyond the meaning of individual words or the organisation of individual words in an utterance. There are obvious implications for the acquisition of language. One, which has often been commented upon, is that part of the skills that children need to use language involves being able to understand an utterance from the context in which it is used. Another consequence of this work has been to draw attention to the importance of intention in relation to communication. These considerations have led to a recognition that communication does not just involve grammatical skills, but more fundamental skills of understanding what others seek to do by communicating. This recognition was taken up in the 1970s and was part of a reaction against purely grammatical accounts of language acquisition (e.g. Bruner, 1975).

One general problem with recognising intentions, which has already been mentioned in Chapter 2, is that communication is often many layered, consequently it is not at all clear what intentions are present or even foremost in the minds of the communicator. For example, the following utterances are likely to convey slightly different intentions: "It would help me if you put away the toys", "Please put away the toys", "Put the toys away!"—the difficulty is to be sure of the intention behind each utterance.

Interwoven with these ideas about intention have been theories about *speech acts*. Speech act theory, initiated by Austin (1962), provided an important new perspective about linguistic communication. Austin observed that in some circumstances speaking can actually perform an action by changing a state of affairs. In certain cases it is even necessary for certain words to be used for an event to be considered to have taken place, as in the example of a vicar performing a marriage ceremony. In other cases, utterances can be considered to involve some element of performing an action because they involve an attempt to make a change (this might be telling, promising, commanding, etc.).

Austin used this insight as a basis for proposing that speech acts have a number of component parts: there is the *locutionary* act of speaking (i.e. the activity of simply saying something whether or not an audience is present—talking to oneself); the *illocutionary* act of attempting to achieve some objective by speaking; and the *perlocutionary* act which involves the effect of speaking (the intended or unintended consequences). As we will see in this chapter, Bates used this scheme in her description of early communication.

Searle (1969) further developed speech act theory. He acknowledged that some speech acts may be direct in their intent, whereas others may involve an indirect speech act. A direct request would be "Please pass the salt", whereas "Can you pass the salt" is usually an indirect request for action, not a question requiring the answer "Yes" or "No". More importantly, he argued that intentions are recognised by the presence of rules and conventions in both speech and gesture. Counter-arguments led Searle to concede that in some circumstances communication can occur without such rules and conventions, but he maintained that to convey complicated messages requires the presence of this knowledge. Thus, Searle argued that contextual information was employed to help establish the meaning of a speech act.

One consequence of this work has been the appreciation that utterances are used to achieve a variety of objectives. Thus, children are not just learning a system of rules to arrange words in an appropriate way, but are also learning how to get things done by using words. As we will see, speech act theory has been used to classify early speech.

A further area of discussion has been the way that conversations achieve coherence and are meaningful despite the content of the words in these utterances. Here the concern is the way meaning is conveyed, not just in a single utterance, but in a conversation. The following sequence identified by Green (1989) and taken from the cartoon strip about Garfield the cat is a good example of this issue:

> (*Garfield is eating*) ARLENE: Do you love me more than you love food, Garfield? (*Garfield stops eating*) GARFIELD: Do chicken have lips? ARLENE: No. GARFIELD: Bingo! (*Garfield resumes eating*)

Most of us understand the meaning of this conversation, but this understanding is achieved not from a simple processing of the semantic content of individual words. This type of problem led Grice (1957) to suggest that speech is regulated by *conversational maxims*. These include such items as: a maxim of quantity, contributions to conversations should be as informative as required; a maxim of quality, be accurate and truthful; a maxim of relation, be relevant; and a maxim of manner, be brief and orderly, avoid obscurity and ambiguity. Grice suggests that these maxims can be violated (as in the case above), as a result of which the *conversational implicature* will be different from the explicit meaning of the utterance.

The application of ideas about intentions and meaning to the problem of reference can be seen, for example, in proposals from Churcher and Scaife (1982). They have argued that reference in adult–infant interaction involves three processes. The first is to identify an object, and this will usually involve the adult indicating or attending to the object. The second process is for the recipient of the message to recognise the intention of the person who indicates. The third process is understanding that the act of referring is part of a broader communicative activity of transmitting information. Thus, Churcher and Scaife argue that the act of reference involves infants recognising the communicative intentions of others rather than just having their attention guided to a particular item by the careful manipulation of activities by adults.

From a similar perspective, Forrester (1992, 1993) has used Grice's account as a starting point for a discussion of the way that overhearing conversations may allow children to understand some of the conversational maxims. Forrester also argues that the "affordances" offered by conversations, that is the many possibilities available for the continuation of conversations, mean that we need to move away from a formal examination of language development to obtain a better understanding of the development of conversational abilities.

The Importance of Relevance

It should be clear by now that it is difficult to maintain that our understanding of speech is simply derived from analysing each word in an utterance. If this was the case sarcasm would not be possible, one would treat "Can you pass the salt?" as a question rather than a request, and so on.

The awareness of this issue has led to proposals that communication by speech involves two major processes, one of which involves the coding and decoding of messages in a mechanical way, and one of which involves the *inference* of meaning from the circumstances and past history of the individuals who are communicating. Sperber and Wilson (1986) suggest that communication involves an inferential process which "starts with a set of premises and results in a set of conclusions which follow logically from, or are at least warranted by, the premises" (p. 12). They use the example of the following three utterances to illustrate the point:

1 Jones has bought *The Times*.
2 Jones has bought a copy of *The Times*.
3 Jones has bought the press enterprise which publishes *The Times*.

Most people hearing 1 would assume that it meant 2, although it could logically also mean 3. We usually infer that 1 means 2.

How does this inferential process operate? One answer has been to claim that the speaker and the hearer share some common assumptions about the world and these are used to make sense of an utterance (Bach & Harnish, 1979). In many respects this is a reasonable claim, but the great difficulty with it is specifying how the common assumptions are identified. One solution to this difficulty is to suppose that the speaker and hearer make assumptions about what is shared knowledge and what is not shared. The problem with this solution is that there is an infinite regress. A set of assumptions about what is shared and what is not shared would call for a further set of assumptions and so on. Sperber and Wilson attack this notion because of the impossibility of establishing exactly what knowledge is shared when interpreting a message. However, this seems to be missing the point in that speakers and hearers often make predictions about shared knowledge, even though they may not be *certain* that it exists (see Bach & Harnish, 1979, p. 93). Furthermore, speakers who do not know one another often select neutral topics about which almost everyone has knowledge—in Britain the topic is often the weather. If conversations are extended, then there is an exploration of topics about which people are likely to have mutual knowledge and experience, for example, children or sport.

The solution to the problem favoured by Sperber and Wilson (1986) is that a

> "speaker who intends an utterance to be interpreted in a particular way must also expect the hearer to supply a context which allows that interpretation to be recovered. A mismatch between the context envisaged by the speaker and the one actually used by the hearer may result in a misunderstanding."
>
> (p. 16)

Their main argument involves the Principle of Relevance, where it is assumed that the speaker ensures that the speech is optimally relevant for the hearer. In this way the meaning of the utterance will not depend on the meaning of individual words, but on the context in which the words are spoken.

The Principle of Relevance is an attractive one and it has developed further the arguments about meaning and understanding. One attraction is that it appears to provide a way of side-stepping some of the criticisms of the notion of communication involving shared assumptions. However, it should be recognised that Sperber and Wilson's approach may encounter similar problems in that the speaker has to guess what the hearer knows in order to make the utterance relevant. This returns us to the problem of shared understandings once again.

Summary

We have seen that by itself the classic view of concepts cannot be used to account for the meaning of words in an utterance, or for the meaning of the whole utterance. An alternative approach has been to consider the speaker's intention as a source of meaning; however, it is not entirely clear how the hearer discovers the speaker's intention. Such discoveries may be made easier by the speaker and hearer conforming to certain conversational maxims as Grice has suggested. Another possibility is that the speaker may attempt to make the utterance relevant to the context in which it occurs, and in this way the hearer can recover the message. What is worth bearing in mind is that the meaning of an utterance may be derived from all these sources of information, from the dictionary-like definition of individual words, from the intention of the speaker, from conversational maxims, and from the context of the utterance. It is also worth noting that a recent approach to the issue of meaning has been to use connectionist networks to explain the process. This is discussed in Chapter 13; although the approach captures a number of important aspects of the way we process speech, at present it raises as many questions as it answers.

ONE WORD SPEECH: INTENTION, MEANING AND DESCRIPTION

This section is concerned with children's one word speech. It starts with a consideration of Bates' ideas about the development of intentionality. She has utilised Searle's ideas to help describe the way children move from non-verbal to one word communication, and this has been connected with advances in cognitive development. This is followed by examination of the ways of describing the meaning of one word utterances. Lastly, there is a discussion about styles of word use which may be present in children's early speech.

The Development of Intention

As we have seen the intention to communicate a message is central to discussions about meaning. How does this intention develop in infants? Elizabeth Bates has provided an integrated perspective about such developments. This is based on a series of studies and theoretical statements which are summarised in Bates, O'Connell and Shore (1987). Underlying her work has been an interest in the relation between intention, cognition and communication.

In one of her first studies Bates examines the way words take on communicative purpose. She used Searle's terminology about speech acts to identify three forms of communication: a *perlocutionary* act which has an unintended effect on the listener (for example crying which results in feeding); an *illocutionary* act which involves the intentional use of non-verbal methods of communication (e.g. pointing to food and thereby obtaining it), and a *locutionary* act which involves using speech to obtain some objective (e.g. saying "drink"). Bates has changed Searle's scheme to emphasise the development from perlocutionary unintentional non-verbal communication to locutionary intentional verbal communication.

Bates and her colleagues have identified two major forms of intentional illocutionary communication. Proto-imperatives involve a child using pointing and vocalisations to obtain something. Proto-declaratives involve infants using their own actions, and at a slightly older age using objects, to obtain an adult's attention. They suggest that illocutionary acts can be identified from infants visually checking that adults are responding to their attempts at communication. They report that these gazes start to occur when infants progress to Piaget's stage 5 of sensorimotor development. This stage is marked by the use of novel means to obtain familiar ends during problem solving and other activities. Thus, intentional communication can be considered as the use of an adult to obtain familiar objectives.

An experimental study by Harding and Golinkoff (1979) confirmed that the beginning of this type of intentional behaviour is associated with cognitive advances. Harding and Golinkoff used a situation where the infants needed their mothers' assistance to obtain a toy. Eleven-month-old infants, unlike younger ones, tended to vocalise and look at their mother. These 11-month-old infants were usually at stage 5 of sensorimotor development, which led Harding and Golinkoff to conclude that these cognitive skills provide a basis for the development of intentional communication.

In one of their later studies Bates and her colleagues employed three criteria to identify pre-linguistic intentions to communicate. These are worth outlining because of the difficulty in identifying intentional behaviour. One criterion concerned the use of gaze alternation by infants; before 9 months if an infant wants an object she will look at it and make straining noises. As a result, intentional communication can be identified by infants not only looking at the goal, but also turning to check the effect of their message on an adult. A second criterion is the repair of failed messages, which occurs when an infant's signalling behaviour fails to result in a change of adult activity. The intention to communicate can be inferred if the infant repeats, adds to, and/or substitutes communicative activities. Such behaviour suggests that the infant has a communicative goal which she is working towards in the face of an unresponsive partner. A third criterion is the ritualisation of behaviours, for example, reaching or straining noises become more economical in presentation and are no longer directed at an object.

The idea that non-verbal communication is similar to Searle's speech acts has met with criticism. Dore (1975) maintains that speech acts involve linguistic processes which are not present before the use of words. Nelson has made a similar point. The suggestion by Bates, O'Connell and Shore that words map on to intentional non-verbal communicative acts also conflicts with proposals in the Vygotskian tradition. Both Lock (1980) and Clark (1978; see Chapter 2) put forward the idea that the first words are not used to communicate intentions. Instead infants imitate words and adult reactions transform the child's use of words. When infants notice the adult's reaction then they start to use the word to obtain the reaction. While this type of process may occur for some children there has been little recent evidence to support the idea. A slightly different perspective has been taken by McShane (1980) who supposed that adult reactions will enable infants to develop communicative intentions, and that words come to be used in the service of these intentions.

Describing One Word Utterances

There has been controversy over the linguistic status, meaning and intention behind one word utterances ever since DeLaguna's (1927) proposal that they are *holophrases* which involve undifferentiated global meanings. Most adults have a strong impression that one word utterances represent a child intentionally attempting to communicate a meaningful message. This can be contrasted with the difficulty of working out objective, consistent and reliable methods of classifying such events. A number of schemes have been devised to categorise one word utterances, and inevitably each categorisation scheme makes certain assumptions about the conceptual and intentional basis of words when inferring their meaning.

One influence on the early studies of child speech during the 1970s was the controversy about the grammar of one word utterances. Some like McNeil (1970) argued that one word utterances were the tip of the iceberg, the child was constructing full sentences, but a limitation presented these full sentences from being produced (see Chapter 11 for more recent theories about early grammar). The full sentences were supposed to follow the principles of Chomsky's transformational grammar (see Chapter 10).

At this time criticisms were being made of transformational grammar because of the difficulties it had in specifying why the semantic characteristics of some utterances made them unacceptable to speakers of the language (e.g. "a hammer broke the glass with a chisel"). This had led to proposals to take greater account of semantics when developing a grammar (McCawley, 1968; Lakoff, 1971). The case grammar of Fillmore (1968) was particularly influential. Thus, the classification schemes of one word utterances reflected the semantic and pragmatic theories of the time. In addition, many of the investigators were interested in the transition from one to two word speech, and used their schemes to explain this transition. Two word speech is considered in more detail in Chapter 8, but theoretical statements about this topic are considered here.

An important landmark in dealing with one word utterances was the detailed observations by Bloom (1973) of her daughter's utterances. Bloom distinguished *substantive* words which involve classes of objects and events, from *functional* words which refer to the operations in relation to objects such as "more" and "away". Bloom used her observations to suggest that one word speech reflects the child's references to the word and argued against McNeil's proposals.

A detailed study by Greenfield and Smith (1976) utilised the case grammar of Fillmore to develop a classification scheme. Central to Fillmore's grammar is the notion that the verb is the pivotal element in an utterance. The other parts of speech have a "case" relationship to the verb. For example, a noun is classified as an agentive because the action specified by the verb is carried out by an active agent (i.e. "the boy kicks the ball"), or a noun might be classified as instrumental when it is inanimate and carries out an action (e.g. "the *wind* blew the paper away").

Greenfield and Smith identified 12 different types of semantic messages in children's single word utterances. For example, they suggested that the utterance "ball" could be dealing with an attempt to communicate about an agent–object relationship when a child observes and describes someone hitting a ball with a bat. Other types of relation include object–location (e.g. commenting on a ball in an unusual location) and possessor–possessed (e.g. commenting on ownership). They argued that the single word is used to communicate part of this relationship, the other part is implicit in the circumstances of the use of the word. Greenfield and Smith also supposed that children's use of words changes. Initially words tend to be used to label entities, i.e. "ball" is said when the object is observed. Later the same word might be used when the child wants to play a game or is commenting on a game using a ball. Thus, they believed that increasingly varied and sophisticated messages were conveyed during the one word period.

After interacting with young children it is easy see the temptation to make these types of interpretations. However, McShane (1980) has criticised Greenfield and Smith for utilising pragmatic features of a message to construct a semantic classification scheme. Furthermore, it is very difficult to establish whether or not children's one word utterances contain this degree of complexity and whether the context can give unambiguous information about the type of message that is being conveyed.

A proposal was made by Dore (1975) who used Searle's ideas as a basis for his theory that one word speech involved *primitive speech acts*. These utterances are supposed to involve a rudimentary method of referring to an entity, together with a device, such as intonation, to indicate the force of the communication. The primitive speech acts include: labelling, repeating, answering, requesting an action, requesting an answer, calling, greeting and so on. Thus, Dore suggested that such functions can be identified in one word speech. Dore believed that innate mechanisms allow these primitive speech acts to become more similar to adult speech acts, and so allow multi-word utterances to emerge.

A slightly different analysis has involved the pragmatic basis of infant communication. Halliday (1973, 1975) identified four functions which occur in non-verbal and sometimes verbal communication, these are:

1   instrumental—to obtain an objective, e.g. obtain a toy;
2   regulatory—to influence the actions of others, e.g. to play a game;
3   interactional—to form a relationship, e.g. greetings;
4   personal—to express feelings, e.g. crying or protesting.

Halliday suggested, on the basis of observations of his son Nigel, that pre-verbal vocalisations can fulfil these four functions and later single word utterances will fulfil the same functions. Two functions are supposed to emerge slightly later: a heuristic function, to ask questions about the world, e.g. "that?"; and an imaginative one, to pretend and play make-believe. Later still, when a child can use word combinations and engage in dialogue, an informative function emerges. This involves communicating facts. Eventually the system evolves to consist of three forms of communication which roughly correspond to Searle's speech acts.

Fundamental to Halliday's proposals is the idea that children are learning how to use words and language to convey meaning, they are learning how to mean. He supposed that the development of word use involves a number of restructurings which result in progress to more sophisticated levels of communication. However, the theory does not identify the processes that would propel such restructurings.

A scheme involving a pragmatic approach to the classification of communication has been proposed by McShane (1980). McShane's scheme is extensive, but easy to follow. He divided utterances into five main groups:

Regulation (attempts to regulate communication in some way)
• *attention* directing to some object, action or group
• *request* an action by another person
• *vocative* a call to come or locate another person
Statement
• *naming* labelling or naming an entity
• *description* a comment about an entity
• *information* a comment about a past or future event
Exchange
• *giving* an utterance used while giving an object
• *receiving* an utterance used when receiving an object

Personal
- *doing* a description of what has been or is being done
- *determination* an utterance said before performing an action
- *refusal*
- *protest*

Conversational
- *imitation*
- *answer*
- *follow on*, a continuation of the conversation which is not an imitation or answer
- *question*

By following up a group of six children between 12 and 24 months old he was able to document changes in the communicative system of the children.

Yet another method of classification has been put forward by Dromi (1987). This seeks to classify words in terms of whether they are: object words, used to refer to single entities or objects; action/state words, used to describe actions or states of objects; modifiers, used to refer to properties of things and events; social words, used in conversations with no referential value; and intermediate words which are unclassifiable. Here again we see an attempt both to categorise words and to take account of their use in various contexts.

As Howe (1976) has argued (about two word utterances), the complexity attributed to children's early speech remains a matter of faith rather than a matter of fact. Disputes are likely to continue about the precise meaning of one (and two) word speech. An added complication to the interpretation of infant utterances is the phenomenon of overextension. Dromi (1987) has pointed out that it is difficult enough to classify the use of words without the added possibility that the child is perhaps knowingly extending their use to similar, but inappropriate entities. For these reasons caution is always needed when using examples of children's utterances to support or refute theories.

As we can see from these various classification schemes there is a tension between the aim either to code the parts of speech or to code the communicative intent of children's one word utterances. Attempts to use parts of speech to code one word utterances have suffered from the criticism that pragmatics are needed to supply the necessary information for the classification process, that the ways of classifying adult speech are applied without proper care about the way the word is used, and it often fails to be acknowledged that the same word may be used in different ways. Attempts to classify the intent and pragmatic aspects of communication have also encountered problems. This coding has to employ detective work in order to be able to classify a word on the basis of the context in which it occurs.

Such issues illustrate the serious problems when investigating this period of development, and also why it is a difficult but interesting area of study.

Vocabulary Development and the Vocabulary Burst

Vocabulary development

Much of the information about children's speech comes from the detailed records of the speech of individual children. This has been an important method in psycholinguistics. Nelson (1973) provided an important step away from this methodology by obtaining parental reports of children's language. The more recent development of the MacArthur Communicative Inventories (CDI) has allowed a standardised form to be used for more extensive findings by asking parents to fill in a check list of the words their children understand and produce.

The findings from the use of the CDI on over 1000 children have revealed some interesting patterns in development (Bates, Marchman, Thal et al., in press). The mean number of words comprehended and produced at 8 months is reported to be 36 and 2 (respectively); at 10 months it is 67 and about 12; at 16 months it is 191 and 64, and by 30 months children are reported to produce 534 words. Considerable caution is needed in interpreting findings on comprehension because parents may have different definitions of what they consider "understanding". Interestingly the early comprehenders were found to have different brain waves when presented with familiar rather than unfamiliar words while no difference was found for late comprehenders (Mills, Coffrey & Neville, 1993). There are other interesting features of the development of productive vocabulary. Below 12 months there is little variability, indicating an absence of early and late development, but this changes after 13 months with some children increasing their vocabulary more than the rest.

A vocabulary burst?

One noticeable feature of children's one word speech involves the rapid expansion of the productive vocabulary after a period of gradual accumulation. McCune-Nicholich (1981) found that this occurred at 19–20 months after a vocabulary of 30–50 words had been reached. Similarly, Bates, O'Connell and Shore (1987) suggest that the vocabulary burst takes place after a child's vocabulary contains about 50 words, so that within a few weeks the vocabulary contains 400 or so words. As the vocabulary expands there is an increase in the number and proportion of verbs, adjectives, and adverbs in children's vocabulary. Bates, O'Connell and Shore (1987) suggest this change marks the beginning of the use of predication (predication involves making a comment about an entity).

There is also evidence that a 50–100 word vocabulary is associated with the beginning of two word speech (Gregory & Mogford, 1981; Bates, Dale & Thal, in press). It may be that some "critical mass" is necessary for two word utterance, although this critical mass alone is not sufficient, since children with Down's syndrome do not show the same association (Bates et al., in press).

Several investigators have suggested that the vocabulary burst is a product of children understanding the nature of words, and so it is at this time that "true" words are first used. For example, Nelson (1988) proposes that after children have gained the ability to produce 30 or more words there is the understanding that words can be used to refer to categories of objects and events. She suggests that this results in the "naming explosion" and the asking for the names for entities. Underlying the changes is believed to be a new insight that all concepts have a relevant word, and all words have a concept in the child's mind. Dore (1978) has termed this the *nominal insight*, an understanding of the relation between words and objects. A related proposal has been made by Nelson (1979) who believes that children begin to collect the names for entities when they understand the properties of words. Similarly, McShane (1980) regarded the vocabulary burst as a product of a naming insight.

A different suggestion is that the vocabulary burst may be linked to general features of cognitive development. Corrigan (1978) found an association between level 6 of the Uzgiris–Hunt scales and the vocabulary burst. The Uzgiris–Hunt scales provide an assessment of cognitive development in terms of Piaget's stages of sensorimotor development. Similarly, Meltzoff and Gopnik (1989) suggest that the vocabulary burst is the result of children understanding that all things can be placed in categories (see also Chapter 16).

Two questions have been raised about the vocabulary burst. First, Goldfield and Reznick (1990) obtained maternal reports and found that the majority of children went through a vocabulary expansion which continued for a period of 3 months, and for these children nearly three-quarters of the items in their vocabularies were nouns. A smaller group of children had a more gradual acquisition of words, and their vocabularies showed a more equal distribution of word types. Nelson (1973) also noted that not all children showed a rapid vocabulary expansion. Goldfield and Reznick suggest that these differences may reflect different acquisition strategies by children, and may reflect differences in the types of speech and the naming routines to which children are exposed. It has also been suggested by Bates et al. (in press) that vocabulary increase follows an exponential curve, so that the vocabulary burst is nothing more than a part of this exponential curve. Such findings and arguments seriously weaken the case for a cognitive change being associated with the vocabulary burst.

Referential–Expressive Styles?

The referential–expressive styles of speech

We have just seen that there are various disagreements about the way to classify children's one word speech. There are also disagreements about whether there are differences between children in their use of one word utterances. The findings from a longitudinal investigation led Nelson (1973) to suggest that infants may acquire language in different ways. She suggested that the *referential* infants tended to have a vocabulary which is predominantly composed of object names, they are early talkers, and social interaction with adults often involves objects. In contrast, *social expressive* infants tended to have fewer object names in their vocabulary, having instead many words which fulfilled a role in regulating social interaction (e.g. bye-bye, ta, and so on), and they sometimes use formulae (words which tend to occur together, e.g. all-gone). Dore (1975) made a similar claim when he speculated that "word babies" concentrate on wordlike sounds when babbling and understand words at an earlier age, while "intonation babies" imitate sound contours.

A study by DellaCorte, Benedict and Klein (1983) employed Nelson's method of classification, and reported that children's style of speech was related to features of maternal conversation. Referential children, in comparison to expressive children, tended to have mothers who produced more utterances per event, more descriptions and fewer prescriptions. In addition, the referential style of maternal speech appears to be prevalent amongst firstborns which may be related to the more tutorial style of interaction often employed with such children (Pappas-Jones & Adamson, 1987).

Nelson's original study concerned children's style of speech when they had a productive vocabulary of 50 words. A claim for the presence of referential and expressive styles at an earlier level of vocabulary development has been made by Goldfield (1985). She found differences in the style of social interaction at 12 months. This was related to the later referential–expressive style of children identified on the basis of their 50 word vocabulary. Two children were studied. The referential child tended to initiate periods of joint attention by showing and giving toys, and her mother tended to label toys. In contrast, the expressive child tended to keep more separate object play and social play. Another study suggested an advantage for those with a referential style as Snyder, Bates and Bretherton (1981) found that children just over a year old who had a high proportion of object names in their comprehension vocabularies tended to have a bigger vocabulary. Both these findings suggest that the referential–expressive styles may be present from the very early stages in the use of speech.

More recently, Bates, Bretherton and Snyder (1988) have contrasted an *analytic* style in language acquisition with a *holistic* style (sometimes termed rote style). The analytic style involves a high percentage of referential words in one word vocabularies, a nominal style of speech with two word utterances, and the later overgeneralisation of grammatical rules. These children often appear to learn words faster, are female, firstborn and come from higher socio-economic status families. The holistic style involves the use of intonation during babbling, many expressive words at the one word stage, the use of formulae in two word speech, and later undergeneralisation and inconsistent application of rules. Bates, Bretherton and Snyder (1988) in their longitudinal study found evidence for three strands of relationships; these involved the abilities of comprehension, analysed production, and rote production. However, later research by Bates and her colleagues (in press) based on parental reports using the CDI with a large sample of children has resulted in the conclusion that the characterisation of styles of speech may be a "substantial oversimplification".

The identification of referential–expressive styles

Nelson classified the content of children's first 50 words in terms of a referential–expressive distinction. The words and their context of use were obtained from a maternal diary. Referential words were considered to involve the labelling of objects. A problem for such a scheme is that children sometimes use object words in a functional way (e.g. the referential word "drink" when asking for some liquid). This type of problem led both McShane (1980) and Pine (1992) to argue that the method of classification is inappropriate. They suggested that the classification system fails because it is partly a functional classification based on the children's word use, and partly a formal classification based on the properties of the word in adult speech.

In some investigations, which expanded on Nelson's work, the referential–expressive distinction was made on the basis of the formal properties of words (e.g. whether a word like "drink" is a noun in adult speech), and the functional use of the words was largely ignored (Snyder, Bates & Bretherton, 1981; Bates, Bretherton & Snyder, 1988; Hampson, 1989). This makes the classification scheme clear and easy to use, but means that little is known about the child's use of words.

Further criticisms of the referential–expressive classification have been made by Pine (1992). He notes that the same words often appear to be used in different ways by the same infant. In addition, Pine and Lieven (1990) argue that it is inappropriate to make the referential–expressive distinction at different stages of speech development, as the proportion of the two types of words will vary with age. Another criticism is that maternal reports may overestimate the number of common nouns used by children.

Pine (1992) presents an analysis employing a more functional classification of referential–expressive words. He found there was little relationship between a functional classification and a classification scheme similar to that used by Nelson. This suggests it may be incorrect to assume that "referential" infants tend to have any consistent conversational style. However, the small sample of seven infants used in his study means there should be caution in interpreting this finding. Furthermore, if one accepts Pine's argument about the multi-functional nature of words then this raises problems about any classification scheme which cannot fully document all examples of word use by infants. Lastly, it should be remembered that some interesting correlations between referential style and linguistic development have been observed, such as the relation between the proportion of object nouns and vocabulary size.

SUMMARY

We have seen in the first part of the chapter that the demise of the classic view has been accompanied by new views about meaning. In some cases this has resulted in the integration of the classic view with approaches that also consider the pragmatics of communication (e.g. Harman, 1971). Much of the more recent work has concerned the importance of intention and the type of actions accomplished by speaking. However, there is a difficulty, even with adult speech, in establishing the subtle nuances of meaning. This difficulty is compounded with young children's speech. Despite such problems, the discussions about intention and meaning have had important influences on the study of one word utterances.

Different perspectives about intention and meaning have been utilised in the description of children's one word speech. The different perspectives are partly a result of the difficulty of establishing the intention and meaning of such utterances. Even so, there is agreement that the one word period involves the development of increasing sophistication in the use of words to communicate messages.

The issue of referential and expressive styles of speech has attracted attention and debate. As with other discussions of single word speech the issue at the heart of the debate is what is meant when a child produces a word, and how observers can recover this meaning. As McShane and Pine have pointed out, it is difficult to classify children's speech in terms of the referential–expressive distinction. Despite this, there do seem to be differences between children in their vocabulary and this is related to other features of language development.

In all these discussions we have seen the problematic nature of describing and classifying one word utterances. One reaction to all these difficulties is to despair at ever reaching a "true" description of children's speech, or of investigators coming to some consensus. Although it is unrealistic to expect to be able to be absolutely sure about what infants mean when they say a word, this need not be a cause of despair. The various descriptions of children's one word utterances provide a number of suggestions about the functions of this speech, and in the future these may be further refined. Furthermore, we are now in a better position to recognise the limitations of some of the earlier schemes, and this should prevent past mistakes from reoccurring.

8

UNDERSTANDING NEW WORDS: CONSTRAINTS AND GRAMMAR

In discussions about children's acquisition of new words it has often been assumed, particularly in the past, that this occurs simply by adults pointing at objects and naming them. However, children are presented with more complex and subtle forms of information which can help them to identify a referent (see Chapter 4). Further, the way children relate a word to some aspect of the referent also involves complex processes of concept formation and understanding meaning (see Chapter 6). In addition, children are faced with the issue of how to relate a new word to existing words in their vocabulary. Despite these complexities children of 2 years and over acquire a very large vocabulary at a very fast rate; it has been estimated that about new 10 words are acquired every day. How can we account for such a rapid rate of acquisition? In particular how can we account for this given that children are often provided with very limited information about the match between word and referent?

One general solution has been to suggest that children have strategies to help them work out the properties of a word in situations where there is only limited information. For instance it has been suggested that there is a *whole object* assumption, so that when young children hear a word they assume it refers to the whole object rather than a part or property of the object. This assumption helps to explain why young children are so efficient in acquiring a large vocabulary of nouns. Commonly, strategies relevant to the word learning process are referred to as *assumptions* or *constraints*. Nelson (1988) has criticised the use of the term constraint because it suggests that a powerful innate mechanism operates, and this may explain why the term assumption is now preferred, which leaves open issues such as power and innateness. I will use the term *strategy* to refer to constraints and assumptions, and will use these latter terms to refer to the particular processes identified by investigators.

There is uncertainty about when strategies are first used. Some have argued that strategies will start to operate after the vocabulary spurt. Both Nelson (1988) and Markman (1991) suggest early speech (before about 18 months) may be different from later speech. Nelson (1988) also points out that cognitive processes may be very different in children who do and do not have a reasonable command of language, and are thereby familiar or unfamiliar with deducing the meaning of words from their context. Similarly, Behrend (1990) suggests that word use before the vocabulary spurt is pre-lexical and therefore not subject to constraints. It has even been proposed by Markman (1991) that the vocabulary spurt may occur because children start to utilise certain strategies and this allows word learning to be faster and more efficient.

The first section of this chapter considers the use of strategies by children of about 2 years or less. At this age one of the most pressing issues is to match a word with its referent and the strategies relevant to this process are outlined and discussed. Many of the proposals about younger children's strategies come from extending findings from 3 to 5 year olds to younger children, and so we should be cautious about the applicability of these ideas. The more extensive and better documented findings about older children are considered in the second section of the chapter. In the third section investigations which have examined the way that grammar can help children to understand the meaning of words are outlined. These investigations reveal that as children increase their understanding of grammar they can start to use cues from it to help them work out the type of new word they hear in an utterance, whether it is a noun, verb or adjective.

INITIAL STRATEGIES WHICH COULD AID WORD ACQUISITION

Initial Strategies

Over the years, various forms of constraint have been proposed to help explain the initial acquisition of words. One of the first claims was made by MacNamara (1972) who believed that children initially assume that words refer to a whole object rather than some part or aspect of the object. Because adults typically talk about whole objects many of the uncertainties of reference are removed by this whole object assumption, but mistakes can be made (e.g. a child refers to an oven as "hot", presumably having often heard "It is hot"). A similar idea has been proposed by a variety of investigators (Behrend, 1990; Markman & Hutchinson, 1984; Markman, 1991; Mervis & Long, 1987; Seidenberg & Petitto, 1987; Clark, 1991).

One problem with the whole object assumption identified by Nelson (1988) is the need to explain how children are able to acquire action and other types of words; early vocabularies do not consist entirely of object words. How do children identify when it is inappropriate to employ the whole object assumption? Behrend (1990) counters this objection by arguing that constraints explain why verbs are less frequent and appear more difficult to acquire, but this appears to miss Nelson's point that there need to be further mechanisms postulated to account for the acquisition of other types of word.

Furthermore, children do violate the whole object assumption when it is appropriate to do so. Research by Soja, Carey and Spelke (1990) revealed that children have different strategies when applying words to solid objects and to non-solid substances. The paradigm employed was to present a *solid* shape, such as a "T" made out of piping, and frequently refer to it with a nonsense word. Then the 2-year-old children were asked whether the nonsense word referred to a similar shape made up of another solid substance, or to parts of the original substance in different smaller shapes (see Figure 8.1). As one might expect from the whole object assumption, 2 year olds applied the nonsense word to solid objects of the same shape as the original referent, rather than to the parts of the original.

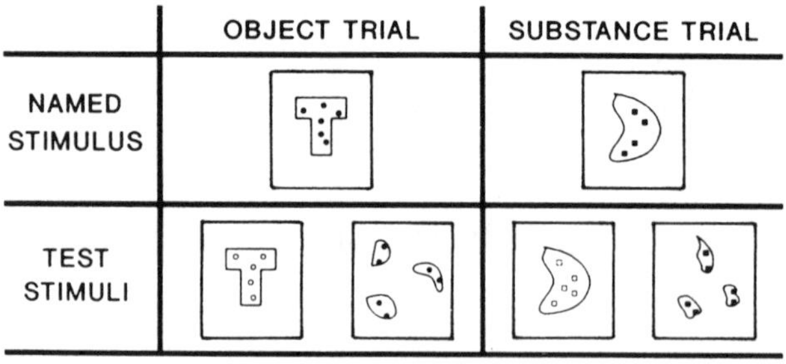

Figure 8.1 The design of Soja, Carey and Spelke (1990) (reproduced with permission from N. N. Soja, S. Carey & E. S. Spelke (1990) Ontological categories guide young children's inductions of word meaning: Object terms and substance terms. *Cognition*, **38**, 179–211. Elsevier Science Publishers)

More interesting findings occurred when the same procedure was used with a *non-solid* substance (e.g. cold-cream). In the test the children were given the same shape made up of a different substance, or smaller elements of the original substance. They were asked to choose which set corresponded to the nonsense word. Children tended to choose the substance rather than the shape. Thus, the study suggests that children, when learning words, have greater flexibility than the whole object assumption would suggest, and that at an early age they use their knowledge about the world to help them make appropriate choices when objects and substances are named.

Another strategy that has been proposed is the *equal detail* assumption (Clark, 1991). Here children are supposed to assume that neighbouring categories are at the same level of specificity (e.g. ducks, chicken and geese involve one level of specificity while birds, mammals and reptiles involve another). In this way children should develop a categorisation system with appropriate entries. However, it is unclear how children are able to identify when it is appropriate and when inappropriate to apply the equal detail assumption, and it is also not clear what rules should be employed (by children and by investigators) to identify referents at the same level of specificity.

A related proposal is the *taxonomic assumption*, that labels will pick out an object as an example of a taxonomic category rather than sets of objects which are thematically or functionally related. The operation of this strategy is seen in studies which have given a child a target picture and the instructions, "See this. Can you find another one?" from an array of other pictures. Typically, children make a choice based on functional or thematic similarities, so that they would choose items like milk to go with a picture of a cow. However, if the target object is referred to as follows, "See this fep? Can you find another fep?", then children usually choose a taxonomically related picture. Backscheider and Markman (1990) have found this effect in 18–24 month olds. In addition, Baldwin (1989) has reported a related effect; this study revealed that when objects are not labelled children are likely to sort them by their colour, when objects are labelled objects are more likely to be sorted by their membership of a category.

However, the taxonomic assumption encounters problems in explaining at least one area of word use. The early vocabularies of children consist of a high number of names of individual people (i.e. Mummy, Mary, Fido) and a high number of context-bound words. An explanation needs to be given of why there are these apparent violations of the taxonomic assumption. Furthermore, Bavin, Ng, Brimmell and Gabriel (1993) have reported that 3 year olds who are acquiring Greek and Chinese do not behave in the same way as children learning English when given Markman and Hutchinson's task.

It has also been suggested that there is a *basic level* assumption. Brown (1958) argued that speech to children usually referred to generic descriptions of entities: "Do you want an apple?" (not "Do you want some fruit?"). The idea of a basic level of categorisation is also present in prototype theory, where it is supposed that at this level members of a category are most easily distinguishable and most easily stand out (Mervis, 1987), so "chair" would be a basic level category in contrast to "furniture" and "high chair". Here also there is controversy; Mandler (1993) has questioned whether there is any rule which can reliably identify basic categories, and she argues instead that basic categories are a result of social convention rather than conceptual analysis. Thus, an item is at a basic level if adults and children use that level to talk about referents. Such a criticism casts doubt on the usefulness of postulating a basic level assumption.

Summary

These proposals provide some interesting possibilities about the acquisition of words and highlight the complexity of the strategies children bring to word learning tasks. However, there is a need for a clearer articulation of the mechanisms which lead to the operation of children's word learning strategies. It is still uncertain whether these are innate or acquired processes. Similarly, we need to know why assumptions are violated as in the cases of proper nouns, verbs, and non-solid substances.

Not only does the theory need to be developed, but the methods are in need of further refinement. Experimental studies can be criticised for providing an artificial situation for word learning. However, there are also problems with data which are based on diary recordings of children's speech because of the uncertainties about the meaning of children's first utterances.

FITTING WORDS INTO AN EXISTING VOCABULARY

The Contrastive Hypothesis

An influential view about the way assumptions can influence the acquisition of words is the *contrastive* hypothesis. This theory was originally developed by Barrett (1978, 1982) and by Clark (1983, 1987, 1991). In essence the hypothesis supposes that as words are acquired they will be differentiated or contrasted with existing words, and that children assume that different words typically have different meanings.

A classic study by Carey (1978) involved an experimenter asking 3- and 4-year-old children to "bring me the chromium tray, not the blue one" (the target tray was in fact olive green and there were only two trays available). Children successfully picked out the tray with the unknown colour, and later on showed some knowledge of the meaning of the unknown colour term. This paradigm involves what has been termed a process of lexical contrast whereby children work out the properties of an unknown word by contrasting it with another known word. Dockrell and Campbell (1986) followed up this investigation and found that 3- and 4-year-old children were successful in acquiring a new name for an unknown toy animal in these conditions, but had more problems with acquiring colour terms. Interestingly, the contrastive assumption does not appear to be species specific. Savage-Rumbaugh (1990) reports that apes are able to infer that a novel symbol refers to a novel food, and will use the novel symbol to request the food.

A useful clarification about the operation of this assumption has been made by Elbers, van Loon-Vervoom and van Helden-Lankhaar (1993) who put forward the *principle of contrast usage*. This suggests that when words are used contrastively children not only assume a difference between words (e.g. in terms of which colour is referred to), but also assume that the words are referring to the same dimension (e.g. colour). Consequently, Elbers, van Loon-Vervoom and van Helden-Lankhaar argue that the usefulness of contrast is in relation to other similar words rather than to the whole of the lexicon. They also suggest that such contrast will aid children's under-standing of the relationship between words.

There have been a number of criticisms of the contrastive hypothesis. Nelson (1990) has pointed out that not all words are used contrastively, she herself claims to use the words "couch" and "sofa" interchangeably (and I am tending to use the words "assumption" and "constraint" interchange-ably!). Furthermore, Nelson also argues that the meaning of a word shifts with its use, rather than being a function of some inherent abstract meaning. In other words, the contrastive hypothesis appears to predict that words have fixed meanings which can then be contrasted with the meanings of other words. However, as we have seen in the last chapter, meanings of words are more complex and flexible than this. The contrastive hypothesis has also received detailed criticism from Gathercole (1987) who argues that children sometimes have words which overlap in their meaning and that a number of other assumptions of the hypothesis are incorrect (see Clark, 1988, for a rebuttal).

Contrast, Conventionality and Mutual Exclusivity

More recently, Clark (1991) has emphasised the operation of the constraint of conventionality as well as contrast. Conventionality is simply a prag-matic principle that words have conventional meanings within the lan-guage community. She supposes "that children appear to recognise very early that language is conventional, that the speakers around them have words for objects, events, states, and relations, and that a major task in acquisition is to map those conventional terms onto appropriate conceptual categories" (Clark, 1991, p. 35). A problem with the idea of conventionality is that, as Clark (1991) herself observes, children violate the principle by creating new words to fill gaps in their lexicon.

The mutual exclusivity assumption proposed by Markman (1991) is closely related to the assumption of contrast. In comparison to contrast, the mutual exclusivity assumption is the more powerful. There is a *contrast* between the words "animal" and "dog", but because the two words can refer to the same thing they violate the mutual exclusivity assumption. Clark (1991) has argued that the assumption of contrast, when coupled with the single level assumption (that words refer to entities at the same level of detail) is in effect the same as the mutual exclusivity assumption.

When do children start to use mutual exclusivity or contrast assumptions? Maratsos (quoted in Merriman & Bowman, 1989) has pointed out that the contrastive hypothesis is unlikely to be correct as a description of the child's first words; logically the first words would have to provide a global description of the world which was gradually contrasted with other words.

Thus, it is interesting that Merriman and Bowman (1989) suggest that this assumption does not become operative until about 30 months. In their study children were allowed to play with a set of unfamiliar objects. They were then presented with an unfamiliar object from this set (e.g. a garlic press), and with a familiar object (e.g. a doll). When asked to "put your finger on the garlic press" 2-year-old children tended to touch the doll. This appears to violate the mutual exclusivity assumption because the children already have a name for this object. But 30-month-old children did follow the strategy predicted by the mutual exclusivity assumption as they touched the garlic press. However, Markman (1991) has criticised these studies for failing to control for the effect of novelty in the session, so that the choice of the younger children was a result of a preference for the unfamiliar. Even if the children were responding to novelty there still remains the issue of why the assumption did not operate in these circumstances.

Mervis (1987), like Merriman and Bowman, has also argued that the mutual exclusivity assumption does not develop until the late pre-school years. She provides examples of violations of the mutual exclusivity assumption. For example, Banigan and Mervis (1988) were able to train 2-year-old children to violate the mutual exclusivity assumption by teaching them a second label for an object (e.g. glasses and goggles). However, Markman (1991) responds to this criticism by emphasising the difficulty of carrying out this procedure. Markman goes on to suggest that the mutual exclusivity assumption will not operate when there is sufficient contrary evidence; this seems to be an attempt to take account of objections and counter examples (Gathercole, 1987; Merriman, 1987; Merriman & Bowman, 1989; Mervis, 1987, 1989; Nelson, 1988). Such a suggestion by Markman makes it extremely difficult if not impossible to test the hypothesis. Thus, the claims by both Clark (1991) and Markman (1991) that these assumptions "normally" operate allow them to account for exceptions, but do not provide a coherent and testable account of the operation of word learning strategies.

Another criticism made of this literature by Nelson (1988) is that investigations usually report a higher probability of responding in a certain way, rather than the totally consistent response by all children that might be expected from the operation of a general principle. A reply to this type of criticism has been made by Behrend (1990) who makes a distinction between constraints which operate as a cognitive process, and the actual behaviour of young children which he regards as the product of a variety of influences. Consequently, he argues that although a constraint may exist it may not govern behaviour because of peripheral influences. However, without a clear statement of the mechanisms that produce the strategies that children employ, any explanations of behaviour can only be made in a post hoc manner and we will fail to understand the operation of these processes.

Assumptions and Inferences

Not only has it been suggested that children's word learning will be directly influenced by particular assumptions, but it is also supposed that children use these assumptions to make inferences about the meaning of a novel word from fairly complex sets of circumstances. A number of investigations have designed studies with the following procedure. The investigator ensures that children know or are given the names of most, but not all, of a set of objects. Then an unfamiliar word is used, but it is unclear which object is being labelled. Children usually assume that the novel word refers to the object for which they do not have a name. These types of findings have been reported by several investigators (Carey, 1978; Dockrell, 1981; Golinkoff, Hirsch-Pasek, Baduini & Lavallee, 1985; Hutchinson, 1986; Markman & Wachtel, 1988). Originally, Carey termed this an odd-name odd-element strategy. Markman (1991) argues that such responses are compatible with the mutual exclusivity principle, as the children appear to make the assumption that the unfamiliar word does not refer to the object they can already name.

There is another set of studies which involve inference and are also claimed to provide an example of the integration of different constraints. Markman (1991) suggests that if the whole object assumption was never violated children would have great difficulty in learning the names for parts of objects and of superordinate or subordinate terms because they would always assume that a word referred to the whole object. However, if children assume that words differ in meaning, because of the mutual exclusivity assumption, then the use of two different words in relation to the same object should lead them to look for differences in meaning of the two words. Thus, the contrastive and mutual exclusivity assumptions provide a mechanism for the acquisition of words which are not the labels for whole objects.

Findings which are compatible with this reasoning come from a study by Taylor and Gelman (1989) with 2 year olds. They found that a second word that was used to describe an object was often treated as a subordinate expression, or treated as a proper noun. The latter strategy was especially likely to occur if this was appropriate, if, for example, the object was a stuffed toy. Similarly, Au and DeWitt (1993) report that when a second word was used to refer to a familiar object made out of an unusual substance then 4 year olds usually assumed that it referred to the substance rather than the object. Interestingly, Au and DeWitt also found that the exclusivity assumption was violated when children were told that the word was from another language; they then treated the "foreign" word as applying to the object and not to the attribute.

Summary and Evaluation

The investigations into the use of strategies during word learning have identified an important dimension of the language acquisition process. The way that children acquire unfamiliar words appears to be governed by a complex set of processes. However, within this literature there is a lack of precision about when these constraints, biases or assumptions operate and when they will fail to operate. Furthermore, the lack of any theoretical account means that we still have to move beyond a redescription of the experimental findings to identify a mechanism to explain these processes.

Another serious worry is that most studies have been concerned with the *fast mapping* of words. Typically children are given minimal exposure to the word and referent and the post-test occurs shortly after the experimental procedure. While such procedures can inform us about the early stages of word learning, they tell us little about the longer term process which involves modifying and increasing the complexity of concepts associated with words. Notable exceptions to this general trend are the studies of Carey (1978) and Dockrell and Campbell (1986). In these studies we see that the word learning is a considerably longer and more variable process than is suggested by simple models of constraints.

In addition, Tomasello and Barton (in press) have rejected an approach to word learning based on a rigid set of assumptions or constraints. Instead they argue that their findings show that children have flexible word learning strategies which utilise a wide range of information sources. This they believe is possible because children have a rich knowledge about the pragmatics of communication which they utilise when attempting to understand new words and expressions. For instance, 2 year olds will use cues from the fact that someone is searching for something to enable them to associate a nonsense word with an object which is not manipulated until some time after the original referential expression, and when the experimenter has handled several objects in the intervening time.

SYNTACTIC BOOTSTRAPPING

A growing body of evidence suggests that children utilise the information in adult utterances to help them understand the semantics and the syntactic category of a new word that they hear. According to this perspective children utilise cues such as word order and affixes (the beginnings or endings of words) to help them obtain more information about an unknown word. Landau and Gleitman (1985) have used the idea of syntactic bootstrapping to explain some of their findings concerning the language development of children who are blind. Syntactic bootstrapping involves using grammatical information from the structure of a sentence to infer the *meaning* of an unknown target word. Obviously, such processes can only operate once children have a command of syntax.

Early Syntactic Influences

Research by Naigles (1990) suggests that syntactic bootstrapping may occur surprisingly early in development and because of the innovative nature of this study it is described in some detail. In it, 2-year-old children were presented with the nonsense word "gorping", in either a transitive or intransitive sentence. A transitive verb requires an object, e.g. "she hit the ball", an intransitive verb does not require an object, e.g. "she swam". While one type of sentence was being said, a video screen presented an action that had *two* components. One component involved causationandtherefore could be associated with transitive verbs: e.g. "the duck is gorping the bunny" where the duck was forcing the bunny into a bending position. The other component of the action involved the bunny and duck making pointing-like arm gestures; this was regarded as an intransitive event as there was no referent of the gesture. Thus, during training the children heard one type of sentence and they saw a picture of a *combined* action.

Subsequently, the children were asked about the nonsense word in the same sentence frame ("where's the gorping now?"). At this point the two component actions were presented separately on two different video screens, so the children either saw the forcing action or the pointing action. The children tended to look at the transitive action when they had heard the transitive sentence, which suggests that they had some understanding of the syntactic information given in the sentence. A similar procedure with intransitive verbs revealed the expected preference for looking at the pointing gestures. Thus, the findings suggest that young children use syntactic information to help them understand words, but as Naigles admits, it is not entirely clear what type of meaning had been deduced from the sentence frames and what from the action. One possibility is that children were applying their knowledge of verbs to identify a relevant transitive or intransitive action during training, and as a result they looked at the appropriate action when tested.

Identifying Common and Proper Nouns

We have already seen that the taxonomic assumption was identified in studies which revealed that naming an object seems to alter children's strategies when selecting objects; children change from choosing objects on the basis of thematic relations to choosing objects on the basis of taxonomic relations. This suggests that children are using some clues from syntax to alter their behaviour (i.e. the difference between "see this" and "see this fep").

A more direct investigation of this issue comes from experimental studies which have investigated whether labelling an object with a common or a proper noun alters children's behaviour towards the object. Most, if not all, languages have words where the category members are usually treated as being similar (i.e. common nouns such as "spoon") and words which refer to an entity which are treated as being unique (i.e. proper nouns such as "Mary"). Thus, the use of a common noun should lead children to treat all similar objects in a similar way, whereas the use of a proper noun should lead children to treat the object as having a unique name.

One of the first studies to examine children's understanding of common and proper nouns was conducted by Katz, Baker and MacNamara (1974). They were interested in the effect on young children's behaviour of whether or not an object is usually treated as an individual entity, and whether it is referred to by a common or a proper noun. To do this they conducted a training study in which 2-year-old children were given a pair of dolls or a pair of blocks—in each case the individuals of the pair were similar, but could be distinguished. One of the pair was referred to with a nonsense word such as "zav". Later the children were instructed to perform actions on the "zav" when the pair of similar objects were present. It was expected that the children would select the named doll because dolls are usually treated as being individual entities, but randomly select the blocks because these are usually treated randomly.

The investigators also varied whether "zav" was employed as a common noun by including the articles (e.g. "Here's a zav") or as a proper name by leaving out the articles (e.g. "Here's Zav"). In English this provides a very useful clue as to whether a proper or common noun is being employed.

The findings revealed that girls tended to treat the dolls as being individuals, but only in the proper noun condition. The same pattern of findings was obtained with younger children who were 17 months old; this occurred even when the dolls and the blocks were clearly different and could have been treated as unique. In other words, the children, at both ages, treated the nonsense word as the name for a doll when they had heard it as a proper noun in utterances like "Here's Zav". There was no evidence that blocks were treated as proper nouns. Thus, understanding of both the world and syntax appeared to influence the way children acted in this study.

Gelman and Taylor (1984) extended this investigation by conducting a training study where 2-year-old children were exposed to two pairs of novel toys at the same time (two toy animals and two block-like toys). One of the toys was named with a nonsense word six times, either as a proper noun or as a common noun. Afterwards the children were tested on their knowledge of the nonsense word by being asked to perform activities (e.g. "Put the kiv in the basket").

The response to instructions about the toy animals was influenced by whether a common or a proper noun was used during training. After use of a proper name during training, children when tested usually chose the previously named object more often than any other. This suggests that they were treating the word as a proper name for the animal. The use of a common noun with an animal during training resulted in both animals being chosen about equally during testing. This suggests that children were, in response to hearing the nonsense word used as a common noun, treating similar objects as having the same name.

The toy blocks presented a more complex pattern of findings. The use of proper nouns during training led to the random selection of toys during testing. Gelman and Taylor speculate that this may have been because the children were confused by the inappropriate use of a proper noun with an object that appeared to be a common noun. The use of a common noun resulted in the equal selection of either block during testing, again suggesting that the children were responding to the syntactic cues in the speech they heard. Thus, this study also suggests that children use syntactic information to provide information about the referent of utterances.

A related area of research has concerned the syntactic properties of count and mass nouns. Count nouns typically take an -s in the plural form, are distinct entities, and can be counted (e.g. two cups). Mass nouns do not usually have an -s in the plural form, do not form distinct entities, and are not counted (e.g. water). Gordon (1985) tested 3–5 year olds' behaviour after they had been given sentences with nonsense words used as either a count or a proper noun. The sentence construction seemed to be a more powerful influence than the perceptual properties of the object on the children's later use of these nouns. Here it was claimed that cues from syntax may be more powerful than the semantic cues about the grammatical category of the novel word.

Nouns, Verbs and Adjectives

Nouns, verbs and adjectives are all important components in children's early speech and there are findings which suggest that children can use syntactic information to help them identify these grammatical categories. Research by Taylor and Gelman (1988) has contrasted the use of nouns and adjectives. In their study they used expressions like "a zav" (i.e. a noun form) and "a zav one" (i.e. an adjective form) when talking about one toy from a set. When tested, the children were asked to select the previously named object and asked whether the name could be applied to a series of objects (e.g. "Is it a tiv?"). After being exposed to noun forms children tended to pick out the named object or a similar object, but after being exposed to adjectives children tended to pick out the named object and an object which was made of the same material, but not necessarily similar in shape. Thus, even 2-year-old children appear to be using syntactic information to help them respond appropriately to test items.

A study of 3–4-year-old children by Dockrell and McShane (1990) examined the way in which the use of nouns and verbs influenced children's understanding of the properties of a novel word. The children were shown a picture with an accompanying commentary. The children then had to choose one of three pictures to match the novel word. Four different commentaries were employed in the study. Two involved a novel word being treated as singular or as a plural version of a noun with an -s affix (e.g. "Do you know what levs are?"). The other two involved a novel word being treated as a present or present progressive form of a verb. The -s ending was also used for present tense verbs, but was of course presented in a different sentence frame, as in "In this picture he levs". In contrast the -ing ending only occurred for the progressive form of a verb ("He is leving"). The test pictures corresponded to the possibilities offered by the different commentaries.

The majority of 3- and 4-year-old children were able to use the information from these instructions to choose the appropriate picture. The findings also indicated that the children did not appear exclusively to attend to the endings of words when making these decisions (or they would have had problems with the -s ending), but also attended to the whole sentence frame.

SUMMARY

In this chapter we have seen that children use a variety of strategies to help them understand the meaning of novel words. There is still considerable uncertainty about when these strategies start to operate and whether or not they are the result of innate biases. The research on children older than 2 years provides a greater range of studies and hypotheses. Here there have been a number of ingenious experiments which indicate that children can make quite complex inferences about the meaning of words. Unfortunately, although the area is rich in findings, there is an absence of theories which go beyond a redescription of the behaviour. As a result, findings can be explained by the operation of this or that strategy, but there is no way of predicting why one strategy should be employed rather than another when there are conflicting demands placed on children.

Thus, research has revealed that children utilise a variety of forms of information, to help them gain an understanding of the semantic and syntactic properties of a novel word. In the future, it may be profitable to think of children as having a variety of strategies to help them understand speech in situations where there is limited information, and that these strategies are acquired from a variety of sources. These sources would include cultural assumptions acquired during interaction, basic abilities involving the way children process information and solve problems, together with the logical and functional properties of any communication system. In doing this it will be important to move away from the idea of a fixed cognitive structure which automatically comes into function in a given set of circumstances, towards seeing children as utilising the pragmatics of the situation to help them understand the speech they hear.

9

WORDS AND THE
BEGINNINGS OF LANGUAGE

Before discussing the beginnings of language it is useful to consider the
ways in which it is similar to, and different from, other forms of communication. There is no easy or agreed answer to this question of definition, a
point which becomes apparent in the first section of the chapter. The next
section considers the beginnings of language in children's speech; the use
of two word utterances, telegraphic speech, and the acquisition of morphology. This provides a description of early speech; the theoretical discussions
about the linguistic status of this early speech are left until Chapter 12. The
third section returns to questions about the nature of language, and outlines
attempts to teach apes to use language.

LANGUAGE AND COMMUNICATION

What is Language?

What is the difference between speech and language? Speech is used to refer
to the production of words by vocalisations, but speech may not always
involve the use of a language. I can speak a set of nonsense words, or
produce a random arrangement of words, neither of which would be
considered as language. In contrast, language does not have to involve the
spoken word, for example the sign languages of the deaf are accepted as
languages.

The definition of the term language is critical to a number of controversies.
These include the issue of when infants start to use language, whether
language is unique to humans, and the related topic of whether apes can
use language. A classic series of papers published by Hockett (1963) set out
to identify the features of language which make it different from most other

forms of communication. The list extended to some 16 items, and included such items as the interchangeability of who is a transmitter and who is a receiver; arbitrariness and creativity. This approach of listing the properties of language has not found favour with linguists, who now concentrate on one or two features to define language. A useful way to think about the properties of language is to compare human language with the communication of other animals.

Similar Features in Language and Animal Communication

It is often supposed that an important distinction between language and other forms of communication is that there is an arbitrary relation between a word and its referent. This is certainly true for most words, there is no apparent relation for example between the word "cat" and the animal, in sight, sound, taste, touch or smell. However, the arbitrary nature of language is not restricted to human speech; many animals communicate by using arbitrary signals. For example, the warning cries of vervet monkeys differ according to whether the threat comes from a snake, an eagle, or a lion; and the monkeys take appropriate evasive action when these sounds are replayed to them via a hidden recorder (Seyfarth, Cheney & Marler, 1980a, b).

One feature of language which makes it different from most other forms of communication is that meaning is conveyed by the organisation of its elements (words and parts of words). For example, "Jack takes Fido for a walk" has a very different meaning from "Fido takes Jack for a walk". In most forms of animal communication the precise organisation of the elements does not influence the message that is conveyed. In fact an intelligent dog is likely to wag its tail and run about happily if the word "walk" is mentioned, irrespective of the precise order of the words in the utterance. The emphasis on the relation between organisation and meaning can be traced back to de Saussure (1959) whose work of 1915 provided an important impetus to modern linguistics.

Human language, however, is not the only form of communication to convey meaning by the organisation and variation of its elements. Perhaps the most famous example of this is the dance of honey bees. The work of Von Frisch (1927) has shown that bees can indicate, to other bees in a hive, the position and distance of a source of nectar by the direction and the tempo—the organisation and variation—of a "dance" that they make. It is unlikely (but not impossible) that we would want to describe the dance of a honey bee as language, and so little weight has been paid to this criterion for identifying whether or not this form of communication is language.

Sometimes it has been suggested that human language is unique because it is the result of cultural transmission, with little or no conscious teaching of the skill. There are, however, a number of examples of cultural-like transmission of methods of communication in animals. The basic song of chaffinches appears to be innate since it will occur in birds that are reared in isolation, but for the full complexity of the song to be produced the young bird needs to be exposed to model songs from adults (Thorpe, 1961, 1963). In addition, as we will see later, a chimpanzee has been reported as teaching signs to a younger animal.

Differences between Language and Animal Communication

One feature of linguistic communication that appears to make it different from other forms of communication is structural-dependency. Structural-dependency refers to the way that the correct organisation of speech depends on the types of elements that are used. For example, one general rule in English is that a statement can be changed into a question by moving the verb to the beginning of the utterance "Jogging is fun" becomes "Is jogging fun?" This operation involves being able to identify the verb irrespective of the length and number of elements in the utterance. In the example "Jogging is fun even if you are overweight", it is necessary to identify the appropriate verb to transform the statement into a question (this process is not usually at a conscious level). As we can see, the rules do not involve a merely mechanical process of taking the first or last word and moving that about. Chomsky (1980, 1986, 1988) regards structural-dependency as one of the aspects of language which make it different from other forms of communication.

Another process which involves structural-dependency is the requirement of languages to have correspondences between elements. For example, in English, verbs are altered according to whether the subject of the verb is one or several entities: "He jogs quickly" vs "They jog quickly". It is worth noting that in special circumstances human speech may involve less reliance on structural-dependency. Where people who use different languages need to communicate there is often the development of a pidgin system. This involves a restricted vocabulary and few morphological forms (i.e. endings to words). Because of the lack of structural-dependency there have been doubts about whether pidgins should be considered as languages in the formal sense of the word.

Another feature, which Chomsky believes is unique to human languages, is the capacity to convey an infinite number of messages using a finite number of elements. As a result, the complexity of linguistic messages appears to be qualitatively different from that possible in animal communication. For example, it is impossible for any known non-linguistic system to communicate a message as complex as "That fat person jogs much better than I ever expected".

The Study of Language

Having considered issues concerned with the definition of language, it is now necessary to consider the terminology used in discussing language and language development. At the core of the terminology is the notion of a grammar. The grammar of a language is a description of the rules that are used to construct utterances in that language. The term grammar, as used by linguists, is not a description of the way language *should* be used, but a description of the way language *is* used. There can be different grammars of the same language, as in the case of dialects, but the linguist does not regard one grammar as any more correct than the others. Furthermore, it is unusual for a person to be conscious of the rules of the grammar. People can usually say whether or not an utterance "sounds correct", but may not be able to explain their decision. For instance, we know that "a beautiful red sauce" is grammatically more appropriate than "a red beautiful sauce", but very few of us would be able to say why! These rules and constraints are complex to describe, and even today there is no agreed grammar for a language.

The term grammar is used to refer to three areas of language. These are: (i) phonology, the way sounds are used (see Chapter 5); (ii) semantics and pragmatics (see Chapters 6 and 7), and (iii) *morphology* and *syntax*, the rules governing the arrangement of the elements of meaning (see Chapter 10). Morphology is concerned with the smallest units of speech that can be used to convey meaning, these are called *morphemes*. Words are not the smallest element, certain tenses can be denoted by the addition of elements to words (e.g. -ed), and plurals can be denoted by the addition of -s. Thus, *bound morphology* is concerned with the study of the rules concerning the use of these elements. Morphology is also sometimes considered to be concerned with the study of words which are morphemes (e.g. pronouns—I, you, we, etc.; auxiliaries—a, the; prepositions—in, on, by, etc.).

The study of syntax involves the study of the "organisation of meaningful elements within the sentence" (Atkinson, Kilby & Roca, 1988, p. 155), that is the way meaning is conveyed by the arrangement of the elements of speech. A major goal in linguistics is to construct a set of rules which will describe the syntax of any sentence. According to some definitions, syntax includes the study of morphology as both are concerned with the elements of speech. Other definitions involve morphology being limited to the study of the morphemes, whereas syntax involves the study of words. I will use the latter definition.

In linguistics a distinction is often made between competence and performance. The linguistic competence of a person is their underlying ability to produce speech. When utterances are spoken they may not correspond to a person's linguistic competence because the speech that is eventually produced is affected and distorted by non-linguistic processes such as attention, memory limitations, slips of the tongue and so on. If there were none of these intervening processes then the speech produced would exactly reflect the linguistic competence of a person, but because there are these intervening processes speech only gives an approximate idea of the underlying linguistic competence. For example, sentences can be of infinite length, there are no linguistic rules to stop this. In practice sentence length is limited by cognitive and discourse constraints. In linguistics the interest is in providing a description of the competence of a speaker, and therefore this description is of an ideal system, one step removed from the utterances that are spoken.

A DESCRIPTION OF THE BEGINNINGS OF LANGUAGE

The Transition from One to Two Words

For about 10 months infants produce only one word utterances. During this time children's communication does change, but such changes are relatively difficult to document (see Chapter 7). At about 18–24 months there is the next clearly recognisable advance, the production of two word utterances. The somewhat surprising feature of this advance is that utterances continue to be restricted to a few words (Braunwald, 1978; Greenfield & Smith, 1976); there are few occasional examples of much longer sentences.

There seem to be a variety of ways in which children move from using one to two words. Scollen (1976) has reported that in an intermediate stage children use *vertical constructions*; this can involve adding a word to complete the meaning of the adult utterance: e.g. "What did the birdie do?" "away"; "Do you want cornflakes?" "milk". It is apparent that answering any question will, to some extent, involve adding to an existing topic, and clearly children are able to do this well before the two word stage. However, when a child does not simply answer a question, but extends the topic by saying "milk", as in the example above, something different is happening. The child seems to be using an implicit answer (i.e. yes), and adding to this to remind the parent that she wants milk with her cornflakes. Furthermore, according to Sperber and Wilson's (1986) ideas about relevance, the child is making considerable progress as she appears to recognise the relevance that will be conveyed by the use of a single word. Scollon argues that there is continuity between one and multi-word utterances because both involve the use of a topic and a comment about it.

Another intermediate step in this transition may involve using words which are said with a pause in between them (Branigan, 1979). Each word is like an individual utterance, but the words can also be considered as similar to a sequence of words in an adult utterance. In such cases the words appear to be semantically related and may share a common intonation pattern: e.g. "Daddy. Car. Garage".

An interesting progression from one to two words has also been described in one French-speaking child by Veneziano, Sinclair and Berthoud (1990). Early constructions by the child predominantly involved two forms. She either produced two words in close proximity which were related to different intentions, or she used separate words which were related to a single intention. In this early stage the child seemed unable to put two words together to express a single intention.

A later transition form appeared to involve the repetitions of the same word to express the same intent (i.e. word-1 + word-1). A slightly more advanced form was considered to be the use of word-1 then the production of word-1 + word-2, giving a more advanced content to the utterance. The repetition of the same word seemed to assist production of these two word utterances. More sophisticated utterances occurred at later ages and these involved two words being said together with related intentions. Veneziano, Sinclair and Berthoud argue that these utterances provide the basis for linguistic development, because children are confronted with the issue of ordering the words in two word and longer sequences.

Why are children able to start to produce two word utterances? One obvious answer is that children simply begin to be able to say longer sequences of words. However, this does not seem to be the case. MacWhinney has reported that Hungarian children will produce one word sounds containing a number of syllables, but be unable to produce two word utterances which could contain words of shorter overall length (cited in Bates, O'Connell & Shore, 1987, p. 178). Furthermore, Bloom (1970) found that her daughter added the sound "wida" to single word utterances. There was no obvious purpose for the addition. This led Bloom to conclude that children may possess some of the skills necessary to produce two word utterances, but that they do not have the syntactic capacities necessary for the process. More recent discussion of the addition of elements by a French child to the beginning of words has suggested these may be part of the children's inappropriate analyses of the sound system of words (Veneziano & Sinclair, 1993). Other evidence against a motor limitation is that during the one word stage children will produce formulaic, that is, multi-word utterances which commonly appear in the language such as "Hello Daddy", but neither word is independently combined with others. Again it would seem that children have the phonological capacity to produce two words in one utterance, but some other restriction is constraining their speech.

One way to account for the change from single to multi-word speech is to suggest that there is some cognitive change which increases children's information processing capacity. Bloom (1973) uses evidence from her diary study of her daughter to argue that single words are simple constructions that are made when a child is focusing on a single aspect of the situation. Only later are they able to consider two entities and this is reflected by the production of two word speech.

Bates has a similar suggestion that there may be a general cognitive change at about 18 months which involves the acquisition of the ability to process two items of information, a change from "oneness to twoness". According to this account, children are able to begin to separate a collection of objects into two groups (Sugarman, 1983); they are able to imitate the building of a simple model which involves remembering two positions (Case, 1985); and they are also able to use symbolic play in a series of acts rather than produce isolated symbolic activities (McCune-Nicholich & Bruskin, 1982). Although these abilities appear to co-occur in children without developmental delays, as we will see in Chapter 16, two word speech appears to lag behind related cognitive development in children with Down's syndrome. Such findings create some difficulties for Bates' theory.

It is important to recognise that the cognitive perspective is not claiming that these general changes are all that is needed for language development to proceed. Rather the perspective claims that without the key advances in cognition language development would stop or at the very least be slowed down.

A Grammatical System?

As soon as children start to produce multi-word speech there is the possibility that some system of rules could describe the ordering and use of word classes in utterances. The identification of such rules would go a long way to establishing that children were truly using language. An early proposal was that two word utterances involved a *pivot-open* grammar (Braine, 1963). It was supposed that children use two main classes of words: pivot words and open words. Pivot words were considered to be a relatively small group that are the first words of an utterance. Open words were considered to be a larger class that occur in the second position in an utterance (e.g. "here car", "here hat", ""here milk"). Initially there was enthusiasm for this proposal, but the enthusiasm diminished as examples came to light of child utterances which could not be described by this scheme.

A review by Braine (1976) of language acquisition in several languages raised serious questions about whether any general grammatical description can be made of early multi-word speech. He found that there were differences between children in whether they produced pivot-open or telegraphic constructions, and in their use of word order principles. This may mean it is necessary to have different grammars for different children. Bloom, Lightbrown and Hood (1975) also found that there were differences in a sample of four children. Two children produced telegraphic speech without the use of inflections (-ed, -s, etc.) or pronouns; this was termed a *nominal style*. The other children used a *prominal style*, which involved implicit references to objects rather than the explicit use of object names. As we will see in Chapter 12 more recent discussions about early speech tend to conclude that two word speech is not organised in terms of linguistic rules and there are proposals that early speech may be determined by children making incorrect assumptions about the speech they hear (see Chapter 10).

Early Multi-word Utterances

Most early child utterances do not contain certain types of words, in particular pronouns, articles, and auxiliary verbs. It is uncertain whether this reflects a difficulty in perceiving these words in adult speech, or a problem in using such words with some, as yet undefined, grammatical system. Because of the absence of these types of words (sometimes called functors or functional words) these utterances are sometimes referred to as telegraphic speech.

A way of describing children's two word utterances has been in terms of meaning. Brown (1973) identified the relations shown in Table 9.1, which are common in children learning a range of different languages. As with the semantic classification of single word utterances this and similar schemes rely on contextual information to identify the semantic role of the words. Howe (1976) has criticised such a rich interpretation of children's speech, and identifies the difficulty in being sure about the meaning behind

Table 9.1 Meaning in two word utterances

Agent	+	Action	John kick
Action	+	Object	Kick ball
Agent	+	Object	John ball
Action	+	Location	Kick there
Entity	+	Location	John there
Possessor	+	Possessed	Adam ball
Entity	+	Attribute	Ball fast
Demonstrative	+	Entity	That ball

any utterance. This has elicited rejoinders from several investigators who have suggested that cues are available about meaning (e.g. Golinkoff & Markessini, 1980).

A classification of early speech which has proved to be popular and depends on a grammatical description has been provided by Brown (1973). The classification is based on the type of morphemes that are used and the length of the utterances (*MLU*). The MLU is calculated from the mean number of morphemes in a sample of 100 utterances of a child. Because morphemes are counted instead of words it is possible for there to be more morphemes than words in an utterance (e.g. "he kick-ed ball" consists of four morphemes). Brown considered Stage I of language development to involve utterances below 2 to 2.5 morphemes; the utterances are mostly nouns and adjectives, with few inflections being used.

Further Developments in Morphology

The further development of language in children is not strictly the focus of this chapter. However, a description of children's later language is useful to provide a context for the subsequent chapters and for this reason will be included here. A classic study, by Cazden (1968) and Brown (1973) described the acquisition of grammatical morphemes. Three children were studied, and they were given the pseudonyms of Adam, Eve and Sarah. Brown used both verbal and non-verbal information to establish whether a particular morpheme should have been used (e.g. "my doll" is appropriate if there is only one doll, but the use of this expression when there are several dolls reveals that the child was not using the obligatory morpheme "-s", needed for most plural nouns). Using this technique the presence and absence of obligatory morphemes were noted, and from this a calculation was made of the percentage of times that morphemes were employed appropriately at different ages. In general, the morphemes appeared to be acquired gradually, and the process was not an all-or-nothing event. The acquisition of the first morphemes was accomplished by between 21 and 34 months, and that of the sixth morpheme by 23 to 38 months (see Table 9.2). Although there was variability in age of acquisition, the order of acquisition was similar across the three children.

Table 9.2   The sequence of acquisition of 14 morphemes investigated by Brown

1	Present Progressive verb	+ -ing
2/3	Prepositions	in/on
4	Plurals	noun + -s
5	Irregular Past Tense	went, swam
6	Possessive	hers
7	Uncontracted Copula (verb "to be")	she was good
8	Articles	the, a
9	Regular Past Tense	looked, talked
10	Third Person Present Tense Irregular	she has
11	Third Person Present Tense Regular	she talks
12	Uncontracted auxiliary verb	she was talking
13	Contracted Copula	she's good
14	Contracted auxiliary	she's talking

A copula involves the use of the verb "to be" as the *main* verb of an utterance and it can be used either in the uncontracted (full) form (e.g. "she *is* good") or in the contracted form (e.g. "she's good"). An auxiliary verb is not the main verb of an utterance and it is used in the presence of another verb (e.g. "she *is* talking"). It can be used in its uncontracted form, or in a contracted form (e.g. "she's talking").

Brown's findings were to a large extent replicated by de Villiers and de Villiers (1973) in a cross-sectional study of 21 children. Thus, it would seem that by 3–4 years children have acquired many of the basic grammatical abilities, which is a comparatively short space of time for such an achievement.

Why should the morphemes be acquired in this order? One possibility is that the order reflects the frequency of the morphemes in speech to children. Careful analysis of maternal speech by Brown provided little support for such a notion. Instead, Brown suggested that the order of acquisition may reflect the linguistic complexity of the morphemes and his analysis provided some support for this notion.

English is a language in which word order is important in conveying meaning, and the use of inflections (the use of morphemes like -ed or -s in relation to the stem of a verb) is relatively restricted. The language of the Greenlandic Eskimos involves the use of a complex morphological system where a word may have a large number of affixes. Up to eight morphemes may be used to accompany the use of a word. One observation of a 2-year-old child by Fortescue (1984/5) revealed that in half an hour 40 separate inflections were produced, with the longest single word utterances containing several elements of meaning. Thus, the rate of language acquisition is clearly influenced by the structure of the language being acquired. Slobin (1985) has suggested that the acquisition of morphemes will be influenced by both the semantic and the syntactic complexity of the form that is being acquired.

Continuity between Children's Pre-linguistic and Linguistic Communication?

We have seen that during the first 30 months of life children make great advances in their ability to communicate. The question naturally arises, what is the relationship between children's early non-verbal communication and their later language? One extreme position maintains that there is little or no relation between language and earlier forms of communication (e.g. Radford, 1990). The most important argument for this position is that language is a unique form of communication which involves structural-dependency of items, and as a result it is very different from other forms of communication. At the other extreme is a position which claims that language is related to other types of communication, but is merely more complicated than them.

Sugarman (1983) takes a pessimistic view about the possibility of answering questions about the relationship between pre-verbal communication and language. She argues that although it is possible to identify antecedent behaviours which will reliably occur before language, this tells us little about the relationship between the earlier behaviours and language (e.g. eating usually occurs before speaking). At another level it is possible to identify precursors, that is behaviours which reliably precede another behaviour and share common features (e.g. pointing and naming). However, she maintains that identifying precursors is simply a matter of opinion, and is not open to empirical verification. Lastly, she suggests that logically there could be prerequisites. These are behaviours that are causally necessary for the emergence of the later behaviour; such claims, she suggests, are impossible to test given the ethical limitation on experimental investigations. Another strand to Sugarman's argument is that the opposition of continuity and discontinuity is meaningless. She argues that the development of communication involves the continuity of some capacities and skills, together with the emergence of new skills.

The later theme has been discussed at greater length by Shatz (1983). Shatz points out that continuity has more to do with explanations than with the presence of similar structures or appearances. She points out that for development to occur there has to be change. If a structure is similar at two ages there has been no development, but a high degree of continuity. She follows Lipsitt (1981) who argues that:

> "The preservation of sameness is not what development and developmental continuity are about. The essence of continuity is *predictable* and *explicable* change. That the tadpole and the frog, or the pupa and the butterfly, do not look like one another or behave like one another does *not* mean that the later stages are discontinuous with the earlier. Nor does it mean that the later stages could not, and cannot, and may not be well predicted and understood in terms of the organism's earlier history. It is the nature of life processes that change will occur, that some later stages of the same organism may only bear superficial resemblances to earlier, and that progressive, orderly, lawful, and understandable rules for these changes will be discovered."
>
> (Lipsitt, 1981)

Furthermore, Snow and Gilbreath (1983) point out that the perception of continuities or discontinuities, in part, depends on the scale of analysis. Observations of children's behaviour taken every day, or even every week, tend to lend support to the idea of continuity. Observations which are placed further apart are more likely to identify more major changes, and thereby there will be a perception of discontinuity.

The implication for language acquisition is that there is likely to be some continuity with previous structures, but also some innovations or transformations which allow the emergence of the new capacity. Interestingly, performance on information processing tasks involving habituation from about 4 to 8 months predicts later verbal ability and intelligence. This suggests that there is some form of continuity in abilities across apparently different domains (Messer, 1993).

The arguments about continuity and discontinuity have resurfaced in terms of whether there are special cognitive modules devoted to the processing of linguistic information, or whether such modules are of a more general nature (see also Chapter 16). Clearly the existence of a linguistic module would support the separation of language from other forms of communication.

TEACHING LANGUAGE TO APES

In psycholinguistics the question of whether or not language is unique to our species is a magnet for debate and argument. For some, the issue goes to the very heart of what it means to be human, which seems to be because in Murphy and Medin's (1985) terms it is part of a theory of what it is to be human. Equally importantly, success in teaching language to apes would force revision of the claim that language is the result of a species-specific inherited capacity.

Apes cannot acquire speech simply because their vocal apparatus does not allow them to produce the appropriate sounds. Parrots and other birds can produce speech, but the words are merely a set of imitations and cannot be considered to convey meaning. The limited vocal capacity of apes has meant that teaching has had to rely on sign languages or on specially devised communication systems.

Teaching Sign Language to Apes

A study which refocused attention on ape language was conducted on a chimpanzee called Washoe who was exposed to American Sign Language (ASL). Allen and Beatrice Gardner, who were responsible for the project, hoped Washoe would acquire the ability to hold conversations in sign language, and towards this end they raised Washoe in a playful and unrestricted environment.

Several methods were employed to help Washoe acquire language. It was planned to train her to imitate signs as a way of increasing her vocabulary. However, although she spontaneously imitated signs it proved to be difficult to make her do this on request. A more successful strategy was to follow Washoe's inappropriate signs with a correct one, and repeat this until she imitated it. Another method was to shape Washoe's hands into the appropriate gesture in circumstances where she wanted something, and the something was then produced if she provided an approximation of the sign. Then closer and closer approximations of the signs were required to produce the desired effect. Such a procedure was used to train Washoe to sign "more" when she wanted to be tickled, a great pleasure for chimpanzees.

Washoe certainly was able to produce and respond to a variety of signs and occasionally this occurred a day or so after seeing the gesture. Washoe sometimes used signs to name or comment on objects much like a young child does. For example, her first sign for toothbrush occurred when she found one in the Gardners' house; as she disliked having her teeth brushed it was unlikely to be a command! When she used signs she was able to generalise these to new circumstances, e.g. using the sign "more" for a variety of needs, or "flower" for a range of referents and circumstances. Although there has been debate about whether Washoe used language there is little evidence that her signs had a rule-based grammatical structure.

Washoe was eventually moved to a primate station because of her size and strength. She was given a baby chimp to adopt and was observed to teach the baby some of the signs she knew. On one occasion she repeated the "chair-sit" sign five times after putting a chair in front of the baby. The infant has now acquired its own repertoire of signs (see Premack, 1986). Thus, quite remarkably some cultural transmission of the sign language appears to have taken place.

A series of other apes have been raised in similar circumstances to Washoe. Nim Chimpsy was brought up from 2 months by Terrace and his colleagues; unlike Washoe, he was given formal tuition in American Sign Language every day. Among the trainers Terrace is unusual in that he eventually denied that his chimpanzee was producing language.

A 1-year-old captive born gorilla, Koko, has been raised by Patterson. She was raised in an unrestricted way (similar to that of Washoe), while being given extensive tuition in sign language for most of the day. By 6 years she had acquired over 650 signs. Although she certainly has the ability to take part in quite sophisticated conversations, linguists are sceptical that she produces structured utterances, especially as she will make signs simultaneously using each hand, which suggests a lack of ordering in the organisation of communication.

Methodological and Conceptual Issues

Criticisms have been made of the claim that the apes were being exposed to and acquiring ASL. Few of the trainers were fluent users of signs, which means that they sometimes made basic translations of English to ASL, and produced a hybrid language without its full potential for expression. In some respects this may have made it more difficult for the apes to acquire language (see Chapter 16 about the acquisition of sign languages in humans).

Other criticisms have been made by Terrace, Petitto and Bever (1979) concerning the under-reporting of errors and of "cleaning-up" the data so that repetitions of elements in strings, imitations of the trainer's strings, ambiguities in strings, or even the actual word order were not always given.

Terrace, Petitto and Bever have also suggested that both Nim's and Washoe's trainers inadvertently cued the chimpanzees with appropriate signs or gestures to help the production of strings of signs. Without more rigorous testing they claim that the findings are ambiguous.

In addition, various other differences have been noted between the apes' and children's communication. In general the apes have been much less spontaneous and willing to communicate than children. They also often failed to observe the turn-taking conventions of discourse (but often so do children). Significantly the apes were not reported to have the curiosity to ask questions about the names of things.

It is undoubtedly true that all the apes acquired an impressive vocabulary, usually of at least 100 signs. What is less clear is whether the apes understood the arbitrary relationship between signs and signified, or whether they were merely making very intelligent use of a tool for instrumental ends, such as obtaining food (Aitchinson, 1989). It is extremely difficult to decide between these alternatives, but the sophistication in some of the communication suggests that sometimes signs were used in a creative and referential way.

We have already seen that the ability to use arbitrary signals to communicate is not usually considered to be a critical feature of language. What is more important is the way in which signs are used together. There is no dispute that the apes do use sequences of signs to communicate, but what is far less certain is whether these strings possess language-like characteristics.

Re-analysis by Terrace, Petitto and Bever (1979) of the length of Nim's sign strings revealed no increase in length with age and experience, or any increasing semantic and grammatical complexity; the proportion of imitations increased with increasing age, and only 12% of Nim's signs were initiated by him, the other 88% being imitations. All this is very different from language development in children.

Similarly, although Washoe produced "open key" to have a door unlocked, "listen dog" on hearing a dog bark, and "gimme tickle" when requesting to be tickled, there was no detectable ordering of the elements of these strings (i.e. "tickle gimme" was just as likely as "gimme tickle"). To be fair to the apes, despite there being reasonable agreement that children's early speech is organised, there is no agreement about the rule system which governs this ordering. Another feature which suggests that the apes' signs are not a rule-based language is the repetition and reordering of elements when a message is not effective, a very different process from that in children (e.g. "give orange me give eat orange me eat orange give me eat orange give me you" from Nim).

Interestingly, the arguments about ape signing parallel some of the arguments about pidgin speech. It would seem that humans do sometimes use less elaborate forms of speech to communicate with one another when there are cultural and linguistic differences. Linguists have usually avoided the term language for these systems. However, the existence of pidgins can be used to argue there is a continuum between language and other forms of communication.

Structured Teaching and Chips

Following the attempts to teach sign language to apes, a different teaching strategy has been tried that involves the use of physical items instead of signs. Premack (1986) used this with Sarah, a 6-year-old chimpanzee. Small plastic chips of different colours and shapes were used for communication. These had to be placed on a magnetic board. The teaching was more formal than in the sign language studies.

For the initial training sessions fruit was placed outside Sarah's cage and she had to use the appropriate chip to be given it. The complexity of the communication was gradually increased so that Sarah could use four chips to produce a string such as "Mary give apple Sarah" which involves a donor + action + object + recipient. She appeared able to understand conditional statements like "if apple then chocolate", by taking the apple to obtain the desired chocolate and able to answer questions such as "quersy cup equals spoon" (one of the chips termed "quersy" by the investigators was used to make a sequence into a question).

Despite the capacity to produce complex messages, Sarah never held spontaneous conversations with her trainers. Furthermore, it is unclear whether Sarah understood that she was using a communication system or was just very clever at producing the correct "chips" to obtain a reward. The debate is made even more complex by the finding that a severely mentally handicapped child who had not acquired speech was able to be taught this method of communication (reported in Premack, 1986). Premack (1986) has concluded that the training, although establishing a complex system of communication, did not teach Sarah language.

Computer technology has been used by Rumbaugh (1977) with Lana, a 2-year-old chimpanzee. Lana could use her computer keyboard to produce effects in her environment, such as the dispensing of food or the operation of music and slides, and she could use the keyboard to communicate with her trainer.

As with the other apes Lana was able to use signs for new messages. She, like Washoe, after learning the sign for "more" was able to use it with a variety of other words. In a similar way after learning the word "put" in the context of putting a ball in a bowl, she produced the string "Tim put milk in machine" when her trainer was late in filling up the vending machine from which she could obtain feedstuffs via the computer. She also created new combinations for unnamed objects, such as "banana which-is green" for cucumber.

In this training regime each type of computer sign had a different coloured background (e.g. objects that can be eaten are red). Lana appears to have produced a more organised system of ordering elements in the strings she produced, and this might have been helped by the more explicit training and the colour coding of the elements. It has even been possible for other chimpanzees who have been trained on this system to communicate with one another to solve problems, a result which is impressive, but which many linguists would not consider a critical feature of language. Despite the claims, by Rumbaugh, that Lana has the ability to use language, the definition of language she uses is broader than the one employed by linguists.

Understanding and Communicating

Further work with a pygmy chimpanzee called Kanzi has refocused attention on what apes can be taught (Savage-Rumbaugh, 1986). Kanzi was able spontaneously to acquire the use of "lexigrams" (geometric shapes) on a keyboard by watching his mother who had been given training. This was followed up with a teaching method that concentrated on communicating in a functional manner and has been carried out with other apes. Savage-Rumbaugh (1991) has attributed the success of her programme to a move away from formal methods of teaching, as had been used previously, to a method in which the lexigrams were introduced into established and meaningful patterns of communication. In particular, Savage-Rumbaugh identifies the establishment of mutually understood routines between trainers and chimpanzees as providing sequences of behaviours which can be understood and anticipated by both individuals, such as changing a nappy/diaper or when to take a bottle of milk when it is being prepared. These routines were accompanied by both speech and lexigrams in a spontaneous manner to provide a higher level of communication with the chimpanzees. As a result, the apes progressed from passive to active participants in the routines; at first initiating the routines and then using lexigrams to communicate intent. This perspective is similar to that proposed by Bruner, except that Savage-Rum-baugh highlights the functional benefits of the learners being able to predict events in their world through the use of routines. She also emphasises the way that an understanding of the referential properties of lexigrams grows out of the use of a lexigram in different routines or similar routines in different circumstances, so that lexigrams can be used independently of routines. Implicit in this account is the way that the development of shared under-standings allows a symbolic system to be acquired.

Unlike the previous training studies, Kanzi was able to use the geometric lexigrams to construct messages, and to comprehend complex messages. In his messages he tended to put agents of actions at the beginning of messages, whereas objects of actions would be put at the end of messages. For instance, "Matata-bite" was used when Matata was biting, but "grab-matata" was used when Matata was grabbed, thereby showing some element of organisation in these messages. A claim which suggests that Kanzi has the rudiments of grammar (Greenfield & Savage-Rumbaugh, 1991).

Seidenberg and Petitto (1987) have challenged the idea that Kanzi was using word-like forms in a symbolic manner. Instead they suggest he was using them in an associationist and problem-solving manner. However, part of Seidenberg and Pettito's argument rests on a misinterpretation of the child literature. They assume that children are inflexible in their use of words, so that they associate them with meaning in a conventional way. As was outlined in Chapter 7, children use words in a flexible way to achieve a variety of objectives, a point made by Savage-Rumbaugh (1987) and Nelson (1987).

The heated debate about whether or not apes can be taught language is likely to continue for some time. The answer to such a question will partly depend on the definition of language which is adopted—so far there is little prospect of a consensus on this topic. Despite there being uncertainty about the answer to this issue, the studies of ape language have been useful in forcing us to ask questions about what we consider are the important characteristics of language, and at what point would we concede that another organism has the ability to use language. The studies have also highlighted aspects of child language development which tend to be taken for granted.

SUMMARY

The discussion about the precise definition of language is likely to continue. Such controversies are important in that they establish the goalposts in arguments about a number of issues. These include the age when children start to use language; whether there is continuity between non-linguistic and linguistic communication and whether animals can be considered to use language. It is ironic that the move away from the classic view of concepts has not been accompanied by a greater appreciation of the uncertainty in the definition of a word like "language". There needs to be a greater recognition of the uncertainty about what constitutes a linguistic communication system. For this reason it may be more fruitful for future research to concentrate on the similarities and differences between communication systems, rather than on whether a communication system is or is not a language.

The uncertainty about when children are able to use a language has not prevented a number of very useful descriptions of the development of their speech. However, a formal description of the syntax of the first multi-word utterances remains elusive, especially as it is likely to be different for different children and different languages. There is also uncertainty about the nature of the abilities that give rise to using multi-word utterances. This topic will be considered again in relation to the speech of children with Down's syndrome (see Chapter 16).

Research into the possibility of teaching language to apes has generated more heat than light. These arguments have provoked a more careful discussion of the essential characteristics of language. The research has also indicated that the gap between human and animal communication is not as large as was previously believed. Apes often use signs in ways similar to the use of words by children; what they do not seem able to do is to spontaneously organise their words into a coherent discourse. However, it should be noted that in the more recent studies the apes are able to respond to quite sophisticated instructions. The debate about ape language is likely to continue and hopefully we will obtain a better picture of the differences and similarities between their communication and ours.

10

GRAMMAR AND ITS BEGINNINGS: A LINGUISTIC VIEWPOINT

A strongly held belief in psychology from the 1920s to the 1950s was that almost all human capacities could be explained in terms of learning. This belief was associated with the large amount of research conducted about learning in rats and mice. By the 1950s the deficiencies of this paradigm were beginning to be more widely recognised. At this time Skinner (1957), probably the most famous advocate of learning theory, published a book, *Verbal Behavior*, which proposed that learning theory could be used to explain language learning. The essence of Skinner's account was that infants' early babbling was a random arrangement of sounds. Certain of these sounds would by chance correspond to the words that parents used. Furthermore, Skinner suggested that parents would reward the use of these sounds—for example, if an infant produced a sound like the word "milk" then he or she would be fed. In this way infants would come to produce words in the correct circumstances, because their previous behaviour (i.e. sound) had been reinforced.

A devastating review of Skinner's book was made by Noam Chomsky in 1959. At the heart of Chomsky's argument was the claim that speech is the result of using a set of rules, which are employed to arrange a limited number of words in an infinite number of combinations. Thus, the process of acquiring language is not a matter of merely learning a set of associations between the environment and words, but involves developing a set of rules which allow the creation of a potentially infinite number of grammatically correct sentences. Chomsky also supposed that by using the same set of grammatical rules humans were able to understand an infinite set of utterances (including of course utterances they had never heard before).

Despite the well known criticisms of learning theory there have been subsequent proposals using it to explain language acquisition (Moerke,

1983; Mowrer, 1960; Stemmer, 1987). Often it is suggested that a process of generalisation can enable children to produce rule-like verbal constructions, by learning for example that "-ed" is associated with the past tense of a particular word, and then generalising this association to other words. It is also suggested that children may imitate adult utterances and in this way acquire new knowledge of the relationships between words (e.g. Whitehurst & Vasta, 1975). However, these proposals have not been part of mainstream discussions and research, and this chapter will concentrate on Chomsky's theories.

TRANSFORMATIONAL GRAMMAR AND LANGUAGE ACQUISITION

An Outline of Transformational Grammar

Since the early 1960s the most important single influence on discussions about language acquisition has come from the ideas of Chomsky. In the 1950s and 1960s Chomsky was concerned with describing the syntax and morphology of adult grammar, and from this perspective he discussed the mechanism of language acquisition. Thus, his interest concerned language as a formal system of rules, and explaining the way that children acquire these rules. Because it would seem that children receive inadequate information to detect the rules of speech (see next section and Chapter 14) Chomsky argued that an innate predisposition must be present to aid the acquisition process. This can be seen as part of Chomsky's wider perspective that language is a capacity present in all people, and a capacity that exists despite disadvantage and lack of education.

Chomsky's primary interest was in linguistic processes that can account for the grammar of a language, and this of course has implications for the way we produce speech. However, it should be realised that the linguistic processes he discussed are not claimed to map directly on to psychological processes. A central idea in Chomsky's theory is that the production of speech begins with a basic message which then undergoes complex linguistic processes to ensure that it consists of a grammatically correct arrangement of words and morphemes. When this is accomplished the message is spoken. Comprehension is believed to involve the reverse sequence, but much less attention has been paid to this.

In Chomsky's early work he proposed that linguistic processing can be portrayed in terms of the set of elements given in Figure 10.1. The deep structure component was an important level of linguistic representation. In some ways it can be thought of as an incompletely formed sentence. In relation to the deep structure component, it is important to understand that

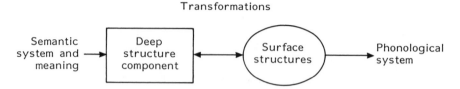

Figure 10.1 The components identified in Chomsky's early work

although it was involved in meaning, many aspects of this were of little concern to Chomsky's theory. For example, little attention was paid to the way an intention to communicate becomes translated into a deep structure. Similarly, there has not been an in-depth description of meaning. Rather it was simply assumed that the deep structure plays a part in determining the meaning of a sentence, and that this representation is transferred using a system of rules to the semantic system.

The creation of deep structures was supposed to take place in part through the operation of phrase structure rules. The *phrase structure* rules specify the way that elements are ordered, and at each stage there is a more detailed identification of the elements (see Figure 10.2). In this way a representation can be created by working from the most general element (a sentence) down to the more specific elements. The rules typically are referred to as PS1 for the first line in Figure 10.2 and PS2 for the second line, and so on.

The final set of rules specify the actual group of words that make up any grammatical category, so the slashes in Figure 10.2 indicate that a whole group of words can be selected to fill the slot. Often the phrase structure rules are displayed as a tree diagram such as the one in Figure 10.3.

S (sentence)	→	NP (noun phrase) + VP (verb phrase)
NP	→	DET (determiner) + N (noun)
DET	→	/The/
N	→	/man/
VP (verb phrase)	→	V (verb) + NP
V	→	/hit/
NP	→	DET + N
DET	→	/the/
N	→	/boy/

Figure 10.2 Phrase structure rules for the sentence "The man hit the boy"

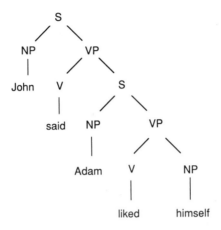

Figure 10.3 Phrase structure tree diagram

Although the phrase structure rules can be thought of as operating in deep structure, their final product is not a fully formed sentence, instead it should be regarded as a more primitive and intermediate version of a sentence which can be altered by other subsequent processes.

A second input to deep structure, besides the phrase structure rules, is the *lexicon* which stores idiosyncratic information about the content of words which is not contained in general linguistic rules. And a third input to deep structure is details about the *subcategorisation* of the words to be used in the sentence. Subcategorisation concerns the types of syntactic relationship a word has with other words. An example of this would be information about whether a verb is transitive or intransitive. A transitive verb usually has a direct object as in "Adam drove a car"; an intransitive verb usually does not have a direct object as in "Adam ran". Thus, the subcategorisation of a word can be an important factor in deciding the structure of an utterance. Together, these three inputs, the rules and information from phrase structure, the lexicon and subcategorisation, enable the creation of a deep structure form of a sentence.

In the production of speech, a deep structure representation is changed to a surface structure by *transformational rules*. The transformational rules were an important innovation and helped to solve some of the problems encountered by grammars which were only based on phrase structure rules. Thus, transformational rules were needed because the complexity of languages could not be created only on the basis of phrase structure rules.

The transformational rules allow the same representation in deep structure to have different surface structures depending on which transformational rules are applied. For example, an active sentence such as "The man hit the boy" or passive utterances such as "The boy was hit by the man" can be produced by the application of different transformations to the same deep structure representation. The surface structure can be thought of as a representation of the words of an utterance which can be used to produce the sounds of a sentence. Further rules are hypothesised to exist to enable a phonological structure (i.e. a sequence of sounds) to be created from the surface structure, but this area of the model was left vague.

Language Acquisition and Transformational Grammar

Transformational grammar was used as a basis for generating hypotheses about the way children acquire language. Because of the complexity of the grammars needed to describe language (there is still no widely accepted grammar of any human language), and because it was assumed that children heard speech which was similar to that between adults (see next section and Chapter 14), it was believed that there must be some innate capacities which would aid language acquisition.

The view Chomsky took in 1965 was that children have an innate LAD (Language Acquisition Device). The LAD was believed to be able to con-struct a grammar of any human language from the speech that children hear. This was supposed to be accomplished by the LAD generating hypo-theses about the grammar and evaluating them (children would not be conscious of this process). In this way increasingly complex hypotheses could be tested and adopted as children's linguistic abilities increased. It is important to recognise that the hypothesis testing ability is not a trivial one, it means that children listen to the stream of sound that they hear and test ideas about the way this stream of sounds is organised.

Chomsky claimed that a knowledge of *language universals* makes this hypothesis testing possible. One aspect of this knowledge involves the ability to recognise what are termed *substantive* universals. These are the elements of language, for example, being able to identify words in the stream of speech, and crucially being able to identify the grammatical classes of words (noun, verb, pronoun, etc.). Another aspect of the knowl-edge concerns *formal* universals, which involves knowledge about the structure of grammar. Here Chomsky supposed that children would have a working knowledge of the transformational nature of language. He also supposed that children assume that the speech they hear has the grammar of one of the limited number of human languages. In this way the set of hypotheses about grammar would be restricted and thereby considerably reduce the complexity of the language acquisition process.

The proposals about transformational grammar provoked investigations to test its predictions in relation to psychological processes involving the production or comprehension of speech. Initially findings provided support for the psychological reality of transformational grammar. For example, it was found that active sentences were understood more quickly than passive sentences, and this agreed with the idea that passive sentences are more linguistically complex than active sentences (Gough, 1966; Slobin, 1966). However, in a later work the opposite pattern of findings was reported and methodological problems have been identified in the original studies (see Glucksberg & Danks, 1975; Stevenson, 1987).

Other problems were revealed in a study of memory by Johnson-Laird and Stevenson (1970). They found that even when sentences should have different representations in deep structure, this does not seem to affect memory. Rather the basic meaning of a sentence is stored, not a syntactic record. So the utterance "John liked the painting and bought it from the duchess" is confused with "the painting pleased John and the duchess sold it to him". Although these sentences refer to similar events their representation in deep structure should be very different (the sentences have different subjects, objects and so on). All this controversy led to a distrust of attempts to match transformational grammar to psychological processes and a move to separate the latter from linguistic processes.

A different problem was encountered with the idea of deletion rules. Deletion rules were necessary to account for utterances like "John was smacked". This short passive utterance was assumed to have originated from a form such as "John was smacked [by someone]". The deletion of the material in square brackets involves an extra transformation and therefore would be considered as more complex than the shorter form. As a result, the longer form should be acquired before the shorter form. In fact the shorter form appears to be produced and comprehended by children before the longer form (Harwood, 1959; Maratsos & Abramovitch, 1974; Stevenson, 1987).

It is also worth noting that the use of syntactic rules by children does not necessarily support the idea of transformational grammar. One general feature of children's speech is the errors made with irregular verbs and nouns. For example, children often say "goed" instead of "went", or "sheeps" instead of "sheep". This shows that children are acquiring a rule structure for their language, but are inappropriately applying the rule to some words by a process of over-regularisation (Brown & Bellugi, 1964). What was not always recognised, however, is that although the observations support the idea that children's speech follows certain rules, it does not follow that the rules have been derived from transformational grammar.

The proposals made by Chomsky about transformational grammar and the application of his ideas to language acquisition had a profound impact on research about children's speech. However, from the mid 1960s onwards more and more problems were detected with the grammatical model that had been proposed. This led to a series of modifications and eventually a new model was developed to take account of various criticisms and problems. Before outlining this model some work which has had an important impact on theorising about language acquisition will be outlined.

LEARNABILITY THEORY

Learnability theory seeks to specify what are the logical conditions necessary for language acquisition to take place. It is useful to consider learnability theory at this point as it explains why so much attention has been paid to the possibility that language acquisition is the result of innate processes.

Learnability theory was first discussed by Gold (1967). In this work attention focused around the logical constraints on the language acquisition process rather than examining the types of constraints present in actual samples of adult–child interaction. Gold distinguished between two possible types of speech input, *information* presentation and *text* presentation. Information presentation involves negative evidence being provided about all the ungrammatical utterances of children (this is unlikely ever to occur). Negative evidence would consist of responses from other people that would tell a child which of their utterances were grammatical and which were ungrammatical. Gold argued that input which contained negative information allowed a much broader range of languages to be acquired than input without such information. Text presentation, on the other hand, involves the learner only being given a list of grammatical sentences, and having to work out the grammar from this list of model utterances. Gold argued that no natural languages could be learned in this way without some additional assistance from innate biases and constraints.

An important principle in learnability theory is that if a language learner chooses a grammar which is too restrictive in relation to the actual grammar (sometimes termed an error of undergeneralisation) then both systems of input (information and text presentation) would provide information necessary to correct this error. However, it is also possible to have errors of overgeneralisation. This would occur when a child chooses a grammar which can describe the language she hears, but her grammatical system also allows her to produce other utterances which adults would consider ungrammatical. In this case learners using text presentation will never detect that their incorrect utterances are not grammatical because the speakers would never receive any information that would allow them to discover their errors. At a very simple level one might think of this as a problem in learning that "sheeps" is the incorrect plural of "sheep", if you are never told that this is incorrect.

The impact of learnability theory was enhanced by findings from a study by Brown and Hanlon (1970). This study examined parental responses to children's grammatical mistakes. Brown and Hanlon set out to test the idea that parents reinforce speech which is grammatically correct, and provide negative reinforcement for speech which is grammatically incorrect. A grammatically incorrect (sometimes termed ill-formed) utterance might involve a child leaving out necessary parts of speech (e.g. "I not going"), using a part of speech incorrectly (e.g. "I goed to the room"), or the word order might be inappropriate. They found that direct feedback about grammatical mistakes rarely occurred (e.g. an adult saying "No, that's wrong", "You can't say that"), in fact the negative feedback was usually given about semantic errors (e.g. "they are goats not sheep"). Brown and Hanlon concluded that there is not "even a shred of evidence that approval and disapproval are contingent on syntactic correctness" (p. 47). Their findings have been interpreted by some humorists as predicting that children should grow up to be very truthful and accurate, but with poor command of grammar; the reverse is invariably the case.

Not only does there appear to be an absence of explicit negative feedback, but even when it occurs it has been reported that this type of feedback is ineffective in assisting grammatical development. There are quite a large number of case reports of children ignoring a correction to their ill-formed utterance, and being unable to imitate correct models. One of the most famous examples is:

"*Child*   Nobody don't like me
Mother   No, say 'Nobody likes me.'
Child   Nobody don't like me. (this sequence was repeated 8 times)
Mother   Now listen carefully, say 'NOBODY LIKES ME.'
Child   Oh! Nobody don't likeS me."

(McNeil, 1966)

These three sets of arguments have led to an assumption by some theoreticians that negative information is not available to assist the language acquisition process. As a consequence a major problem for them has been to explain how language acquisition takes place when children could produce ungrammatical utterances by overgeneralisation and never know that they were incorrect.

One way to solve this problem has been to suppose that learners have certain biases or constraints. Perhaps the most important example of this approach is the *subset* principle which was developed in relation to Chomsky's later PPT theory (Wexler & Manzini, 1987). The principle assumes that if there is more than one grammatical description of a certain type of utterance, then children will assume that the most elementary representation is the correct one. In other words they will always choose the least complex subset grammar during language development. As a result, they will not produce utterances by a process of overgeneralisation. Of course this principle neatly avoids the problems of the absence of negative information about grammatical errors.

One difficulty with the subset principle is that it is not at all clear what constitutes a more simple representation of grammatical structure as we do not have a measure of the complexity of grammars. This makes testing the subset principle difficult (Fodor & Crain, 1987). Furthermore, there is also a lack of clarity about why some types of overgeneralisations occur and not others. One way of testing this idea might be to compare different languages and discover whether children adopt an incorrect, but more simple, hypothesis about the grammatical structure of the speech they hear.

As we will see in Chapter 14 the assumptions of learnability theory have been questioned. Furthermore, although parents may not give consistent feedback about children's errors, it is likely that if persistent errors occurred that would not be expected in a child of a certain age, then some type of feedback would occur. This might be peers laughing or mocking the unfortunate child, teachers intervening, or parents deciding that something was amiss and was in need of correction.

GB THEORY AND PPT

Language Acquisition and Parameter Setting

Chomsky's (1981, 1986) more recent ideas about grammar are often referred to as Principles and Parameters Theory (PPT) or Government and Binding theory (GB theory). The former term captures the general nature of the approach, while the latter term is taken from the title of Chomsky's book published in 1981 and refers to two features of the theory.

In PPT it is supposed that there are a number of *modules*. Each module concerns a set of linguistic *principles* (i.e. rules). These principles are employed to construct a grammatically correct sentence. For instance there is a module which is mainly concerned with the appropriate use of pronouns (i.e. he, she, himself, themselves, etc.). Most of the principles in this module consist of rules governing particular aspects of pronoun use. Thus, modules can be thought of as collections of related rules (the modules are outlined in the next section).

Some of the principles in the modules are fixed and can operate from the beginning of the language acquisition process. Other principles involve a set of possible structures and these are known as parameters. Parameters play a crucial part in accounting for the way that children acquire language. Languages, of course, vary along a number of dimensions. For example, there are differences in word order. In English the subject–verb–object word order is typically used. In Japanese the subject–object–verb order is more typical. This difference is known as *parametric variation.*

If children identify and follow the appropriate parameters then they will be able to produce an adult language. How is this accomplished? PPT theory supposes that identification of parameters is relatively easy because children already have a knowledge of all the linguistic possibilities from the information in UG (Universal Grammar, the child's innate knowledge about human languages). More precisely, it is suggested that the information in UG means that each parameter contains settings which correspond to the range of linguistic structures in human languages. When a grammatical structure is identified in speech heard by a child then the appropriate setting is switched on, once the switch has been set in this way children can produce the relevant structures in their speech. Thus, there might be a parameter for subject–verb–object and subject–object–verb orders which is set differently in English and Japanese.

Often it is assumed that setting a parameter can have consequences beyond the particular module to other parts of the linguistic system and similarly assumed that the switch setting or parameter setting allows the acquisition of crucial grammatical principles on the basis of limited evidence. As we will see in the next chapter, there is considerable discussion about the way parameters are set.

Thus, the PPT approach assumes that language acquisition is possible because children have access to all the crucial grammatical differences across all human languages. At present these differences are not yet known and one goal of PPT is to identify them. Further, the PPT approach assumes that exposure to the speech of others is sufficient to set the relevant parameter, and feedback about errors is not necessary.

A general problem with the parameter setting approach to language acquisition is the absence of clear a priori specifications of the parameters and what is required to set them—this makes testing a difficult enterprise!

Another issue which continues to create controversy is the proposal that the cognitive processes which concern language are largely separate from other processes, so that language involves autonomous module(s) of operations. Both these issues are considered in subsequent chapters.

An Outline of the GB/PPT Modules and Levels

PPT has involved a new set of proposals. In the new theory there is still the notion of deep structure and surface structure. There is also the notion that linguistic representations are built up and changed as they pass through a number of processes on the way to the production of a grammatical utterance. However, in the new theory the terminology has changed, the function of the components has changed and there are new elements. In this section I will outline the structures used in PPT to give a flavour of the theory, this is of necessity sketchy and it should be possible to understand the next chapter without a detailed understanding of these structures. The most important modules are usually considered to be:

1. $\bar{X}$ theory;
2. Theta theory;
3. Control theory;
4. Binding theory;
5. Case theory;
6. Bounding theory.

Figure 10.4 provides an outline of the new levels of linguistic representation. At each level, the representation is affected by particular modules, consequently, as a linguistic representation progresses through the levels it becomes more sentence-like in structure.

As can be seen in Figure 10.4 the lexicon and phrase structure specifications provide an input to d-structures (d-structures are similar to deep structures and will be considered shortly). The lexicon, as its name suggests, contains information similar to a dictionary. The type of information stored in the lexicon concerns idiosyncratic features of a word that are not covered by general rules. For instance, the lexicon might contain information to treat "data" as a plural noun (but it also seems to be the case that information is often absent!).

In PPT the information in the lexicon has a more important role to play than in transformational grammar. The information in the lexicon is utilised throughout the system. As a result the lexicon can have an influence on the structure of the whole utterance. This idea is stated in the *projection principle*

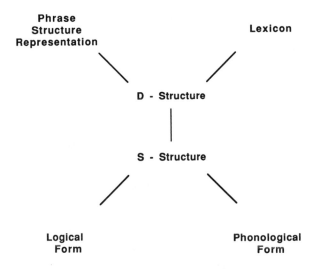

Figure 10.4   The levels of representation in PPT

which specifies that the details about lexical items are sent to all levels from d-structure to logical form. This includes semantic details, phonological details, details about subcategorisation, and details about thematic structure.

Some idea of the dimensions of all these variables, except thematic structure, should have been gained from sections in this and previous chapters. However, it should also be recognised that in PPT there is not a comprehensive enumeration of all these dimensions, so for example, little has been written about the way phonological details have an impact on the system as a whole.

Thematic structure and thematic roles have not been dealt with before. There has been a lot of discussion about their precise nature; in general it is agreed that thematic roles involve variables such as agent, patient, experiencer, location and so on. One concern of *Theta theory* is to ensure that there is a match between the different thematic roles that are present in the words of an utterance. As a result this theory helps to specify the organisation of the elements in d-structures and by the projection principle the roles have implications for s-structures and higher levels of representation.

To give an example, one principle of theta theory is that each appropriate thematic role associated with a verb must be filled by an element in the d-structure representation. For example, some verbs require an agent and a patient (e.g. the verb "kiss" in "Sid kissed Mary"), while others may only require an agent (e.g. "Sid swam"), and others only require an experiencer (e.g. "Sid died"). Part of the rules of theta theory are concerned with making sure the information in the lexicon is utilised in the construction of linguistic representations. It should be noted that subcategorisation involves a similar process, but is concerned with syntactic relations; thus in our examples "kiss" requires an object as it is a transitive verb, while "swam" does not require an object because it is an intransitive verb. Thus, although theta theory and subcategorisation may operate on the same utterance, and have a similar outcome, they are involved with subtly different processes.

The phrase structure specifications in PPT are now supplied by the module concerned with $\bar{X}$ theory, these produce syntactic representations which are utilised in d-structure. $\bar{X}$ theory (spoken of as X-bar theory) consists of general principles rather than the former more detailed phrase structure rules. The one essence of $\bar{X}$ theory is that a phrase will contain an element of that type of phrase, thus noun phrases will contain a noun at some position in the phrase. Furthermore, this is seen as a component of universal grammar. Surprisingly this obvious notion has not been specified in phrase structure grammars. Other elements of $\bar{X}$ theory are believed to be acquired during development.

Information from $\bar{X}$ theory and the lexicon is used to create representations of a message in d-structure. In d-structure there can be null pronoun elements which are referred to as PRO. The presence of a PRO element enables an intermediate representation to be produced even though the final sentence will not contain the null element. A PRO element is required when one of the verbs in a sentence does not have an associated noun phrase. For example, in "Adam promised [PRO to be good]", PRO can be thought of as a pronoun structure which is related to the element "to be good". *Control theory* is concerned with the use of PRO.

Movement rules change d-structures to s-structures. The s-structures provide a representation of the linear order of elements of the original d-structure. The elements in s-structure can contain trace or empty elements that are not produced when spoken. One purpose of the traces is to assist under-standing.

The movement between the d-structure and the s-structure does not in-volve a complex set of transformational rules, instead it is assumed that an element can move to any other position. Because this rule is very powerful, without any other constraints it would produce ungrammatical utterances (i.e. the word order of a sentence could be jumbled up). Such power is limited by general principles contained in the various modules. Thus, the structure of an utterance is constrained by principles rather than by the movement rules.

The *s-structure* contains elements of speech that influence semantic interpretation. Binding theory rules operate on s-structures and produce representations at the level of logical forms. Part of binding theory deals with the identification of the referent of elements such as pronouns. Considerable interest has been paid to the rules related to the use of pronominals (he, she, it) and anaphors (herself, himself). These will be considered in more detail in the next chapter.

Case theory also is applied to s-structures. This module provides markings of case (roughly object, dative, possessive, etc.) for noun phrases. These markings give a further set of restrictions which help to ensure that the final sentence is grammatical. In English, case relations are not often marked by morphological elements, but one exception is possession, e.g. "Chomsky's theory". A case filter prevents ungrammatical utterances from being produced. This operates at the level of s-structure. Case theory and theta theory are related and Chomsky suggests that ultimately case theory may be reduced to theta theory.

Movement between the s-structure and the *logical form* (LF), allows a further rearrangement of elements. These rearrangements mostly involve question words. This movement enables potentially ambiguous utterances to be interpreted. Thus, the logical form allows the relationship between words to be understood. Movement from s-structure also enables a *phonological form* to be generated. The latter is only briefly discussed by Chomsky and corresponds to the spoken utterance.

In addition to the theories already described there is *bounding theory*. This is concerned with the structure of the elements in a message, and is important in restricting some movements. A particular area of concern for this theory is the rearrangement of sentences which occur as the result of the use of wh-expressions (i.e. "what", "where").

SUMMARY

This chapter has given an outline of Chomsky's ideas about language and language acquisition. His original ideas about transformational grammar have been superseded by a new model. The new model bears some similarities to the old, but there are important differences in that more of the "work" of the grammatical system is contained in the lexicon and the movement rules themselves are now very general. PPT theory still assumes that language acquisition is possible in humans because of innate dispositions, and there now are few investigators who would disagree with this claim in its very general form. What some find implausible is the idea of parameter setting. However, if this is translated into a more psychological process of predispositions for learning, and predispositions for learning certain types of structure, then the idea may appear more reasonable. PPT has had a major impact on linguistic research. The focus of this research has been to identify the parameters which are set during language acquisition and to describe the parameter setting process in more detail. Some of this literature will be discussed in the next chapter.

11

APPLYING PPT TO LANGUAGE ACQUISITION

The previous chapter outlined the theoretical underpinnings of PPT. This chapter illustrates the way these ideas have been used to explain the language acquisition process. The first section has three parts which examine an area of research which has obtained findings in support of the PPT approach. The first two parts attempt to account for the structure of children's early speech. The third examines the employment of principles from universal grammar to govern pronoun use in older children. In all three parts we see that the application of PPT to children's language development has uncovered further questions, and as a result there are considerable uncertainties about how parameter setting could explain the emergence of any particular linguistic form. The second section considers theories which have attempted to deal with some of these uncertainties. Here debates about the precise nature of the parameter setting process are outlined; this highlights different views and disagreements about the precise way that a parameter is set.

USING PARAMETERS AND PRINCIPLES TO DESCRIBE LANGUAGE ACQUISITION

Early Parameter Setting

One issue that has attracted the interest of investigators is the initial process of parameter setting. A basic difference between some languages is the way that additional elements can be added to sentences. In English, extra elements can be added to the right of a verb phrase (see Figures 10.1 and 10.2), and this makes the end of the sentence longer (e.g. "*Ben saw John* who thought that Richard had spoken to Adam who...."). This is an example of a right-branching language. Such languages often have a subject–verb–object word order. The opposite pattern occurs in left-branching languages, where extra phrases are usually added to the left of the verb phrase, which can be thought of as adding material to the beginning of the sentence. These languages frequently possess a subject–object–verb order.

One of the first parameters to be set might be expected to involve features such as these, because they are basic to the whole structure of a language. This possibility was examined by Lust (1977). One way to assess children's ability to process an utterance is to ask them to repeat it. Lust (1977) asked 2–3-year-old children to repeat two different forms of an utterance. One form had extra right-branching material and this should make English sentences easier to process (e.g. "The teddy bear *walks and sleeps*"). The other form had extra material at the beginning of the sentence making it like a left-branching structure (e.g. "*The kittens and dogs* hide"). Lust found that English children were better at repeating sentences which had a right-branching structure which suggests that they already had a parameter set for this basic feature of English. Furthermore, when the same type of test was used with Japanese children the opposite pattern of results was found, as one would expect for a left-branching language (Lust & Wakayama, 1979).

Thus, there is evidence that at an early age children are already sensitive to important aspects of the grammar of their language. Such findings are compatible with PPT theory and can be interpreted in terms of there being parameters set by linguistic experience. However, it is important to recognise that such findings do not provide a test of PPT. If children had not been found to be sensitive to these grammatical structures, the conclusion could simply be made that the relevant parameter is acquired at a later age.

Prodrop Languages and Parameter Setting

One interesting proposal in some forms of PPT is that parameters have a default setting; thus if children do not detect examples which would set any of the relevant parameters, then the default switch (usually termed an unmarked value) would control the production of speech. Such a mechanism could explain why children who hear different languages produce similar forms of speech at the beginning of language acquisition. Because there has been considerable discussion about this proposal I will go into this in detail to illustrate some of the features of the PPT approach.

An unmarked parameter?

The possibility of a default parameter setting has attracted interest in relation to a group of related phenomena involving the elements at the beginning of an utterance (termed prodrop sentences, subjectless sentences, or null subject sentences). Some languages, like English, require a subject to be present at the beginning of the main clause. This is not required in other languages such as Italian (the equivalent of "Am going to the shop" would be permitted in Italian).

Hyams (1986) claimed that there is a parameter that controls the generation of prodrop utterances and the unmarked value of this parameter will produce prodrop utterances. As a result, at the beginning of language acquisition, English children were supposed to assume that they should employ a prodrop grammar. The benefit of this proposal is that it explains why English children leave out subjects in telegraphic speech. Later on, when children identify sentences which are incompatible with the parameter, it is reset.

More recently, Hyams (1992) has modified her original view to suggest that the prodrop parameter is set on the basis of more complex features of a language. These involve, for example, the presence of inflections for all the different forms of a verb, which seems to be generally associated with prodrop grammars (in English inflections are seldom employed for different forms of a verb, e.g. "I/we/you/they *take*", but in Italian each subject is associated with a different verb inflection). She also suggests that the initial selection of a prodrop grammar is consistent with the subset principle that children will tend to select the simpler grammar. However, Weissenborn, Goodluck and Roeper (1992) present examples which show that French and German children produce verb inflections which should indicate to them that their language allows subjects, but they still continue to produce utterances without subjects.

Problems with the unmarked value hypothesis

A challenge to a Hyams' parameter setting explanation has been provided by Valian (1990a, b). She found that young English-speaking children use subjects more frequently than Italian children. Even though English-speaking children will often omit the subject they do say things like "I fall", "He go out". This could be interpreted as suggesting that English children acquire the relevant parameter, but it is not used very accurately. Alternatively, the findings might be thought of as failing to provide convincing evidence for the presence of some type of prodrop parameter, since children's speech contains utterances which should not occur if this parameter is set.

Valian (1993) has developed a "balance scales" account of the setting of the prodrop parameter. She argues that if the parameter is incorrectly set children will not be able to detect linguistic structures incompatible with their present grammar. Thus, if the prodrop parameter is set they will not recognise the significance of adult utterances containing a subject. Because of this she reasons that the parameter setting is much like a balance scale which is set level at birth. As children process adult speech one pan of the scale will receive a higher weight as a result of the predominance of one form of speech input. However, another parameter may also be identified as being able to account for the structure of some adult utterances. If this parameter is increasingly successful at accounting for the adult speech then it will accumulate a greater weight and eventually may come to be the parameter with the heaviest weight. In the case of children speaking English, Valian supposes that children will eventually change from the prodrop setting and this will then govern the production of speech.

Discussion has also concerned the precise nature of the parameter. More careful cross-linguistic comparisons have revealed that English and Italian differ not only in the use and absence of the null subject, but Italian also has syntactic agreement between the verb and the null subject (i.e. the ending of the verb indicates the type of subject of the sentence, single, plural, etc.). Thus, it is difficult to maintain that an English child's telegraphic speech is similar to Italian (i.e. can be set by the same parameter). In fact more recent discussions have been concerned with the possibility that the telegraphic speech of English children is more similar to Chinese in which verb inflections are rare and null subjects are allowed (Hyams, 1992), and it has also been argued that there is greater variation between languages than the prodrop parameter would suggest (Weissenborn, Goodluck & Roeper, 1992).

There are also uncertainties about why a parameter is not set appropriately from the start of language production. After all, the speech to English children contains linguistic forms which should result in the setting of correct parameters for any dimension of the language which is heard. One way to explain this anomaly is to assume that some aspect of the perceptual or grammatical structure matures, and in this way the information would only be utilised at a later point in development (Hyams, 1986, 1987; see also the later section on maturation).

It might be supposed that the absence of functional words (pronouns, articles, auxiliary verbs, and so on, see Chapter 9) in telegraphic speech is due to some general effect of setting the parameter to the prodrop value. When the switch is reset correctly these other functional elements should appear. However, there does not seem to be a sudden appearance of these forms as a switch-setting explanation might imply. Pronouns and other functional words slowly enter children's language over several months (O'Grady, Peters & Masterson, 1989). Furthermore, in general, the acquisition of linguistic forms occurs more slowly than a switch-setting analogy might imply. Although, even about this matter there are disagreements over what is considered slow or quick (cf. Aitchinson, 1989; Atkinson, 1992).

Furthermore, the characteristics of telegraphic speech can be explained in terms of processing limitations without recourse to parameter setting. Children may simply omit the unstressed words that they hear, or there may be processing constraints. Bloom (1990) has reported that the use of subjects tended to occur in longer utterances with English-speaking children. Thus, it may be that subjects are omitted from children's utterances because of some performance limitation. When this limitation is removed the subjects are then inserted into utterances. All these uncertainties serve to illustrate the difficulty of identifying what forms of a parameter are set during language acquisition.

Pronouns and Language Acquisition According to PPT

One feature of PPT which has attracted a lot of attention is binding theory and the acquisition of the appropriate use of pronouns. Before examining studies dealing with this issue it is useful to explain why there has been this interest in binding theory. Transformational grammar encountered problems in dealing with the relation between the subject of a sentence and a later pronoun. For example, the utterance "Everyone hoped that he would win" is ambiguous, since it is not clear whether each person hoped that they themselves would win, or whether everyone in a group of people hoped a particular person would win. Transformational grammar failed to give a satisfactory explanation of why such utterances are ambiguous.

Binding theory was developed by Chomsky to take account of considerations such as these. In English it was proposed that pronominals (i.e. a pronoun such as him, they—these are sometimes called non-reflexives) do not refer to a noun in the same *local domain*. A local domain roughly corresponds to the clause of a sentence. If we consider a sentence like "John said that Adam likes him", "him" is likely to refer to John as "him" and "John" are in different local domains. "Him" does not refer to "Adam" as the two words are in the same local domain (technically nouns and pronouns show a structural relationship to one another, but for the sake of simplicity I will use the term "refer").

In the same way it was supposed that anaphors, such as himself or themselves, are used where the referent is in the same local domain (anophers are sometimes termed reflexives). Consequently, in the sentence "John said that Adam likes himself", "himself" refers to Adam and not John. Thus, in English pronominals and anaphors have the opposite set of constraints governing their reference.

One way to evaluate these ideas has been to present children with potentially ambiguous instructions. The aim is to determine whether their interpretation of the instructions corresponds to principles of binding theory. Usually children have to act out an instruction on a group of toys.

Solan (1983) and Deutsch, Koster and Koster (1986) found that 5 year olds will correctly interpret anaphors. Anaphors were found to be understood at an earlier age than pronominals, and there was a much higher number of misinterpretations for the latter. Such findings indicate that the principles of binding theory are only fully acquired by 6–7 years.

Not all findings agree with the idea that binding theory is applied to pronominal and anaphoric structures. Matthei (1981) asked children (4–6 years) to perform actions in the following sentence "the chickens said that the pigs tickled each other". In this sentence "each other" is an anaphor, and so would be expected to refer to the pigs as they are in the same local domain. In fact, the children often made the chickens and the pigs tickle one another. This would not be expected, according to binding theory and universal grammar, as the children do not appear to be treating "each other" as either an anaphor or a pronominal.

However, it is possible to argue that their error might be due to problems in processing complex utterances such as these, rather than a problem of linguistic competence. This is backed up by a study by Stevenson (1992) who found that adults made similar errors to those of the children in Solan's (1983) study. She draws the conclusion that the adults in her study and the children in Solan's study know the appropriate principle, but their performance with complex sentences does not always reflect this knowledge.

A different principle of binding theory concerns the "backward" reference of an anaphor. Given a suitable non-verbal context, the sentence, "When he ate the hamburger, the Smurf was in the box", involves "he" and "Smurf" referring to the same entity. Crain and McKee (1985) used a task where an action was carried out by an adult, and then the child had to decide whether or not a sentence said by a puppet was correct. This is a useful innovation in assessing children's understanding of an utterance as problems of children acting out complex instructions are avoided. When using this methodology it was found that 2–5-year-old children did not simply interpret a sentence based on the order of words, but were able to understand sentences where a pronoun referred to a noun that occurred later on in the sentence (i.e. backward reference). This would seem to indicate that children have a fairly complex principle of grammar quite early on in development.

How should findings such as these concerned with anaphors and pronominals be interpreted? A common interpretation is that children use the principles of PPT from the time they start to use the relevant linguistic structures (see Goodluck, 1991; Atkinson, 1992). However, it should be remembered that in general the findings reveal that at certain ages children are able to use the principles specified in the modules of PPT, and that this is in itself unsurprising as PPT is a description of an adult language that children acquire.

Can PPT Account for All Speech?

Some children appear to produce utterances which do not conform to the principles of a universal grammar (UG). A report by Wilson and Peters (1988) about Seth, who is partially sighted, gives the following examples:

> "we're gonna look at some houses with johnnie" "what are we gonna look for some?" "what are we gonna look for some with johnnie?"

In the last two examples Seth appears to have left the word "some" behind, when moving "what" to the front of the utterance to make a question. According to PPT children should not split up phrases and move half of them in this way. Furthermore, Wilson and Peters do not believe that the utterances were the result of performance errors, because they occurred on a number of occasions and were stable even when Seth was questioned about what he had said. Wilson and Peters do, however, suggest that there might have been features of the language Seth heard which could have led to this pattern, in particular, the tendency of his father to leave sentences unfinished so Seth could complete them, and the father's flexible use of sentence fragments. The important point that Wilson and Peters make is that these utterances appear to violate the assumptions of UG, and this raises questions about the power of UG to limit grammatical constructions.

Specific Language Impairment

Specific language impairment (SLI) occurs when language abilities are below other cognitive abilities. SLI appears to cover a range of difficulties with language and there is still uncertainty about the best way to identify subgroups within this population. One way of explaining SLI is in terms of a lack of appropriate principles in the grammatical system. For instance, Gopnik and Crago (1991) have identified a family who have difficulty with regular verb inflections (e.g. -ed), but can produce irregular past tenses (e.g. went). From this they claim there might be a separate processor for regular and irregular verbs. However, this claim is controversial as Vargha-Khadem and Passingham (1990) report that the same family has more extensive language problems. Studies by van der Lely and Harris (1990) suggest that some of the difficulties of SLI children may be caused by their failing to identify grammatical characteristics in the speech they comprehend and, in particular, the module may involve government of the relations between elements in an utterance (van der Lely, in press). Van der Lely and Howard (1993) also fails to find evidence to support the idea that short-term memory or phonological processing problems are responsible for this deficit. In addition, Rice and Wexler (1993) have suggested that the difficulties of SLI children may be because of specific impairments to modules in the syntactic system.

In contrast to these claims, Kursten and Scholer (1992) conclude that the gradual improvement of linguistic abilities in children with SLI is not compatible with a parameter-setting viewpoint. Research into the characteristics of SLI in different language groups suggests that the type of impairment is variable and may depend on the syntactic and auditory characteristics of the language (Rom & Leonard, 1990; Lindner & Johnston, 1992). These findings are taken further by Dromi, Leonard and Shteiman (in press) who argue that the lack of grammatical morphemes in SLI children may be because these elements are unstressed in the speech that children hear, or because children ignore characteristics which are infrequent in the grammar of a language (such as inflections in English). Both these characteristics are believed to be due to limited processing capacities and Gathercole and Baddeley (1990) present evidence suggesting that SLI children have deficits in short-term phonological memory, while similar arguments have been advanced by Speidel (1993).

Summary

The studies that have been reviewed provide a very useful description of language acquisition in terms of PPT. The ages at which principles are adopted can be identified. But as I have already noted, the problem is that the formal testing of PPT theory is difficult. This is because one can simply explain any pattern of findings as being caused by one of a number of factors. Consequently, such findings are not enough to convince sceptics of the developmental mechanisms of parameter setting. In the next section we will see that matters have become even more complicated.

FURTHER DEVELOPMENTS IN PPT

The Operation of Parameter Setting

The original formulation about parameter setting did not account for the intermediate stages in the development of children's language. From a very simple interpretation of parameter setting one might suppose that, from the beginning, children would produce grammatically correct speech. Clearly this is not the case. In response to this problem two broad solutions have been proposed, and within each approach different emphases and proposals can be identified. These two approaches have become known as the continuity and maturity hypotheses. However, it is worth bearing in mind that Weissenborn, Goodluck and Roeper (1992) note that although it is easy to identify different theoretical positions, in practice, the issues often become blurred when specific aspects of development are considered.

The continuity hypothesis

In the continuity hypothesis (Pinker, 1984) it is assumed that the principles of UG are available from the start of language learning, but that the setting of parameters is dependent on triggering from the speech children hear. Felix (1992) has characterised this position as involving "perceptionism" because parameter setting is governed by perceiving the relevant characteristic in the language input. One form of the continuity hypothesis has involved the claim that children will incorrectly set a parameter because they mistakenly perceive the speech they hear as being a language with a different parametric setting, as in Hyam's suggestions about telegraphic speech (see above). Basic to all forms of the continuity hypothesis is the assumption that each stage of child grammar corresponds to the principles of UG and so child speech always corresponds to a possible human language.

In the PPT approach it is generally accepted that changes in adult speech as children become older cannot be sufficient to account for the changes in children's grammar (though there is little empirical evidence about this). Consequently, a problem for the continuity view is explaining these grammatical changes, especially as it is also supposed that children have access to UG from the beginnings of language use (Borer & Wexler, 1987). In response to these issues Clahsen (1992) has recently argued that the children's intake (i.e. perception) of language may change with development of memory size and processing abilities, and in this way the same speech may have different effects on children of different ages. He also argues that lexical learning may involve the restructuring of child grammars as new forms are acquired and new relationships between words identified. He sees lexical learning as providing triggers for the setting of parameters. Thus, he predicts that the emergence of some syntactic structures will occur at the same time as certain classes of words and morphemes are acquired. In these and other ways proponents of the continuity hypothesis are able to account for the fact that children's speech does not necessarily correspond to the grammar of the relevant adult language.

Another recent proposal in the continuity tradition is Randall's catapult hypothesis (Randall, 1992). She believes that parameter setting will involve an "either/or process", so that parameters must be set in one of two ways with the result that both forms of a parameter cannot be operational at once. As a consequence, if children set a parameter incorrectly, they will encounter adult utterances which are not compatible with the parameter setting. Randall suggests that the child's perception of the forms which are incompatible with their grammar results in their resetting the parameter to the appropriate form. This, she argues, allows positive information to result in the rejection of a previously incorrectly set parameter. Such a proposal assumes that UG is organised in ways that enable mutually exclusive operations to govern the development of language.

The maturational hypothesis

The maturational hypothesis suggests that the grammatical system matures and thereby enables children, at particular ages, to adopt more and more aspects of the adult linguistic system. Within this approach it is possible to identify "weak" and "strong" forms. According to the weak hypothesis the setting of UG parameters is constrained by factors external to UG, for example memory size (Borer & Wexler, 1987). This position has similarities to the form of the continuity hypothesis proposed by Clahsen (1992) who suggests that advances in the perception of speech may allow new parameters to be set.

According to a "strong" maturational hypothesis the various principles of UG become operational at different ages so that the process of language acquisition is internally driven (Felix, 1987, 1992). In the latter case the emergence of new principles is supposed to force a restructuring of the inadequate child grammar. Thus, Felix (1987, 1992) has argued that child grammars temporally violate UG principles and this provides support for the strong maturational view. An interesting example is the use of expressions such as "no Fraser drink all tea" where the negative is placed at the beginning of the utterance. This feature does not appear to be present in any naturally occurring adult language, and consequently seems to violate UG principles. However, many of the examples of violations given by Felix are drawn from two word utterances and, as Stevenson (1992) points out, there is considerable uncertainty about whether or not this stage can be considered as a product of a syntactic system (see the first section of this chapter). In addition, Clahsen (1992) in a technical argument disputes that the examples provided by Felix demonstrate that children's speech violates UG principles. Furthermore, Stevenson (1992) points out that some of the naturally occurring failures of children to follow UG principles are probably the result of peripheral non-linguistic processes and that experimental studies are needed to validate claims made on the basis of descriptions of children's speech. This doubt about the validity of UG errors she sees as undermining the maturational hypothesis.

SUMMARY

PPT continues to provoke research designed to provide a more detailed picture of language acquisition within this framework. The results of such research have led to clearer proposals about parameter setting. However, the changes and flexibility of this model mean that critics not only have to understand an extremely complex system, but often have to hit a moving target.

Much of the study of language development in the PPT tradition has resulted in post hoc conclusions. If an adult-like grammatical capacity is present in children then it is assumed that the relevant parameter has been set or this is one of the principles of UG, but if another non-adult form is present then it is assumed that some other setting is being used or that the relevant parameter needs to "mature". Research in this tradition allows one to fit PPT to children's linguistic development, but it makes a test of the model extremely difficult. Furthermore, it is important to bear in mind that the more extreme models have been presented in this chapter. Stevenson (1992) in her comments about the positions taken by Felix (1992) and Clahsen (1992) makes the point that logically there can be a number of intermediate views between the extreme positions of continuity and maturation.

Thus, in this research domain investigators have different objectives. The majority of studies have used PPT as a framework for studying language development, which has resulted in interesting descriptions of children's linguistic abilities. Moving outside this framework to test it is much more difficult for the reasons I have already outlined. Here I would like to identify two crucial areas for future research. One is reaching agreement about the mechanism of parameter setting. The other is discovering how well parameter setting can describe development with different languages. There are many important questions to be answered by cross-linguistic research, including: Can a universal set of principles be identified? and Do the same parameters become operational with different settings at similar ages across languages?

One last comment about PPT is that while it provides a very useful description of children's competence it is less successful in accounting for developmental processes. Chapter 13 considers an alternative description of development which has come from work in cognitive science. However, before this, the next chapter outlines some of the processes that may enable children to crack the linguistic code, and enable children to progress from telegraphic speech to more sophisticated levels of language.

12

EXPLANATIONS ABOUT STARTING TO USE LANGUAGE

In the last two chapters the PPT approach to language acquisition has been discussed. This chapter provides a broader perspective about early multi-word speech, and includes some work in the PPT tradition. There are two major issues covered in this chapter. The first one concerns the question of how children break into the linguistic system; this is a difficult question to answer and perhaps for this reason, the topic has been somewhat neglected. The task facing the pre-linguistic child, from any account of language acquisition, is to be able to identify the linguistic properties of individual words (whether a word is a noun, verb and so on) and the linguistic structure of utterances. This is necessary, for instance, to enable children to utilise their knowledge of UG in order to set parameters. Another issue running through this chapter is the linguistic status of early multi-word speech. There has been discussion of whether early telegraphic speech has a syntax, and whether true language emerges at a slightly later age. The chapter provides details about a number of perspectives which consider this transition.

PROSODIC INFORMATION ABOUT LINGUISTIC STRUCTURE

Children are presented with a stream of sounds. To acquire language they need to be able to work out the way utterances are structured in terms of their phrase structure (see Figure 10.3). How do children do this? One type of answer is to suppose that speech to children contains prosodic clues that help them work out the grammatical structure of utterances. In particular, it is supposed that phrases may be marked by the pauses and intonation in speech. Such information, if used by children, would give them an important aid in identifying the general structure of the language that they hear.

The prosodic characteristics of speech could help children identify the grammatical structure of utterances. Pinker has termed this prosodic boot-strapping. A more specific term is the Bracketed Input Hypothesis, which Morgan (1986) used to describe his theory. At the core of the theory is the idea that the speech to children contains clues which mark out the phrase structure of words in utterances. Thus, if the structure of the sentence such as the one given in Figure 10.3 could be identified from prosodic markers then children would be provided with information about the syntactic organisation of the speech they are attempting to acquire.

There is reasonably good evidence that the speech to children contains such patterning. Newport, Gleitman and Gleitman (1977) found that much of the speech to young children consists of well formed phrases, which are not part of a larger utterance. In addition, there are prosodic cues, the ends of phrases are marked by vowel lengthening and by a longer pause (Cooper & Paccia-Cooper, 1980), and the ends of clauses tend to be marked by a rise or fall in fundamental frequency and by stress (Garnica, 1977).

An ingenious study by Hirsch-Pasek, Kemler Nelson, Jusczyk et al. (1987) revealed that 7–10-month-old infants preferred to listen to speech which had pauses inserted at clause boundaries than to speech which had pauses inserted within a clause. Furthermore, this preference appears to be confined to A–C speech and did not occur with A–A speech (Hirsch-Pasek et al., 1987). It has sometimes been objected that even if the speech to children contains bracketing information and even if this information is processed by children, this does not establish that children use the information to help language acquisition. While it is true that Hirsch-Pasek et al. do not show that children use the information from clause boundaries in language acquisition, the study indicates that children do perceive these boundaries. Furthermore, compared to many theories, the bracketing hypothesis has collected an impressive array of supporting evidence. Included in this is the finding that input information which highlights the phase structure of sentences assists adults to acquire artificial languages (Morgan, 1986). It should also be remembered that pre-linguistic infants appear able to comprehend some syntactic structures (Golinkoff, Hirsch-Pasek, Cauley & Gordon, 1987; see Chapter 8). Thus, features of the input may help children acquire language by providing information about the syntactic structure of utterances.

Semantics to Syntax

A common first reaction to reading the literature on the one word stage and the literature about transformational grammar is that meaning may provide a bridge between the communicative intentions of infants and the use of a formal grammar by older children. Infants appear to have meanings to convey by the use of words, but they do not yet appear to have a formal system of rules to govern the production of speech.

Several attempts have been made to apply this common sense notion to the acquisition of language. As we have already seen in the discussion of one word utterances there is not necessarily a one-to-one correspondence between classification of words in terms of their meanings (e.g. agent, recipient, patient) and the classification of words in terms of their syntactic categories (e.g. noun, verb, adjective; subject, object, etc.). If children were simply to assume that the agent of a sentence, which they can infer from non-linguistic information, is always the subject of the sentence then they would make profound errors. For instance, in the utterance "The girl caught the ball", the girl is both the agent and the subject, but children may have difficulty in using this coincidence as a basis to identify syntactic classes as there are also utterances like "The ball was caught by the girl" where the subject is not the agent.

The idea that there is a transition from a semantic to a syntactic basis for language receives support from work conducted by Bowerman (1982) who suggests that there is a cognitive reorganisation which enables this change to take place. An example involving the use of prefixes can be used to illustrate her ideas. In English the prefix un- is often used with words that involve a reversible action (e.g. undo, untie, unblock, unstuck). Consequently, at first sight it would appear that the use of the prefix is governed by a semantic rule. However, un- cannot be used with all words which involve a reversible action (e.g. unsmear—clean, unlose—find). This and more careful analyses suggest that there is not a clear semantic category to identify words which have un-added to them. So it would seem that the use of the prefix is governed by linguistic not semantic rules. Given these assumptions, do children employ a semantic or a syntactic basis for extending the use of un-?

Observations made by Bowerman revealed that children initially only use the prefix un- with appropriate words, but soon afterwards they start to add the prefix to inappropriate words (e.g. "undraw", meaning rub out). Bowerman argued that as the children were applying the prefix to reversible actions they seem to have been using a semantic category. Bowerman claims that these overextensions are followed by a cognitive reorganisation which results in the prefix being applied only to words of the appropriate syntactic category. Thus, there is evidence that there is a change from a semantic to a syntactic system during the language acquisition process.

A study of deaf children acquiring sign language by Petitto (1987) also suggests a transformation in the communication system. Petitto found that the signs for "I" (pointing at the other) and "me" (pointing at oneself) were initially acquired by the two children who were studied, and seem to have been acquired as part of a non-linguistic gestural system. However, this was followed by a period of avoidance and errors which Pettito argues was due to the children assimilating these signs to a linguistic system. From this Pettito argues that there is discontinuity between early non-linguistic communication and language.

Other research conducted by Gordon (1985) has suggested that a change from semantics to linguistic processing may occur at an early stage in language acquisition. In English a distinction can be made between *mass* nouns and *count* nouns. Mass nouns include "gold", "fruit", "love" and "water"; these nouns do not usually have -s added to them in their plural form (e.g. "two waters" is incorrect, but note "fruit" is somewhat unusual as it is acceptable to say "two fruits" and also say "there was a lot of fruit"). In contrast, count nouns have a plural form when they are counted, e.g. "two glasses". In general, mass nouns involve substances that do not occur as obvious individual entities; there is no quantity which would correspond to "one water". The opposite is clearly the case for count nouns.

Some mass nouns can, however, involve the identification of individual items (e.g. a fruit). Thus, the distinction between mass nouns and count nouns seems to involve a syntactic rather than a semantic basis. Gordon tested whether young children would add -s to mass nouns which can refer to individual items (e.g. fruit). If children's speech had a semantic basis then one would expect them to incorrectly add -s to make a plural. Children between 2 and 5 years old, who knew the nouns, made very few errors in the tasks. For example, when they were asked the question "Do you know what you get in the vegetable/fruit section?" they would typically reply, "fruit"/"vegetables". This study has raised important issues and is often quoted as evidence against a semantic basis in early language. However, as we will see later from the work of Tomasello and Olguin (in press) children appear to have a syntactic category for nouns before 2 years. Consequently, a full answer to the question of whether there is any semantic organisation in early speech requires further research with younger children.

Thus, there is evidence that children progress from a semantic to a syntactic linguistic system according to the work by Bowerman. In addition, it would seem from the work of Gordon that the syntactic system is in place at a very early age.

Semantic Bootstrapping

Another important question is how do children identify the different syntactic classes of words (nouns, verbs, etc.) when these are not always clearly marked in the speech they hear? For example, in English, there does not seem to be any consistent linguistic clue which will enable children to identify nouns. A noun can appear at various positions in an utterance, and there is no morpheme which will invariably identify a noun (i.e. the plural affix for nouns is -s, but -s is also an ending for some verbs and adjectives).

Proposals about a semantic basis for the initial entry into language were made by a variety of investigators in the early 1980s (Wexler & Culicover, 1980; Grimshaw, 1981; MacNamara, 1982; Pinker, 1982, 1984). Pinker's proposal about semantic bootstrapping (pulling oneself up by the bootstraps—self-initiation) is one of the most detailed and I will concentrate on this.

Initial proposals

The starting point for Pinker's argument is that children have to discover which words are nouns, verbs and so on, if they are to learn language. Even if children have innate constraints on the way they process speech, without a means to identify the classes of words such constraints would be of little or no use. Pinker in 1984 suggested that the semantic bootstrapping hypothesis involves four assumptions:

1. The meanings of many words can be acquired independently of grammatical rules.
2. A child can form a semantic representation of an utterance from the context and the meaning of individual words.
3. There are a limited number of *substantive* linguistic universals for expressing certain semantic concepts and relations. These make up the basic sentences of all languages. For example, names for concrete objects and people are universally nouns.
4. The basic sentences of a language are accompanied by non-linguistic information which will enable their meaning to be understood, and non-basic sentences are rarely used with children (e.g. passive utterances are rarely used). A basic utterance would correspond to the most usual type of utterance in a language; in English it would be a subject–verb–object sentence.

Pinker believed that the lexical entry of a word is inferred from its semantic properties (e.g. object words and names are taken to be nouns). Also coded in the lexical entry are the grammatical functions of a word. These are inferred from the thematic relation of the word (e.g. the subject of a sentence is often an agent of an action, cause of an event, etc.). Phrase structure rules are learnt by use of $\bar{X}$ theory, which involves making use of the semantic relations between the words in an utterance and the phrase structure configuration (i.e. the semantics of the utterance help determine which particular grammatical tree best represents the organisation of the utterance).

Once a child has established a first set of rules, these can be used to help deduce the properties of unknown words. If an unknown word has a recognisable set of syntactic relations with the other words in an utterance, then children are assumed to be able to deduce the syntactic class of the unknown word. This explains how children are able to take an unknown word like "wug", and produce appropriate plurals (Berko, 1958). Support for this model comes from Pinker's own work and from studies like that of Ingham (1993) who has found that the acquisition of transitive and intransitive verbs is influenced by the context in which they are used (i.e. whether there is an object which is acted upon), and this seems to override information from syntax itself.

According to Pinker's account, once children can identify classes of words they can then look for the grammatical features which are associated with such words, so for instance by identifying nouns they can look for the way verbs or other words vary with the use of nouns in systematic ways. The identification of associations is assisted by UG which limits the hypotheses that are needed. As a result a child does not need to examine the relationship of every linguistic element with every other one.

A constraint satisfaction model

Pinker (1984, 1987) admits to problems with the semantic bootstrapping model and lists them. These include: that some or all of the regularities between semantics and syntax are not universal; that the input may include a number of non-basic utterances which would considerably complicate the child's task; that incorrect interpretation of contextual information by a child may occur; no account is taken of individual differences; that sometimes it seems reasonable for children to make the best guess rather than wait for a watertight deduction. Pinker considers his previous scheme "aesthetically unpleasing" because the deterministic nature of the scheme gives children little opportunity for creative deductions.

Because of these difficulties Pinker (1987) proposed a revised theory. In this he supposes that children make best guesses rather than waiting for watertight evidence. In consequence, rules will be tentative and subject to revision. Pinker also moves away from the claim that semantics provides the only way into syntax. Instead he suggests that semantics, prosody and word order might all contribute to the process, but that semantics is the earliest and most important influence.

An interesting feature of his newer proposals is that inferences are made by the analysis of all the elements of an utterance (i.e. semantics, prosody, word order, etc.), rather than taking one part of the input and then working out the relation it has to the others. The latter analytic process, Pinker reasons, may be impossible because of the interdependency of the elements to each other.

Pinker argues that in other biological processes, deductions are made on the basis of an analysis of the whole of the input. Examples he gives are the perception of binocular depth where the relationship between the two different retinal images of an object can give a clue to distance only if one can identify the two images as being of the same thing, and vice versa. Interestingly one might also include the problem of identifying which things are included in a category; we need an idea of the category to identify a relevant attribute, and we need a relevant attribute to obtain a notion of the category. In such cases there is no distinction between the premises and the conclusions, both seem to be needed to solve the problem. In analysis of visual perception relaxation models are used, and these models require iterative processing (Ullman, 1979). The relaxation notion is used by Pinker to develop a constraint satisfaction model which forms the basis for his revised proposals.

The essence of the model is that children have an incomplete representation of grammatical structure. However, UG provides a set of constraints on the analysis of utterances so that not all logically possible sets of relationships are evaluated. At the start of language learning incomplete representations of utterances are formed. The parser (processor of utterances) assigns every word to underspecified lexical categories, groups of adjacent lexical categories are assigned to phrases, and so on. In this way a temporary syntax is constructed.

There is also a pattern matching process. The pattern matching occurs as both a bottom-up and a top-down process. The words in the input are matched to rule prototypes based on UG. In this way sequences of words and morphemes will be aligned with certain rules. Furthermore, a match between a rule prototype which has already been activated and a new underspecified input will lead to a further strengthening of the connection.

Significantly, Pinker uses a symbol manipulating network as a basis for his proposal. As we will see later, Pinker has argued vehemently against the possibility of using connectionist networks to explain language acquisition. He claims that his model could not operate in a connectionist network where there are no representations of rules or grammatical categories.

Thus, Pinker's influential proposals have moved away from a purely semantic bootstrapping model to a model which includes other types of information. In addition, he favours a process which involves both a top-down and a bottom-up processing of information, to enable children to make progress with this very difficult problem.

Dividing up the World: Linguistic and Non-Linguistic Divisions

In this section I will briefly consider another aspect of the way children understand the properties of words. Slobin (1985) has followed Talmy (1985) in distinguishing between *closed-* and *open-class* items in language. A closed-class item is similar to a functional item, it involves grammatical forms which code such things as time (e.g. present, past, future), space (e.g. containment, position, etc.), force, causation and so on. Slobin claims that children are constrained by the meanings they can apply to these closed-class items, in other words they have a set of innate dispositions for dealing with these dimensions and the language they hear is mapped onto these dimensions. For example, some languages mark the subject of a transitive sentence (e.g. "Adam-SUBJ ate the bun"), and others mark the object of the sentence (e.g. "Adam ate the bun-ACC"). Slobin claims that in such cases children initially attach the relevant ending only with verbs that involve a direct physical effect on the object. This is because children have a prototype conception of groups of events which involve an agent intentionally and physically changing a patient. Other evidence to back up this idea comes from Budwig (1986) who reports that children learning English will use "my" for their actions ("my blew the candles out", "my cracked the eggs"), and will use "I" for experiences (e.g. "I like peas", "I wear it"), suggesting they are creating a non-existent distinction.

Bowerman (1989) has shown that across different languages different terms are used to code relations of objects in space (e.g. in, on, under, tightly contained, loosely contained). She uses this evidence to question the idea that there are universal dispositions. For instance, children learning Korean and English have different linguistic categories for the relationship between objects, involving the idea of in/on (English) and tight/loose containment (Korean). Bowerman reports that these words about spatial relations are not mapped onto a common core meaning, but are already used in different ways by 18–24 month olds. The reason for this is unclear, one possibility being that children of this age already comprehend these relationships from their experience with language. Another possibility is that the marking of non-verbal actions, and of adult speech in relation to such, will tend to highlight the type of linguistic relation employed in the culture and the language.

Thus, we see again that there are complex processes involved in the relation of cognitive and linguistic structures. What is important to register from these findings is that some form of experience as well as some form of innate disposition could play a part in assisting the acquisition of words.

ANALYSIS OF SYNTACTIC FEATURES

Detecting Correlations

There have also been proposals that children do not need to utilise non-linguistic information from semantics or prosody to acquire syntax, but can utilise the redundancy already present in syntax. An important suggestion along these lines was made by Maratsos and Chalkley (1980).

Maratsos and Chalkley believed that telegraphic speech reflects a child's perception of the world and this is translated into the ordering of words. From this stance, telegraphic speech is not considered to be structured by a grammar. However, the beginning of a grammatical system is believed to present at about 3 years when children start to use morphemes (e.g. the plural ending -s). Morphemes such as these are supposed to provide clues about syntactic groups (e.g. nouns can have -s, verbs can have -ed). Furthermore, it is possible that more detailed correlations may be noticed, for example that some verbs are transitive and need to be followed by a noun, e.g. "he hit her", while other verbs are intransitive and do not require a noun to follow them, e.g. "he ran". Thus, children are believed to develop grammatical categories by noticing the features associated with particular words, and the way that particular words have similar sets of relations with other words.

This account can explain the occurrence of words like "gooses" or "sheeps" in children's speech. The explanation is that children identify these words as nouns based on the way that they are used in their singular form, and apply the general rule that nouns are made plural by adding -s. This account can also explain why children do not usually confuse words which are similar in meaning, but are different parts of speech. An example of this is "like" which is a verb, but has a similar meaning to "fond" which is an adjective. Children's awareness of this distinction provides an explanation of why fond is not used in error as a verb (typically children do not produce the past tense "fonded").

However, Bowerman (1982) has reported errors in children's speech which should not occur according to Maratsos and Chalkley's predictions. And I too have heard one of my children say "higher my saddle", where high is being used incorrectly as a verb. A possible rejoinder to such criticisms from Maratsos and Chalkley is that these errors may reflect innovation on the child's part because they do not have in this example the verb "raise". Another criticism made by Pinker (1982, 1989) is that there are so many possible ways of looking for common features across utterances (sound patterns, position in the utterance, intonation, etc.) that without an a priori basis for detecting the correlations children would be faced with an impossible computational task (this argument being similar to those about identifying a category from a range of entities). For example, even in the case of affixes, as Gleitman and Wanner (1982) have observed, there is an imperfect correspondence between the affixes and their grammatical category; some verbs end in -s, and some adjectives will end in -ed. In defence of Maratsos and Chalkley it should be remembered that there are the findings which indicate that children as young as 17 months are influenced by syntactic information during training sessions (see Chapter 8), thus they do appear to notice some of the correlations in the data to which they are exposed.

The Acquisition of Grammatical Abilities

We have already seen that Maratsos and Chalkley suggest that telegraphic speech constitutes a pre-linguistic stage in communicative development. This raises the question of when do infants begin to treat words as grammatical categories? Of course the answer to this question depends on what we mean by grammatical categories. Grammatical categories, such as noun, verb and adjective, can be identified when children start to position words of a certain class appropriately in an utterance, and start to employ the appropriate morphemes when using that class of words.

There is broad agreement that sometime in the third year of life children start to employ grammatical categories from observations of naturally occurring speech. An analysis of noun use in 24–30-month-old children's speech by Valian revealed the appropriate employment of singular and plural forms. Bloom (1990) has also found that at this age, nouns are used appropriately with adjectives and determiners. Similarly, over the same age the -ed ending is spontaneously used to produce the past tense of verbs (Brown, 1973), and children over 3 years can produce appropriate endings for new verbs in experimental circumstances (e.g. "he is ricking...yesterday he —"; Berko, 1958; Perez-Pereira, 1989).

Tomasello and Olguin (in press) have argued that a problem with these studies is that one can never be sure whether the speech produced by a child is a result of imitation or the result of genuinely treating a word as a member of a grammatical class, and being able to generate appropriate grammatical forms which the child has never heard (e.g. singular to plural forms). For this reason Tomasello and Olguin introduced children to four nonsense words which referred to four novel objects. A child heard a different type of utterance associated with each word and no other grammatical structure was associated with the novel word; this ensured that if children produced other grammatical expressions it could not be the result of imitation. The children's speech was observed and tested to discover if 2 year olds could use the appropriate plural morpheme after hearing the singular form (i.e. "peri-s"), and could use the nouns as both agents and patients when they had only heard the other form (e.g. "Ernie is brushing the Wuggy" where Ernie is the agent and Wuggy is the patient). The findings confirmed that most of the children were able to correctly attach -s to these novel words, and to put the words into new and appropriate sentence frames.

A similar study was carried out by Olguin and Tomasello (in press) to investigate verb categorisation. Their findings revealed that 22–25 month children were not able to reliably generate new verb forms if they had not heard that form before. They did not add the -ed past tense inflection even though they used this form with other verbs. This ties in with Tomasello's (1992) case study where his daughter at first restricted her use of verbs, and developments in syntax seemed to occur on a word-by-word basis, rather than across all verbs at about the same age.

The investigators interpret their findings as indicating that children have more difficulty with forming grammatical categories for verbs than for nouns, and that before 2 years children's sentences are not organised around a verb as a grammatical category. From this Olguin and Tomasello argue that children do not use grammatical categories from the beginning of word production as might be predicted by some linguistic accounts. Instead they suggest that children analyse the functional use of different word forms and in this way notice regularities in the speech they hear. A problem noted by Olguin and Tomasello is the findings of Naigles (1990; see Chapter 8) that 25–28 month children can relate the use of new transitive and intransitive verbs to appropriate pictures, thereby showing some understanding of the properties of transitive and intransitive verbs. An obvious explanation of this discrepancy is that comprehension may occur earlier than production because there are lower processing demands.

Discontinuity Between Early and Later Speech

The functional parameterisation hypothesis

A strand of argument within the maturational approach of PPT is the suggestion that before certain ages child speech may not be constrained by the principles of universal grammar (e.g. Radford, 1990; Felix, 1987, 1992). Such proposals often suggest that early speech is agrammatical and not a true language, and imply discontinuity between early and later structures (Weissenborn, Goodluck & Roeper, 1992). The *functional parameterisation hypothesis* of Radford (1990) is a prominent example of this type of explanation (other similar proposals are made by Lebeaux, 1988, and Guilfoyle & Noonan, 1989).

Functional words are considered to be the parts of speech which do not refer to a particular class of entities, examples of such words are pronouns and articles. These words are functional from a linguistic perspective, and they are the semantically less important words which are absent from telegraphic speech. Functional words can be contrasted with substantive words such as nouns, adjectives and verbs, which have a conventional semantic content. A dimension on which languages differ is the way that functional words are employed. This has given rise to the idea that the differences between languages might be captured by the way the functional words operate, and this is known as the functional parameterisation hypothesis.

Radford (1990) has suggested that telegraphic speech is at a pre-functional stage, and this is the result of young children using only a few of the modules present in PPT. These modules are concerned with semantic processes (e.g. thematic roles), and the modules influence the word order used in telegraphic speech. The change from a pre-functional to a functional system is supposed to be the result of maturation; this maturation takes place at about 20–24 months and allows the employment of many of the modules in PPT. As Radford admits, functional words are sometimes produced in telegraphic speech, but he argues that this is the result of children's incorrect analysis of the lexical properties of words—such words he terms imposters.

Radford's proposal that there is a pre-functional stage during the use of two word utterances has been disputed by Deuchar (1992). She provides examples from her bilingual daughter which involve the use of noun phrases and other intermediate expressions (e.g. "juice no", "oh dear Panda", "mas juice"). Deuchar reasons that these intermediate expressions ("no", "oh dear", "mas") are not substantive words, and appear similar to functional words. Consequently, she rejects Radford's idea that two word utterances are limited to substantive words, and argues that cognitive developments may allow the use of salient words within the repertoire of two word utterances. Similarly, Bavin (1993) has reported the use of inflections (endings marking case) on verbs in an 18-month-old Greek child, and there was a dramatic increase in their use at 20 months.

It should also be remembered that there is predictability between early vocabulary and later speech, suggesting some type of continuity in functioning (Bates, O'Connell & Shore, 1987). In addition, children may comprehend more about grammar than they are able to produce. A study, using a novel technique, has provided evidence that older children at the two and three word stage of production are able to comprehend multi-word utterances (Golinkoff et al., 1987). The technique used was to present a child at the one word stage with an utterance that directs attention to the activities shown on one of two video monitors. If the child looked at the appropriate action more than the inappropriate action then it seems safe to conclude that she understood the multi-word utterance. Using this technique, in a carefully controlled manner, it was possible to examine whether children understood the difference between "Cookie Monster is tickling Big Bird" and "Big Bird is tickling Cookie Monster". They did look at the appropriate actions when each utterance was said. Such findings suggest that children are able to use word order to help them understand speech and that they have some of the abilities necessary for the production of multi-word utterances.

The lexical parameterisation hypothesis

Another important proposal about early language acquisition in the PPT approach is the lexical parameterisation hypothesis. This suggests that parameters are set for individual lexical items (i.e. the representation of words), rather than classes of items as in the original PPT (Borer, 1984; Wexler & Manzini, 1987). An advantage of this hypothesis is that idiosyncratic syntactic information about words is stored with other information about the word. This helps to explain how irregular words are used. In the same way, it helps to explain why in some languages there are different sets of operations for the same class of words. For example, in Japanese some anaphors operate in different ways to others.

The disadvantage of this theory is that it requires a syntactic entry for every word and clearly this involves much greater information processing demands than PPT. Newson (1990) has suggested that such demands would not occur if the syntactic information was generalised to all relevant lexical entries, and to all future entries. However, there needs to be further specification of why some items are generalised and others are not.

SUMMARY

In this chapter I have discussed various proposals about the possible links between pre-linguistic communication and syntax. We need to know more about these processes if we are to understand the way that children begin to use language. It would seem obvious that children are likely to utilise several sources of information to accomplish this transition. Another important point is that long before children start to produce a recognisable language they have clues, at least from prosody and semantics, which could help them to identify the syntax of the speech they hear.

I have also discussed the transition from telegraphic speech to a more conventional linguistic system that contains inflections and functional words. There is agreement that there is a qualitative difference between these two levels of linguistic sophistication from a variety of different perspectives (e.g. Maratsos & Chalkley, 1980; Radford, 1990; Olguin & Tomasello, in press). Inevitably there are different views about why this change should come about. Maratsos and Chalkley believe that this is a result of children analysing the relations inherent in the linguistic input; Radford believes that this is a result of the maturation of parameters; and Olguin and Tomasello suggest that there may be a stage of rote learning followed by an identification of categories which follow common patterns of use. In the next chapter a very different perspective about the acquisition of syntax is discussed; this has come from the work in cognitive science and seeks to explain such transitions by general principles of learning.

13

CONNECTIONIST MODELS OF LANGUAGE ACQUISITION

The previous two chapters have outlined the PPT approach to language acquisition. This chapter examines a new perspective about language acquisition involving connectionist networks. It has usually been assumed that the production of speech is the result of serial processes, so cognitive operations take place sequentially. Recently there has been increasing interest in the possibility that language and cognition involve parallel processes where there are several operations occurring at the same time. When networks of processors are linked together these are called *parallel distributed processors* (PDPs) or *connectionist networks*.

A connectionist network can acquire new responses by comparing the output it generates with a desired outcome. If the generated outcome is incorrect then the network can be adjusted to make the system more likely to be able to produce the correct outcome. In this way the responses of the system can change.

Information is transmitted through a system from one node to another (see Figure 13.1). When a node is activated it can in turn activate other nodes. In some cases the firing of a node may be governed by a threshold value. There is debate about the extent to which such systems mirror any neurological structure and the consensus is that for something like language acquisition there is little evidence for such matching. Thus, it is important to recognise that connectionist models can show what can be learnt using these systems, but it does not follow that the human brain operates in the same way.

The use of connectionist networks has reopened controversies about the role of learning in the language acquisition process. This is not a return to theories about reinforcement, but a view that cognitive systems using general operating principles can learn to process information in new ways

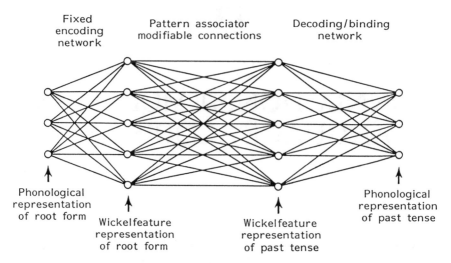

Figure 13.1 Rumelhart and McClelland's connectionist network (reproduced with permission from D. E. Rumelhart & J. L. McClelland (1986) On learning the past tense of English verbs. In J. L. McClelland, D. E. Rumelhart & the PDP Research Group (1986) *Parallel Distributed processing: Explorations in the Microstructure of Cognition*, vol. 2 *Psychological and Biological Models*. Cambridge, MA: MIT Press, p. 222)

and acquire new abilities. Such proposals have been roundly condemned as unworkable or unrealistic by some linguists. The first part of this chapter outlines several connectionist models. One is the already classic work by Rumelhart and McClelland on the acquisition of the past tense for verbs in English. The second part of the chapter examines the competition model which provides a more general proposal about applying connectionist networks to the processing and acquisition of language.

CONNECTIONIST MODELS OF THE ACQUISITION OF SYNTAX

Rumelhart and McClelland's Model of Past Tense Formation

Rumelhart and McClelland (1986) applied connectionist principles to the acquisition of one area of grammar, the past tense. They explicitly stated that their approach involved a system where the regularities of speech were acquired on the basis of general principles of learning. Such a proposal is in direct conflict with the idea that speech is processed and acquired by a set of cognitive operations which are specially adapted for language. In addition, Rumelhart and McClelland stated that their system did not involve any grammatical rules, nor did it process information in terms of the usual grammatical categories. This also is in direct conflict with the traditional psycholinguistic approach where morphemes provide a basis for the construction of grammars. Thus, the system involves a very different mechanism for the acquisition of grammar than that traditionally adopted, and it has attracted a great deal of attention because it is an important challenge to this tradition.

Observation of the acquisition of the past tense by English-speaking children has revealed that there appear to be three phases (Brown, 1973; Ervin, 1964; Kuczaj, 1977). In the first phase children correctly produce the past tense for a small group of both regular and irregular verbs (e.g. arrive–arrived, go–went). In the second phase children over-regularise the -ed ending, as a result of which incorrect forms of irregular verbs are produced (e.g. go–goed). These errors are eliminated in the third phase when correct forms are produced for both regular and irregular verbs, although there might be the production of words like "ated" and "wented".

Rumelhart and McClelland developed a computer simulation that could acquire the past tense of English verbs and which followed the pattern of errors produced by children. The input to the network consisted of a series of verbs in the present tense, and the output was either a correct or an incorrect form of the past tense. Nodes in the network could either be "on" or "off" (see Figure 13.1). Learning occurred through the system's comparing the output verb with the correct version. If the two versions differed then the weights on connections between nodes were adjusted so that the appropriate past tense form would be produced for the last incorrect example. As a result, the system acquired the ability to give high weights to patterns that were common in the input, such as adding -ed to the base. It is important to note that the comparison process between the teacher and the model does not correspond to the type of input children receive, although it is possible to argue that children might compare their own speech with models they have obtained from listening to adult speech—in this way the role of a teacher could be preserved. Such suggestions have the disadvantage of being cumbersome in the sense that a more efficient system would be one where the adults' speech had a direct influence on the system.

The model was able to learn to produce the past tense form from the present tense. The learning process produced over-regularisation, that is there were errors after an initial period of success, and this was similar to the development of verb use in children's speech.

Criticisms of Rumelhart and McClelland's model

The apparent success of the model provoked a detailed critique by Pinker and Prince (1988). Some of these criticisms addressed the design of the learning process, others involved more fundamental concerns, the most important of which are discussed. One of the major concerns of Pinker and Prince was that any analysis of language acquisition needs to consider the way that the formal rules of grammar change.

Pinker and Prince argued that the computer model imitated the pattern of verb development in children merely because of the type of words it was given. Rumelhart and McClelland initially provided 8 irregular and 2 regular verbs, then they exposed the model to 56 irregular and 344 regular verbs. The precise nature of verb use by parents in relation to developments in children's own verb use is still uncertain, but it would appear that the dramatic change in input given to the model is unlikely to occur in speech to children (Ullman, Pinker, Hollander, Prince & Roseen, 1989).

This criticism led Plunkett and Marchman (1991) to experiment with various inputs to their connectionist model. Different training sessions were used. Plunkett and Marchman found that the proportion of regular and irregular verbs did influence the type of past tense forms that were learnt. A high percentage of regular verbs resulted in these forms being learnt and a failure to learn the irregulars. A high percentage of irregulars resulted in a failure to learn the general pattern. Given a more reasonable distribution of regulars and irregulars the system did show U-shaped curves for particular verbs, but not a general phase when irregular verbs were over-regularised. Interestingly, this would seem to be the pattern that actually occurs during learning according to more recent and detailed analyses of speech development (Plunkett & Sinha, 1992).

Another criticism of Rumelhart and McClelland's network was its inability, at the end of training, to identify any output for a set of new verbs. Such an inability, as pointed out by Pinker and Prince, is uncharacteristic of children's responses. Children are usually prepared to generate new grammatical forms for a novel word even if it is incorrect. Pinker and Prince also noted that a rule-based system should have little problem in generating new grammatical forms, at the most simple this could be adding -ed to the new form. More recent models have avoided this criticism and Plunkett and Sinha (1992) have pointed out that rule-based systems have difficulty in accounting for the production of forms like "wented" and "ated" which involve over-regularisation of the irregular past tense form.

A serious problem with connectionist models as a realistic description of language acquisition is the assumption that children receive a correct version of any mistake. Even if children do receive subtle forms of feedback about grammatical errors (see Chapter 14), it is implausible to suggest that every mistake receives an overt correction. Parisi (1993) has argued that future connectionist models should adopt an ecological approach where the method of teaching corresponds to the information available to the child. One way of dealing with this problem is to suggest that a system could be designed to utilise more probabilistic information (see Bohannon, MacWhinney & Snow, 1990). A second way, mentioned by Parisi, is to suppose that merely hearing adult speech influences the production network. It might be that in processing speech children register the features of the input in a connectionist network, and this information may then be used to govern the production of words in an output network. Such a process is termed unsupervised learning. Alternatively, it could be that children make predictions about what words will be used in the speech they hear so that this provides a match between an expected and an actual value.

A general riposte to the detailed criticisms of Pinker and Prince and others is that a more elaborate and sophisticated model can overcome implementation problems (e.g. Clark, 1988; Bechtel & Abrahamsen, 1991). One idea is to incorporate morphological analysis into the system. Such proposals create further arguments. Pinker and Prince anticipate this idea and maintain that such an incorporation would result in a symbolic processing system, so that the operations of the system would be on symbols rather than distributed elements; they argue this would make it needless to have a connectionist network. An alternative view is that an element of symbol processing is an acceptable and useful part of a connectionist network (Norman, Rumelhart & LNR, 1985). Some in the connectionist camp regard such proposals as a needless return to innate constraints (Plunkett & Sinha, 1992). Thus, the disagreements and debates have become even more complex as there has been a differentiation of approaches within the connectionist camp.

More Models of Language Development

In recent years a number of investigators have made findings which illustrate the way that the output of connectionist models corresponds to some aspect of language development. This strengthens the argument that connectionist models involve a process that corresponds to the one used in language development. Plunkett and Sinha (1992) have developed an interesting model about concept formation and word learning of random dot images. The model shows a prototype effect, comprehension being in advance of production, and a vocabulary burst, together with under- and overextension.

Another interesting finding has come from the work of Elman (1991) who has designed a network which has a restricted initial memory that increases with learning, which he claims corresponds to the development of children's memory abilities. The surprising feature of this network was that it was able to acquire a grammar of an artificial language when a network with a larger initial memory was unsuccessful in the task. Elman attributed this to the possibility that a large initial memory meant that the input presented too many possible structures for analysis. Elman (1989) has also devised networks which are able to use distributional evidence to identify classes of words such as noun and verb, and can acquire grammatical dependencies which involve a correspondence between words which are some distance from one another in an utterance. Both these findings challenge the notion that only a rule-based system will be able to generate the syntax of a language.

An innovation by Marchman (1993) is the lesioning of connectionist networks to mimic the effects of brain damage and impairment. The random elimination of between 2% and 44% of the network at various points of the learning process produced learning curves similar to those of children with lesions. In addition, the network had greater problems in acquiring regular than irregular verb forms and this suggests that general learning problems can result in specific impairments, contrary to the position adopted by those who favour a rule-based account.

Pinker (1991) and Marcus, Ulman, Pinker et al. (1992) have claimed there is a dual processing mechanism for the acquisition of the past tense of verbs. Pinker suggests that the irregular forms of verbs are acquired by a rote learning mechanism and the regular forms by rule system. Furthermore it is proposed that the rule system will become operational due to the maturation of appropriate structures which are independent of vocabulary size. Marcus et al. present evidence that the reduction in the number of "bare stems" in children's speech marks the beginning of the use of a rule-based system.

In contrast Marchman and Bates (in press) favour a connectionist account where there is only one learning mechanism and to re-examine this issue they used information from parent reports on the CDI. Their findings reveal that there is a steady increase in the use of correct irregular past tense forms, and that there is also a period when there is a decline in the production of just the verb stem (as Marcus et al. describe). However, these changes also appear to be linked to verb vocabulary size, the decline occurring with a vocabulary of about 90 verbs. Thus, they argue that the acquisition of past tense forms may be the result of a single process, an argument that is likely to continue.

Are Connectionist Accounts Useful?

The work on connectionism has raised wider issues. Pinker and Prince (1988) believe that this type of approach must fail to provide an adequate model because it is arbitrary in relation to linguistic structure and therefore fails to process information at the appropriate level of detail.

This line of reasoning is also presented in general terms by Fodor and Pylyshyn (1988). At the heart of their argument is the belief that models which do not use symbolic representations cannot provide an adequate description of cognitive processes, such as those involving language. They use the following two sentences to illustrate their argument, "John loves the florist" and "The florist loves John". They propose that a symbolic account can explain why the two sentences are related, but have different meanings; in contrast they argue that connectionist models will fail to capture these relationships.

Another part of their case is that connectionist models are at an inappropriate level of analysis. They see the connectionist models as similar to attempts to study molecular changes in the brain and argue that both are unlikely to provide a basis for explaining cognitive operations. A similar analogy is used by Pinker and Prince who compare the rule-based account to computer software, and the connectionist account to electrical changes in the computer hardware.

In reply, it has been pointed out that rule-based systems have to account for exceptions by adding additional rules, in an ad hoc manner. It has also been suggested by Elman (1991) that the distinction between rule-based and non-rule is related to issues about the extent to which the rules are explicit or implicit, and that such distinctions are difficult to apply. In addition, with language, the rule system has been concerned with competence rather than performance. As a result the grammatical description fails to account for the actual performance of real speakers. In contrast, connectionist models attempt to describe the performance of an individual, and do not attempt to specify competence. Another possible advantage of connectionist accounts is that they describe a process and mechanism of acquisition, whereas rule-based accounts of behaviour tend to describe behaviour in terms of whether a rule is or is not present. For instance, Plunkett and Sinha (1992) claim that a single connectionist model can encompass rule-learning and rote-learning aspects of the acquisition of past tense forms. Rule-based accounts have to postulate a separate rote-learning process for irregular forms. There is another intriguing argument, that the distributed knowledge of connectionist accounts has the benefit of giving an explanation of why people follow grammatical rules, but are not conscious of them. This lack of consciousness would be expected from a distributed system, but not necessarily from a rule-based grammatical system.

These discussions about symbolic and connectionist models raise issues about the way any model is related to the original mental process. One response to the tension between traditional representational accounts of language and connectionist accounts, is to suggest that they both provide an approximate description of language processes. In these terms the representational accounts describe rules and principles which can account for the structure of language. In contrast, the connectionist account provides a summary of the mechanisms involved in processing information. Smolensky (1988) makes a similar type of distinction between symbolic systems and subsymbolic systems (i.e. connectionist).

Disputes occur when advocates of both approaches seek to claim that their descriptions are a more accurate account of psychological processes—in terms either of innate parameters or connectionist networks in the brain. Although both approaches claim that there is a biological basis for the operations they describe, in reality neither approach to language is grounded in neurobiology. Furthermore, in both cases criticisms of the models tend to lead to revisions, not to questioning of the fundamental assumptions of the approach.

THE COMPETITION MODEL

An Overview of the Competition Model

The competition model has been developed by Bates and MacWhinney (Bates & MacWhinney, 1987; MacWhinney, 1987; MacWhinney & Bates, 1989). The model contains two important assumptions. First, there is the assumption that the analysis of language should reflect the uses to which it is put. This is a functionalist approach which assumes that: "The forms of natural languages are created, governed, constrained, acquired and used in the service of communicative functions" (Bates & MacWhinney, 1987, p. 160). In other words communicative function and linguistic structure are seen as opposite faces of the same coin.

Second, Bates and MacWhinney wish to develop a model which provides a link between child language and cognitive science. This is associated with their belief that the processing of language is similar to other cognitive operations; a view in direct opposition with the idea that there are separate and special cognitive modules which are devoted to language.

It will be apparent by now that the communication of verbal messages is related to the syntactic structure of utterances. Furthermore, languages differ in the way that syntax is related to meaning. In English the identification of subject, verb and object is related to the order of the words. Consequently, use of this cue leads English speakers to interpret the anomalous and ungrammatical sentence "The eraser are chasing the boys", as the eraser being the subject and actor, despite such an action being very unlikely. The equivalent utterance said in Italian, tends to be interpreted in terms of the boys being the subject and actor, and it is they who do the chasing. In Italian word order is not a powerful cue to meaning, but the agreement between the subject ("boys") and the verb ("are") provides a strong cue for comprehension.

These differences illustrate a fundamental assumption of the competition model that the meaning of an utterance is inferred from the presence of both linguistic and non-linguistic cues. Unlike rule-based grammars it is supposed that these cues will operate in a probabilistic fashion to influence the production and comprehension of speech. Thus, in the previous example, for the English speakers, there is a conflict between several possibilities: erasers do not usually chase boys, the agreement between the eraser and the verb is incorrect, but the eraser is located in a position usually taken by the subject. In English this last cue appears to beat its competitors. It is proposed that a connectionist network provides a mechanism for competition between alternative interpretations to take place. Some networks have already been developed to model component processes (see MacWhinney & Bates, 1989).

The Structure of the Competition Model

In the competition model there is believed to be a functional level, which is similar to the deep structure of transformational grammar. Here the meanings and intentions of an utterance are represented. There is also a formal level, where the linguistic surface structure is represented. Originally it was supposed that these two levels are directly connected in a network, but revised versions of the model propose that there are intervening layers. The connectionist network is designed to allow cues to be combined in a non-linear fashion, the presence of one cue can affect the operation of a second cue by augmenting it, reversing it, or affecting it in other ways.

In Figure 13.2 it can be seen that when processing or producing an utterance there are a number of potential influences between the formal and functional levels. There are horizontal connections between items at the same level, which represent redundancies in the association between words and morphemes. There are also vertical connections between form and function.

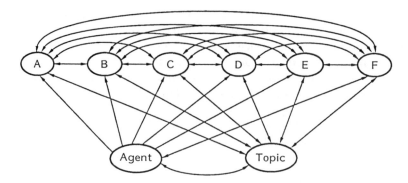

Figure 13.2 Connections in the competition model (reproduced with permission from B. MacWhinney & E. Bates (1989) *The CrossLinguistic Study of Sentence Processing*. Cambridge: Cambridge University Press)

These represent the connection between the intent to say something and the words that are used to convey this message. The strength of any pattern of connections will vary from language to language.

Bates and MacWhinney believe that their model can account for the variable nature of initial grammars across different languages. Unlike some of the PPT approaches (e.g. Hyams, 1986; Radford, 1990) they believe that the initial grammar used by children will vary from language to language, and this grammar will reflect the strength of cues present in speech to children. For example, data indicate that Turkish children respond to case morphology by 2 years, but appear to ignore word order until 4–5 years (Slobin & Bever, 1982). In contrast English children, who are learning a language in which word order is important and morphology less important, at first appear to ignore morphology and respond to word order. Bates and Mac-Whinney argue that these differences reflect the functional importance of word order and morphology in the two systems of communication.

It is supposed that the way cues assist language acquisition changes with development (McDonald, 1989). Initially *cue availability* is a major determinant of the child's use of language. Thus, the proportion of occasions when a cue is present in appropriate situations will influence the linguistic structure of children's early speech. Then *cue reliability* becomes more influential, this is the proportion of occasions when the cue leads to the correct interpretation. This is the basis for progress during the first years of language development. Sometime in the early school years, *conflict validity* influences the fine tuning of the linguistic system. A conflict occurs when two cues make different predictions about the interpretation of an utterance, so that conflict validity is the proportion of times a particular cue is accurate when it is in competition with other cues.

Cross-linguistic research provides support for the model. It is possible to examine the strength of cues in terms of their ease of detection and ease of computation. These will affect when and how the grammatical form is acquired. In Hungarian, case affixes which have a strong vowel that can easily be identified are acquired before those with a consonant cluster that is harder to identify (MacWhinney, Pleh & Bates, 1985). It is also supposed that the vertical connections between form and function will not be established until a function is understood and represented by the child. For example, understanding of past and future events needs to occur before the appropriate tenses can be acquired.

Lexical representations and syntax

In the competition model a lexical representation provides details about the auditory properties of a word and details about its semantic functions. The semantic properties concern information about particular events or objects, experiences and so on, which can vary considerably from person to person. In contrast, semantic concepts are the result of the extraction of a common core from different experiences and this provides the basis for the concept of particular words.

In the model it is assumed that there are four basic types of lexical items, these are nominals, verbals, operators (i.e. adjectives and adverbs), and connectives (e.g. and, or, but). A lexical representation contains information about a word's *valence description*. This consists of details about the way a lexical item is connected to roles it can have in an utterance. Thus, the valence description provides information about the way a lexical item combines with other words to form larger units, and the specification of the type of item that can fill the roles. For each lexical representation at least one role is identified. Thus, a lexical representation of a verb will usually specify that it requires a subject. MacWhinney (1989a, b) suggests that a number of roles are identified, these consist of subject, object, and indirect (i.e. "toy" is an indirect object in the utterance "Jessica gave Nicola a toy"). Other roles operate in relation to groups of words, a head concerns the relation between a noun and its adjective, a complement concerns the relation between a verb and the clauses which act as objects or subjects. Using these and other roles MacWhinney suggests that a grammar can be built up from the redundancy and specifications contained in the lexical representations of words; in other words acquired by experience. It is interesting to note that in some ways this proposal is similar to the lexical parameterisation hypothesis. What is different from a parameter setting approach is that the competition model does not suppose that there is the same detailed innate knowledge about the types of grammar which are available.

Meaning and competition

The competition model also describes the way words are selected when speaking and how comprehension operates. According to MacWhinney (1989b) during speech words are selected by a process of competition. One level of competition concerns classification issues. For example, MacWhinney suggests a person may distinguish between a "cup", "mug" and "demitasse" (a type of small cup) on the basis of size, thickness, and cylindricality. If the object being referred to is large, thick and cylindrical it will be called a mug. Objects which are ambiguous will be classified according to the type and strength of the cues available; as a result a very small cylindrical cup would often be called a demitasse, even though it is mug-shaped.

In comprehension another type of competition occurs which involves choosing which is the appropriate meaning from a number of possibilities. "She has a beautiful mug" has two competing meanings, a beautiful cup-like object or a beautiful face. MacWhinney suggests that when a word is heard all the different possible interpretations are activated, and all are in competition. The interpretation with the strongest cue strength wins. Thus, "She has a beautiful mug which is kept away from the children" would result in a decision to interpret "mug" as something to drink from.

Experiments with adults support the idea that the interpretation of a word reflects the content of the whole utterance. People tend to interpret "container" differently in the following two utterances: (i) "The Coca-Cola poured all over the table, and then the container was empty" and (ii) "The apples rolled all over the table, and then the container was empty". In the first utterance "container" is usually interpreted as meaning bottle, whereas in the second utterance the same word is interpreted as referring to a basket (Anderson, Reynolds, Schallert & Goetz, 1977).

The competition model provides an intuitively appealing description of the way we process speech. What is lacking from the model is an explanation of how the material is encoded into a connectionist network. This is the major problem for all models of production and comprehension.

Evaluating the Competition Model

Bates and MacWhinney are explicit in the way they wish their model to be judged. They see their model as providing a framework which cannot be destroyed by a single finding, since such findings would typically lead to further modification of the details of the model. Instead, they propose that the success of the model should be judged in terms of its coherence, its ability to generate further research, and its ability to provide a satisfactory account vis-à-vis other theories. This is much like the approach in PPT, where the model is seen as a proposal for development rather than a final product which can be tested. Thus, in all cases, there is no quick and easy way to establish the validity of the models. Instead, there has to be a long-term research strategy which will result either in further modifications to the model, revisions to the model, or the demise of the model because of the contradictions inherent within it and the difficulty in testing the proposals.

SUMMARY

This chapter has outlined connectionist ideas which have often been regarded as in direct conflict with the PPT approach to language acquisition. The PPT approach assumes an innate knowledge of language and has a rule-based representational system. This approach has difficulty in accounting for the gradual development of new grammatical forms. In contrast, the connectionist approach usually assumes a general purpose learning mechanism, a system which does not contain formal rules, and which can provide a mechanism to account for change in grammatical ability. Between these "pure" forms intermediate positions are possible. Indeed, there are now attempts to use connectionist networks to provide modular descriptions of PPT.

The competition model is an interesting application of connectionist and linguistic principles to the language acquisition process. The competition model gives emphasis to the possibility that cues from the input allow children to acquire the grammatical structure of their home language. The value of the competition model is that it is beginning to provide an alternative explanation to that of PPT. Interestingly, in both cases there is the realisation that the study of the acquisition of different languages is essential either for an understanding of what parameters are set in what order, or for an accumulation of evidence of the ways that the cues present in a language influence its acquisition.

Much is still uncertain about the value of connectionist work. At the very least these studies force us to examine the type of information and processing that occurs in language acquisition and development. The work also forces us to look in more detail at previous observations and claims—as witnessed by the debate about past tense acquisition. We have seen that most of the technical objections about Rumelhart and McClelland's model have been overcome. Connectionist models can now mimic the process of children learning past tenses. The lack of consensus now concerns the value of such approaches.

So far most networks have modelled particular aspects of language acquisition, which produces very useful models which can summarise the material about the relevant process. However, it remains an open question about how far this can be taken when there are attempts to model different aspects of syntax together with semantic, phonological, and pragmatic processes. If such models work then this will represent an advance in the way of conceptualising children's language, but there is the danger that such attempts will become meaningless because at each stage there are a number of possible alternative ways to construct a system, and so with increasing the size of a model the uncertainty will increase in a corresponding manner.

14

SPEECH TO CHILDREN

During the 1960s it was usually supposed by psycholinguists that speech to children (A–C speech, sometimes called motherese or adultese) was in many ways similar to that between adults (A–A speech). For example, Fodor (1966, p. 109) claimed that "the language environment of the child does not differ in any useful way from that of an adult…it must contain a very substantial number of false starts, slips, grammatical mistakes and so forth". Chomsky (1965) supposed that "a record of natural speech will show numerous false starts, deviations from rules, changes in plan… The problem…for the child…is to determine from the data of performance the underlying system of rules". Such claims implied that language acquisition must be very difficult, thus strengthening the argument that some innate capacity is necessary for the process to take place. Chapters 10 and 11 have presented explanations of language acquisition in this tradition. A contrasting tradition which seeks to show that speech to children helps language acquisition is presented in this chapter.

The claims about the complexity of adult speech to children came under close scrutiny during the early 1970s. A number of investigators described the ways in which speech to young children is simplified. These studies are reviewed in the first section of this chapter. Naturally enough, such findings led to questions about whether or not such speech aids language development. As the second section shows, it has not been possible to obtain a clear answer to this question. The third section describes patterns of social interaction in families who are not made up of middle-class Western members. Here we see that the adaptations made in middle-class Western families may not be universal. Such findings question the importance of speech modifications for the acquisition of language. The final section considers the possibility that adults may provide different responses to children's grammatically correct and incorrect utterances. These responses, according to learnability theory, would be of vital assistance in the language acquisition process. Here again we see controversy about whether such information is universal and whether it helps language acquisition.

THE MODIFICATIONS IN SPEECH TO CHILDREN

If you listen to adults talking to young children it is clear that their speech is not like normal adult-to-adult conversation (A–A speech). Two of the first investigations to document this behaviour were conducted by Phillips (1972) and by Snow (1973). The typical paradigm employed in these and other similar studies was to compare a mother speaking to her child with the same mother in conversation with another adult (usually the experimenter). These utterances were then written down for later analysis. Transcribing utterances is a time-consuming process since it can easily take an hour to transcribe 5 or 10 minutes of conversation.

One of the most commonly used measures of grammatical complexity has been the MLU (mean length of utterance, see page 153). This measure has been assumed to provide a rough indication of grammatical complexity, because a higher MLU is associated with longer utterances and with a higher probability of the utterance containing more sophisticated grammatical expressions (subclauses, connectives, and so on). In fact, this assumption has been questioned (Hickey, 1988), but we can accept that the measure has some limited validity for English at least.

As can be seen from Table 14.1 the MLU of A–C speech is much shorter than that found in A–A speech. In addition, other measures of grammatical complexity show that A–C speech is simpler than A–A speech. Such measures include the number of verbs per utterance and the number of conjunctions. In both cases a higher incidence of these would be expected to occur with more complex (and longer) utterances. Speech to children also tends to be in the present tense—this means that young children do not have to be troubled with verb forms that refer to past and future events.

In addition, A–C speech appears to be easier for children to process than A–A speech (see Table 14.1). One characteristic often noted by those who transcribe speech is that it is very much easier to identify when an utterance to a child begins and ends; in A–A speech pauses are interspersed through the utterance. Any model of language would predict that slower speech would be less difficult for children to process, and this is precisely what they receive. Furthermore, A–C contains a high proportion of repetitions. As a result, children often have a "second chance" to process what is said to them. In addition, these characteristics (slower rate, more repetitions, and exaggerated form) all appear in maternal signs used with children who are deaf (Masataka, 1992).

Table 14.1 A comparison of A–C with A–A speech

	A–C speech	A–A speech	
Syntax			
MLU	6.5 (to 10 yr olds)	9.3	Snow (1973)
	3.7	8.5	Phillips (1972)
Transformations of verbs	95% present tense	–	Snow (1977)
Verbs/utterance	0.8	1.5	Phillips (1972)
Percent of utterances with conjunctions	20%	70%	Remick (1976)
Content			
Modifiers/utterance	0.7	2.6	Phillips (1972)
Use of single words	15%	–	Broen (1972)
Type–token ratio	0.35	0.52	Phillips (1972)
Processing			
Percent of pauses at end of sentence	75%	51%	Broen (1972)
Speed, words/min.	70	132	Broen (1972)
Repetitions	18%	–	Snow (1977)
Emphasis of names	50%	–	Messer (1981)

The content of A–C speech is more simple than A–A speech. As has already been pointed out, A–C speech is usually in the present tense and concerns the "here and now", that is the things children can see or events that are happening (see also Chapter 4). A–C speech contains more concrete nouns (nouns which do not concern abstract entities), has fewer modifiers (adjectives and adverbs), and has a lower type–token ratio (the latter measure is calculated by dividing the total number of words that are different by the total number of words—as a result the higher the type–token ratio the greater the range of vocabulary). In addition, there is a tendency to use proper names rather than pronouns (Conti-Ramsden, 1989). All of these features make the content of A–C speech less difficult to understand than A–A speech.

Another notable feature of A–C speech is its unusual vocabulary. Ferguson (1964) pointed out that a variety of languages (English, Spanish, Arabic, Comachi, Gilyak, and Syrian) contain special words for use with children. These words refer to kin names, nicknames, body parts, body functions, animals, games, and taboo subjects. The words typically involve a simplification of difficult consonants, for example the use of "tummy" rather than "stomach"; and the reduplication of parts of words, for example "dada" and "mama".

Ferguson argued that these modifications make it easier for young children to produce words. An interesting example of this in English is the shortened forms of some names, as in "Bob" for "Robert", "Bill" for "William"; not only has the name been shortened, but an easy to say consonant has been substituted for a more difficult one. Another feature of the baby talk in English is the use of the -ey and -ie endings with proper nouns, as in horsey and doggie; such a device may alert young children to a grammatical class. Both types of modification could help children to start to use words.

The complexity of A–C speech appears to change with children's communicative and cognitive abilities. Mothers use the most simple speech to infants who are about 8–12 months old (Sherrod, Friedman, Crawley, Drake & Devieux, 1977; Murray, Johnson & Peters, 1990; Stern et al., 1983; Phillips, 1972). Phillips suggested that this occurs because prior to this age children are not able to understand the content of speech, and after this age they become more able to deal with increasingly complex speech. It would also seem, from comparisons of children with different capacities, that adult speech is related to children's language skills rather than to their chronological age or cognitive ability (Cross, Johnson-Morris & Nienhuys, 1980), and in particular children's expressive abilities (Whitehurst et al., 1988). Furthermore, the precise nature of A–C speech appears to differ with first-borns and later-borns, and depends on whether or not siblings are present (Pappas-Jones & Adamson, 1987; Hoff-Ginsburg, 1992).

THE EFFECT OF A–C SPEECH

A very basic aspect of language input is the amount of adult speech to young children. In a number of studies, a positive correlation between the amount of maternal speech and later language development has been reported. The importance of this relation has been confirmed by Huttenlocher, Haight, Bryk, Seltzer and Lyons (1991). Their study revealed that the amount of maternal utterances at 16 months was related to a faster rate of vocabulary growth between 14 and 26 months. The rate of vocabulary growth was calculated by using a hierarchical linear model, rather than the simple subtraction model used in most previous studies. In addition, the order of acquisition of different types of words in the children's vocabulary was related to the relative frequency of these words in the mothers' speech. Such findings would be predicted by most theories of language acquisition.

As we have seen, adults simplify their speech to young children. This raises the question of whether such simplifications help or hinder language acquisition. Sometimes it has been suggested that these simplifications are of no help to children and may even be detrimental as A–C speech provides an inappropriate grammatical model (Newport, Gleitman & Gleitman, 1977). In contrast, other research workers believe that simplification is likely to assist language development. What has emerged from over a decade of work is that it is surprisingly difficult to obtain an answer to this controversy.

Scepticism about the Benefits of A–C Speech

A notable publication in the controversy about A–C speech was written by Newport, Gleitman and Gleitman (1977). These authors argued against the idea that A–C speech helps language acquisition. As A–A speech predominantly consists of declarative sentences (87%), they reasoned that the most logical language teaching strategy would be first to concentrate on teaching declaratives. In fact, A–C speech has a more equal distribution of questions, declaratives and imperatives (44%, 30%, and 18% respectively), and therefore appears to be a less than ideal model. Newport, Gleitman and Gleitman also argued that on some measures A–C speech seems to be more complex than A–A speech, although the authors admit that the psychological reality of such measures is difficult to establish. For example, questions could be considered as more complex than declaratives because they involve movement of the auxiliary verb to the beginning of the utterance (e.g. "Can you eat?"), despite which questions are more frequent in speech to children. Another line of argument developed by Newport, Gleitman and Gleitman was that the characteristics of A–C speech are the result of a need to communicate effectively with an inattentive listener rather than a teaching strategy.

Newport, Gleitman and Gleitman presented findings from their longitudinal study which suggested that modifications in A–C speech do not aid language development. The study involved measuring the mothers' speech at one age (Time 1), and measuring the children's language at a later age (Time 2). Correlations were then calculated between the measures to see if there was a relation between maternal speech and later child language. Newport, Gleitman and Gleitman studied 15 children who were divided into three age groups: 12–15 months, 18–21 months and 24–27 months. The actual analysis was based on 100 utterances of mothers' speech.

Gain scores were calculated, that is the difference between the children's language ability at Time 1 and Time 2. In addition, the child's age and linguistic ability at Time 1 were taken into account when calculating correlations. The measures of maternal speech included the frequency of: declaratives, yes–no questions, imperatives, wh-questions, interjections, deixis (i.e. utterances which indicate an entity—using this, that, here, there, etc.), expansions (utterances which repeat and add to the previous child utterance) repetitions, and MLU. No significant correlations were found between these measures and three measures of children's later speech at Time 2: MLU; the number of noun-phrases, and the number of verb-phrases per utterance. Newport, Gleitman and Gleitman interpreted these findings as showing that children's general linguistic development was unaffected by the properties of the speech they heard.

Although no relationships were found with general measures of linguistic development, several specific correlations were identified. These were interpreted as indicating that A–C speech may assist the acquisition of limited and specific features of a language. For example, the frequency with which mothers used verbal auxiliaries in the first position of an utterance (e.g. "*Can* you kiss her") was related to the later use of verbal auxiliaries in children's speech (auxiliary verbs are ones which can be attached to main verbs such as *am* or *have*, as in "I am eating"). Newport, Gleitman and Gleitman argued that when the speech input corresponds to biases in children (attention to the beginning of utterances) then A–C speech may assist in the acquisition of particular aspects of language.

Controversy about A–C Speech

The conclusions from Newport, Gleitman and Gleitman's study have been questioned by Furrow, Nelson and Benedict (1979). They criticised them for having a sample of children with a range of ages, which creates methodological problems as linguistic changes (such as increase in MLU) may not be equally likely at all points in development. If this is the case then statistical adjustments by the use of partial correlations will not be satisfactory. For these reasons Furrow, Nelson and Benedict conducted a study where each of their seven children had an MLU of 1 and all were of a similar age.

Children were seen at 18 and 27 months in their homes. Overall there were 20 significant correlations between maternal speech at 18 months to later child speech, and 11 between maternal speech and child speech at the older age. Furrow, Nelson and Benedict interpret this as indicating that earlier speech had a greater influence on child language than concurrent speech.

The significant correlations appeared to be due to less complex maternal speech (fewer pronouns and more yes–no questions) being associated with faster linguistic progress as assessed by MLU. In contrast, more complex maternal speech, as assessed by the number of words, number of pronouns, number of verbs, and number of copulas, was related to children having a smaller MLU.

Furrow, Nelson and Benedict concluded that the environment must be considered a significant contribution to all aspects of the language learning process. They also suggested that a simple style of maternal speech was positively related to faster linguistic development, and that the benefits of simple speech came from successful communication.

A further paper by Gleitman, Newport and Gleitman (1984) continued the controversy. They accepted some of the criticisms of their work, but also criticised Furrow, Nelson and Benedict for using a small sample in which the receptive language could have varied (i.e. even though all the children had an MLU of 1, some could have better understanding of speech than others).

Gleitman, Newport and Gleitman reanalysed their data in a similar way to before, but only considered two age groups in an effort to reduce the range of ages and linguistic ability. In their analysis they conducted split half correlations to establish whether there was consistency in two halves of the data. They discarded any correlations which were not significant in both halves. This questionable strategy meant that some significant correlations were ignored (i.e. those that occurred in only one half of the data). The overall findings were similar to before.

Counter-arguments were produced in another paper by Furrow and Nelson (1986). Furrow and Nelson stated that Gleitman, Newport and Gleitman had misinterpreted the case for A–C speech by their emphasis on syntactic complexity. Instead, Furrow and Nelson proposed that children gain access to grammar through meaning, and therefore simplifications in maternal speech aid the acquisition of syntax by making utterances easier to understand. As a result, Furrow and Nelson claim that there is not necessarily a direct relation between forms present in A–C speech and language acquisition.

Further Studies of A–C Speech

Other studies have also been conducted to investigate the effects of A–C speech. These have produced a mixed set of findings. An interesting study by Barnes, Gutfreund, Satterly and Wells (1983) involved automatic recordings of speech in homes, using a radio microphone. At Time 1 the 32 children were very close to an MLU of 1.5 morphemes and there was a range of ages with the mean being 2 years. Nine months later the observations at Time 2 were obtained.

Adult MLU at Time 1 was not significantly correlated with any later child language measure. Somewhat surprisingly adult directives were found to be related to child MLU, semantic complexity (the number of different meanings in a child's speech) and syntactic complexity (the number of clause constituents in an utterance such as subject, auxiliary verb, etc.). Barnes et al. suggested that directives may be important at this stage of linguistic development because they will ensure some response. Another finding was that adult extensions of child utterances were related to later child MLU; Barnes et al. suggested that this might be because a shared conversation is established. In addition, various complex relationships were found that involved auxiliary verbs. Lastly, the amount of maternal speech was found to be related to later child MLU and to semantic complexity.

Despite the finding of a reasonable degree of relationship between adult and later child speech, Barnes et al. are cautious about regarding this as the product of a causal relationship. They show that a number of the adult measures at Time 1 were also correlated with measures of child speech at Time 1. Their conclusion was that language learning is strongly determined by the characteristics of the learner, although the nature of the input does have some impact on this process.

An investigation by Scarborough and Wyckoff (1986) failed to find any effect of maternal speech. They examined maternal speech to nine children who were 2 years old, and its relationship to the children's linguistic ability at 30 months. Of the 85 correlations that were calculated only 2 were significant. However, the small sample size limited the power of the statistical tests, and made the detection of significant findings much less likely.

A study of younger children has revived the case for the effectiveness of A–C speech. Murray, Johnson and Peters (1990) report that a lower maternal MLU at 9 months and a higher number of maternal utterances predicted more advanced receptive language at 18 months. Child characteristics (being a girl and, surprisingly, having a lower expressive ability at 9 months) were also related to more advanced expressive language at the older age. Murray, Johnson and Peters speculate that other studies, which have observed older children, may not have chosen the most appropriate age to detect the effects of a shorter MLU. They believe that simplified speech may be especially important at this age because infants are just starting to comprehend speech.

Experimental Studies of the Effect of Speech to Infants

Over the years there have been a variety of studies conducted for a variety of reasons to examine experimentally whether adult responses to child utterances aid language development. One of the first studies was conducted by Cazden (1965) who found no significant difference between three types of experience: a condition which received expansions, a condition which received well-formed replies which were not expansions, and a control group. Similarly, Feldman (1971) failed to find a significant difference in child language as the result of using expansions and move-ons (an adult utterance which did not repeat the child's utterance). It should be noted that in both cases the experimenters were not concerned with providing a differential response to well- and ill-formed utterances, a topic dealt with in the last section of this chapter.

A more successful training study was carried out by Nelson, Carskaddon and Bonvillian (1973) who compared the effects of training sessions involving the provision of: (i) recasts, which were either expansions of children's incomplete utterances, or the recasting of correct utterances into a new form; (ii) new sentences which had a different content to the previous child utterance; and (iii) a control group. The 32–40-month-old children were seen twice a week for 20 minutes over 11 weeks. The recast condition did better than the controls in a post-test by using more verbs and more auxiliary verbs, and they were better able to imitate utterances. Although the study found an effect of adult response, it does not exactly map onto the responses of adults in natural conversations. Similarly, Nelson (1977) provided recasts for two different forms of syntax and found that there was more use of the form in the target condition. Interestingly, Farrar (1990) reports that the adding of missing morphemes to child (C) utterances by mothers (M) (e.g. C "phone ring", M "the phone is ring*ing*") was related to the acquisition of the same morphemes later on in development, while the use of expansions (e.g. C "the phone", M "yes the phone is ringing") and topic continuations (e.g. C "the phone", M "yes pick it up") were related to the acquisition of other morphemes.

Summary

The majority of studies have failed to find strong support for the effects of A–C speech. But all studies find some relationship between adult speech and later language development. Unfortunately there are a number of methodological issues which make interpretation of the findings problematical. The first is that all the studies have implicitly assumed that the more frequently a mother simplifies her speech the faster will be her child's acquisition of language. This may not in fact be the case, it could be that children need to be exposed to a certain degree of simplification, but that the precise degree of simplification is not important. The important comparison might be between parents who modify their speech, and parents who do not. In the next section I will discuss some studies which have a bearing on this issue.

A second, more general, issue is that even if all the studies had found significant correlations, this would not mean that one could conclude that A–C speech causes faster language development. The classic problem with studies which employ correlations is that they cannot be used to establish the direction of causality. It is perfectly possible that children who are more linguistically able would affect their mother's speech at Time 1. This could result in a spurious correlation between maternal speech at Time 1 and children's speech at Time 2 (see Figure 14.1). Some effort to minimise this effect has been attempted in most of the studies, although in practice it is difficult to be sure that such an effect was not present.

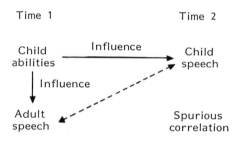

Figure 14.1 Problems with longitudinal studies

An additional problem has been the large number of correlations which have been calculated in these studies. The more correlations that are calculated the more likely one is to obtain a spurious correlation just by chance. As Schwartz and Camarata (1985) have pointed out, it would be far better to conduct factor analyses on the maternal and child speech measures, and to use the information from such an analysis to reduce the number of correlations that are calculated (Barnes et al. adopted this methodology).

Lastly, it may well be that combining all speech together for the purposes of analysis is an inappropriate strategy (Harris, 1993). The studies described in Chapter 4 indicated that not all experiences are equally likely to result in vocabulary growth, in particular the use of speech during episodes of joint attention appears to be particularly effective. In the same way it may well be that certain verbal input, in particular contexts, is needed to facilitate children's language development.

UNIVERSAL PROCESSES?

Most of the research on adult–infant social interaction has been conducted on white, middle-class, Western mothers and infants. Without counter-evidence it has been easy to assume that behaviours observed in these samples reflect universal patterns. If such patterns are not found to be universal then this would destroy the argument that A–C speech is essential for language acquisition. Is language acquisition and development possible without such modifications?

The assumption of universality has been challenged by a number of reports about childrearing practices in other cultures (see also Chapter 1). In reviewing this material Ochs and Schieffelin (1984; Schieffelin, 1990) have suggested that social interaction between infants and adults reflects cultural attitudes and beliefs about children. They suggest that Western culture adapts behaviour and objects to the capacities of infants, and infants are treated as if they have the capacity to engage in communication. By way of contrast they draw attention to quite different childrearing practices in Samoa and in Papua New Guinea.

Samoan society is highly stratified according to a person's rank and various features of childrearing practice appear to reflect this. During the first 6 months infants stay close to their mothers, but are often looked after by lower status members of the household, such as older siblings. Infants of this age are not treated as conversational partners, but are usually "spoken to" in songs or rhythmical high-pitched vocalisations. Speech tends to be directed at the infant in a loud and sharp voice, and adults do not simplify their speech towards infants.

Another feature of Samoan interactions is that low ranking individuals, including children, are expected to adapt to the needs of higher ranking individuals. Consequently, caretakers rarely attempt to clarify children's unintelligible utterances. Instead children are expected to make the clarification for the adult's benefit. In addition, Ochs and Schieffelin claim that Samoans believe that actions are open to one interpretation only. As a result, caregivers tend to treat children's utterances as either intelligible or not, and if they are not intelligible then it is for the child to clarify them. These observations draw attention to the diversity of childrearing practices that are employed in human societies and challenge assumptions that particular features of adult–infant interaction found in the West are important to later communicative development.

The other pattern of childrearing described by Ochs and Schieffelin involves the Kaluli of Papua New Guinea. Their society assigns an important role to conversation. Conversations take place against a complex pattern of relationships based on obligation and reciprocity. Ochs and Schieffelin state that acquiring language and independence is an important goal of Kaluli childrearing. However, the Kaluli do not talk about the feelings or thoughts of others, a norm which has consequences for childrearing practices.

The Kaluli infant's mother is the primary caregiver and she is responsive, attentive and constantly present. Infants are not treated as conversational partners because of the belief that they are not capable of understanding verbal exchanges. As a result, few utterances are addressed to infants, and those that are involve calling his or her name or the use of expressive vocalisations. Although the mothers do not talk *to* their infants they will talk *for* their infants. For example, if another child addresses an infant, the mother of the infant will reply in a high-pitched, nasalised voice. In these cases, the mother's speech will be appropriate for the older child, not similar to the baby speech used in Western homes. Unlike the attempts at conversation in Western families, the speech of the Kaluli mother appears unrelated to the activities of the infant. Ochs and Schieffelin suggest that these exchanges are designed to foster social relationships rather than to teach language. Another feature of these early interactions is that Kaluli mothers do not engage in mutual gaze. Instead, they usually put their infants in a position where they can observe, and be observed, by others.

When the infants are between 6 and 12 months old, adults start to speak to them using short utterances. Imperatives are often used and the infants are expected to comply with the instructions. Questions are used infrequently and tend to be rhetorical with no verbal response being required. These limited verbal interactions continue until children start to use the words for "mother" and "breast", at which point it is considered that the children can be taught to speak. Teaching involves providing a model utterance and instructing the child to repeat it. Such utterances are usually concerned with the social uses of language rather than object labelling. These model utterances are not modified according to the child's linguistic ability. In fact, mistakes by the child are corrected by adults in an apparent effort to make the child a more competent speaker. It is worth noting that this strategy appears to be similar to the informant presentation of language in learnability theory (see page 170 of Chapter 10). Such findings might be taken to suggest that modified A–C speech is not necessary when other forms of interaction and feedback are available to assist language development.

Some caution should be exercised before concluding on the basis of these cross-cultural studies that modified A–C speech is not important for language acquisition. It should be remembered that modification of speech to infants appears to occur in a wide variety of cultures (Ferguson, 1964); that these modifications are made even by children of 3 or 4 years of age (Shatz & Gelman, 1973); and that the modifications appear finely tuned to infants' perceptual capacities (Fernald et al., 1989). Furthermore, doubts have been expressed about the accuracy of these cross-cultural studies because of the lack of quantitative data (Harris, 1992).

Given these cross-cultural studies of social interaction, what can we conclude about the role of A–C speech in developing language? To begin with, it would appear that by 2 years of age infants have not only become sensitive to verbal and non-verbal communication, but this sensitivity reflects the pattern of communication that occurs in the culture to which the child belongs. This latter process occurs because the communication of adults to children reflects the wider assumptions of the culture. It would also appear that the acquisition of language is not necessarily through adaptation to the child's needs, but through an emphasis on certain patterns of culturally-appropriate exchanges. Different cultures emphasise different functions to which language can be put, and these functions are emphasised in speech to children.

MISTAKES AND FEEDBACK

Do Children Receive Feedback in any Form?

It is often assumed, following the work of Brown and Hanlon (1970; see Chapter 10) that children do not receive feedback about grammatical errors. This assumption has had important consequences, because of the perceived need to postulate powerful innate processes which will allow language acquisition to proceed despite the absence of feedback. Such assumptions can be seen in most of the work in the PPT tradition.

This issue was reopened in a study by Hirsch-Pasek, Treiman and Schneiderman (1984). They coded adult feedback using the same measures as Brown and Hanlon, but also recoded maternal repetition of children's utterances (this included all forms of repetition and expansion). There was a replication of Brown and Hanlon's findings and, more interestingly, the findings also revealed that for 2-year-old children 21% of ill-formed utterances were followed by a repetition, while 12% of well-formed utterances were followed by a repetition. An ill-formed utterance had one or more of the following features: incorrect word order, incorrect matching of elements, for example "they is mad", or missing obligatory articles. Thus, at this age (but not at the older ages) grammatical errors received a special response from mothers, and inspection suggested that the repetitions often contained a correction of the mistake.

Demetras, Post and Snow (1986) provided a more detailed analysis of this issue with a smaller sample of four children. They employed a broad category of repetition similar to Hirsch-Pasek, Treiman and Schneiderman's, but also used a category of clarification questions that involved asking about what had been said (e.g. C "elevator", M "it's an elevator isn't it?", or "you went where?"). Any other utterances were considered to be a *move-on*, that is an utterance that kept the conversation moving. Ill-formed utterances were usually followed by a clarification question, and Demetras and colleagues argue that because clarification questions involve a break in the flow of conversation this might be frustrating to the child and be a form of negative feedback. Well-formed utterances were usually followed by a move-on and so the conversation would smoothly continue. In addition, there was an interesting difference in the forms of repetitions that followed well- and ill-formed utterances. Well-formed utterances were most often followed by an exact repetition, while ill-formed utterances were most often followed by a repetition which extended the information in the child's utterance.

A further study by Penner (1987) obtained similar findings to the two previous ones. Penner investigated children who had an MLU of between 2 and 3.5 words. Her categories of maternal replies also included *expansions* which involved the repetition of child utterance with additional words. Ill-formed utterances received more expansions (15%) than well-formed utterances (5%). Another category used by Penner was topic extension. Well-formed utterances received more *topic extensions* (36%) than ill-formed utterances (25%); topic extensions involved continued speech about a topic (similar to move-ons).

Bohannon and Stanowicz (1988) replicated and extended the previous findings. Their study involved data from an existing study of the speech of mothers and fathers to their 27-month-old children, and students interacting with a 30-month-old child. Three types of child error were identified: semantic, syntactic, and phonological. The child utterances were coded as having single errors or multiple errors.

The analyses of children's speech revealed that semantic errors were infrequent and only the parents responded to these with an overt correction. The main analyses concerned differences in the response to well-formed, ill-formed syntactic and ill-formed phonological utterance of the children. These are given in Table 14.2. An interesting finding was that all the adults were more likely to respond with a correct version to a single error than to a multiple error and the investigators argued that this would help children to pinpoint the nature of their error.

It was estimated that about a third of the children's flawed speech (syntactic errors and mispronunciations) received some form of differential feedback

Table 14.2 Responses to well- and ill-formed child utterances

Percentage of adult responses to each type of child utterance	
Child utterance	Adult response
Ill-formed	3% Exact repetitions
(syntactic)	15% Recasts and expansions
	21% Clarification questions
Well-formed	12% Exact repetitions
	10% Recasts and expansions
	8% Clarification questions

(recasts, expansions, clarification questions). Moreover, over 70% of the recasts and expanded utterances followed ill-formed utterances. In contrast, over 90% of the exact repetitions followed well-formed utterances. The authors suggest that these patterns of responses would help the child to distinguish reliably between ill- and well-formed utterances. They also argue that recasts not only provide the child with information that utterances may be incorrect, but also often provide the correct version.

Summary

We have seen that over these different studies there is consistency in the finding that children's ill-formed utterances tend to be followed by more repetitions and expansions (Hirsch-Pasek, Treiman and Schneiderman, 1984; Demetras, Post & Snow, 1986; Penner, 1987; Bohannon & Stanowicz, 1988), by more clarification questions (Demetras, Post & Snow, 1986; Bohannon & Stanowicz, 1988), and by recasts (Bohannon & Stanowicz, 1988). In contrast, well-formed utterances tend to be followed by more exact repetitions (Demetras, Post & Snow, 1986; Bohannon & Stanowicz, 1988), more move-ons (Demetras, Post & Snow, 1986), and more topic extensions (Penner, 1987). The relevance of these findings to language development is discussed in the next section.

Arguments about the Effectiveness of Feedback

A challenge to the proposal that adults provide useful feedback for language development has been made by Morgan and Travis (1989). They reanalysed Brown's data on Adam, Eve and Sarah looking at parental responses to inflectional over-regularisation (e.g. "goed") and wh-question auxiliary verb omissions (i.e. leaving out "is" from "what-that"). They argued that these types of errors are the most difficult to overcome without negative feedback.

Morgan and Travis discovered that expansions and clarification questions occurred more often following ill-formed utterances than well-formed utterances with Adam and Eve, but not with Sarah. However, these corrective responses formed only a small proportion of all adult responses to errors. In addition, the responses stopped as the children became older, even though the errors continued. However, it should also be noted that the two children who acquired language most quickly had mothers who were the most frequent users of expansions.

Pinker (1989) has listed a series of reasons why adult responses do not provide *negative evidence* (i.e. negative feedback) which would enable the children to discover their grammatical errors. These reasons include the probabilistic nature of the feedback which makes it difficult to identify an error, the possibility that some children do not receive any differential responses (e.g. the families observed by Ochs and Schieffelin and by Heath), that to make use of feedback children would need to store relevant contingencies over time and compare information about equivalent types of sentences, and that children resist overt corrections of their speech (see Chapter 10). A paper by Gordon (1990) has made similar points. In addition, Bowerman (1987) has questioned the usefulness of negative evidence about errors which appear to occur because of a lack of rules, rather than incorrect rules (e.g. "I help him yesterday" is incorrect because the child does not appear to know the appropriate rules, rather than because the child has applied the rules incorrectly). These arguments have been amplified and extended by Marcus (1993), who makes the important point that children would have to use the utterance about 85 times and monitor the adult's response before they could be sure whether the utterance was either well- or ill-formed.

A response to these criticisms is contained in papers by Bohannon, Mac-Whinney and Snow (1990), and by Moerke (1991). Bohannon, MacWhinney and Snow argue that even if feedback is given only on a percentage of trials this can contribute to learning. They cite evidence that concepts can be learnt with less than 25% of trials involving feedback (Levine, 1959, 1963). Nor do they consider it a problem that well-formed utterances are sometimes followed by recasts. This, it was argued by Pinker, could lead to children discarding appropriate hypotheses about grammar since they have negative feedback about a correct utterance. Bohannon, MacWhinney and Snow reply that the recasts may provide a more appropriate way of expressing the message, even if the original message was grammatically correct.

The suggestion that feedback is absent in some cultures led Bohannon, MacWhinney and Snow to question the validity of the original observations. They argue that there is still a need to examine the populations in more detail to investigate whether subtle parental responses are present. Furthermore, it should be noted that the Samoans and Kaluli have explicit reactions to incorrect utterances, either ignoring them or asking for the correct version to be repeated. However, there is at least one case which suggests that language acquisition can occur even when feedback is not available. Richard Boydell was not able to speak because of cerebral palsy. At the age of 30 years he was given a foot-operated typewriter (Fourcin, 1975). Within 9 days he was able to compose elegant and grammatical sentences. He appeared to have acquired language by listening to it, and this occurred despite the absence of feedback about ill-formed utterances.

Thus, there are doubts whether feedback is necessary for language development. However, its absence is implicated in problems of language development. Sachs and Johnson (1976) report that hearing children of deaf parents who watch a lot of television show considerable delay in acquiring language and also show language deviance (see Chapter 16). This occurs until they are provided with a conversational language environment. Similarly, children in Europe who watch television in another language are not found to acquire that language (Snow, 1977). Furthermore, some studies of A–C speech have found the use of expansions to be positively correlated with later linguistic abilities (e.g. Newport, Gleitman & Gleitman, 1977).

SUMMARY

It is apparent that in many if not all cultures children are exposed to modified speech rather than normal A–A conversation. Many of the modifications are of a type that might be expected to aid linguistic development. Investigations of the effect of these modifications have not produced a clear message, some studies failing to find any major effect, while others have reported that there could be some beneficial consequences of A–C speech. However, there are notable methodological problems in investigating these issues, and the studies of the effects of A–C speech should be seen as providing a cautionary note about similar types of investigation.

Another reason to doubt the benefits of A–C speech is that language acquisition occurs in families who do not adopt the middle-class Western approach to childrearing. But even here, there are disputes about whether the studies of non-Western childrearing practices are sufficiently detailed to allow firm conclusions to be made. A serious concern with such studies is that there would appear to be a universal need to carry out a variety of joint activities with infants. These include activities such as feeding, changing clothes, sleeping, stopping dangerous activities, keeping them entertained, stopping crying and so on.

Thus, it may be that all adults and infants engage in joint activities, but that the joint activities will vary from culture to culture. As a result, children will be learning about what is important and relevant in their culture, and they are likely to be exposed to conversation which reflects these values. However, the controversy about the socialisation in different cultures is likely to continue until we have more complete observations of this process.

Not only has there been controversy about the effect of the content of A–C speech on language development, but there has also been controversy about the way mothers respond to children's grammatical errors. In Western families there do seem to be typical, if probabilistic, patterns of response to children's well- and ill-formed utterances. What is in dispute is whether these responses are universal, the arguments being similar to those about the modifications in A–C speech. Although feedback is of a probabilistic nature, and language development may occur in its absence, this does not mean that it has no effect.

All these controversies stem from a dispute about nature–nurture issues. Investigators in the PPT tradition reject the idea that the environment provides information necessary to allow children to acquire the complexity of syntactic structures. In the other camp it is generally accepted that humans are born with the potential to develop certain cognitive abilities which will enable language to be acquired. Consequently, discussion has moved to consider the role the environment can play in this process. Unfortunately, the arguments have been reduced to claims and dismissal of the claims. We still do not have satisfactory experimental data in relation to this issue, and given the methodological problems of the experimental studies into A–C speech this is going to be difficult to obtain.

15

SENSORY DEPRIVATION AND THE DEVELOPMENT OF COMMUNICATION

What happens to language development when there is sensory deprivation either because of isolation or because of sensory impairments? The answer to this question is important for two reasons: first, it gives a better understanding of what can be done to assist children's development, and second, it helps us to understand the importance of sensory input in relation to the language acquisition process.

Three important forms of sensory deprivation are isolation, blindness, and hearing loss. A simple model about the effects of environmental input predicts that these forms of deprivation should disrupt and delay language acquisition. The research findings generally fail to support this prediction. Instead, language acquisition appears to be remarkably resilient. However, there are also findings which indicate that there are subtle effects of sensory loss. For example, it would appear that children who are blind have difficulties over certain syntactic forms and this can be attributed to the lack of visual input.

PROBLEMS WITH THE SPEECH INPUT

In this section three types of problem with the speech input are considered, those caused by isolation, by temporary hearing loss, and by parents having a poor command of speech. The main question being addressed is whether these forms of deprivation preclude or impair language acquisition and development.

Isolation

Over the centuries there have been a number of reports of children who have been raised in isolation, either by wild animals, as a deliberate experiment, or as the result of severe neglect. For instance, there is a report of an Egyptian pharaoh who raised children in isolation to discover what language they would naturally use; reports of children being raised by wild animals, such as Casper Hauser, and more recent reports about Genie—a child who was raised in isolation in an attic until her teenage years.

We already know that young children can recover from early and extreme deprivation if they are subsequently given a more stimulating and enriched environment (Clarke & Clarke, 1976). The same appears to be true of the acquisition of speech after years without any language input. Such findings suggest that the speech acquisition process is a relatively robust one, and that it is sufficiently flexible for recovery after a number of years of isolation. An implication of this is that normal language acquisition is limited by the maturation of cognitive structures, because language acquisition is relatively fast once the deprivation is removed.

Recovery, however, does not always occur, and in such cases it is difficult to know whether there were some features of the isolation which prevented recovery (e.g. age of isolation, age of detection, type of isolation) or whether the child had learning disabilities when he or she was isolated. Indeed it has sometimes been suspected that behavioural and/or cognitive problems may have contributed to ill treatment of the victim. Consequently, if there is acquisition of language then we can draw inferences about the flexibility of the language acquisition mechanism, but if there is no recovery then there will be uncertainty about the precise reason for this.

I will limit the description of the cases of isolation to three more recent examples as there is greater confidence in the accuracy of these reports. The first case I will outline is that of Isabelle. She had been kept in isolation in a darkened room with her mother who was deaf and without speech (Mason, 1942; Davis, 1947). Isabelle had been given an inadequate diet and had severe rickets. During her isolation she communicated with her mother through gestures.

The mother escaped from the isolation when Isabelle was about 6 years old. On her admission to hospital Isabelle behaved like a wild animal and only made croaking sounds. After one week in the hospital she started to make speech sounds and seemed to pass rapidly through the normal stages of speech. After 18 months she had a vocabulary of over 2000 words, could read and write, and could compose imaginative stories.

The second case involves two Czechoslovakian, male, monozygotic twins whose mother died after giving birth (Koluchova, 1972, 1976). The children then went to a children's home for 11 months, spent 6 months with their aunt, and next went to stay with their father and stepmother. The father was of low intelligence and the stepmother was exceptionally cruel. The boys were never allowed out of the house and were kept in a small unheated closet, or in a cellar. When discovered at 7 years old the children could hardly walk, had acute rickets, were very fearful, and their spontaneous speech was very poor. After placement in a hospital and then in a foster home excellent gains were made in social adjustment and speech. The children are now adults and appear well adjusted and cognitively able (Clarke, personal communication).

Genie, the third case, was found when she was 13 years old (Curtiss, 1977). Her history was one of isolation, severe neglect, and physical restraint; she was kept strapped to a child's potty in an attic. Her father punished her if she made any sound. On discovery her appearance was of a 6–7-year-old child. She was described by Curtiss as "unsocialised, primitive, and hardly human", making virtually no sounds and being hardly able to walk. Genie has not achieved good social adjustment or language despite intervention and being placed with a foster family.

These cases have relevance to the claim that there is a critical period for language acquisition so that it is difficult to acquire language after puberty (Lenneberg, 1967). The studies provide some support for this idea in that all the children who were discovered before puberty acquired language, whereas Genie, who has failed to acquire language, was discovered during her adolescent years. However, caution is needed before accepting this conclusion as Genie may have had a learning disability before her isolation. Another interpretation of the difference between Genie and the other cases is that they had had some minimal social interaction which may have helped to develop rudimentary social skills, and these provided a template for their later, rapid linguistic progress.

The most important and surprising finding from these studies is that some children can, after profound deprivation, make remarkable recovery in general and linguistic abilities. Needless to say the recovery depends on placing the child in a supportive and stimulating environment. Such findings highlight the adaptability of human functioning, and in particular, the adaptability of the systems concerned with language acquisition.

Otitis Media

Otitis media is a condition which results in temporary hearing impairments. The middle ear contains three small bones which communicate vibrations from the ear membrane to the inner ear. Otitis media involves the accumulation of fluid in the middle ear and reduces the efficiency of sound transmission. The fluid is often caused by an infection, but can also be due to fluid accumulation from the eustachian tube. The condition is often termed "glue ear" in Britain. The degree of otitis media (OM) can be identified in a variety of ways, from methods involving the child having to signal that they have heard a sound, to examining the movement of the tympanic membrane. Therefore different definitions of severity are present in the literature.

The amount of hearing loss is variable, but it has been estimated that 92% of sufferers have a loss of around 15–40 dB (Ruben, Downs, Jerger et al., 1985). A loss of 10 dB would mean that most speech sounds can be heard; a loss of 40 dB would mean that only some louder voiced sounds can be heard and there would be difficulty with the unvoiced sounds such as "f", "th", "p". Thus, the condition results in a muffling of sounds and the degree of impairment is variable.

Examinations of the incidence of OM suggest that about 90% of children experience the condition at some time. Furthermore, about half of the sufferers first have the condition when they are less than 1 year old (Howie, Ploussard & Sloyer, 1975; Lous, 1987; Casselbrant, Brostoff, Flaherthy et al., 1985). Each infection is likely to last, on average, about 4 weeks, and the infections are likely to reoccur. By 2 years of age sufferers usually have had about 6 infections (Teele, Klein, Rosner et al., 1984; Roberts, Sanyal, Burchinal et al., 1986).

Given that the auditory input is affected by OM, and given that the condition is often recurrent, what effect does this have on children's language acquisition and development? Retrospective studies have found differences between children who have had OM and control children. The differences include the ability to recognise monosyllabic words (Jerger, Jerger, Alford & Abrams, 1983), reduced sequential auditory memory, attention deficits and poor selective attention (Brandes & Ehinger, 1981; Gottlieb, Zinkus & Thompson, 1979; Sak & Ruben, 1981). However, criticism has been made of the methods of these retrospective studies mainly because of problems in matching children and of the difficulty in eliminating other explanations of the deficits (Paradise, 1981; Ventry, 1980).

Prospective studies, where a group of children are investigated as they develop, are usually considered to be methodologically more satisfactory. In these studies children with OM typically score within the normal range on language skills. However, there appear to be some deficits when comparisons are made between children with OM and matched children who do not have the condition. This suggests the children with OM may be falling slightly short of their full potential; alternatively the increased power of statistics using a matched design may account for finding significant small effects. The investigations often also reveal problems in attentional behaviour (e.g. Feagans, McGhee, Kipp & Blood, 1990).

Studies which have examined the relation between the number of episodes of OM and later language development have found in general that the greater the duration of hearing loss the poorer the subsequent language development of the child. A detailed investigation of a middle-class sample by Friel-Patti and Finitzo (1990) found that the incidence of early OM was related to receptive abilities at 12 months, and expressive abilities at 18 months. Gravel, McCarton and Ruben (1988) have also reported impaired expressive abilities in the second year, but these were no longer present by 4 years (Wallace, Gravel, McCarton & Ruben, 1988; Wallace, Gravel & Ganon, 1991).

Similarly, a positive relation between the amount of early OM and speech abilities at 3 years has been reported by Klein, Teele, Mannos, Menyuk and Rosner (1984), and by Teele et al. (1984). The occurrence of OM during the first year has been found particularly important for predictions. When this sample was divided according to SES, it was found that the children from higher SES families, who typically had more advanced speech, were affected by the amount of OM. However, children from lower SES families, who typically had less advanced language, were unaffected by the amount of OM. Thus, the advantages of being in a higher SES family were reduced by the presence of OM. A follow up of these children at 7 years revealed that the amount of OM was associated with poorer abilities to discriminate sounds (Menyuk, 1986).

As might be expected from the previous study, an examination of a lower SES sample by Roberts et al. (1986) and Roberts, Burchinal, Koch, Footo and Henderson (1988) revealed no association between the amount of OM and scores on standardised tests of verbal and non-verbal intelligence during the pre-school years. When these children were followed up at 7 years there was still no effect of the amount of OM on children's MLU, but the amount of OM was found to be associated with poorer narrative skills and poorer attentional behaviour (Feagans, Sanyal, Henderson, Collier & Applebaum, 1987).

There also appear to be some effects on processing abilities. For example, although Wallace et al. (1988, 1991) found no significant difference in comprehension or cognitive abilities at 4 years in children with and without OM, they needed a higher signal to comprehend utterances with a background noise (their hearing was normal on the day of testing).

Summary

There is still debate and uncertainty about the precise effects of OM on development. This uncertainty seems to be a result of any effect being comparatively weak, depending on the amount of time infections last, the severity of infection, and the SES of the family. Given that OM results in hearing losses, the surprising feature of these findings is that the deficits are not stronger and more obvious, and the lack of gross effects again points to the resilience of the language learning system.

Hearing Children of Deaf Parents

Hearing children of deaf parents will usually be exposed to less speech than other children. The parents will often communicate by sign language, and although the parents may produce some oral language they are likely to have problems in speaking in a similar way to hearing adults. Does all this affect the children's language development?

A cross-sectional study of vocabulary size by Brelje (1971) involved 56 children of deaf parents, 13 of whom were pre-schoolers. He found that the children's performance on the Peabody Picture Vocabulary Test was within the normal range. In this test a word is said and the child has to point to the corresponding picture from an array of four. Surprisingly the articulation of the children was better than that of the general population.

A more extensive study by Schiff and Ventry (1976) concerned 52 children of deaf parents, with an age range of 6 months to 12 years. Nearly half were considered to be developing language normally on the basis of a variety of tests. Just under half of the rest of the sample had speech delays of at least a year but some of the children in this group also had hearing or other problems. Further checking revealed that about a fifth of the children had speech problems where there was no obvious physical cause for the delay and most of these children had poor comprehension and small vocabularies.

Schiff and Ventry noted that the actual amount of speech input did not appear to be as significant as one might expect. For example, sibling status and time spent with normally speaking adults did not predict which children had problems. A similar point has been made by Murphy and Slorach (1983) who failed to find a correlation between children's language skills and the amount of time spent with hearing speakers. Furthermore, although the intelligibility of the mother's speech appeared to be important, it was not an essential contributor to language development. Some children whose mothers produced unintelligible speech had normal language development whereas other children whose mothers' speech was more intelligible had delayed language.

There have been a number of other more detailed reports with smaller cross-sectional samples. Mayberry (1976) assessed eight children of 3–7 years with a battery of tests. There was little evidence of any delay, and it was concluded that the children heard enough speech outside the home for adequate language development. In contrast, Murphy and Slorach (1983) suggest that some of the six children in their sample had problems with language; these included shorter utterances (two children), poorer comprehension (five children), smaller vocabulary (two children), and the presence of unusual word orders (e.g. "that a daddy bring my"). However, a clear definition of the criteria of a delay was not provided.

A valuable longitudinal study of five children was conducted by Schiff (1979). The parents were profoundly deaf and there were no other hearing individuals living in the home. The children were first seen at about 2 years. Only a small proportion of the mothers' speech was intelligible, and their MLU was 4 or less. The children watched about 2 hours of television a day, and four of the children spent a minimum of 10 hours a week with hearing individuals (usually grandparents). Despite this restricted speech input the children appeared to be following the normal course of language acquisition, although in two cases there may have been some delays in development. From this Schiff concluded that minimal exposure to speech is sufficient for early language acquisition.

Three of the same children were assessed at about 8 years. All were found to be within the normal developmental range for their age on a battery of standardised language tests. It was particularly interesting that the speech articulation of children was not problematic despite the restricted and non-standard speaking of their mothers. However, there were some worrying features of one child's speech which included grammatical errors, word-finding problems and a reluctance to talk; these may have been connected with family problems or with the child having less frequent contact with hearing speakers (about 5 hours per week).

Summary

The findings suggest that hearing children of deaf parents can develop a satisfactory standard of oral language. In some cases, children do less well than would be expected from the norms of development. However, in these cases it is difficult to know whether it is a characteristic of the child which causes delays or some characteristic of the environment. There may be some minimum amount of exposure to hearing speakers needed for adequate language development, but the available evidence suggests this may be an amount as low as 5 hours per week (Schiff-Myers, 1988).

DEAFNESS

In discussing deafness the first point to be made is that it is a far from uniform condition. There are different degrees of auditory impairment and there is variation in the age of onset. There are also differences in the language learning environment. The parents of about a tenth of deaf children are deaf and use sign language, but in the majority of cases deaf children have hearing parents who do not know sign language. To complicate matters even further, hearing parents may learn sign language or more often learn a signed version of their own oral language. Before discussing the communication of deaf children it is worth noting that the term *language* is used to refer to both oral and sign languages, while *speech* is used to refer to oral communication. A feature of the literature about language development in deaf children has been the sometimes heated arguments between advocates of different methods of teaching language. The major methods are outlined in Table 15.1.

The *oralist* tradition has as its goal making the deaf child an effective communicator with hearing individuals. As a result, emphasis is placed on developing skills in lip reading and on the complicated training necessary to achieve the ability to produce recognisable words. In the past the use of sign languages has been actively discouraged, as it was thought to interfere with the development of lip reading and producing words. Such discouragement has received criticism because it threatens the language of the deaf community, and is often seen as an outside attack on a system which works very well for many deaf individuals.

There are a number of reports of the successful use of the oralist method (e.g. Quigley & Paul, 1987). However, it also seems to be the case that a large proportion of children, despite assistance and training in oralist methods, fail to develop the ability to produce recognisable words. They also have problems in reading skills, and many do not progress beyond the reading age of 10 years (Trybus & Karchmer, 1977). Similarly, written communication is often marked by grammatical errors. Thus, although oralist methods are successful in some cases, there also are many deaf children who are not able to communicate effectively after having received this method of training.

The traditional alternative to the oralist tradition comes from advocates of the acquisition of sign language. Sign languages such as British Sign Language (BSL) and American Sign Language (ASL or Ameslan) are equivalent to and as complex as oral languages (Klima & Bellugi, 1979; Wilbur, 1987). The syntax of these sign languages does not correspond to spoken English, but is independent and different from it. In sign languages there

Table 15.1 Types of communication systems used with hearing impaired children

ORAL ENGLISH	
Aural-Oral	Concentration on auditory and visual capacities, by using any minimal hearing, lip-reading and productive capacities.
Cued Speech	Handshape and hand location are used to provide information about those sounds which are very difficult to identify from lip reading (e.g. m, p, and b).
SIGN LANGUAGES	Languages which rely on the use of gestures to communicate. These languages have their own syntax and morphology and do not simply map onto the syntax (e.g. word order) of the hearing community.
MANUALLY CODED ENGLISH	These systems are designed to reflect the structure of English rather than that of a sign language. The systems are designed to be used at the same time as speech.
Finger Spelling	Twenty-six handshapes match the letters of the alphabet (sometimes known as the Rochester method). The slowness of the method has limited its use.
Signed English	Signed items correspond to English words, these are employed with sign markers which give the 14 most common inflections in English. Finger spelling is used for some words where there is no sign equivalent.
SEE (I & II)	Seeing Essential English (SEEI) and Seeing Exact English (SEEII) have involved the invention of new signs where there is no English equivalent in ASL, particularly for functional elements (e.g. pronouns, inflections).
Pidgin Signed English	This involves the informal use of signs in an English-like structure, more complex syntactic elements are omitted.

are commonly four major components: the shape of the hand; the location of the hand in relation to the body; the movement of the hand; and the orientation of the hand (Stokoe, 1960; Kyle & Woll, 1985).

In cases where deaf children have deaf parents sign language is readily acquired as a first language. A problem for deaf children of hearing parents is that the rest of the family are not usually fluent in the use of signs, and as a result the input will be less than ideal. Quigley and Paul (1987) regard the main arguments for using sign languages as being that it is the method of communication of the deaf community, and that it would also seem to provide as good a starting point as any for the development of literacy skills.

A third and more recent approach to communication with deaf children is the use of sign systems which correspond to the words and the structure of an oral language (see items about manually coded English in Table 15.1). An advantage of manual signs, in comparison with sign language, is that it is easier for parents and teachers to learn. However, the sign systems are not as rich as sign languages, and even when using the simpler system, adults often fail to include a number of relevant syntactic elements. Quigley and Paul (1987) comment that despite extensive use there is little evidence for sign systems resulting in competent literacy skills. It is often suggested that the sign systems should be used in conjunction with spoken language. However, there are numerous comments about the difficulty of using signs at the same time as speech, especially as adults often have an imperfect knowledge of the sign system. For this reason there is concern that adults may not provide an adequate signed system for language acquisition.

Related to the use of sign systems has been the method of *total communication*; this has been defined in various ways, but is perhaps best seen as an attitude to use any available method to communicate effectively (Stewart, 1992). This has been a popular approach to teaching (Quigley & Paul, 1987), and has sometimes been regarded as simply using signs together with speech to communicate. In practice, sign languages, as opposed to manually signed English, are infrequently employed in total communication programmes. Indeed, Stewart (1992) suggests that the predominant form of manual communication is pidgin signed English, and argues that there is a tendency for adults to use whatever method of communication is easiest for them rather than what may be most suitable for the deaf person. For example, Gregory and Barlow (1989) have questioned the effectiveness of hearing parents using total communication. They worry that it may be difficult for parents to simplify the new language they are using in the same way they would a spoken language, and that unless the whole family learns sign language the child may become isolated from conversation with the result of being unable to "oversee" conversations.

Lastly, it should be noted that one group of investigators have distanced themselves from such arguments about the method of communication by suggesting that the extent of the hearing loss and the child's ability are more important to educational success than the programme employed (Musselman, Lindsay & Wilson, 1988).

The Acquisition of Signs

In a minority of cases deaf children are born to deaf parents. Here the acquisition of sign language occurs at a similar rate to oral language, and may even be faster (Bonvillian, Orlansky & Novack, 1983; Prinz & Prinz, 1981; Schlesinger & Meadow, 1972). There has been some uncertainty as to whether or not signs are produced earlier than words, and whether the early signs can be treated as being equivalent to words (Kyle & Woll, 1985).

A study by Maestas y Moores (1980) observed that the modification of signs by deaf parents was equivalent to that in A–C speech; in particular, signs were adapted in ways that made them more visible to the deaf infants. Adults also appear to use more single signs (Kyle & Woll, 1985) and produce fewer signs (Harris, Clibbens, Chasin & Tibbitts, 1989) than one would expect from A–C speech to hearing children. Harris (1993) attributes these phenomena to the need to gain the child's attention to the referent and the sign, and has observed that a common strategy is to make the signs in the child's visual field. She also speculates that failing to gain the child's attention when signing, and directing rather than following the child's interest, may impair the acquisition of signs.

Gregory and her colleagues have argued in a series of reports (e.g. Gregory & Barlow, 1989) that there is a different degree of attunement between deaf infants and their deaf mothers, than between deaf infants and their hearing mothers. She suggests that this stems from the difficulties and uncertainties of having to adapt to a different mode of communication by the hearing mothers. For instance, deaf mothers in comparison to hearing mothers spent more time with the same focus of attention as the child (94% vs 75%) and were more likely to "reply" to a child behaviour (50% vs 23%). Gregory and Barlow argue that this failure to develop effective pre-linguistic communication has consequences for later language development. They also speculate that the frequent problems of deaf children of hearing parents come not from the fact that the hearing parents are unfamiliar with signs, but because they have difficulty in using a different mode of communication with a different set of constraints.

A study by Folven and Bonvillian (1991) has attempted to minimise problems and criticisms of earlier studies of the rate of sign acquisition. The nine infants studied were mostly hearing infants of deaf parents who used sign language. The findings were based on detailed parental reports. The first signs were found to occur at 8 months, earlier by several months than is typically reported for words. Similarly, the age of having 10 different signs at 13.5 months, is earlier than the 15 months reported by Nelson (1973), with the items in both sets of vocabularies being broadly similar. However, unlike some verbal diary records, signs were included when they were imitations or were part of a routine.

Folven and Bonvillian (1991) also classified the signs produced by children in terms of their iconicity. Inspection of the first words revealed that some of the early gestures were not iconic (i.e. having a visual similarity to the thing that was signed) and so this cannot be a complete explanation of the early acquisition of signs. Nor was it found that the initial signs were based on pointing gestures as Petitto (1988) has suggested.

Interestingly, the referential use of signs to label and comment on objects did not appear until about 12 months, a similar age to the referential use of words in children who use speech. Folven and Bonvillian suggest that this correspondence could be caused by general cognitive limitations which are overcome at the same age. At 12 months children also began to combine signs with gestures such as pointing, a process which is sometimes believed to precede the use of two word speech in oral language development (Lock, 1980). The use of two sign communication was found to begin at about 17 months, again slightly ahead of the typical age in speaking children. However, as Meier and Newport (1990) argue, there are a number of methodological problems in ensuring equivalence between the two types of communication (e.g. the use of formulae and the use of pointing with signs). Later progress in oral and signed language appears to be equivalent and this may be because cognitive factors limit progress (Folven & Bonvillian, 1991; Meier & Newport, 1990).

What explanations might account for signs being produced before words? One is that motor control of the hands may develop earlier than the control of the vocal apparatus (Bonvillian, Orlansky & Novack, 1983; Locke, 1983). A related suggestion is that parents may be able to mould and structure their children's hands to produce an appropriate sign in a way that is not possible with speech (Bonvillian, Orlansky & Novack, 1983). However, there also remains the possibility that signs are employed in a different way to words. Given the problems of identifying the function of one word utterances (see Chapter 7), the problems of detecting an exact equivalence between signs and words should not be underestimated (Gregory & Mogford, 1981; Kyle & Woll, 1985).

Deaf Children of Hearing Parents

Deaf children of hearing parents may not be exposed to sign language until quite late in their development. Observation of children in these circumstances has led to the claim that they may be developing a linguistic system of their own. In other words children may be acquiring a systematic way of organising their communication with others in the absence of a structured external example. Such a claim has important implications for the whole of the study of language acquisition.

Goldin-Meadow and her colleagues have studied a sample of 10 deaf children of hearing parents (Goldin-Meadow & Feldman, 1975; Goldin-Meadow, 1985, 1987; Goldin-Meadow & Moreford, 1985). The children, who were aged between 16 months and 70 months, were trained in the oralist tradition and made minimal progress in the comprehension and production of speech. The children were observed every 2 to 4 months at home during play sessions.

Goldin-Meadow and Mylander (1990) identified three types of sign. *Deictic signs* are used to indicate entities (e.g. by pointing), and are supposed to correspond to words such as "that" and "there". It is also suggested that in some way deictic signs may refer to the entity being pointed at, e.g. "mother", "blocks", etc. Goldin-Meadow and Mylander (1990) admit that deictic signs do not have an exact correspondence to words as, unlike words, they direct the partner's gaze at an object, and it is more difficult to refer to a class of objects rather than to a particular entity (e.g. "I like cakes" vs "I like that cake"). Thus, there are considerable uncertainties about their communicative status.

Characterising signs are the second type. These have verb- and adjective-like properties because they seem to refer to actions and attributes (e.g. a fist held by the mouth plus chewing to signify "eat"). Unlike the gestures in sign language, these usually bear a relatively clear visual relationship to the referent. The third type of signs are *markers* which are used to negate, affirm or control conversation (e.g. headshakes, or holding finger to signify "wait").

Goldin-Meadow (1987) claims that signs are combined in ways that produce the usual semantic relations observed in early child speech (requests, comments, etc.). An example she gives is of a child who pointed at a block tower and then signed "hit" by swatting his fist in the air to indicate that the tower had been knocked down. Furthermore, she believes that the signs have semantic case roles such as actor and recipient (much like two word utterances which have been assumed to have certain semantic or syntactic characteristics). Goldin-Meadow reports that all the children she observed produced utterances where there was some consistency in the ordering of the signs. Across the 10 children the following patterns occurred: patient–act (e.g. signs for "tower + fall down"), patient–recipient (e.g. "hat + cowboy's head"), and act–recipient (e.g. "move-to + table").

Furthermore, there were regularities in which types of signs were included in particular messages. Goldin-Meadow argues that this indicates that children were not randomly producing gestures. For example, in the children's communication an actor was unlikely to be identified by a sign, but the patient was likely to be identified, as a result the signs for "apple eat" were more likely to be produced than "boy eat".

More recently, Goldin-Meadow and Mylander (1990) have suggested that there may be morphological components which are similar to those occurring in sign languages. The data from one child revealed that he not only produced a gesture, but also incorporated motion with the gesture to indicate that the object was moving. Similarly, characterisation gestures tended to be made near to the object of the action, either the actual object itself or the position where the sign for the object had been made. Again this is similar to the system used in sign languages.

Goldin-Meadow (1985) rejects the possibility that these language-like features were the result of input from the parents. Firstly, the vocabulary of gestures between mother and child overlapped at most in a third of the items. Secondly, mothers produced many single string gestures, but typically produced fewer multiple string gestures than their child, and there was no identifiable ordering of these gestures. It was observed that the mothers' use of two gesture strings became more noticeable after their child had already begun producing them.

These are important and fascinating observations. However, it should be recognised that we do not have unequivocal evidence that the children had created their own language. Investigators have found it difficult to identify any grammar to describe early multi-word utterances in children who speak and even if ordering occurs it may be on semantic rather than syntactic principles (see Chapter 12). In other words there is uncertainty about knowing how far it is appropriate to extrapolate from the circumstances of the message to identify its structure. For example, Goldin-Meadow supposed that the sequence of signs "knife David knife sister" could be glossed as "she gave knife to me and knife to you". The context may supply much of the evidence to support this interpretation, but there are well known dangers in this rich interpretation of communication. However, in defence of Goldin-Meadow's analyses it should be noted that the same problems occur when interpreting the speech of children, which suggests some equivalence between the two modes of communication. An additional and different worry is that some investigators have failed to observe the creation of a sign language (Gregory & Mogford, 1981). Similarly, Volterra (1983) failed to find evidence in Goldin-Meadow's data of progress to using two referential signs in an utterance, and Volterra argues that this is a distinctive aspect of sign language acquisition in other circumstances.

Goldin-Meadow argues that her investigations indicate the resilience of language in the absence of an adequate model. Interestingly she concludes that although a language input may be unnecessary, it is essential to have a communicative partner. The reason for this is clear, since without the presence of an understanding parent who can interpret the child's signs it is difficult to believe that the system she has described would develop.

If we accept, for the moment, that a language is created by deaf children what are the implications for theories about language acquisition? Such a conclusion does not at first seem to create problems for the PPT approach. It is reasonable to assume that the linguistic system observed by Goldin-Meadow is a product of the use of principles or unmarked parameters. However, it also follows that a linguistic system does not have to be based on speech, and this suggests that PPT modules must function on the basis of more general processing characteristics than is commonly accepted by advocates of PPT. Such findings call into question the specificity of linguistic modules. However, the observations also create difficulties for connectionist accounts because it is assumed that language develops as a result of feedback. The answer to this problem, in connectionist terms, could be that the language network starts with some biases.

VISUAL DISABILITIES

As in the case of the other sensory impairments there are a variety of forms and degrees of visual disability. In this section I will be concentrating on studies about children who have very little or no visual perception. Children who are blind often have other disabilities and the early studies of communication failed to take account of this. As a result they typically reported delays in language development which could have been due to other factors. Consequently, I will discuss the more recent studies of children who are blind.

Early Communication

Blind infants have no access to the obvious cues provided by faces or facial expressions that signal the very existence of adults with whom they can communicate. Their contact with people is through vocalisations and touch, and for many blind infants these modalities appear sufficient to provide a basis for the beginnings of communication. Research into precisely how this occurs will provide valuable insights into the genesis of children's communication.

One of the pioneers of research with blind children was Selma Fraiberg. As I have already noted, Fraiberg (1979) recognised that the absence of eye contact and cues about interest from infant gaze makes interaction with a blind infant especially difficult (Chapter 3). For this reason she suggested that parents should pay careful attention to the hands of blind children, because the manipulation of objects gives vital information about a child's interest and preferences. If such interventions are used Fraiberg reports that blind children can make normal linguistic progress. Another strategy suggested by Urwin (1978) is the introduction of routines involving nursery rhymes in the second year. These routines when accompanied by actions such as clapping appear to provide a basis of social co-ordination and for the child to control part of the interaction.

The onset of first words in blind children is sometimes reported to be delayed by several months, but this is within the normal range of variation. Furthermore, a study by Mulford (1987), which carefully screened the children to exclude those with other disabilities, found no major delays in lexical milestones. Similarly, Urwin (1978) and Andersen, Dunlea and Kekelis (1984, 1993) in their case studies report no obvious delays in early linguistic skills.

Differences in Speech between Blind and Sighted Children

Although the major milestones in speech may be reached at similar ages in sighted and blind children, there appear to be some more subtle differences concerning the quality of speech and type of conversations that occur. Indeed, Andersen, Dunlea and Kekelis (1984) question whether overestimates may have been made of the speech capabilities of young blind children because insufficient attention has been paid to the qualitative aspects of language use.

In the case of vocabulary there appears to be agreement that although the words used by blind children are broadly similar to those of sighted children there are differences which probably reflect the experiences of these children (Andersen, Dunlea & Kekelis, 1984; Bigelow, 1986; Dunlea, 1989). Blind children tend to have more names of household objects and fewer names for animals, presumably because of the difference in the ease of locating these two forms of referents (Dunlea, 1989).

Another feature of early word use of blind children is that three-quarters of the words remain context-bound (see Chapter 5), a much larger proportion than that commonly reported in sighted children (Andersen, Dunlea & Kekelis, 1984). This leads Andersen, Dunlea and Kekelis to speculate that blind children are not producing hypotheses about the meaning of words in the same way as sighted children. Furthermore, words rarely fell into disuse as happens with sighted children (Dunlea, 1989).

In later language development there are other subtle characteristics of the speech of blind children which can be attributed to their lack of sight. For a blind child it may be easier to share and refer to past events than to aspects of the "here and now". Andersen, Dunlea and Kekelis (1984) suggest that this results in the ability to use past tense verb forms (e.g. -ed) before sighted children, and the delay in learning locative prepositions (e.g. in, on, under, etc.). Similarly, Perez-Pereira and Castro (1992) found speech to be more concerned with her own actions in a twin who was blind, than was the case with her sighted sister.

A problem that has often been noted in blind children is the reversal of the meaning of personal pronouns (i.e. you, I: Andersen, Dunlea & Kekelis, 1984; Fraiberg, 1977; e.g. a child might say "you wanna go outside?" as a request to go outside herself: Dunlea, 1989), but such problems are not always present (Perez-Pereira & Castro, 1993). Andersen, Dunlea and Kekelis suggest that this may be because blind children are using speech before they fully understand its meaning. Similar problems occur in the use of deictic pronouns (e.g. this, that, here, there), where blind children may use the forms interchangeably (Andersen, Dunlea & Kekelis, 1993). In this case the difficulty of identifying the distance of objects, together with the use of speech before it is fully understood, may contribute to this problem.

There are also reports of general differences in content and style of conversation. Rowland found that three blind pre-verbal children were best able to communicate feelings and emotions by vocalisations but, not surprisingly, had difficulty communicating about objects when they were not in physical contact with them. Rowland also found that the children tended to be silent after an adult had said something, perhaps because they needed to listen to what was going on and therefore tried to avoid overlapping vocalisations.

Andersen, Dunlea and Kekelis (1993) have suggested that blind children have more difficulties with the pragmatics of conversation. This may be partly due to confusions about personal pronouns, but seems also to be a result of problems about introducing a topic. In conversations with blind children most of the topics were initiated by the mother, not the child. Furthermore, when blind children introduce a new topic it is sometimes at inappropriate points in the conversation, by changing a topic when a partner has just asked a question. Andersen, Dunlea and Kekelis suggest that this is because blind children will be more focused on their own activities than on those of a partner. Findings which back this up come from Dunlea (1989) who observed a tendency for blind children to talk about their possessions, their own actions and about past events, while they seldom produced descriptions of events (Dunlea, 1989).

An area where the lack of visual input has unexpected consequences for language development is in the production of speech sounds. It has sometimes been said that babbling in blind and sighted children occurs at a similar age around 6–7 months. For 1–2-year-old blind infants more errors have been found with sounds which have highly visible mouth movements (e.g. b/m/f: Mills, 1987). No difference was found between blind and sighted children in the articulation of sounds where there is no obvious mouth movement (e.g. j/k/x/h), showing that this finding is not the result of a general delay. This suggests that seeing the mouth movements helps infants to produce the sounds. Mulford (1987) reports that blind children have fewer words in their vocabulary which include a sound with visible mouth movements than sighted children. This indicates a bias in word selection according to phonological ability.

Findings about blind children are relevant to debates about the role of speech input and cognition in language development. Chomsky (1980) predicted that blind children should not be delayed or deviant in their language acquisition if they were being exposed to speech. In contrast, Piaget (see Piattelli-Palmarini, 1980) has claimed that the lack of sight would affect cognitive development, which in turn would affect language development. At first sight the research findings provide stronger support for Chomsky's predictions. Given the lack of sight, it is striking that there are not greater problems in the acquisition of speech. However, some caution should be exercised before making too hasty a conclusion; the speech of blind children is not the same as that of sighted children. In addition, the input to blind children may not be the same as that to sighted children, it may often be specifically adapted to the needs of the children. Consequently, the matching of adult speech with child interest may overcome some of the problems associated with the lack of a visual input.

Summary

It would seem that although language delays often occur in blind children this may well be due to factors other than the loss of sight. Blind children who do not have other disabilities appear to acquire language at much the same rate as sighted children. However, there are a number of subtle differences between the speech of blind and sighted children. These can often be attributed to difficulties in understanding the function of particular linguistic forms as a result of the lack of sight.

SUMMARY

This chapter has examined children who have lacked sensory information relevant to the development of communication. The most surprising feature of the findings is that in many cases children's language development is relatively unaffected by quite dramatic absences of sensory information. However, it is important to note that there is a great deal of variability in the effects that have been discussed, so that it cannot be presumed that all children will remain unaffected. However, it is also worth remembering that communication can occur even despite both blindness and deafness. The famous example of Helen Keller, who was both deaf and blind, shows it is possible to develop linguistic communication in the most adverse circumstances, in this case through the use of touch spelling.

Children who have been isolated can acquire language once they are rehabilitated. Impaired speech input as a result of otitis media or because of an absence of speech from parents typically does not seem to have major or profound effects on language development. In a similar manner deafness and blindness present no insurmountable barrier to the acquisition of language. Such findings emphasise the resilience of the language acquisition process.

Thus, these findings give some support to Chomsky's view that language acquisition will be able to take place more or less automatically provided a sufficient amount of language is heard. Particular support comes from the studies of some blind children who can develop language despite their problems of relating speech to the external world. However, other findings indicate that language is not acquired from the automatic processing of decontextualised speech. In Chapter 4 we saw that the initial language of some twins is delayed apparently because they are not receiving communication which is finely tuned to their interests, and there is other evidence that language is not acquired from the provision of speech in the absence of a communicative context (e.g. children who are isolated, and see Chapter 15). Thus, the speech delays in twins are surprising when set against the finding that blind children seem able to make largely normal progress with speech even though they are restricted in the sorts of relations they can detect between words and objects. This seems to indicate that the nature of the support provided by parents may be crucial in helping children start to use language—relating speech to joint activities and sharing experiences. This is a topic which deserves to receive much more attention.

DEVELOPMENTAL DISABILITIES AND LANGUAGE ACQUISITION

This chapter focuses on conditions where there are delays in language acquisition and development. The study of children with learning disabilities can both be of assistance to the development of appropriate intervention programmes and can assist our understanding of communicative development. There are a number of important methodological issues in such investigations and these are considered in the first section. The second section considers a specific syndrome, that of autism. Children with autism have difficulty in relating to people and in communicating with them, and the reasons for this are discussed. The third section outlines the communication of children with Down's syndrome and particular attention is paid to the relationship between cognitive and communicative development. The fourth section discusses conditions where there is delay, but language ability is in advance of cognition. The last section considers adult communication to children with disabilities; this reveals that adults use a more directive style and different views about the effects of this are evaluated.

GENERAL METHODOLOGICAL ISSUES

One issue that is often addressed in the literature on disabilities concerns whether development is similar but delayed in comparison to other children, or whether there is a different pattern of development. As we will see it is difficult to give a straightforward answer to this question. Part of the difficulty lies in there being different meanings of difference. Sometimes children with learning disabilities go through approximately the same developmental sequence as non-delayed children. This at first sight would tend to support the delay hypothesis. However, more careful examination of the profile of development often reveals that language is discrepant in relation to other cognitive milestones. Such a discrepancy would tend to support a weak form of the deviance hypothesis.

Another issue of theoretical and practical interest is the relation between language and cognition. This allows a test of the modularity hypothesis that language is independent of other cognitive processes (Fodor, 1983). If, for example, language is found to be significantly different from other abilities then this would support the position that language involves a separate area of cognitive functioning.

A critical issue in the research on children with disabilities concerns the characteristics of comparison groups. Early studies tended to match target children who had learning disabilities with those of a similar chronological age; usually these comparisons revealed that children with learning disabilities were delayed relative to children of a similar age, an unsurprising finding! A more typical comparison, in more recent research, is between children with disabilities and a group matched with those of a similar mental age (MA). Such comparisons can be used to answer questions about, for instance, whether language is less developed than one would expect according to the children's general mental age.

Unfortunately, there are still problems with the interpretation of these comparisons. Children with learning disabilities may lack the motivation to attempt standardised tests in the same way as other children, they also may be less attentive and less able to keep attention during a relatively long testing session. Thus, mental age scores may underestimate the cognitive abilities of children with learning disabilities. Another problem is that the performance on standardised tests is usually heavily influenced by the understanding and production of speech, so that MA scores are often strongly influenced by verbal ability; this makes for a circular process when one examines the relation between language and mental age. In addition, it has been suggested that if development is deviant, then standardised tests are inappropriate as the profile of scores will differ from that of non-delayed children. All this makes for difficulties when interpreting comparisons with mental age matched groups.

Dissatisfaction with mental age scores has resulted in comparison groups being chosen on the basis of having similar specific abilities relevant to the dimension being considered (e.g. when language is being investigated a similar MLU or vocabulary size is often used to match children). Even these comparisons can be criticised; for example, MLU provides only an approximate indication of language ability (Hickey, 1988). Thus, there are no simple or obvious methods of choosing comparison groups when studying children with learning disabilities—this is what makes the topic so fascinating for some, and so frustrating for others.

CHILDREN WITH AUTISM

An Overview of the Characteristics of Children with Autism

There is a range in the severity of autism. Some children show withdrawal from social interaction, and dislike change in their environment, and there is either a lack of speech or speech which is not particularly communicative. Such characteristics were described by Kanner (1943) in his identification of the condition. A broader definition has been given by Wing (1988) and this includes children who seek social contact, but lack the skills to interact effectively. A feature of autism which is often commented on by observers and by the individuals themselves is a difficulty in understanding the pragmatics of communication. Children with autism generally perform poorly on IQ tests and two-thirds of them have scores below 70 (DeMyer, Barton & Alpern et al., 1974); their linguistic ability is, however, very variable. In addition, some children with autism show areas of average or above average functioning: these abilities include drawing skills, remembering names and dates, performing complex calculations, and the ability to play a musical instrument. In the form identified by Kanner (1943) autism is a rare condition (0.002% of children, see Gilberg, 1990) but, however, there has been a great deal of research interest in this condition and there is an impossibly large literature to discuss.

Many children with autism do not speak (DeMyer et al., 1974), and there is commonly an absence of pre-verbal gestures such as pointing and problems with the pragmatics of communication (for more details see Chapter 4). About three-quarters of the children who do speak go through a stage of echolalia (Ricks & Wing, 1975). Echolalia involves repeating utterances or parts of utterances, and the repetition may occur some while after the model. Another common feature of the speech of children with autism is problems with the personal pronouns (i.e. I/you, me/he, she, they). These last two characteristics also occur in children who are blind (see Chapter 15).

Explanations of Childhood Autism

Why do children with autism have an impaired ability to communicate and why do many have problems with acquiring language? There have been a number of answers to these questions, sometimes at different levels of analysis. Originally the parents were blamed and thought to have impersonal relationships with their children (Kanner, 1943); it has also been proposed that there may be a genetic cause. The explanation that I will concentrate on is the idea that children with autism lack the ability to attribute mental states to themselves and others, which provides one account of why these children have difficulties with the pragmatics of communication. According to this type of explanation children with autism lack a theory of mind—the understanding that other people have mental states which can involve different conceptions of the world. There is much current interest in this possibility and about the way that such ideas can explain many features of autism.

The theories that have been put forward to account for the characteristics of autism may sometimes seem divorced from issues related to communication. What needs to be constantly borne in mind is that answers to questions about the causes of autism will also help us to understand processes involved in the development of communication. Although, as always, caution is needed. Jordan (1993) has pointed out that there may be a complex interplay between the characteristics of autism, the reactions of people to these characteristics, and the development of the condition.

An Inability to Understand Triadic Relationships?

Autism is not usually identified until problems in communication become obvious. However, it is known that joint gaze rarely occurs in infants with autism (Mundy & Sigman, 1989). This finding has been incorporated into a model about early representation developed by Baron-Cohen (1993). He believes that non-delayed infants have an eye direction detector module (EDD) which develops representations of others' intentions between 9 and 14 months (see Chapter 4). He goes on to suggest that some children with autism are not able to use eye direction information to deduce a person's attentional interest or their mental states. In the terms of his theory this means they are unable to build triadic representations of joint attention, and so are unable to relate their own representation to that of another person.

Baron-Cohen's model has the advantage of accounting for problems in joint attention which occur before 18 months. Previous theoretical work by Leslie (1987; see next section) supposed that autism is the result of difficulties of forming secondary representations such as those that occur in pretence and symbolic play. Consequently, the deficits at younger ages in joint attention could not be explained by Leslie's theory.

One problem for Baron-Cohen is accounting for why children with autism can follow the direction of points and be successful in visual perspective-taking tasks (Baron-Cohen, 1989a; Hobson, 1984). He simply explains this by postulating that children with autism can establish where another is looking, but do not relate such information to where they themselves are looking.

Baron-Cohen believes that impairment in EDD results in a failure to develop the more advanced representational capacities involved in developing a theory of mind. In an added complication, Baron-Cohen also suggests that there may be a subgroup of children with autism who have an operating EDD, but whose more advanced representational abilities are impaired.

An Inability to Decouple from Reality?

A model of the capacities necessary for pretence and symbolic play has been developed by Leslie (1987) and this has been used to explain the difficulties of children with autism. He suggested that pretence is possible because of the operation of a *decoupler*. Prior to about 18 months, when the decoupler becomes available, infants are supposed to perceive the world in a literal way. The activation of the decoupler changes this and allows new cognitive operations involving pretence.

The decoupler has three components: an expression raiser, a manipulator and an interpreter. The expression raiser allows a person to copy a representation based on normal perceptual processes for further use in the decoupler system. The copy can then be "manipulated" to provide alternative representations of events such as pretence and symbolic activity. Thus, the interpreter can take the perception of an object such as a banana, and manipulate this representation so that it is treated as a telephone. In addition, an "interpreter" allows the decoupling process to be related to stored memories and concurrent perceptions, which can then be passed back to the manipulator. For instance, past memories of a telephone can be used to provide a more elaborate scenario.

According to this model the absence of symbolic play and other related deficits in children with autism (Wulff, 1985) is due to their inability to decouple their perceptions. However, it should be noted that Lewis and Boucher (1988) report that children with autism exhibit a similar amount of elicited symbolic play to matched children, although there has been discussion of the appropriateness of the methodology of this study and whether elicited symbolic play is equivalent to spontaneous symbolic play (Baron-Cohen, 1989a, b, 1990; Boucher & Lewis, 1990).

An interesting set of suggestions concern the implications that the decoupler has for language use. Leslie points out that the decoupler allows us to appreciate that the sentence "Sarah-Jane believes that Mrs Thatcher lives at No. 10 Downing Street" refers to Sarah-Jane's belief about the world and does not tell us anything about the accuracy of the statement. Similarly, the decoupler allows one to understand that someone can believe something that is not true, thus, Sarah-Jane may still believe the statement about Mrs Thatcher, but the statement is no longer true (or at least not true at the time of writing this!). In addition, the decoupler allows statements to be made about things that do not exist (e.g. "The king of France is bald"). Consequently, the more sophisticated uses of language can be related to our ability to decouple information about other people's representations from reality. However, Perner (1991) has reservations on the degree of similarity between symbolic play and language.

What is the relation between EDD and the decoupler? Baron-Cohen has suggested that EDD activates a theory of mind mechanism (ToMM which includes the decoupler mechanism) and transfers its triadic representations to this mechanism. The ToMM is more complex than EDD because it can represent more complicated mental states (e.g. pretend, know, think, and believe) and can use deceit. Thus, Baron-Cohen claims the two modules are similar in character, but have different levels of functioning.

Baron-Cohen admits that EDD is not necessary or sufficient for the activation of ToMM. He notes that children who are blind cannot develop an EDD module, yet they can possess a ToMM, and he believes that this is possible because they establish joint attention in some other modality. Such an admission suggests that we either have to construct a series of modules or that EDD is not specific to gaze.

An Inability to Form a Theory of Mind?

For children to possess a theory of mind (ToM) they must be able to understand that someone else may have a different perspective or understanding to their own. The classic study in this area involved testing children's understanding of stories in what has become known as a false belief task. One such story was as follows. Maxi puts his chocolate in a green cupboard and then goes to play outside. Unknown to Maxi his mother moves the chocolate to a blue cupboard. The children are asked where they think Maxi will look for the chocolate when he comes back. Children younger than 4 years typically say the blue cupboard and therefore do not seem to take account of the fact that Maxi does not know that the chocolate has been moved. Among investigators in this area it is generally agreed that the ability to answer questions like this signals an important cognitive and social development indicating that children can now view what people know in a very much more sophisticated way (Moses & Chandler, in press).

Children with autism typically fail ToM tasks even though their mental age is above 4 years, and a number of investigators have suggested that many of the problems experienced by children with autism (e.g. inability to deceive, lack of personal relationships, difficulty with communicating) can be attributed to a lack of ToM (e.g. Baron-Cohen, Leslie & Frith, 1985; Tager-Flusberg, 1992).

Leslie links his decoupler model with the literature on children's theory of mind as both are concerned with the creation of secondary hypothetical representations, and he suggests that theory of mind may be dependent on the presence of secondary representations. One problem with this is explaining why symbolic activity is present at 2 years, but most studies report that a ToM emerges at about 4 years. Leslie (1987) originally suggested that this age difference can partly be accounted for by the additional complexity of the ToM task, especially the need to make inferences about another person's beliefs. Furthermore, the age gap between these two processes may be smaller than was originally thought, and may simply be due to young children's problems in remembering all the components in the ToM tasks. Leslie has also suggested that the ToM task may require a deeper understanding of the way that mental states can be the cause of actions, and this is needed for successful performance in ToM tasks. Perner (1991) has used these terms in a slightly different way from Leslie. He believes that secondary representations involving pretence together with an understanding of past and future emerge from 18 months onwards, while metarepresentations which involve deception and the abilities needed for ToM tasks emerge at about 4 years.

An Inability to Detect and Respond to Emotions?

An alternative to both the decoupler and ToM accounts of cognitive development has been provided by Hobson (1984, 1991, 1993). As we have seen in Chapter 3, Hobson argues that children develop an understanding of people as a result of their capacity to directly perceive the emotional states of others. This is achieved through their ability to react to these perceptions, and through the experience of social interaction. He also supposes, as we have seen in Chapter 4, that towards the end of the first year children develop the ability to understand the perspective of others during activities like following the direction of another's point and showing toys to others. This he believes provides the basis for the development of symbolic activities where children can operate with different representations of the same entity.

Furthermore, Hobson claims that children's ToM emerges as a result of coming to understand that there can be accurate and inaccurate representations of the world. This may be achieved by discovering that success is more likely when accuracy is maximised, and by observing that people often engage in heated discussion about what is "true", as in family arguments over whose turn it is to do domestic chores. Here he emphasises that children develop an understanding that agreement between people helps to identify when a viewpoint is accurate.

Hobson accounts for autism in terms of an inability to perceive and react to the emotions of others. This he believes results in the problems with non-linguistic and linguistic communication, as children fail to develop metarepresentational abilities and fail to develop a more sophisticated communicative perspective. Thus, Hobson agrees with the previous proposals that children with autism have difficulties with metarepresentations, but he believes that the cause of these difficulties is because of a lack of socio-emotional understanding. The other theories propose that the lack of socio-emotional understanding is the result of cognitive deficits. Unfortunately, the critical observations about the very early socio-emotional and cognitive development of children with autism are lacking because diagnosis is not usually made until a much later age.

One of the pieces of evidence that Hobson cites in support of his ideas is the presence in children who are both blind and who have autism of features such as echolalia and pronoun reversal. He believes that blind children show these conditions mainly because of the lack of shared visual reference and the inability to see the partner's emotional response to an object or event. In this way the evidence from children who are blind supports his general argument.

Challenges and New Proposals

The ToM-based explanation of autism is made more complicated by debates about the abilities that are necessary for success in these tasks. As Moses and Chandler (in press) have pointed out, children who fail the false belief task appear to attribute a belief to Maxi, but unfortunately it is not the attribution that adults and older children would make. In addition, there are investigators who subscribe to the view that some form of ToM is present before 4 years. Evidence to support this argument comes from such observations as: children younger than 3 years interact with adults in ways that appear to suggest they can understand the intentions, beliefs and knowledge of the adults (Reddy, 1991); children younger than 3 years use words referring to cognitive states of themselves and others (Wellman, 1990); there appear to be methodological shortcomings in the false beliefs task (Chandler et al. 1989; Freeman et al., 1991; Robinson & Mitchell, in press).

Another challenge has come from Leekam and Perner (1991) who dispute the view that children with autism lack a metarepresentational ability. In the task they used, a picture was taken with a Polaroid camera of a doll in a red dress, and while the picture was being developed the doll's dress was changed to a green one. The children had to predict the colour of the dress "in the picture". Children with autism were successful in this task, but failed the false belief task. This led Leekam and Perner to conclude that children with autism can form metarepresentations in some circumstances. The fact that children make representational drawings also suggests that they have a metarepresentational capacity (Charman & Baron-Cohen, 1993).

Recently, yet another explanation about the deficits of children with autism has been proposed. This concerns executive functioning. Space does not permit a detailed review of this account, but in essence the idea is that children with autism have difficulties in making plans, and inhibiting responses (Bishop, 1993; McEvoy, Rogers & Pennington, 1993). Such an explanation can account for a large number of findings about children with autism.

Looking at Some of the Evidence

Attempts to make a decision about the accuracy of these viewpoints are fraught with difficulty. Hobson (1991) points out that, given many of the similarities between Leslie's and his own ideas, it will be difficult to identify a critical test to distinguish between them. Thus, the accounts of Baron-Cohen, of Leslie, and of Hobson can all be used to explain a number of the observations about children with autism. For instance, in children with autism there is a striking absence in the words and the signs that refer to attention and to cognitive states (Jordan, 1993; Tager-Flusberg, 1992); all the three accounts would predict this. Similarly, children with autism seem unable to decouple themselves from reality and as a result have difficulty in deceiving, again such findings are amenable to explanations from the three accounts (Russell, Mauthner, Sharpe & Tidswell, 1991). There are, however, disputes about some features of the behaviour of children with autism in relation to the theoretical approaches which I have just outlined. For instance, there is debate about whether children with autism are able to understand the desires of others, to understand that desires can be linked to an emotional action, and to understand the nature of simple emotions (Baron-Cohen, 1991; Tager-Flusberg, 1992; but see Hobson, 1993).

In relation to all these arguments it is important to return to the range of abilities of children with autism. Tager-Flusberg (1992) has observed that in many studies between a fifth and a half of the children with autism are able to pass the false belief task. However, Baron-Cohen (1989c) points out that even in these cases, there may be an inability to make second-order belief attributions (e.g. Maxi thinks that his mother thinks that...). Similarly, Eisenmjer and Prior (1991) have found a range of abilities on ToM-related tasks in children with autism, and suggest that there may be a delay rather than a permanent ToM deficit in these children. Thus, there is considerable variability in the performance of children with autism. In future theories should address the nature of these discrepancies.

The research into children with autism has had an important impact on our understanding of cognitive processes and their relation to communication. One obvious implication from this research is that language development does not simply depend on linguistic skills, but also depends on skills that involve the ability to understand the mental states of other people. At present there is some uncertainty about the precise cause of the difficulties in children with autism. However, discussion of this issue has been associated with the development of more detailed models about the way that cognition, emotion, and communication are interrelated.

CHILDREN WITH DOWN'S SYNDROME

An Outline of the Characteristics of Children with Down's Syndrome

Children with Down's syndrome (DS) have an extra chromosome and this has consequences for health and cognition. In these children there is a higher incidence of respiratory and heart problems together with a susceptibility to infections. Their cognitive abilities seldom surpass those of a 5 year old and the maximum potential is usually reached by 12 to 15 years (Rondal, 1988). Furthermore, language abilities typically do not progress beyond those of a non-delayed 3 year old (Fowler, 1990). However, it is extremely important to note that the problems and the degree of disability in children with Down's syndrome are highly variable, so that there will be exceptions to any generalisation. (The term Down syndrome is used in the US, and Down's syndrome in the UK; both terms are used in this book.)

Children with Down's syndrome often possess more specific disabilities which could make language acquisition more difficult. They have a small mouth cavity in relation to their tongue. In addition, they appear to have less control of the movements of the tongue, lips and respiratory muscles (Buddenhagen, 1971). There also may be problems with vision and particularly hearing (the latter is often caused by otitis media).

The Development of Communication and Language

How is it best to characterise the communicative development of children with DS? There has been a debate about whether it is deviant or delayed. Cicchetti and Mans-Wagener (1987) have presented evidence for children with Down's syndrome being generally delayed in their development, and Fowler (1988, 1990) has claimed that language development in children with DS shows delay without deviance. The delay position does seem to describe the broad outlines of development, but when more detailed observations are made this description becomes less convincing. For example, Miller (1988) argues that as children with Down's syndrome become older there is an increasing gap between linguistic and cognitive abilities and language becomes increasingly delayed and deviant.

An understanding of this debate requires a review of communicative development in these children. If we start by examining early communicative development, given the possible problems in producing sounds, it is surprising that the babbling of children with Down's syndrome is similar to that of non-delayed (ND) children and begins at roughly the same age (Smith, 1977). Furthermore, later phonological development appears to follow a similar course to that of ND children (Menn, 1985; Rondal, 1978; Smith, 1977).

Even though early vocal development appears similar to that in ND children there seems to be a delay and difference in the use of sounds during interaction. Observations by Berger and Cunningham (1981) have revealed that in the first few months children with DS vocalise less than ND infants, but there is a rapid increase in vocalisations at about 4 months with the result that the total duration of vocalisation is considerably higher than that in ND infants. A consequence of the higher amount of vocalisations may be more vocal overlaps with adult partners as reported by Jones (1977). There are also differences in the quality of the sounds that are produced by infants with DS. Non-delayed infants start to produce melodic sounds at about 2 months, these melodic vocalisations being similar in sound pattern to speech. In children with DS melodic vocalisations emerge at the later age of 4 months, there are fewer melodic vocalisations, and they make up a smaller proportion of all infant vocalisations (Legerstee, Bowman & Fels, 1992). The investigators speculate that this may create problems for the development of communication because parents have greater difficulty in constructing social responses to the vocalisations of children with DS. In addition, there is a different pattern of gaze interaction in infants with DS in relation to both chronological and MA matches. The peak of mutual looking during interaction occurs at a later age in infants with DS (4–5 months) and continues until a much older age (Berger & Cunningham, 1981).

The use of gestural communication by children with DS (aged 10–19 months) is delayed, but appropriate for their mental age (Greenwald & Leonard, 1979), and they start using words at about 24 months (Fischer, Share & Koch, 1964; Share, 1975). The early vocabularies of children with DS are comparable to those of ND children (Gillham, 1979), and this similarity continues through Brown's stage I (Coggins, 1979; Dooley, 1977) and into the use of multi-word utterances (Rondal, 1978; Layton & Sharifi, 1979). These findings suggest similar, but delayed, vocabulary acquisition in children with DS.

In relation to pragmatic abilities children with DS at Brown's stage I were not found to differ from MA matched controls in these abilities (types of speech acts based on Dore's codes, see Chapter 7) or in their ability to take part in a sustained conversation. In fact these children were more able than MLU matched children in language skills. Thus, the pragmatic ability of children with DS seems to be ahead of their language, but appropriate for their cognitive abilities.

This pattern seems to be a more general phenomenon, in children with DS there is often a delay in the production of communication in relation to other cognitive skills. Once words start to be used, vocabulary acquisition in children with DS occurs more slowly than in samples with similar MA and linguistic abilities (Cardoso-Martin, Mervis & Mervis, 1985); this was interpreted as being due to the difficulty in forming associations between words and referents. Miller (1988) also reports an absence of multi-word utterances and fewer different words being produced by children with DS in relation to 18 month MA matched children. Older children with DS (MA = 3 years), in comparison to MA matched samples, are reported to have a lower MLU and a smaller degree of variation in the words which are used together (Miller, 1988). This may be because these syntactic skills require more sophisticated cognitive processing so that experience alone does not provide a basis for increasing MLU. More recently, Bellugi, Wang and Jernigan (in press), using parental reports from the CDI, have found a delay in grammatical development relative to vocabulary size.

Miller (1988), reviewing this complex set of findings, concluded that the vocabulary size and syntax of children with DS is less developed than would be expected on the basis of mental age, but that their vocabulary is larger than would be expected on the basis of their language skills as assessed by MLU. Fowler (1990) in her review makes a similar point that syntax is further delayed than vocabulary and she suggests that these dimensions may involve separate areas of functioning.

In still older children it is possible that there is yet another pattern of development. Rondal (1978) reports that children with DS have a higher type–token ratio (i.e. use a greater range of words) than ND children matched for MA or for linguistic development. This was interpreted as being due to the DS children having greater experience of speech than the matched sample (i.e. they were chronologically older). Similar findings have been reported by Miller (1988).

Thus, there is support for both the delay and the deviance descriptions of the development of children with DS. In relation to this, Rondal (1988) has argued that even though one dimension of communication may follow the same *sequence* of development, it may be "out of step" with related abilities. When this is the case, he argues that the pattern of development as a whole could be considered deviant. Rondal also questions the usefulness of such terms. As we will see in the next section, an added complication to the delay/deviance debate is that the appropriateness of the terms may also depend on the period of development which is being considered, making simple holistic descriptions of delay and deviance inappropriate.

Patterns of Communicative Development

Two general trends in language development of children with DS have been identified by Miller (1988). He observed that before the chronological age of 3–4 years the relationship between children's language and cognitive skills is similar to that in ND children. However, once children with DS reach this age he suggests that language progressively falls behind other cognitive achievements. These claims are backed up by a cross-sectional study. This revealed that below a chronological age of 25 months and an MA of 18 months, only a fifth of children with DS showed a delay in production relative to comprehension and non-verbal cognitive abilities; over this age nearly 70% showed a delay (Miller, 1988). Fowler (1990) has developed a similar argument.

Miller investigated various possible explanations of this discrepancy. No evidence was found for hearing difficulties or health problems being associated with delayed production and he reasons that different patterns of adult language input are unlikely to account for delays that only occur in production. He proposes that the pattern of development could be the result of a neurological dissociation between the development of speech production and comprehension, or simply due to motor problems in speech production. Support for the motor problem explanation comes from Smith (1977) who reports a low proportion of intelligible vocalisations in children with Down's syndrome, and from Messer and Hasan (in press) who found a low incidence of vocalisations in these children. In addition, older individuals with DS appear to have difficulty in articulating real and pseudo-words compared to children matched for short-term memory (Racette & Fowler, 1993). These motor problems may be compounded by muscle hypertonia which results in difficulties in control of movement. However, the motor problem explanation should not be accepted uncritically as Beeghly, Weiss-Perry and Cicchetti (1990) failed to find differences in the intelligibility of speech between children with DS and a matched sample at Brown's stage I. Furthermore, surgical intervention to reduce tongue size does not always appear to have been effective in assisting the production of sounds and normal speech can occur in other individuals with anatomical problems (Hamilton, 1993). Thus, some other deficit, such as problems in planning the muscle movements (Frith & Frith, 1974), may be the cause of the delay in production. There may also be problems in the development of the phonological system so that children with DS are delayed or deviant in the way they produce sounds. A recent examination of speech production by Hamilton (1993) has concluded that the speech production problems may be due to a multitude of causes which are present at every stage of the speech production process. Interestingly, older children with DS appear to have greater difficulties in the sequencing of auditory information than visual information (Pueschel, Gallagher, Zartler & Pezzullo, 1987; Ellison & Gillis, 1993), and it would appear that the development of reading can assist the development of language (Buckley & Bird, 1993).

Another suggestion about there being a general pattern in communicative development of children with DS has been made by Fowler (1988). In her first study Fowler recorded the language development of a girl with DS between 4 years and 7 years. The general characteristics of development were found to be similar to those observed by Brown (1973) in the rate of MLU increase and content. However, once stage III had been reached at about 66 months there was little progress for a further 10 months, and later development was erratic. Fowler suggests that this plateau may be the extent of language development in children with DS, and that this may be related to the chronological age of the children.

Fowler (1988) backed up her argument by following up a group of 10 children with DS for a minimum of 4 years. Language development was found to gradually increase up to an MLU of 3.5 which was achieved between 4 to 8 years. There was then a plateau between 8 to 15 years of age with little further progress being made. This was followed by a slight increase to an MLU of 4.0 that was reached at about 19 years. These ages correspond to suggestions by Gibson (1966, 1981) that there are three periods of cognitive growth in children with Down's syndrome which are surrounded by plateaux in development. The plateaux are believed to occur between 4–6 years, 8–11 years and 12–17 years; the mental ages at these plateaux are approximately 18 months, 30 months and 48 months. As yet we do not know the reason why these plateaux occur, but clearly the answer to the question will be of considerable practical and theoretical interest.

The Cognitive Hypothesis

The finding of a dissociation between speech and language in children with DS is of further interest because it provides a way of testing the "cognitive hypothesis". What has sometimes been termed the Piaget–Werner cognitive hypothesis is that language advances are dependent on cognitive advances (Piaget, 1962; Werner & Kaplan, 1963), thus for language to proceed general cognitive developments have to take place. For instance, according to this view, at about 18 months there are general cognitive changes which involve the emergence of symbolic play and enable children to divorce words from their original context and associations. However, studies which correlated the emergence of cognitive skills and communication have failed to provide convincing support for this model (see Bates, O'Connell & Shore, 1987).

As a consequence, proposals have been put forward that there are particular, rather than general, links between communication and cognitive development. Two prominent proposals are the *local homology model* (Bates, O'Connell & Shore, 1987) and the *specificity hypothesis* (Gopnik & Meltzoff, 1986). Support for these proposals has come from investigations which have documented the way that cognitive and language abilities emerge at the same age in ND children. A more severe test of such ideas is to examine whether the relationship also occurs in children with DS, which will be considered in the next two sections.

The local homology model

The local homology model unlike the specificity hypothesis claims that general changes in cognitive functioning, at particular points in development, will affect a range of capacities and this includes communicative abilities. One prediction of the local homology model is that the transition from one to two word speech is the result of a general advance which enables children to process two items rather than one item of information (Bates, O'Connell & Shore, 1987). Following the work of Case (1985), Bates and colleagues suppose that this change occurs because children become more efficient at processing information, rather than because their memory capacity is increased. In ND children there are a number of changes which accompany the beginning of two word speech. These include the ability to sort objects into two groups, the use of symbolic play, and the ability to use two relations when copying a brick model.

The development of symbolic play in children with DS follows a similar course to that in ND children and there appears to be a similar pattern of links between developments in sensorimotor functioning and symbolic play. For example, the findings of Hill and McCune-Nicholich (1981) and Beeghly, Weiss-Perry and Cicchetti (1990) can be summarised as follows: pre-linguistic children with DS do not engage in symbolic play; children who produce one word utterances only produce single symbolic schemes during play; and children who combine words are also able to combine symbolic schemes. These findings broadly support the local homology model.

An investigation which provides a more precise test of the change from processing one to two items was conducted by Pat Hasan and myself. We examined the chronological relationship between the use of two word utterances and three abilities. These were the ability to construct a "train" where one of two relationships had to be remembered, the ability to remember where two toys were located in a line of 10 small boxes, and the ability to sort objects into two groups (Hasan & Messer, 1990). The findings revealed that the accomplishment of "twoness" occurred at about the same age in the three cognitive tasks, but that the production of two word speech was delayed behind these accomplishments by about 12 to 16 weeks. Thus, the prediction that two word speech would occur at the same age as the other cognitive changes was not supported. However, these findings are not as damaging to the local homology model as would first appear. Bates has suggested that when there are developmental delays "comprehension obtains custody of cognition", meaning that changes in cognition will be associated with the ability to comprehend rather than the ability to produce speech.

The specificity hypothesis

Piaget's work provided a starting point for Gopnik and Meltzoff's model. Piaget supposed that at about 18 months children are able to form symbolic representations and as a result there are related cognitive developments involving vocabulary expansion, symbolic play and deferred imitation, all of which require the representation of an entity in a more abstract way. However, Gopnik and Meltzoff have reasoned that children achieve the ability to form symbolic representations before 18 months; before this age they are already using words and are able to imitate actions after having seen them. This has led Gopnik and Meltzoff to propose that underlying the changes at 18 months is the ability to construct hypothetical representations about things that have never been experienced. For example, they suppose that the ability to form hypothetical representations allows children on object permanence tasks not only to understand that an object continues to exist, but also to develop hypotheses about where it is located.

Meltzoff and Gopnik (1989) have provided details of three sets of specific relations between cognition and speech. One involves a link between the use of cognitive relational words about disappearance (e.g. "all-gone") and the ability to pass object-permanence tasks which require children to understand that an object can be positioned in several locations. A second and similar link is between cognitive relational words which signal an understanding of success or failure in relation to an event (e.g. "oh dear" or "good") and the ability to pass means-ends tasks where children have to work out which of several strategies will be successful. Gopnik and Meltzoff (1986) believe both these abilities require the capability to consider different hypothetical outcomes. The third link is between the ability to sort objects into groups and the sudden vocabulary burst which occurs at about 18 months. Gopnik and Meltzoff have presented a number of studies of non-delayed children which indicate that these changes occur at about the same age.

In order to test the specificity hypothesis Pat Hasan and I examined the development of these three sets of skills in children with DS. Our investigations revealed that some children produced cognitive-relational words several months before they had mastered the appropriate sensorimotor tasks. Nor did we find any evidence of a vocabulary burst accompanying the ability to sort objects into groups.

Our difficulty has been in knowing precisely how to interpret these findings. The most negative interpretation for the specificity hypothesis is that these relations between cognition and speech are not invariant, and that the correlations observed in ND children are purely fortuitous. Alternatively, our findings could be interpreted as indicating that development in children with DS is different from that in other children so that the same associations across cognitive domains do not occur. It could even be argued that there are the same underlying associations across cognitive domains in children with DS, but that peripheral problems result in a delay in the productive language of these children. Thus, our findings reinforce the conclusion from earlier studies about the delay in productive speech in children with DS and raise questions about the cognitive changes identified in the specificity hypothesis.

Summary

In reviewing the development of communication in children with DS it is apparent that a simple delay–deviance description is inadequate and inappropriate. In addition, there are proposals about general patterns of development which provide challenges for intervention and theoretical understanding. Lastly, we have seen that delay in language production, relative to other abilities, means children with Down's syndrome do not show the same linkages between cognition and language which are found in ND children.

LANGUAGE IN ADVANCE OF COGNITION

Children with developmental disabilities typically show similar delays in language and cognition, or as in the case of children with DS their productive language may be more delayed than other areas of functioning. In other syndromes the use of language has been reported to be in advance of cognitive functioning. This finding suggests that language can function independently of these other cognitive capacities and thus gives support for a modular approach to cognition. For example Cromer (in press) has reported the case of a 16-year-old girl with internal hydrocephalus. Although measures of cognitive functioning indicated she had the abilities of a 6 year old, her speech appeared much more sophisticated than this, and her speech also appeared to be more advanced than indicated by standard measures of linguistic ability. Cromer and Lipka (1990) have argued that this may be because even the standard language tests involve non-linguistic abilities; other tests which involved making grammatical judgements indicated a level of understanding compatible with the speech that was produced. From these findings Cromer argues that there is an independent language module which is allowing more advanced speech to be produced than would be expected from this person's other cognitive abilities.

Children with Williams syndrome (WS) have a marked asymmetry between cognition and language (the condition is also known as infantile hypercalcemia; Williams, Barratt-Boyes & Lowe, 1961). The condition involves problems in the metabolism of calcium and calcitonin, mental retardation, failure to thrive, hyperacusis (increased sensitivity to sound) and a characteristic facial pattern (Jones & Smith, 1975; Meyerson & Frank, 1987; Bertrand, Mervis, Rice and Adamson, 1993).

The speech of children with WS is delayed relative to their chronological age, but their speech is usually reported as being in advance of their mental age (although some studies have failed to identify this, see Arnold & Yule, 1985; Kataria, Goldstein & Kushnick, 1984). A typical report is that of Bennett, La Veck and Sells (1978) who found relatively higher scores for verbal and memory scales, with relatively lower scores for perceptual and motor skills. Bellugi et al. (1988) has given a summary of the abilities of three adolescents with Williams syndrome. The individuals were unable to lead independent lives as they had difficulty dressing themselves, remembering routines, and dealing with money. The three adolescents were assessed on Piagetian tasks and it was found that they were not capable of solving concrete operational tasks (e.g. conservation of liquid and seriation which are typically solved at 7–8 years). They were also found to have difficulties with tasks involving the visual-spatial organising of elements such as drawing, but performed at adult levels on a task involving the identification of familiar and unfamiliar faces.

The three individuals were found to have mental ages of between 5 to 9 years. In contrast the productive and receptive vocabularies were about two years in advance of their mental ages. Not only was the conversation of these young people fluent, but they also showed advanced syntax and morphology. An assessment of comprehension of sentence structure from the TROG (Test for Reception of Grammar) revealed scores that were again about two years in advance of their mental age, although similar gains were not found in a test of grammatical understanding. There also seems to be a marked difference in narrative skills, with WS children giving interesting and attention-worthy stories in comparison to children of matched MA (Reilly, Klima & Bellugi, 1991).

More recently, Bellugi, Wang & Jernigan (in press) have used the CDI to obtain parental reports about children with WS and DS between 1 and 6 years of age. Both groups showed delayed speech development until they reached the equivalent language level of 16–30 month olds. After this age the linguistic abilities of children with WS increased in relation to their vocabulary size. This suggests that there may need to be a set of cognitive abilities which are necessary (but not sufficient) for language to proceed. Once these are in place the relative advances in language skills of children with WS are possible, but without these abilities speech development will not occur. Bates (1993) uses the findings to argue against a modularity account of language acquisition as certain basic cognitive abilities appear to be needed for language acquisition to proceed. However, there remains the possibility that once these basic cognitive abilities are present then the language module can operate. Although Bates herself would probably argue that these cognitive abilities simply allow the further development of language.

SPEECH TO CHILDREN WITH DISABILITIES

It has become apparent that adults' speech to children with both physical and learning disabilities tends to differ from that to other children. The adults' speech, although it is modified to the children's level of language or cognitive functioning (Rondal, 1978; Cunningham, Reuler, Blackwell & Deck, 1981), has often been observed to be more directive and less responsive than to children without learning disabilities (Cunningham et al., 1981; Mahoney & Robenalt, 1986; Tannock, 1988), and there is report of a high percentage of directives in maternal speech to blind children (Andersen, Dunlea & Kekelis, 1993). Broadly speaking, directiveness involves the use of instructions and commands, responsiveness concerns the replies to child communication. There has been discussion about whether this phenomenon is an appropriate or inappropriate adaptation to children's needs, whether it is caused by the lack of conversational responsiveness and inattention on the child's part, and whether the lack of child responsiveness is the result of the adults' conversational style. This section outlines research which is related to these questions.

The Characteristics of Speech to Children with Disabilities

The global characterisation of speech to children as directive has given way to more detailed observations of this style. For instance, Maurer and Sherrod (1987) found that directives tended to be used to encourage appropriate object-related play and compliance in children with DS. In contrast, mothers of non-delayed children tended to use directives to gain attention and encourage further exploration. Similar findings have been reported by Mahoney (1988b).

Mahoney (1988a) has speculated that there are different styles of maternal conversation to children with disabilities. One style may be because mothers see their role as "attenders", this involves adopting a teacher–director's role with the frequent use of behavioural prompts, seeking attention, elaborating their own topic, and the use of grammatical utterances. Another group may consist of "responders", these mothers frequently use one word utterances, smile and laugh, use exaggerated facial expression, and use more exclamations. A third group of "ignorers" are unresponsive and seem to lack a sensitivity to the child's communication. Such findings emphasise the problems of global descriptions of speech to children with disabilities.

Appropriate or Inappropriate?

Marfo (1990) has argued against a too ready acceptance of the hypothesis that directive styles are an inappropriate and harmful aspect of interaction with children who have disabilities. She admits that studies with non-delayed children suggest that a responsive style facilitates language development (see Chapter 4), but reasons that such findings cannot be unquestioningly extrapolated to other children, especially as we have good evidence that in general mothers are sensitive to the communicative needs of their children.

As we have seen, Maurer and Sherrod's (1987) findings suggest that directives are used appropriately by mothers of children with DS. In addition, the use of adult directives is not necessarily associated with a generally negative style of interaction (e.g. lack of sensitivity, inappropriate pacing, intrusiveness, and so on: Crawley & Spiker, 1983; Tannock, 1988; Mahoney & Robenalt, 1986; Marfo & Kysela, 1988). More recently, research by Cielinski, Vaughn and Seifer (unpublished) has suggested there are different patterns of association between directiveness and quality of play for non-delayed children and children with DS. Maternal intrusiveness was associated with lower play quality in the non-delayed sample, while maternal directiveness was associated with sustained attention in children with DS. Such findings highlight the dangers of simple extrapolations of findings from non-delayed to delayed samples.   Findings which appear to create problems for Marfo's argument have been presented by Herman and Shantz (1983) and by Mahoney (1988a). In both studies, directive strategies were found to be associated with poorer performance on another task. However, there is some evidence to suggest that in cases when there is an adverse effect of adult interactional style this may be due to a combination of characteristics. Marfo builds on observations of Crawley and Spiker to suggest that directiveness when combined with low sensitivity to children's communication may be detrimental to development.

Children with learning disabilities are less likely to sustain attention in a topic and less likely to initiate conversation, characteristics which appear to be related to maternal directiveness and responsiveness (Crawley & Spiker, 1983; Mahoney and Robenalt, 1986; Mahoney, 1988a, b). Such correlations imply an effect of maternal speech on child characteristics, but it is equally possible for the direction of causality to run the other way. However, it should be noted that findings from children who are deaf suggest that a directive style of interaction can have effects on the conversational abilities of children. Power, Wood and Wood (1990) report that an intervention study which reduced the directiveness of teachers of deaf children had the indirect effect of increasing child initiative and loquaciousness. Thus, there is still uncertainty about whether a directive style of interaction is an inappropriate strategy with children who have learning disabilities and whether such a style impairs development. Like the study of the effects of adult–child speech (see Chapter 14), it is going to be difficult to obtain an answer to these seemingly simple questions. Even so, it is also clear that such answers are important for giving advice to parents and for the design of intervention programmes.

SUMMARY

The study of children with developmental disabilities is difficult because of both practical and methodological issues. However, such research can be both personally and theoretically rewarding. Currently, there is almost an obsession in British psychology about the study of autism. This research has refocused attention on issues about the development of interpersonal understanding; the competing theories about the causes of autism have become easier to identify, but more difficult to resolve. In contrast, research into children with DS is a smaller enterprise despite there being a larger population of these individuals. In DS, like autism, there remains an unanswered central question—why is the language of these individuals delayed?—but here the type of hypothesis is very different from that put forward about autism, as the problem is much more likely to be directly related to speech processing or production. Another condition which has received increasing research interest in the last decade is WS. Children with WS appear to show a dissociation between language and cognition, but this does not seem to occur until a cognitive platform of a certain height has been built, a finding which is compatible with modular and non-modular accounts of language development. In the last section of this chapter we have seen that the speech to children with disabilities differs from that to non-delayed children. There is still controversy about whether this is an appropriate or inappropriate adaptation. Furthermore, such findings serve to reinforce the point that children with disabilities affect their social environment, and this in turn may affect their development. A simple but suitable message with which to end this book.

REFERENCES

Abravanel, E. & Sigafoos, A.O. (1984) Exploring the presence of imitation during early infancy. *Child Development*, **55**, 381–392.

Ahrens, R. (1954) Beitrag zur entwicklung des physiognomie und mimikerkennens. *Z. exp. angew. Psychol.*, **2**, 412–454.

Ainsworth, M. D. S., Blehar, M., Waters, E. & Wall, S. (1978) *Patterns of Attachment: A Psychological Study of the Strange Situation*. Hillsdale, NJ: Erlbaum.

Aitchinson, J. (1989) *The Articulate Mammal*. London: Unwin Hyman.

Akhtar, N., Dunham, F. & Dunham, P. J. (1991) Directive interactions and early vocabulary development: The role of joint attentional focus. *J. Child Language*, **18**, 41–49.

Ambrose, J. A. (1961) The development of the smiling response in early infancy. In B. M. Foss (Ed.), *Determinants of Infant Behaviour*, vol. 1. London: Methuen.

Andersen, E., Dunlea, A. & Kekelis, L. (1984) Blind children's language: Resolving some differences. *J. Child Language*, **11**, 645–664.

Andersen, E. S., Dunlea, A. & Kekelis, L. (1993) The impact of input: Language acquisition in the visually impaired. *First Language*, **13**, 23–49.

Anderson, B., Vietze, P. & Dokecki, P. (1977) Reciprocity in vocal interactions of mothers and infants. *Child Development*, **48**, 1676–1681.

Anderson, R. C., Reynolds, R. E., Schallert, D. L. & Goetz, E. T. (1977) Frameworks for comprehending discourse. *American Educational Research Journal*, **14**, 367–381.

Arnold, R. & Yule, W. (1985) The psychological characteristics of infantile hypercalcemia: A preliminary investigation. *Developmental Medicine and Child Neurology*, **27**, 49–59.

Aslin, R. N. (1987) Visual and auditory development in infancy. In J. D. Osofsky (Ed.), *Handbook of Infant Development*. New York: Wiley.

Atkinson, J., Hood, B., Wattam-Bell, J., Anker, S. & Tricklebank, J. (1988) Development of orientation discrimination in infants. *Perception*, **17**, 587–595.

Atkinson, M. (1987) Mechanisms for language acquisition: Learning, parameter-setting and triggering. *First Language*, **7**, 3–30.

Atkinson, M. (1992) *Children's Syntax: An Introduction to Principles and Parameters Theory*. Oxford: Blackwell.

Atkinson, M., Kilby, D. & Roca, I. (1988) *Foundations of General Linguistics*. London: Unwin Hyman.

Au, T. K. (1990) Children's use of information in word learning. *J. Child Language*, **17**, 393–416.

Au, T. K. & DeWitt, J. E. (1993) Acquiring object and attribute names: Preschoolers' use of mutual exclusivity within one language and across two languages. Society for Research in Child Development Conference, New Orleans, 24–28 March.

Austin, J. (1962) *How to do Things with Words*. Oxford: Oxford University Press.

Bach, K. & Harnish, R. M. (1979) *Linguistic Communication and Speech Acts*. Cambridge, MA: MIT Press.

Backscheider, A. & Markman, E. M. (1990) Young children's use of the taxonomic assumption to constrain word meanings. Unpublished manuscript.

Baillargeon, R. (1992) The object concept revisited: New directions. In C. E. Granrud (Ed.), *Visual Perception and Cognition in Infancy: Carnegie-Mellon Symposium on Cognition*. Hillsdale, NJ: Erlbaum.

Baldwin, D. A. (1989) Priorities in children's expectations about object label reference: Form over color. *Child Development*, **60**, 1291–1306.

Baldwin, D. A. (1991) Infants' contribution to the achievement of joint reference. *Child Development*, **62**, 875–890.

Baldwin, D. A. & Markman, E. M. (1989) Mapping out word–object relations. A first step. *Child Development*, **60**, 381–398.

Balogh, R. D. & Porter, R. H. (1986) Olfactory preferences resulting from mere exposure in human neonates. *Infant Behavior and Development*, **9**, 395–401.

Banigan, R. L. & Mervis, C. B. (1988) Role of adult input in young children's category evolution: II An experimental study. *J. Child Language*, **15**, 493–504.

Barnes, S., Gutfreund, M., Satterly, D. & Wells, D. (1983) Characteristics of adult speech which predict children's language development. *J. Child Language*, **10**, 65–84.

Baron-Cohen, S. (1989a) Perceptual role-taking and protodeclarative pointing in autism. *Brit. J. Developmental Psychology*, **7**, 113–127.

Baron-Cohen, S. (1989b) The autistic child's theory of mind: A case of specific developmental delay. *J. Child Psychology and Psychiatry*, **30**, 285–298.

Baron-Cohen, S. (1989c) The autistic child's theory of mind: a case of specific development delay. *J. Child Psychology and Psychiatry*, **30**, 285–298.

Baron-Cohen, S. (1990) Instructed and elicited play in autism: A reply to Lewis & Boucher. *Brit. J. Developmental Psychology*, **8**, 207.

Baron-Cohen, S. (1991) The theory of mind deficit in autism: How specific is it? *Brit. J. Developmental Psychology*, **9**, 301–314.

Baron-Cohen, S. (1993) *Origins of Theory of Mind: The Eye-Direction Detector*. SRCD Conference, New Orleans.

Baron-Cohen, S., Leslie, A. M. & Frith, U. (1985) Does the autistic child have a "theory of mind"? *Cognition*, **21**, 37–46.

Barrett, M. (1978) Lexical development and overextension in child language. *J. Child Language*, **5**, 205–219.

Barrett, M. (1982) Distinguishing between prototypes: the early acquisition of the meanings of object names. In S. A. Kuczaj (Ed.), *Language Development*, vol. 1, *Syntax and Semantics*. Hillsdale, NJ: Erlbaum.

Barrett, M. (1986) Early semantic representations and early semantic development. In S. A. Kuczaj & M. Barrett (Eds), *The Development of Word Meaning*. New York: Springer-Verlag.

Barrett, M. (in press) Early lexical development. In P. Fletcher & B. MacWhinney (Eds), *Handbook of Child Language*. Oxford: Blackwell.

Barrett, M., Harris, M. & Chasin, J. (1991) Early lexical development and maternal speech: A comparison of children's initial and subsequent uses of words. *J. Child Language*, **18**, 21–40.

Bates, E. (1993) Modularity, domain specificity and the development of language. *Project in Cognitive Neuroscience Technical Report* 9305, Center for Research in Language University of California, San Diego.

Bates, E., Benigni, L., Bretherton, I., Camaioni, L. & Volterra, V. (1979) *The Emergence Symbols: Cognition and Communication in Infancy.* New York: Academic Press.

Bates, E., Bretherton, I. & Snyder, L. (1988) *From First Words to Grammar: Individual Differences and Dissociable Mechanisms.* Cambridge: Cambridge University Press.

Bates, E., Bretherton, I., Snyder, L., Shore, C. & Volterra, V. (1980) Vocal and gestural symbols at 13 months. *Merrill-Palmer Quarterly,* **26**, No. 4.

Bates, E., Camaioni, L. & Volterra, V. (1975) The acquisition of performatives prior to speech. *Merrill-Palmer Quarterly,* **21**, No. 3, 205–226.

Bates, E., Dale, P. & Thal, D. (in press) Individual differences and their implications for theories of language development. In P. Fletcher & B. MacWhinney (Eds), *Handbook of Child Language.* Oxford: Blackwell.

Bates, E. & MacWhinney, B. (1987) Competition, variation, and language learning. In B. MacWhinney (Ed.), *Mechanisms of Language Acquisition.* Hillsdale, NJ: Erlbaum.

Bates, E., Marchman, V., Thal, D., Fenson, L., Dale, P., Reznick, J. S., Reilly, J. & Hartung, J. (in press) Developmental and stylistic variation in the composition of early vocabulary. *J. Child Language.*

Bates, E., O'Connell, B. & Shore, C. (1987) Language and communication in infancy. In J. Osofsky (Ed.), *Handbook of Infant Development,* 2nd edn. New York: Wiley.

Bates, J. E., Maslin, C. A. & Frankel, K. A. (1985) Attachment security, mother–child interaction, and temperament as predictors of behavior problem rating at age 3 years. *Monographs of the Society for Research in Child Development,* No. 50, 167–193.

Baumwell, L., Tamis-LeMonda, C., Kahana-Kalman, R. & McClure, J. (1993) Maternal responsiveness and infant language comprehension as predictors of language development. SRCD Conference, New Orleans.

Bavin, E. L. (1993) The acquisition of functional categories: A case study from Greek. Paper presented at the International Congress for the Study of Child Language, Trieste, Italy.

Bavin, E. L., Ng, B. C., Brimmell, T. & Gabriel, B. (1993) A crosslinguistic study on the acquisition of word meaning. Presented at the International Congress for the Study of Child Language, Trieste, Italy.

Bechtel, W. & Abrahamsen, A. (1991) *Connectionism and the Mind.* Cambridge, MA: Blackwell.

Beeghly, M., Weiss-Perry, B. & Cicchetti, D. (1990) Beyond sensorimotor functionism. In D. Cicchetti & M. Beeghly (Eds), *Children with Down Syndrome.* Cambridge: Cambridge University Press.

Behrend, D. A. (1990) Constraints and development: A reply to Nelson (1988). *Cognitive Development,* **5**, 313–330.

Bell, R. Q. (1968) A reinterpretation of the direction of effects in studies of socialization. *Psychological Review,* **75**, 81–95.

Bellugi, U., Marks, S., Bihrle, A. M. & Sabo, H. (1988) Dissociation between language and social functions in Williams Syndrome. In K. Mogford and D. Bishop (Eds), *Language Development in Exceptional Circumstances* (pp. 177–189). New York: Churchill Livingstone.

Bellugi, U., Wang, P. & Jernigan, T. (in press) Williams Syndrome: An unusual neuropsychological profile. In S. Broman and J. Grafman (Eds), *Cognitive Deficits in Developmental Disorders: Implications for Brain Function.* Hillsdale, NJ: Erlbaum.

Benedict, H. (1979) Early lexical development: Comprehension and production. *J. Child Language,* **6**, 183–200.

Bennett, F. C., La Veck, B. & Sells, C. J. (1978) The Williams elfin faces syndrome: The psychological profile as an aid in syndrome identification. *Pediatrics,* **61**, 303–305.

Berger, J. & Cunningham, C. C. (1981) The development of eye contact between mothers and normal versus Down's syndrome infants. *Developmental Psychology,* **17**, No. 5, 678–689.

Berko, J. (1958) The child's learning of English morphology. *Word,* **14**, 150–177.

Bertenthal, B. I. & Proffitt, D. R. (1986) The extraction of structure from motion: Implementation of basic processing constraints. Paper presented at the International Conference on Infant Studies, Los Angeles, 1986. Abstract in *Infant Behavior and Development,* **9**, 36.

Bertenthal, B. I., Proffitt, D. R., Kramer, S. J. & Spetner, N. B. (1987) Infants' encoding of kinetic displays varying in relative coherence. *Developmental Psychology,* **23**, 171–178.

Bertenthal, B. I., Proffitt, D. R., Spetner, N. B. & Thomas, M. A. (1985) The development of infant sensitivity to biomechanical motions. *Child Development,* **56**, 531–543.

Bertrand, J., Mervis, C. B., Rice, C. E. & Adamson, L. (1993, March) Development of joint attention by a toddler with William's syndrome. Paper presented at the Gatlinburg Conference on Research and Theory in Mental Retardation and Developmental Disabilities, Gatlinburg, TN.

Bigelow, A. (1986) Early words of blind children. *J. Child Language,* **14**, 47–56.

Birdwhistle, R. L. (1970) *Kinesics and Context.* Philadelphia: University of Pennsylvania Press.

Bishop, D. (1988) Language development in children with abnormal structure or function of the speech apparatus. In D. Bishop & K. Mogford, *Language Acquisition in Exceptional Circumstances.* Edinburgh: Churchill Livingstone.

Bishop, D. V. M. (1993) Annotation: Autism, executive functions and theory of mind. A neuropsychological perspective. *J. Child Psychology and Psychiatry,* **34**, No. 3, 279–293.

Blake, J. & De Boysson-Bardies, B. (1992) Patterns in babbling: A cross-linguistic study. *J. Child Language,* **19**, 51–74.

Bloom, K., Russell, A. & Wassenberg, K. (1987) Turn-taking affects the quality of infant vocalizations. *J. Child Language,* **14**, 211–227.

Bloom, L. (1970) *Language Development: Form and Function in Emerging Grammars.* Cambridge, MA: MIT Press.

Bloom, L. (1973) *One Word at a Time: The Use of Single Word Utterances before Syntax.* The Hague: Mouton.

Bloom, L., Lightbrown, P. & Hood, L. (1975) Structure and variation in child language. *Monographs of the Society for Research in Child Development,* No. 40, Serial No. 160.

Bloom, P. (1990) Subjectless sentences in child language. *Linguistic Inquiry,* **21**, 491–504.

Boen, P. A. (1972) The verbal environment of the language learning child. *Monographs of the American Speech and Hearing Association,* No. 17.

Bohannon, J. N., MacWhinney, B. & Snow, C. (1990) No negative evidence revisited: Beyond learnability or who has to prove what to whom. *Developmental Psychology,* **26**, 221–226.

Bohannon, J. N. & Stanowicz, L. (1988) The issue of negative evidence: Adult responses to children's language errors. *Developmental Psychology,* **24**, 684–689.

Bomba, P. C. & Siqueland, E. R. (1983) The nature and structure of infant form categories. *J. Experimental Child Psychology,* **35**, 295–328.

Bonvillian, J., Orlansky, M. & Novack, L. (1983) Development milestones: Sign language acquisition and motor development. *Child Development,* **54**, 1435–1445.

Borer, H. (1984) *Parametric Syntax.* Dordrecht: Foris.

Borer, H. & Wexler, K. (1987) The maturation of syntax. In T. Roeper & E. Williams (Eds), *Parameter Setting*. Dordrecht: Reidel.

Bornstein, M. H. & Krinsky, S. J. (1985) Perception of symmetry in infancy: The salience of vertical symmetry and the perception of pattern wholes. *J. Experimental Child Psychology and Psychiatry*, **39**, 1–19.

Bornstein, M. H. & Ruddy, M. (1984) Infant attention and maternal stimulation: Prediction of cognitive and linguistic development in singletons and twins. In H. Bouma & D. Douwhuis (Eds), *Attention and Performance: Control of Language Processes*. London: Erlbaum.

Boucher, J. & Lewis, V. (1990) Guessing or creating? A reply to Baron-Cohen. *Brit. J. Developmental Psychology*, **8**, 205–206.

Bower, T. G. (1974) *A Primer of Infant Development*. San Francisco: Freeman.

Bowerman, M. (1978) The acquisition of word meaning: An investigation into some current conflicts. In N. Waterson & C. A. Snow, *The Development of Communication*. Chichester: Wiley.

Bowerman, M. (1982) Reorganizational processes in lexical and syntactic development. In E. Wanner & L. Gleitman (Eds), *Language Acquisition: The State of the Art*. Cambridge: Cambridge University Press.

Bowerman, M. (1987) Commentary: Mechanisms of language acquisition. In B. MacWhinney (Ed.), *Mechanisms of Language Acquisition*. Hillsdale, NJ: Erlbaum.

Bowerman, M. (1989) Learning the semantic system: What role do cognitive predispositions play? In M. Rice & R. Schiefelbusch (Eds), *The Teachability of Language*. Baltimore: Brooks.

Braine, M. D. S. (1963) On learning the grammatical order of words. *Psychological Review*, **70**, 323–348.

Braine, M. D. S. (1976) Children's first word combinations. *Monographs of the Society for Research in Child Development*, No. 41 (1).

Brandes, O. & Ehinger, D. (1981) The effects of middle ear pathology on auditory perception and academic achievement. *J. Speech and Hearing Disorders*, **22**, 301–307.

Branigan, G. (1979) Some reasons why successive single words are not. *J. Child Language*, **6**, 411–421.

Braunwald, S. (1978) Context, word and meaning: Toward a communicational analysis of lexical acquisition. In A. Lock (Ed.), *Action, Gesture and Symbol: The Emergence of Language*. London: Academic Press.

Brazelton, T. B, Koslowski, B. & Main, M. (1974) The origins of reciprocity: The early mother–infant interaction. In M. Lewis & L. Rosenblum (Eds), *The Effect of the Infant on the Caregiver*. New York: Wiley.

Brelje, H. W. (1971) A study of the relationship between articulation and vocabulary of hearing impaired parents and their normally hearing children. Doctoral dissertation, University of Portland, Oregon.

Broen, P. A. (1972) The verbal environment of the language-learning child. *Monographs of the American Speech and Hearing Association*, No. 17.

Brown, R. (1958) How shall a thing be called? *Psychological Review*, **65**, 14–21.

Brown, R. (1973) *A First Language, the Early Stages*. Cambridge, MA: Harvard University Press.

Brown, R. & Bellugi, U. (1964) Three processes in the child's acquisition of syntax. *Harvard Educational Review*, **34**, 133–151.

Brown, R. & Hanlon, C. (1970) Derivational complexity and the order of acquisition in child speech. In J. R. Hayes (Ed.), *Cognition and the Development of Language*. New York: Wiley.

Bruner, J. S. (1975) From communication to language—a psychological perspective. *Cognition*, **3**, 255–287.

Bruner, J. S. (1976) Learning how to do things with words. In J. Bruner & A. Garton (Eds), *Human Development*. Oxford: Oxford University Press.

Bruner, J. S. (1981) Intention in the structure of action and interaction. *Advances in Infancy*, **1**, 41–56.

Bruner, J. (1983) *Child's Talk: Learning to Use Language*. New York: Norton.

Buckley, S. & Bird, G. (1993) Teaching children with Down's syndrome to read. *Down's Syndrome Research and Practice*, **1**, 34–41.

Buddenhagen, R. G. (1971) *Establishing Vocal Verbalizations in Mute Mongoloid Children*. Research Champaign Press. I, 11.

Budwig, N. (1986) Agentivity and control in early child language. Unpublished doctoral dissertation, University of California, Berkeley.

Bushnell, E. W. (1982) Visual-tactual knowledge in 8 and $9\frac{1}{2}$ and 11 month old infants. *Infant Behavior and Development*, **49**, 1163–1173.

Bushnell, I. W. R., Sai, F. & Mullin, J. T. (1989) Neonatal recognition of the mother's face. *Brit. J. Developmental Psychology*, **7**, 3–15.

Butterworth, G. (1990) Self-perception in infancy. In D. Cicchetti and M. Beeghly (Eds), *The Self in Transition: Infancy to Childhood*. Chicago: University of Chicago Press.

Butterworth, G. E. & Grover, L. (1988) The origins of referential communication in human infancy. In L. Weiskrantz (Ed.), *Thought without Language*. Oxford: Oxford University Press.

Butterworth, G. E. & Grover, L. (1989) Joint visual attention, manual pointing and pre-verbal communication in human infancy. In M. Jeannerod (Ed.), *Attention and Performance*, vol. XIII. New York: Erlbaum.

Butterworth, G. E. & Jarrett, N. (1991) What minds have in common is space: Spatial mechanisms serving joint attention in infancy. *Brit. J. Developmental Psychology*, **9**, 55–72.

Camarata, S. & Leonard, L. B. (1986) Young children pronounce object words more accurately than action words. *J. Child Language*, **13**, 51–65.

Campbell, R. N., Macdonald, T. B. & Dockrell, J. E. (1982) The relationship between comprehension and production and its ontogenesis. In F. Lowenthal, J. Vandamme & J. Cordier (Eds), *Language and Language Acquisition*. New York: Plenum.

Campos, J. J., Barrett, K. C., Lamb, M. E., Hill, H., Goldsmith, H. & Stenberg C. (1983) Socio-emotional development. In P. Mussen (Ed.), *Handbook of Child Psychology*, vol. 4. New York: Wiley.

Camras, L. A., Malatesta, C. & Izard, C. (1991) The development of facial expression in infancy. In R. Feldman & B. Rime (Eds), *Fundamentals of Non-verbal Behavior*. New York: Cambridge University Press.

Cardoso-Martin, C., Mervis, C. B. & Mervis, C. A. (1985) Early vocabulary acquisition by children with Down Syndrome. *American J. Mental Deficiency*, **90**, 177–184.

Carey, S. (1978) The child as word learner. In M. Halle, J. Bresnan & G. A. Miller (Eds), *Linguistic Theory and Psychological Reality* (pp. 264–293). Cambridge, MA: MIT Press.

Carey, S. (1982) Semantic development: The state of the art. In E. Wanner & L. Gleitman, *Language Acquisition: The State of the Art*. Cambridge: Cambridge University Press.

Carnap, R. (1947) *Meaning and Necessity*. Chicago: University of Chicago Press.

Carpenter G. C. (1974) Mother's face and the newborn. *New Scientist*, 21 March, 742–744.

Case, R. (1985) *Intellectual Development: From Birth to Adulthood*. New York: Academic Press.

Casselbrant, M. L., Brostoff, L. M., Flaherthy, M. R., Bluestone, C. D., Cantelkin, E. I., Doyle, W. J. & Fria, T. J. (1985) Otitis media with effusion in preschool children. *Laryngoscope*, **95**, 428–436.

Cazden, C. (1965) Environmental assistance to the child's acquisition of grammar. Unpublished doctoral dissertation, Harvard University.

Cazden, C. (1968) The acquisition of noun and verb inflections. *Child Development*, **39**, 433–438.

Cernoch, J. M. & Porter, R. H. (1985) Recognition of maternal axillary odours by infants. *Child Development*, **56**, 1593–1598.

Chandler, M. (1991) Alternative readings of the competence–performance relation. In M. Chandler and M. Chapman (Eds), *Criteria for Competence: Controversies in the Conceptualization and Assessment of Children's Abilities*. Hillsdale, NJ: Erlbaum.

Chandler, M. J., Fritz, A. S. & Hala, S. M. (1989) Small scale deceit: Deception as a marker of 2-, 3- and 4-year-olds' early theories of mind. *Child Development*, **60**, 1263–1277.

Chapman, K. L., Leonard, L. B. & Mervis, C. B. (1986) The effects of feedback on young children's inappropriate word usage. *J. Child Language*, **13**, 101–117.

Charman, T. & Baron-Cohen, S. (1993) Drawing development in autism: The intellectual to visual realism shift. *Brit. J. Developmental Psychology*, **11**, 171–185.

Chomsky, N. (1959) Review of *Verbal Behavior*, by B. F. Skinner. *Language*, **35**, 26–58.

Chomsky, N. (1965) *Aspects of the Theory of Syntax*. Cambridge, MA: MIT Press.

Chomsky, N. (1980) Rules and representations. *Behavioural and Brain Sciences*, **3**, 1–15; 42–61.

Chomsky, N. (1981) *Lectures on Government and Binding*. Dordrecht: Foris.

Chomsky, N. (1986) *Knowledge of Language: Its Nature, Origins and Use*. New York: Praeger.

Chomsky, N. (1988) *Language and Problems of Knowledge*. Cambridge, MA: MIT Press.

Churcher, J. & Scaife, M. (1982) How infants see the point. In G. Butterworth & P. Light (Eds), *Social Cognition*. Brighton: Harvester.

Cicchetti, D. & Mans-Wagener, L. (1987) Stages, sequences, and structures in the organization of cognitive development in Down Syndrome infants. In I. Uzgiris & J. McV. Hunt (Eds), *Research with Scales of Psychological Development in Infancy*. Urbana: University of Illinois Press.

Cielinski, K. L., Vaughn, B. E. & Seifer, R. (unpublished) Relations among sustained attention in play, quality of play, and mother–child interaction in samples of children with Down syndrome and normally developing toddlers. Unpublished Ms.

Clahsen, H. (1992) Learnability theory and the problem of development in language acquisition. In J. Weissenborn, H. Goodluck & T. Roeper (Eds), *Theoretical Issues in Language Acquisition*. Hillsdale, NJ: Erlbaum.

Clark, A. (1988) Thoughts, sentences, and cognitive science. *Philosophical Psychology*, **1**, 263–78.

Clark, A. (1989) *Microcognition*. Cambridge, MA: MIT Press.

Clark, E. V. (1973) What's in a word? On the child's acquisition of semantics in his first language. In T. E. Moore (Ed), *Cognition and the Development of Language*. New York: Academic Press.

Clark, E. V. (1978) Strategies for communicating. *Child Development*, **49**, 953–959.

Clark, E. V. (1983) Meanings and concepts. In J. H. Flavell & E. M. Markman (Eds), *Handbook of Child Psychology*: vol. 3. *Cognitive Development* (pp. 787–840). New York: Wiley.

Clark, E. V. (1987) The principle of contrast: A constraint on language acquisition. In B. MacWhinney (Ed.), *Mechanisms of Language Acquisition: The 20th Annual Carnegie Symposium of Cognition* (pp. 1–33). Hillsdale, NJ: Erlbaum.

Clark, E. V. (1988) On the logic of contrast. *J. Child Language*, **15**, 317–335.

Clark, E. V. (1990) On the pragmatics of contrast. *J. Child Language*, **17**, 417–431.

Clark, E. V. (1991) Acquisition principles in language development. In S. A. Gelman & J. A. Byrnes (Eds), *Perspectives on Language and Thought*. Cambridge: Cambridge University Press.

Clark, R. A. (1978) The transition from action to gesture. In A. Lock (Ed.), *Action, Gesture and Symbol*. London: Academic Press.

Clarke, A. M. & Clarke, A. B. D. (1976) *Early Experience: Myth and Evidence*. London: Open Books.

Clibbens, J. & Harris, M. (1993) Phonological processes and sign language development. In D. Messer & G. Turner (Eds), *Critical Influences on Language Acquisitions and Development*. London: Macmillan.

Coggins, T. E. (1979) Relational meaning encoded in the two-word utterances of Stage 1 Down's Syndrome children. *J. Speech and Hearing Research*, **22**, 166–178.

Cohn, J. F., Matias, R., Tronick, E. Z., Connell, D. & Lyon-Ruth, D. (1986) Face-to-face interactions of depressed mothers and their infants. In E. Z. Tronick & T. Field (Eds), *Maternal Depression and Infant Disturbance* (pp. 31–45). San Francisco: Jossey-Bass.

Cohn, J. F., Matias, R. & Tronick, E. (1990) Face-to-face interactions of depressed mothers and their infants. In E. Tronick & T. M. Field (Eds), *New Directions for Child Development*, vol. 34. San Francisco: Jossey-Bass.

Cohn, J. F. & Tronick, E. Z. (1983) Three month old infants' reaction to simulated maternal depression. *Child Development*, **54**, 185–193.

Collis, G. M. (1977) Visual co-orientation and maternal speech. In H. R. Schaffer (Ed.), *Studies in Mother–Infant Interaction* (pp. 355–375). London: Academic Press.

Collis, G. M. (1981) Social interaction with objects: A perspective on human infancy. In K. Immelman, G. Barlow, L. Petrinovich & M. Main (Eds), *Behavioural Development*. Cambridge: Cambridge University Press.

Collis, G. M. (1985) On the origins of turn-taking: Alternation and meaning. In M. Barrett (Ed.), *Children's Single-Word Speech*. Chichester: Wiley.

Condon, W. S. & Sander, L. W. (1974) Synchrony demonstrated between movement of the neonate and adult speech. *Child Development*, **45**, 456–462.

Conti-Ramsden, G. (1989) Proper name usage: Mother–child interactions with language-impaired and non-language-impaired children. *First Language*, **9**, 271–284.

Cooper, R. P. & Aslin, R. N. (1990) Preference for infant directed speech in the first month after birth. *Child Development*, **61**, 1584–1595.

Cooper, W. E. & Paccia-Cooper, J. (1980) *Syntax and Speech*. Cambridge, MA: Harvard University Press.

Corrigan, R. (1978) Language development as related to state 6 object permanence development. *J. Child Language*, **5**, 173–189.

Corte, M. D., Benedict, H. & Klein, D. (1983) The relationship of pragmatic dimensions of mothers' speech to the referential-expressive distinction. *J. Child Language*, **10**, 35–43.

Crain, S. & McKee, C. (1985) Acquisition of structural restrictions on anaphora. In S. Berman, J. W. Choe & J. McDonough (Eds), *Proceedings of the 16th North Eastern Linguistics Society Meeting*. Amherst, MA: Graduate Linguistics Student Association.

Crawley, S. B. & Spiker, D. (1983) Mother–child interactions involving two-year-olds with Down's syndrome: A look at individual differences. *Child Development*, **54**, 1312–1323.

Cromer R. F. (in press) A case study of dissociations between language and cognition. To appear in H. Tager-Flusberg (Ed.), *Constraints on Language Acquisition: Studies of Atypical Children*. Hillsdale, NJ: Erlbaum.

Cromer, R. & Lipka, S. (1990) Problems in testing linguistic knowledge. Paper presented at the 5th International Congress for the Study of Child Language, Budapest, Hungary.

Cross, T. G. (1977) Mothers' speech adjustments: The contribution of selected child listener variables. In C. E. Snow & C. A. Ferguson (Eds), *Talking to Children: Language Input and Acquisition* (pp. 151–188). Cambridge: Cambridge University Press.

Cross, T. G., Johnson-Morris, J. E. & Nienhuys, T. G. (1980) Linguistic feedback and maternal speech: Comparisons of mothers addressing hearing and hearing-impaired children. *First Language*, **1**, 163–189.

Cross, T. G., Nienhuys, T. G. & Kirkman, M. (1985) Parent–child interaction with receptively disabled children: Some determinants of maternal speech style. In K. E. Nelson (Ed.), *Children's Language*, vol. 5. Hillsdale, NJ: Erlbaum.

Cunningham, C. C., Reuler, E., Blackwell, J. & Deck, J. (1981) Behavioural and linguistic developments in the interactions of normal and retarded children with their mothers. *Child Development*, **52**, 62–70.

Curtiss, S. (1977) *Genie: A Psycholinguistic Study of a Modern-day "Wild Child"*. London: Academic Press.

Dannemiller, J. L. & Stephens, B. R. (1988) A critical test of infant pattern preference models. *Child Development*, **59**, 210–216.

Davidson, D. (1986) A coherence theory in truth and knowledge. In E. LePore (Ed.), *Truth and Interpretation*. Oxford: Blackwell.

Davis, E. A. (1937) The development of linguistic skill in twins, singletons and sibs, and only children from 5 to 10. University of Minnesota Institute of Child Welfare, Monograph No. 14.

Davis, H. (1978) A description of aspects of mother–infant vocal interaction. *J. Child Psychology and Psychiatry*, **19**, 379–386.

Davis, K. (1947) Final note on a case of extreme isolation. *American J. Sociology*, **52**, 432–437.

Day, E. J. (1932) The development of language in twins. 1. A comparison of twins: their resemblances and differences. *Child Development*, **3**, 179–199, 298–316.

De Boysson-Bardies, B., Sargart, L. & Durand, C. (1984) Discernible differences in the babbling of infants according to target language. *J. Child Language*, **11**, 1–15.

DeCasper, A. J. & Fifer, W. P. (1980) Of human bonding: Newborns prefer their mothers' voices. *Science*, **208**, 1174–1176.

DeCasper, A. J. & Spence, M. J. (1986) Prenatal maternal speech influences newborns' perception of speech sounds. *Infant Behavior and Development*, **9**, 133–150.

DeLaguna, G. (1927) *Speech: Its Function and Development*. New Haven, CT: Yale University Press.

DellaCorte, M., Benedict, H. & Klein, D. (1983) The relationship of pragmatic dimensions of mothers' speech to the referential expressive distinction. *J. Child Language*, **10**, 35–44.

de Maio, L. J. (1982) Conversational turn-taking: A salient dimension of children's language learning. In N. J. Lass (Ed.), *Speech and Language: Advances in Basic Research and Practice*. New York: Academic Press.

Demetras, M. J., Post, K. N. & Snow, C. E. (1986) Feedback to first language learners: The role of repetitions and clarification questions. *J. Child Language*, **13**, 275–292.

DeMyer, M. K., Barton, S. & Alpern, G. D. et al. (1974) The measured intelligence of autistic children. *J. Autism and Childhood Schizophrenia*, **4**, 42–60.

de Saussure, F. (1959) *Course in General Linguistics*. New York: McGraw-Hill. (Original work published 1915.)

Deuchar, M. (1992) Can government and binding theory account for language acquisition? In C. M. Vide (Ed.), *Lenguajes Naturales y Lenguajes Formales*, vol. VIII.

Deutsch, W., Koster, C. & Koster, J. (1986) What can we learn from children's errors in understanding anaphora? *Linguistics*, **24**, 203–225.

de Villiers, J. G. & de Villiers, P. A. (1973) A cross-sectional study of the acquisition of grammatical morphemes in child speech. *J. Psycholinguistic Research*, **2**, 267–278.

Dockrell, J. E. (1981) The child's acquisition of unfamiliar words: An experimental study. Unpublished doctoral dissertation, University of Stirling, Stirling, Scotland.

Dockrell, J. & Campbell, R. (1986) Lexical acquisition strategies in the preschool child. In S. A. Kuczaj & M. D. Barrett (Eds), *The Development of Word Meaning*. New York: Springer-Verlag.

Dockrell, J. & McShane, J. (1990) Young children's use of phrase structure and inflectional information in form–class assignments of novel nouns and verbs. *First Language*, **10**, 127–140.

Donnellan, K. (1972) Proper names and identifying descriptions. In D. Davidson & G. Harman (Eds), *Semantics of Natural Language*. Dordrecht: Reidel.

Dooley, J. (1977) Language acquisition and Down's syndrome: A study of early semantics and syntax. Unpublished doctoral dissertation, Harvard University.

D'Ordrico, L. & Franco, F. (1991) Selective production of vocalization types in different communication contexts. *J. Child Language*, **18**, 475–499.

Dore, J. (1975) Holophrases, speech acts and language universals. *J. Child Language*, **2**, 21–40.

Dore, J. (1978) Conditions for the acquisition of speech acts. In I. Markova (Ed.), *The Social Context of Language*. New York: Wiley.

Dowd, J. M. C. & Tronick, E. Z. (1986) Temporal co-ordination of arm movements in early infancy. *Child Development*, **57**, 762–776.

Dromi, E. (1987) *Early Lexical Development*. Cambridge: Cambridge University Press.

Dromi, E., Leonard, L.B., Shteiman, M. (in press) The grammatical morphology of Hebrew-speaking children with specific language impairment: Some competing hypotheses. *J. Speech and Hearing Research*.

Dunlea, A. (1984) The relation between concept formation and semantic development. In L. Feagans, C. Garvey & R. Golinkoff (Eds), *The Origins and Growth of Communication* (pp. 224–244). Norwood, NJ: Ablex.

Dunlea, A. (1989) *Vision and the Emergence of Meaning: Blind and Sighted Children's Early Language*. Cambridge: Cambridge University Press.

Dunlea, A. & Andersen, E. (1992) The emergence process: Conceptual and linguistic influences on morphological development. *First Language*, **12**, 95–115.

Dunn, J. (1991) Understanding others: Evidence from naturalistic studies of children. In A. Whiten (Ed.), *Natural Theories of Mind*. Oxford: Blackwell.

Dziurawiec, S. & Ellis, H. (1986) Study reported in M. Johnson & J. Morton (1991) *Biology and Cognitive Development*. Oxford: Blackwell.

Eimas, P. D., Siqueland, E. R., Jusczyk, P. & Vigorito, J. (1971) Speech perception in infants. *Science*, **171**, 303–306.

Eisenberg, R. B. (1976) *Auditory Competence in Early Life*. Baltimore: University Park Press.

Eisenmjer, R. & Prior, M. (1991) Cognitive linguistics correlates of "theory of mind" ability in autistic children. *Brit. J. Developmental Psychology*, **9**, 351–364.

Ekman, P., Levenson, R. W. & Friesen, W. V. (1983) Autonomic nervous system activity distinguishes among emotions. *Science*, **221**, 1208–1210.

Elbers, L., van Loon-Vervoom, A. & van Helden-Lankhaar, M. (1993) "Contrastive Usage" and the development of lexical organization and innovative labelling. In M. Verrips and F. Wijnen (Eds), *The Acquisition of Dutch*. Amsterdam Series in Child Language Development, 1, Report No. 60, General Linguistics Institute, University of Amsterdam.

Ellias, G., Hayes, A. & Broerse, J. (1986) Maternal control of co-vocalisation and inter-speaker silences in mother–infant vocal engagements. *J. Child Psychology and Psychiatry*, **27**, 409–415.

Ellison, D. & Gillis, B. J. (1993) Developmental changes in the cognitive functioning of children with Down syndrome. Paper presented at SRCD, New Orleans.

Elman, J. L. (1991) Distributed representations, simple recurrent networks, and grammatical structure. *Machine Learning*, **7**, 195–225.

Elman, J. L. (1991) Incremental learning, or the importance of starting small. CRL Technical Report 9101.

Ervin, S. (1964) Imitation and structural change in children's language. In E. H. Lenneberg (Ed.), *New Directions in the Study of Language*. Cambridge, MA: MIT Press.

Ervin-Tripp, S. (1973) Some strategies for the first two years. In T. Moore (Ed.), *Cognition and the Development of Language*. New York: Academic Press.

Fagan, J. F. III & Singer, L. T. (1979) The role of simple feature differences in infant face recognition. *Infant Behavior and Development*, **2**, 39–46.

Fantz, R. L. (1966) Pattern discrimination and selective attention as determinants of perceptual development from birth. In A. H. Kidd & J. L. Rivoire (Eds), *Perceptual Development in Children*. New York: International Universities Press.

Fantz, R. L., Fagan, J. F. & Miranda, S. B. (1975) Early visual selectivity. In L. B. Cohen & P. Salapatek (Eds), *Infant Perception: From Sensation to Cognition*. New York: Academic Press.

Fantz, R. L. & Miranda, S. B. (1975) Longitudinal development of visual selectivity and perception in Down's syndrome and normal infants. Cited by R. L. Fantz, J. F. Fagan and S. B. Miranda, Early visual selectivity: As a function of pattern variables, previous exposure, age from birth and conception, and expected cognitive deficit. In L. B. Cohen and P. Salapatek (Eds), *Infant Perception: From Sensation to Cognition*. vol.1. *Basic Visual Processes*. New York: Academic Press.

Farrar, M. J. (1990) Discourse and the acquisition of grammatical morphemes. *J. Child Language*, **17**, 607–624.

Feagans, L. V., McGhee, S., Kipp, E. & Blood, I. (1990) Attention to language in day-care attending children: A mediating factor in the developmental effects of otitis media. Paper presented at the Meeting of the International Conference on Infancy Studies, Montreal, Canada.

Feagans, L., Sanyal, M., Henderson, F., Collier, A. & Applebaum, M. (1987) Relationship of middle ear disease in early childhood to later narrative and attentional skills. *J. Pediatric Psychology*, **12**, 581–594.

Feldman, C. (1971) The effects of various types of adult responses in the syntactic acquisition of two to three year olds. Unpublished paper, Department of Psychology, University of Chicago.

Felix, S. (1987) *Cognition and Language Growth*. Dordrecht: Foris.

Felix, S. (1992) Language acquisition as a maturational process. In J. Weissenborn, H. Goodluck & R. Roeper (Eds), *Theoretical Issues in Language Acquisition*. Hillsdale, NJ: Erlbaum.

Ferguson, C. A. (1964) Baby talk in six languages. *American Anthropologist*, **66**, 103–113.

Fernald, A. (1989) Intonation and communicative intent in mothers' speech to infants: Is the melody the message? *Child Development*, **60**, 1497–1510.

Fernald, A. (1991a) Prosody in speech to children: Prelinguistic and linguistic functions. *Annals of Child Development*, **8**, 43–80.

Fernald, A. (1991b) Approval and disapproval: Infant responsiveness to vocal effect in familiar and unfamiliar language. Unpublished Ms.

Fernald, A. & Kuhl, P. (1987) Acoustic determinants of infant preference for motherese speech. *Infant Behavior and Development*, **10**, 279–293.

Fernald, A. & Mazzie, C. (1991) Prosody and focus in speech to infants and adults. *Developmental Psychology*, **27**, 209–221.

Fernald, A., Taeschner, T., Dunn, J., Papousek, M., Boysson-Bardies, B. & Fukui, I. (1989) A cross-language study of prosodic modifications in mothers' and fathers' speech to preverbal infants. *J. Child Language*, **16**, 477–501.

Field, T. M. (1980) Interactions of high-risk infants: Quantitative and qualitative differences. In D. B. Sawin, R. C. Hawkins, L. O. Walker & H. H. Penticuff (Eds), *Exceptional Infant: Psychosocial Risks in Infant–Environment Interactions*, vol. 4 (pp. 120–143). New York: Brunner/Mazel.

Field, T. M. (1984) Early interactions between infants and their postpartum depressed mothers. *Infant Behavior and Development*, **7**, 527–532.

Field, T. (1985) Attachment as psychobiological attunement: Being on the same wavelength. In M. Reite & T. Field (Eds), *The Psychobiology of Attachment and Separation*. Orlando: Academic Press.

Field, T. M., Cohen, D., Garcia, R. & Greenberg, R. (1984) Mother–stranger face discrimination by the newborn. *Infant Behavior and Development*, **7**, 19–25.

Field, T., Healy, B., Goldstein, S., Perry, S., Bendell, D., Schanberg, S., Zimmerman, E. A. & Kuhn, C. (1988) Infants of depressed mothers show "depressed" behaviour even with nondepressed adults. *Child Development*, **59**, 1569–1579.

Fifer, W. P. & Moon, C. (1989) Psychobiology of newborn auditory preferences. *Seminar in Perinatology*, **13**, 430–433.

Fillmore, C. (1968) The case for case. In E. Bach & T. Harms (Eds), *Universals in Linguistic Theory*. New York: Holt, Rinehart & Winston.

Fischer, K., Share, J. & Koch R. (1964) Adaption of Gesell development scales for evaluation of development in children with Down's syndrome. *American J. Mental Deficiency*, **68**, 642–666.

Flax, J., Lahey, M., Harris, K. & Boothroyd, A. (1991) Relations between prosodic variables and communicative functions. *J. Child Language*, **18**, 3–19.

Fodor, J. A. (1966) How to learn to talk: Some simple ways. In F. Smith & G. A. Miller (Eds), *The Genesis of Language*. Cambridge, MA: MIT Press.

Fodor, J. A. (1983) *Modularity of Language*. Cambridge, MA: MIT Press.

Fodor, J. A. & Pylyshyn, Z. (1988) Connectionism and cognitive architecture: A critical analysis. In S. Pinker & J. Mehler (Eds), *Connections and Symbols*. Cambridge, MA: MIT Press.

Fodor, J. D. & Crain, S. (1987) Simplicity and generality of rules in language acquisition. In B. MacWhinney (Ed.), *Mechanisms of Language Acquisition*. Hillsdale, NJ: Erlbaum.

Fogel, A. (1993) Two principles of communication: Co-regulation and framing. In J. Nadel and L. Camaioni (Eds), *New Perspectives in Early Communicative Development*. London: Routledge.

Fogel, A. & Hannan, T. E. (1985) Manual expressions of 2- to 3-month-old human infants during social interaction. *Child Development*, **56**, 1271–1279.

Fogel, A., Toda, S. & Kawai, M. (1988) Mother–infant face-to-face interaction in Japan and the United States: A laboratory comparison using 3-month-old infants. *Developmental Psychology*, **24**, 398–406.

Folven, R. J. & Bonvillian, J. D. (1991) The transition from nonreferential to referential language in children acquiring American sign language. *Developmental Psychology*, **27**, No. 5, 806–816.

Forrester, M. (1992) *The Development of Young Children's Social Cognitive Skills*. Hove: Erlbaum.

Forrester, M. (1993) Affording social-cognitive skills in young children: The overhearing context. In D. Messer & G. Turner (Eds), *Critical Influences on Child Language Acquisition and Development*. London: Macmillan.

Fortescue, M. (1984/5) Learning to speak Greenlandic: A case study of a two-year old's morphology in a polysynthetic language. *First Language*, **5**, 101–113.

Fourcin, A. J. (1975) Speech production in the absence of speech productive ability. In N. O'Connor (Ed.), *Language, Cognitive Deficits, and Retardation*. London: Butterworth.

Fowler, A. (1988) Determinants of rate of language growth in children with Down syndrome. In L. Nadel (Ed.), *The Psychobiology of Down Syndrome*. Cambridge, MA: MIT Press.

Fowler, A. (1990) Language abilities in children with Down syndrome: Evidence for a specific syntactic delay. In D. Cicchetti & M. Beeghly (Eds), *Children with Down Syndrome*. Cambridge: Cambridge University Press.

Fraiberg, S. (1977) *Insights from the Blind: Comparative Studies of Blind and Sighted Infants*. New York: Basic Books.

Fraiberg, S. (1979) Blind infants and their mothers: An examination of the sign system. In M. Bullowa (Ed), *Before Speech*. Cambridge: Cambridge University Press.

Franco, F. & Butterworth, G. (1991a) Evidence for the "geometric" comprehension of manual pointing. Paper presented at a meeting of the SRCD, Seattle.

Franco, F. & Butterworth, G. (1991b) Infant pointing: Prelinguistic references and co-reference. Paper presented at the SRCD Biennial Meeting, Seattle.

Freeman, H. H., Lewis, C. & Doherty, M. J. (1991) Preschooler's grasp of a desire for knowledge in false-belief prediction: Practical intelligence and verbal report. *Brit. J. Developmental Psychology*, **9**, 139–157.

Freeman, N. H. (1974) *Human Infancy: An Evolutionary Perspective*. Hillsdale, NJ: Erlbaum.

Frege, G. (1970) On sense and reference. In P. Geach and M. Black (Eds), *Translations from the Philosophical Writings of Gottlob Frege*. Oxford: Blackwell.

Fremgen, A. & Fay, D. (1980) Overextensions in production comprehension: A methodological clarification. *J. Child Language*, **7**, 205–211.

Friel-Patti, S. & Finitzo, T. (1990) Language learning in a prospective study of otitis media with effusion in the first two years of life. *J. Speech and Hearing Research*, **33**, 188–194.

Frith, U. & Frith, C. D. (1974) Specific motor disabilities in Down's Syndrome. *J. Child Psychology and Psychiatry*, **15**, 293–301.

Frodi, A. (1985) Variations in parental and nonparental response to early infant communication. In M. Reite & T. Field (Eds), *The Psychobiology of Attachment and Separation*. New York: Academic Press.

Frye, D., Rawling, P., Moore, C. & Myers, I. (1983) Object–person discrimination and communication at 3 and 10 months. *Developmental Psychology*, **19**, No. 3, 303–309.

Furrow, D. & Nelson, K. (1986) A further look at the motherese hypothesis: A reply to Gleitman, Newport & Gleitman. *J. Child Language*, **13**, 163–176.

Furrow, D., Nelson, K. & Benedict, H. (1979) Mothers' speech to children and syntactic development: Some simple relationships. *J. Child Language*, **6**, 423–442.

Garnica, O. (1977) Some prosodic and paralinguistic features of speech to young children. In C. E. Snow & C. A. Ferguson (Eds), *Talking to Children: Language Input and Acquisition*. Cambridge, MA: Cambridge University Press.

Gathercole, S. E. & Baddeley, A. D. (1990) Phonological memory deficits in language disordered children: Is there a causal connection? *J. Memory and Language*, **29**, 336–360.

Gathercole, V. C. (1987) The contrastive hypothesis for the acquisition of word meaning: A reconsideration of the theory. *J. Child Language*, **14**, 493–531.

Gelman, S. A. & Taylor, M. (1984) *Child Development*, **55**, 1535–1540.

Gibson, D. (1966) Early developmental staging as a prophecy index in Down's syndrome. *American J. Mental Deficiency*, **70**, 825–828.

Gibson, D. (1981) *Down's syndrome. The Psychology of Mongolism*. Cambridge: Cambridge University Press.

Gibson, J. J. (1979) *The Ecological Approach to Visual Perception*. Boston, MA: Houghton Mifflin.

Gilberg, C. (1990) The neurobiology of infant autism. *J. Child Psychology and Psychiatry*, **29**, 257–266.

Gillham, B. (1979) *The First Words Language Programme*. London: Allen & Unwin.

Gleitman, L. R., Newport, E. & Gleitman, H. (1984) The current status of the Motherese Hypothesis. *J. Child Language*, **11**, 43–79.

Gleitman, L. R. & Wanner, E. (1982) Language acquisition: The state of the state of the art. In E. Wanner & L. R. Gleitman (Eds), *Language Acquisition: The State of the Art*. Cambridge: Cambridge University Press.

Glucksberg, S. & Danks, J. H. (1975) *Experimental Psycholinguistics*. Hillsdale, NJ: Erlbaum.

Gold, E. M. (1967) Language identification in the limit. *Information and Control*, **10**, 447–474.

Goldfield, B. A. (1985) Referential and expressive language: A study of two mother–child dyads. *First Language*, **6**, 119–131.

Goldfield, B. A. & Reznick, J. S. (1990) Early lexical acquisition: Rate, content and vocabulary spurt. *J. Child Language*, **17**, 171–183.

Goldin-Meadow, S. (1985) Language development under atypical learning conditions: Replication and implications of a study of deaf children of hearing parents. In K. Nelson (Ed.), *Children's Language*, vol. 5. Hillsdale, NJ: Erlbaum.

Goldin-Meadow, S. (1987) Underlying redundancy and its reduction in a language developed without a language model: Constraints imposed by conventional linguistic input. In B. Lust (Ed.), *Studies in the Acquisition of Anaphora*, vol. II. Dordrecht, MA: D. Reidel.

Goldin-Meadow, S. & Feldman, H. (1975) The creation of a communication system: A study of deaf children of hearing parents. *Sign Language Studies*, **8**, 225–234.

Goldin-Meadow, S. & Moreford, M. (1985) Gesture in early child language: studies of deaf and hearing children. *Merrill-Palmer Quarterly*, **31**, 145–176.

Goldin-Meadow, S. & Mylander, C. (1990) The role of parental input in the development of a morphological system. *J. Child Language*, **17**, 527–563.

Golinkoff, R. M., Hirsch-Pasek, K., Baduini, C. & Lavallee, A. (1985, October) What's in a word? The young child's predisposition to use lexical contrast. Paper presented at the Boston University Conference on Child Language, Boston.

Golinkoff, R. M., Hirsch-Pasek, K., Cauley, K. & Gordon, L. (1987) The eyes have it: Lexical and syntactic comprehension in a new paradigm. *J. Child Language*, **14**, 23–45.

Golinkoff, R. M. & Markessini, J. (1980) "Mommy sock": The child's understanding of possession as expressed in two-noun phrases. *J. Child Language*, **7**, 119–135.

Goodluck, H. (1991) *Language Acquisition: A Linguistic Introduction.* Oxford: Blackwell.

Gopnik, A. & Meltzoff, A. (1986) Relations between semantic and cognitive development in the one-word state—the specificity hypothesis. *Child Development*, **57**, 1040–1053.

Gopnik, M. & Crago, M. (1991) Familial aggregation of a developmental language disorder. *Cognition*, **39**, 1–50.

Gordon, P. (1985) Evaluating the semantic category hypothesis: The case for a count mass/distinction. *Cognition* **20**, 209–242.

Gordon, P. (1990) Learnability and feedback. *Developmental Psychology*, **26**, 217–220.

Goren, C. C., Sarty, M. & Wu, P. Y. K. (1975) Visual following and pattern discrimination of face-like stimuli by newborn infants. *Paediatrics*, **56**, 544–549.

Gottlieb, M. I., Zinkus, P. W. & Thompson, A. (1979) Chronic middle ear disease and auditory perceptual deficits: Is there a link? *Clinical Pediatrics*, **18**, 725–732.

Gough, P. (1966) The verification of sentences: Effects of delay and sentence length. *J. Verbal Learning and Verbal Behavior*, **5**, 492–496.

Gravel, J. S., McCarton, C. M. & Ruben, R. J. (1988) Otitis media in NICU graduates: A one-year prospective study. *Pediatrics*, **82**, 44–49.

Gravel, J. S. & Wallace, I. F. (1992) Listening and language at 4 years of age: Effects of early otitis media. *J. Speech and Hearing Research*, **35**, 588–595.

Green, G. M. (1989) *Pragmatics and Natural Language Understanding.* Hillsdale, NJ: Erlbaum.

Greenfield, P. & Savage-Rumbaugh, E. S. (1991) Imitation, grammatical development, and the invention of protogrammar by an ape. In N. Krasnegor, D. Rumbaugh, R. Schiefelbusch and M. Studdert-Kennedy (Eds), *Biological and Behavioural Determinants of Language Development.* Hillsdale: NJ: Erlbaum.

Greenfield, P. & Smith, J. (1976) *The Structure of Communication in Early Development.* New York: Academic Press.

Greenwald, C. & Leonard, L. (1979) Communicative and sensorimotor development of Down's Syndrome children. *American J. Mental Deficiency*, **84**, 296–303.

Gregory, S. & Barlow, S. (1989) Interaction between deaf babies and hearing mothers. In Woll, B. (Ed.), *Language Development and Sign Language*, Monograph No. 1. International Sign Linguistics Association, University of Bristol.

Gregory, S. & Mogford, K. (1981) Early language development in deaf children. In B. Woll, J. Kyle & M. Deuchar (Eds), *Perspectives on British Sign Language and Deafness.* London: Croom Helm.

Grice, H. P. (1957) Meaning. *Philosophical Review*, **66**, 377–388.

Grimshaw, J. (1981) Form, function, and the language acquisition device. In C. L. Baker & J. J. McCarthy (Eds), *The Logical Problem of Language Acquisition* (pp. 165–187). Cambridge, MA: MIT Press.

Grossman, K., Grossman, K. E., Spangler, G., Suess, G. & Unzner, L. (1985) Maternal sensitivity and newborns' orientation response as related to the quality of attachment in northern Germany. *Monographs of the Society for Research in Child Development*, No. 50, Serial No. 209, 233–256.

Guilfoyle, E. & Noonan, M. (1989) Functional categories and language acquisition. Unpublished Ms, McGill University.

Haith, M. M., Bergman, T. & Moore, M. J. (1977) Eye contact and face scanning in early infancy. *Science*, **198**, 853–855.

Halliday, M. (1973) Explorations in the function of language. In J. Lyons (Ed.), *New Horizons in Linguistics*. Harmondsworth: Penguin.

Halliday, M. (1975) *Learning How to Mean: Explorations in the Development of Language*. London: Edward Arnold.

Hamilton, C. (1993) Investigating the articulatory patterns of young adults with Down's syndrome using electropalatography. *Down's Syndrome Research and Practice*, **1**, 15–28.

Hampson, J. (1989) Elements of style: maternal and child contributions to referential and expressive styles of language acquisition. Unpublished doctoral dissertation, City University of New York.

Harding, C. & Golinkoff, R. (1979) The origins of intentional vocalizations in prelinguistic infants. *Child Development*, **50**, 33–40.

Harman, G. H. (1971) Three levels of meaning. In D. Steinberg & I. L. Jakobovits (Eds), *Semantics*. Cambridge: Cambridge University Press.

Harris, M. (1992) *Language Experience and Early Development*. Hillsdale, NJ: Erlbaum.

Harris, M. (1993) The relationship of maternal speech to children's first words. In D. Messer & G. Turner (Eds), *Critical Influences on Language Acquisition and Development*. London: Macmillan.

Harris, M., Barrett, M., Jones, D. & Brookes, S. (1988) Linguistic input and early word meaning. *J. Child Language*, **15**, 77–94.

Harris, M., Barlow-Brown, F. & Chasin, J. (1993) Pointing and the understanding of object names: A brief report. Proceedings of the 1993 Child Language Seminar, University of Plymouth.

Harris, M., Clibbens, J., Chasin, J. & Tibbitts, R. (1989) The social context of early sign language development. *First Language*, **9**, 81–97.

Harris, M. & Davies, M. (1987) Learning and triggering in child language: A reply to Atkinson. *First Language*, **7**, 31–39.

Harris, M., Jones D., Brookes, S. & Grant, J. (1986) Relations between the nonverbal context of maternal speech and rate of language development. *Brit. J. Developmental Psychology*, **4**, 261–268.

Harris, M., Jones, D. & Grant, J. (1983) The nonverbal context of mothers' speech to children. *First Language*, **4**, 21–30.

Harris, M., Jones, D. & Grant, J. (1984/85) The social-interactional context of maternal speech to infants: An explanation for the event-bound nature of early word use? *First Language*, **5**, 89–100.

Harter, S. & Zigler, E. (1974) The assessment of effectance motivation in normal and retarded children. *Developmental Psychology*, **10**, 169–180.

Harwood, F. W. (1959) Quantitative study of the speech of Australian children. *Language and Speech*, **2**, 236–270.

Hasan, P. & Messer, D. (1990) Communication and cognition in children with Down's syndrome. Paper presented at the IV European Developmental Psychology Conference, Stirling University.

Hayes, A. & Elliott, T. (1979) Gaze and vocalization in mother–infant dyads: Conversation or coincidence? Paper presented at the biennial meeting of the Society for Research in Child Development, San Francisco.

Hayes, L. A. & Watson, J. S. (1981) Neonatal imitation: Fact or artifacts? *Developmental Psychology*, **17**, 655–660.

Heath, S. B. (1983) *Ways with Words*. Cambridge: Cambridge University Press.

Hepper, P. G. (1991) An examination of fetal learning before and after birth. *Irish J. Psychology*, **12**, 95–107.

Herman, M. S. & Shantz, C. U. (1983) Social problem solving and mother–child interactions of educable mentally retarded with cerebal palsy, or nonretarded children. *J. Applied Development Psychology*, **4**, 217–226.

Hickey, T. (1988) Mean length of utterances and the acquisition of Irish. Paper presented at the Child Language Seminar, University of Warwick.

Hill, P. M. & McCune-Nicholich, L. (1981) Pretend play and patterns of cognition in Down's syndrome children. *Child Development*, **52**, 1168–1175.

Hirsch-Pasek, K., Kemler Nelson, D. G., Jusczyk, P. W., Cassidy, K. W., Benjamin, D. & Kennedy, L. (1987) Clauses are perceptual units for young infants. *Cognition*, **26**, 269–286.

Hirsch-Pasek, K., Treiman, R. & Schneiderman, M. (1984) Brown & Hanlon revisited: Mothers' sensitivity to ungrammatical forms. *J. Child Language*, **11**, 81–88.

Hobson, R. P. (1984) Early childhood autism and the question of egocentrism. *J. Autism and Developmental Disorders*, **14**, 85–104.

Hobson, R. P. (1986) The autistic child's appraisal of expresssions of emotion. *J. Child Psychology and Psychiatry*, **27**, 321–342.

Hobson, R. P. (1991) Against the theory of "Theory of Mind". *Brit. J. Developmental Psychology*, **9**, 33–51.

Hobson, R. P. (1993) Perceiving attitudes, conceiving minds. In C. Lewis & P. Mitchell (Eds), *Origins of an Understanding of Mind*. Hillsdale, NJ: Erlbaum.

Hockett, C. F. (1963) The problem of universals in language. In J. H. Greenberg (Ed.), *Universals of Language*. Cambridge, MA: MIT Press.

Hoff-Ginsberg, E. (1992) Methodological and social concerns in the study of children's language-learning environments: A reply to Pine. *First Language*, **12**, 251–254.

Howe, C. J. (1976) The meanings of two-word utterances in the speech of young children. *J. Child Language*, **3**, 29–47.

Howie, V. M., Ploussard, J. H. & Sloyer, J. (1975) The "otitisprone" condition. *American J. Disease in Children*, **129**, 676–678.

Hutchinson, J. E. (1986, April) Children's sensitivity to the contrastive use of object category terms. Paper presented at the Stanford Child Language Research Forum. Stanford University, Stanford, CA.

Huttenlocher, J. (1974) Origins of language comprehension. In R. Solso (Ed.), *Theories in Cognitive Psychology: the Loyola Symposium*. Potomac, MD: Erlbaum.

Huttenlocher, J., Haight, W., Bryk, A., Seltzer, M. & Lyons, T. (1991) Early vocabulary growth: Relation to language input and gender. *Developmental Psychology*, **27**, No. 2, 236–248.

Hyams, N. (1986) *Language Acquisition and the Theory of Parameters*. Dordrecht: Reidel.

Hyams, N. (1987) The theory of parameters and syntactic development. In T. Roeper & E. Williams (Eds), *Parameter Setting*. Dordrecht: Reidel.

Hyams, N. (1992) A reanalysis of null subjects in child language. In J. Weissenborn, H. Goodluck & T. Roeper (Eds), *Theoretical Issues in Language Acquisitions*. Hillsdale, NJ: Erlbaum.

Ingham, B. (1993) Critical influences on the acquisition of verb transitivity. In D. Messer & G. Turner (Eds), *Critical Influences on Language Acquisition and Development*. London: Macmillan.

Isabella, R. A., Belsky, J. & von Eye, A. (1989) Origins of infant–mother attachment: An examination of interactional synchrony during the infant's first year. *Developmental Psychology*, **25**, 12–21.

Izard, C. E., Hembree, E. & Huebner, R. (1987) Infants' emotional expressions to acute pain: Developmental changes and stability of individual differences. *Developmental Psychology*, **23**, 105–113.

Izard, C. E. & Malatesta, C. Z. (1987) Perspectives on emotional development 1: Differential emotions theory of early emotional development. In J. Osofsky (Ed.), *Handbook of Infant Development* (pp. 494–554). New York: Wiley.

Jacobson, S. W. (1979) Matching behaviour in the young infant. *Child Development*, 50, 853–860.

Jakobson, R. (1968) *Child Language, Aphasia, and Phonological Universals*. The Hague: Mouton.

Jasnow, M. & Feldstein, S. (1986) Adult-like temporal characteristics of mother–infant vocal interactions. *Child Development*, 57, 754–761.

Jerger, S., Jerger, J., Alford, B. R. & Abrams, S. (1983) Development of speech intelligibility in children with recurrent otitis media. *Ear and Hearing*, 4, 138–145.

Johnson, M. H. & Morton, J. (1991) *Biology and Cognitive Development: The Case of Face Recognition*. Oxford: Blackwell.

Johnson-Laird, P. N. & Stevenson, R. J. (1970) Memory for syntax. *Nature*, 337, 412–413.

Jones, C. P. & Adamson, L. B. (1987) Language use in mother–child and mother–child–sibling interactions. *Child Development*, 58, 356–366.

Jones, K. L. & Smith D. W. (1975) The William's elfin faces syndrome: A new perspective. *J. Pediatrics*, 86, 718–723.

Jones, O. H. M. (1977) Mother–child communication with pre-linguistic Down syndrome and normal infants. In H. R. Schaffer (Ed.), *Studies in Mother–Infant Interaction*. London: Academic Press.

Jones, S. S. & Smith L. B. (1991) Object properties and knowledge in early lexical learning. *Child Development*, 62, 499–516.

Jordan, R. (1993) The nature of the linguistic and communicative difficulties of children with autism. In D. Messer & G. Turner (Eds), *Critical Influences on Child Language Acquisition and Development*. London: Macmillan.

Kanner, L. (1943) Autistic disturbances of affective contact. *Nervous Child*, 2, 217–250.

Kataria, S., Goldstein, D. J. & Kushnick, T. (1984) Developmental delays in William's (Elfin Faces) syndrome. *Applied Research in Mental Retardation*, 5, 419–423.

Kato, M. & Fernald, A. (1993) The frequency and timing of Japanese and American mothers' vocal responses to infant vocalizations. Presentation at the Biennial Meeting of SRCD, New Orleans.

Katz, N., Baker, E. & MacNamara J. (1974) What's in a name? A study of how children learn common and proper names. *Child Development*, 45, 469–473.

Kaye, K. (1977) Toward the origin of dialogue. In R. H. Shaffer (Ed.), *Studies in Mother–Infant Interaction*. New York: Academic Press.

Kaye, K. (1982) *The Mental and Social Life of Babies*. Chicago: University of Chicago Press.

Kaye, K. & Fogel, A. (1980) The temporal structure of face-to-face communication between mothers and infants. *Developmental Psychology*, 16, 454–464.

Keil, F. C. (1991) Theories, concepts, and the acquisition of word meaning. In S. A. Gelman & J. P. Byrnes (Eds), *Perspectives on Language and Thought*. Cambridge: Cambridge University Press.

Kessen, W., Haith, M. & Salapatek, P. (1970) Human infancy: A bibliography and guide. In P. H. Mussen (Ed.), *Carmichael's Manual of Child Psychology* (3rd edn). New York: Wiley.

Kim, K. & Warren S. F. (1993) Running head: Balanced maternal speech. Presented in poster form at SRCD, New Orleans.

Klein, J., Teele, D., Mannos, R., Menyuk, P. & Rosner, B. (1984) Otitis media with effusion during the first three years of life and development of speech and language. In D. Lim, C. Bluestone, J. Klein & J. Nelson (Eds), *Recent Advances in Otitis Media: Proceedings of the Third International Symposium*. Philadelphia: Decker.

Kleiner, K. A. (1987) Amplitude and phase spectra as indices of infants' pattern preferences. *Infant Behavior and Development*, **10**, 49–59.

Kleiner, K. A. & Banks, M. S. (1987) Stimulus energy does not account for 2 month olds' face preferences. *J. Experimental Psychology*, **13**, 594–600.

Klima, E. & Bellugi, U. (1979) *The Signs of Language*. Cambridge, MA: Harvard University Press.

Koepke, J. E., Hamm, M. & Legerstee, M. (1983) Neonatal imitation: Two failures to replicate. *Infant Behavior and Development*, **6**, 97–102.

Koluchova J. (1972) Severe deprivation in twins: A case study. *J. Child Psychology and Psychiatry*, **13**, 107–114.

Koluchova, J. (1976) The further development of twins after severe and prolonged deprivation: A second report. *J. Child Psychology and Psychiatry*, **17**, 181–188.

Kripke, S. (1972) Naming and necessity. In D. Davidson & G. Harmon (Eds), *Semantics of Natural Language*. Dordrecht: Reidel.

Kuczaj, S. A. (1977) The acquisition of regular and irregular past tense forms. *J. Verbal Learning and Verbal Behavior*, **16**, 589–600.

Kuczaj, S. A. (1982) Young children's overextension of object words in comprehension and/or production: Support for a prototype theory of early object meaning. *First Language*, **3**, 93–105.

Kuhl, P. K. (1981) Auditory category formation and developmental speech perception. In R. Stark (Ed.), *Language Behavior in Infancy and Early Childhood*. New York: Elsevier.

Kuhl, P. K. & Miller, J. D. (1975) Speech perception by the chinchilla: Phonetic boundaries for synthetic VOT stimuli. *J. Acoustical Society of America*, **57**, series 49 (abstract).

Kursten, F. & Scholer, H. (1992) Specific language impairment theoretical approaches and some empirical data. (Preprint will appear in a book edited by Melita Kovacevic.)

Kyle, J. & Woll, B. (1985) *Sign Language*. Cambridge: Cambridge University Press.

Lakoff, G. (1987) *Women, Fire and Dangerous Things: What Categories Reveal About the Mind*. Chicago: University of Chicago Press.

Lakoff, G. (1971) On generative semantics. In D. Steinberg & L. Jakobivitz (Eds), *Semantics: An Interdisciplinary Reader in Philosophy, Linguistics, and Psychology*. Cambridge, Cambridge University Press.

Landau, B. & Gleitman, L. R. (1985) *Language and Experience*. Cambridge, MA: Harvard University Press.

Landau, B., Jones, J. & Smith, L. (1992) Discussion. Perception, ontology and naming in young children: Commentary on Soja, Carey & Spelke. *Cognition*, **43**, 85–91.

Landau, B. & Stecker, D. S. (1990) Objects and places: Geometric and syntactic representations in early lexical learning. *Cognitive Development*, **5**, 287–312.

Lasky, R., Syrdal-Lasky, A. & Klein, R. (1975) VOT discrimination by four to six and a half month infants from Spanish environments. *J. Experimental Child Psychology*, **20**, 215–225.

Layton, T. L. & Sharifi, H. (1979) Meaning and structure of Down's syndrome and non-retarded children's spontaneous speech. *American J. Mental Deficiency*, **83**, 439–445.

Lebeaux, D. (1988) Language acquisition and the form of the grammar. University of Massachusetts Doctoral Dissertation.

Leekam, S. R. & Perner, J. (1991) Does the autistic child have a metarepresentation deficit? *Cognition*, **40**, 203–218.

Legerstee, M. (1990) Infants use multimodal information to imitate speech sounds. *Infant Behavior and Development*, **13**, 343–354.

Legerstee, M., Bowman, T. G. & Fels, S. (1992) People and objects affect the quality of vocalizations in infants with Down syndrome. *Early Development and Parenting,* **1** (3), 149–156.

Lempers, J. D. (1976) Production of pointing, comprehension of pointing and understanding of looking behavior in young children. Unpublished doctoral dissertation, University of Minnesota.

Lenneberg, E. (1967) *Biological Foundations of Language.* New York: Wiley.

Leslie, A. M. (1987) Pretence and representation: The origins of "Theory of Mind". *Psychology Review,* **94**, No. 4, 412–426.

Leslie, A. M. (1991) The theory of mind impairment in autism: Evidence for a modular mechanism of development? In A. Whiten (Ed.), *Natural Theories of Mind: Evolution, Development and Stimulation of Everyday Mindreading.* Oxford: Blackwell.

Leung, E. & Rheingold, H. (1981) The development of pointing as a social gesture. *Developmental Psychology,* **17**, 215–236.

Levine, M. (1959) A model of hypothesis behavior in discrimination learning set. *Psychological Review,* **66**, 353–366.

Levine, M. (1963) Mediating processes in humans at the outset of discrimination learning. *Psychological Review,* **70**, 254–276.

Levitt, A. G. & Utman, J. G. A. (1992) From babbling towards the sound systems of English and French: A longitudinal two-case study. *J. Child Language,* **19**, 19–49.

Lewis, V. (1987) *Development and Handicap.* Oxford: Blackwell.

Lewis, V. & Boucher, J. (1988) Spontaneous instructed and elicited play in relatively able autistic children. *Brit. J. Developmental Psychology,* **6**, 325–339.

Lifter, K. & Bloom, L. (1989) Object knowledge and the emergence of language. *Infant Behavior and Development,* **12**, 395–423.

Lindner, K. & Johnston, J. (1992) Grammatical morphology in language-impaired children acquiring English or German as their first language: A functional perspective. *Applied Psycholinguistics,* **13**, 115–129.

Lipsitt, L. (1981) Presidential Address to division 7 of the American Psychological Association, reported in M. Shatz, On transition, continuity and coupling. In M. Golinkoff (Ed.) (1983) *The Transition from Prelinguistic to Linguistic Communication.* Hillsdale, NJ: Erlbaum.

Lleo, C. (1990) Homonymy and reduplication: On the extended availability of two strategies in phonological acquisitions. *J. Child Language,* **17**, 267–278.

Lloyd, V. L., Werker, J. F. & Cohen, L. B. (1993) Age changes in infants' ability to associate words with objects. Poster presentation at Society for Research in Child Development, New Orleans.

Lock, A. (1978) *Action, Gesture, and Symbol.* New York: Academic Press.

Lock, A. (1980) *The Guided Reinvention of Language.* New York: Academic Press.

Locke, J. L. (1983) *Phonological Acquisition and Change.* New York: Academic Press.

Locke, J. L. (1989) Babbling and early speech: Continuity and individual difference. *First Language,* **9**, 191–206.

Lous, J. (1987) Screening for secretory otitis media. *International J. Pediatric Otorhinolaryngology,* **13**, 85–97.

Lust, B. (1977) Conjunction reduction in child language. *J. Child Language,* **4**, 257–287.

Lust, B., Loveland, K. & Kornet, R. (1980) The development of anaphora in first-language: Syntactic and pragmatic constraints. *Linguistic Analysis,* **6**, 359–392.

Lust, B. & Wakayama, T. K. (1979) The structure of coordination in children's first-language acquisition of Japanese. In F. Eckman & A. Hastings (Eds), *Studies in First- and Second-Language Acquisition.* Rowley, MA: Newbury House Press.

Lyons, J. (1977) *Semantics*. Cambridge: Cambridge University Press.

Lytton, H. (1980) Parent–child interaction. The socialization process observed in twin and singleton families. New York: Plenum.

MacFarlane, A. (1975) Olfaction in the development of social preferences in the human neonate. In Ciba Foundation Symposium (Ed.), *Parent–Infant Interaction*. New York: Elsevier.

MacNamara, J. (1972) Cognitive basis of language learning in infants. *Psychological Review*, **79**, No.1.

MacNamara, J. (1982) *Words for Things*. Cambridge, MA: MIT Press.

MacWhinney, B. (1982) Basic syntactic processes. In S. Kuczaj (Ed.), *Language Acquisition*, vol. 1. *Syntax and Semantics*. Hillsdale, NJ: Erlbaum.

MacWhinney, B. (1987) The competition model. In B. MacWhinney (Ed.), *Mechanisms of Language Acquisition*. Hillsdale, NJ: Erlbaum.

MacWhinney, B. (1989a) Competition and teachability. In M. Rice & R. Schiefelbusch (Eds), *The Teachability of Language* (pp. 63–104). Baltimore: Brooks-Cole.

MacWhinney, B. (1989b) Competition and connectionism. In B. MacWhinney & E. Bates (Eds), *The Crosslinguistic Study of Sentence Processing*. Cambridge: Cambridge University Press.

MacWhinney, B. & Bates, E. (1989) *The Crosslinguistic Study of Sentence Processing*. Cambridge: Cambridge University Press.

MacWhinney, B. & Leinbach, J. (1991) Implementations are not conceptualizations: Revising the verb learning model. *Cognition*, **40**, 121–157.

MacWhinney, B., Pleh, C. & Bates, E. (1985) Cue validity and sentence interpretation in English, German, and Italian. *J. Verbal Learning and Verbal Behavior*, **23**, 127–150.

Madole, K. L. (1993) The role of functional properties in infants' categorization of objects. Poster presented at SRCD, New Orleans.

Madole, K. L., Oakes, L. M. & Cohen, L. B. (1993) Development changes in infants' attention to function and form–function correlations. *Cognitive Development*, **8**, 189–209.

Maestas y Moores, J. (1980) Early linguistic environment: Interactions of deaf parents with their infants. *Sign Language Studies*, **26**, 1–13.

Mahoney, G. (1988a) Maternal communication style with mentally retarded children. *American J. Mental Retardation*, **92**, 352–359.

Mahoney, G. (1988b) Enhancing the developmental competence of handicapped infants. In K. Marfo (Ed.), *Parent–Child Interaction and Development Disabilities: Theory, Research and Intervention* (pp. 203–219). New York: Praeger.

Mahoney, G. & Robenalt, K. (1986) A comparison of conversational patterns between mothers and their Down's syndrome and normal infants. *J. Division for Early Childhood*, **10**, 171–180.

Mandler, J. M. (1992) How to build a baby: II. Conceptual primitives. *Psychological Review*, **99**, 587–604.

Mandler, J. (1993) Perceptual and conceptual categories. Presentation at BIRG Conference.

Mandler, J. M., Bauer, P. J. & McDonough, L. (1991) Separating the sheep from the goats: Differentiating global categories. *Cognitive Psychology*, **23**, 263–298.

Mandler, J. M. & McDonough, L. (in press) Concept formation in infancy. To appear in *Cognitive Development*.

Maratsos, M. & Abramovitch, R. (1974) How children understand full, truncated, and anomalous passives. *J. Verbal Learning and Verbal Behavior*, **14**, 145–157.

Maratsos, M. & Chalkley, M. (1980) The internal language of children's syntax: The ontogenesis and representation of syntactic categories. In K. Nelson (Ed.), *Children's Language*, vol. 2. New York: Gardner.

Marchman, V. (1993) Constraints on plasticity in a connectionist model of the English past tense. *J. Cognitive Neuroscience*, 5, 215–234.

Marchman, V. A. & Bates, E. (in press) Continuity in lexical and morphological development: A test of the critical mass hypothesis. To appear in *J. Child Language*.

Marcus, G. F. (1993) Negative evidence in language acquisition. *Cognition*, 46, 53–85.

Marcus, G. F., Ulman, M., Pinker, S., Hollander, M., Rosen, T. J. & Xu, F. (1992) Overregularization in language acquisition. *Monographs of the Society for Research in Child Development*, No. 57(4), Serial No. 228.

Marfo, K. (1990) Maternal directiveness in interactions with mentally handicapped children: An analytical commentary. *J. Child Psychology and Psychiatry*, 31, 531–549.

Marfo, K. & Kysela, G. (1988) Frequency and sequential patterns in mothers' interactions with mentally handicapped and nonhandicapped children. In K. Marfo (Ed.), *Parent–Child Interaction and Developmental Disabilities: Theory, Research, and Intervention* (pp. 64–89). New York: Praeger.

Markman, E. M. (1989) *Categorization and Naming in Children: Problems of Induction*. Cambridge, MA: MIT Press.

Markman, E. M. (1991) The whole-object, taxonomic and mutual exclusivity assumptions as initial constraints on word meanings. In S. A. Gelman & J. A. Byrnes (Eds), *Perspectives on Language and Thought*. Cambridge: Cambridge University Press.

Markman, E. M. & Hutchinson, J. E. (1984) Children's sensitivity to constraints on meaning: Taxonomic versus thematic reactions. *CognitivePsychology*, 16, 1–27.

Markman, E. M. & Wachtel, G. F. (1988) Children's use of mutual exclusivity to constrain the meanings of words. *Cognitive Psychology*, 20, 121–157.

Masataka, N. (1992) Motherese in a signed language. *Infant Behavior and Development*, 15, 453–460.

Maskarinec, A. S., Cairns, G. F., Butterfield, E. C. & Weamer, D. K. (1981) Longitudinal observations of individual infant's vocalizations. *J. Speech and Hearing Disorders*, 46, 267–273.

Mason, M. K. (1942) Learning to speak after six and one half years of silence. *J. Speech and Hearing Disorders*, 7, 295–304.

Masur, E. F. (1982) Mothers' responses to infants' object-related gestures: Influences on lexical development. *J. Child Language*, 9, 23–30.

Matthei, E. H. (1981) Children's interpretation of sentences containing reciprocals. In S. Tavakolian (Ed.), *Language Acquisition and Linguistic Theory*. Cambridge, MA: MIT Press.

Maurer, D. & Barrera, M. (1981) Infants' perception of natural and distorted arrangements of a schematic face. *Child Development*, 47, 523–527.

Maurer, D. & Salapatek, P. (1976) Developmental changes in the scanning of faces by young infants. *Child Development*, 47, 523–527.

Maurer, H. & Sherrod, K. B. (1987) Context of directives given to young children with Down's syndrome and nonretarded children: Development over two years. *American J. Mental Deficiency*, 91, 579–590.

Mavilya, M. P. (1972) Spontaneous vocalization and babbling in hearing impaired infants. In G. Fant (Ed.), *International Symposium on Speech Communication Abilities and Profound Deafness*. Washington: A. G. Bell Association for the Deaf.

Mayberry, R. (1976) An assessment of some oral and manual language skills of hearing children and deaf parents. *American Annals of the Deaf*, 121, 507–512.

Mayer, N. K. & Tronick, E. Z. (1985) Mothers' turn-taking signals and infant turn-taking in mother–infant interaction. In T. Field & N. A. Fox (Eds), *Social Perception in Infants* (pp. 199–216). Norwood, NJ: Ablex.

Mayerson, M. & Frank, R. (1987) Language, speech and hearing in William's syndrome: Intervention approaches and research needs. *Developmental Medicine and Child Neurology*, **29**, 258–270.

McCawley, J. D. (1968) The role of semantics in a grammar. In E. Bach and R. T. Harms (Eds), *Universals in Linguistic Theory* (pp. 124–169). New York: Holt, Rinehart & Winston.

McCormick, K. & Dewart, H. (1986) Three's a crowd: Early language of a set of triplets. *Proceedings of the Child Language Seminar 1986* (pp. 286–287), Durham University.

McCune-Nicholich, L. (1981) Towards symbolic functioning: Structure in early pretend games and potential parallels with language. *Child Development*, **52**, 785–797.

McCune-Nicholich, L. & Bruskin, C. (1982) Combatorial competency in play and language. In K. Rubin (Ed.), *The Play of Children*. Basel: Karger.

McDonald, J. (1989) The acquisition of one-category mappings. In B. MacWhinney & E. Bates (Eds), *The Crosslinguistic Study of Sentence Processing* (pp. 375–96). Cambridge: Cambridge University Press.

McDonald, J. & MacWhinney, B. (1989) Maximum likelihood models for sentence processing. In B. MacWhinney & E. Bates (Eds), *The Crosslinguistic Study of Sentence Processing*. Cambridge: Cambridge University Press.

McDonald, M. & Lang, K. (1993) Children's comprehension and production of locative expressions. In D. J. Messer & G. Turner (Eds), *Critical Influences on Language Acquisition*. London: Macmillan.

McEvoy, R. E., Rogers, S. J. & Pennington, B. F. (1993) Executive function and social communication deficits in young autistic children. *J. Child Psychology and Psychiatry*, **34**, No. 4, 563–578.

McGurk, H. & MacDonald, J. (1976) Auditory-visual co-ordination in the first year of life. *Int. J. Behavioral Development*, **1**, 119–239.

McIntire, M. L. (1977) The acquisition of American Sign Language hand configurations. *Sign Language Studies*, **16**, 247–266.

McKenzie, B. & Over, R. (1983a) Young infants fail to imitate facial and manual gestures. *Infant Behavior and Development*, **6**, 85–95.

McKenzie, B. & Over, R. (1983b) Do neonatal infants imitate? A reply to Meltzoff & Moore. *Infant Behavior and Development*, **6**, 109–111.

McNamara, T. P. & Sternberg, R. (1983) Mental models of word meaning. *J. Verbal Learning and Verbal Behavior*, **22**, 449–474.

McNeil, D. (1970) The development of language. In P. H. Mussen (Ed.), *Carmichael's Manual of Child Psychology*, vol. 1 (3rd edn). New York: Wiley.

McNeil, J. D. (1966) *The ABC Learning Activity: Language of Instruction*. New York: American Books.

McShane, J. (1980) *Learning to Talk*. Cambridge: Cambridge University Press.

McShane, J. (1990) *Cognitive Development*. Oxford: Blackwell.

Meier, R. P. & Newport, E. L. (1990) Out of the hands of babes: On a possible sign advantage in language acquisition. *Language*, **66**, 1–23.

Melhuish, E. (1982) Visual attention to mother's and stranger's faces and facial contrast in 1 month old infants. *Developmental Psychology*, **18**, 229–231.

Meltzoff, A. N. (1988) Infant imitation after a 1-week delay: Long-term memory for novel acts and multiple stimuli. *Developmental Psychology*, **24**, No. 4, 470–476.

Meltzoff, A. N. & Gopnik, A. (1989) On linking nonverbal imitation, representation, and language learning in the first two years of life. In G. E. Speidel & K. E. Nelson (Eds), *The Many Faces of Imitation in Language Learning* (pp. 23–51). New York: Springer-Verlag.

Meltzoff, A. & Gopnik, A. (1993) The role of imitation in understanding persons and developing a theory of mind. In S. Baron-Cohen, H. Tager-Flusberg & D. Cohen (Eds), *Understanding Other Minds—Perspective from Autism*. Oxford: Oxford University Press.

Meltzoff, A. N. & Moore, K. M. (1977) Imitation of facial and manual gestures by human neonates. *Science*, **198**, 75–78.

Meltzoff, A. N. & Moore, K. M. (1983a) New born infants imitate adult facial gestures. *Child Development*, **54**, 702–709.

Meltzoff, A. N. & Moore, M. K. (1983b) Methodological issues in studies of imitation: Comments on McKenzie and Over et al. *Infant Behavior and Development*, **6**, 103–108.

Meltzoff, A. N. & Moore, M. K. (1992) Early imitation within a functional framework: The importance of person identity, movement, and development. *Infant Behavior and Development*, **15**, 479–505.

Menn, L. (1985) Phonological development: Learning sounds and sound patterns. In J. Berko-Gleason (Ed.), *The Development of Language*. Columbus, Ohio: Merrill.

Menyuk, P. (1986) Predicting speech and language problems with persistent otitis media. In J. Kavanagh (Ed.), *Otitis Media and Child Development* (pp. 83–96). Parkton, MD: York Press.

Merriman, W. E. (1987 April) Lexical contrast in toddlers: A reanalysis of the diary evidence. Paper presented at the biennial convention of the Society of Research in Child Development, Baltimore.

Merriman, W. E. & Bowman, L. L. (1989) The mutual exclusivity bias in children's word learning. *Monographs of the Society for Research in Child Development*, No. 54 (3–4), Serial No. 220.

Mervis, C. B. (1987) Child-basic object categories and early lexical development. In U. Neisser (Ed.), *Concepts and Conceptual Development: Ecological and Intellectual Factors in Categorization* (pp. 201–233). Cambridge: Cambridge University Press.

Mervis, C. B. (1989) Early lexical development: The role of operating principles. Unpublished Ms, Emory University, Atlanta, GA.

Mervis, C. B. & Long, L. M. (1987, April) Words refer to whole objects: Young children's interpretation of the referent of a novel word. Paper presented at the biennial meeting of the Society for Research in Child Development, Baltimore.

Messer, D. J. (1978) The integration of mother's referential speech with joint play. *Child Development*, **49**, 781–787.

Messer, D. J. (1980) The episodic structure of maternal speech to young children. *J. Child Language*, **7**, 29–40.

Messer, D. J. (1981) The identification of names in maternal speech to infants. *J. Psycholinguistic Research*, **10**, 69–77.

Messer, D. J. (1983) The redundancy between adult speech and non-verbal interaction: A Contribution to Acquisition? In R. Golinkoff (Ed.), *The Transition from Prelinguistic to Linguistic Communication*: Hillsdale, NJ: Erlbaum.

Messer, D. J. (1986) Adult–child relationships and language acquisition. *J. Social and Personal Relationships*, **3**, 101–119.

Messer, D. J. (1993) Mastery, attention, I.Q. and parent–infant social interaction. In D. Messer (Ed.), *Mastery Motivation in Early Childhood*. London: Routledge.

Messer, D. & Hasan, P. (in press) Early communication and cognition in children with Down's syndrome. *Down's Syndrome Research and Practice*.

Messer, D. J. & Vietze, P. M. (1984) Timing and transitions in mother–infant gaze. *Infant Behavior and Development*, 7, 167–181.

Messer, D. J. & Vietze, P. M. (1988) Does mutual influence occur during mother–infant social gaze? *Infant Behavior and Development*, 11, 97–110.

Meyerson, M. D. & Frank, R. A. (1987) Language, speech and hearing in William's Syndrome: Intervention approaches and research needs. *Developmental Medicine and Child Neurology*, 29, 258–270.

Miller, G. A. (1962) Some psychological studies of grammar. *Americana Psychologist*, 17, 748–762.

Miller, J. F. (1988) The developmental asynchrony of language development in children with Down syndrome. In L. Nadel (Ed.), *The Psychobiology of Down Syndrome*. Cambridge, MA: MIT Press.

Mills, A. E. (1987) The development of phonology in the blind child. In B. Dodd & R. Campbell (Eds), *Hearing by Eye: The Psychology of Lip-reading*. Erlbaum: London.

Mills, D., Coffrey, S. & Neville, H. (1993) Changes in cerebral organization in infancy during primary language acquisition. In G. Dawson & K. Fischer (Eds), *Human Behaviour and the Developing Brain*. New York: Guilford Publications.

Mitchell, P. R. & Kent, R. (1990) Phonetic variation in multisyllable babbling. *J. Child Language*, 17, 247–265.

Mittler, P. (1970) Biological and social aspects of language development in twins. *Development Medicine and Child Neurology*, 12, 741–757.

Miyake, H., Chen, S. & Campos, J. (1985) Infant temperament, mothers' mode of interaction, and attachment in Japan. *Monographs of the Society for Research in Child Development*, No. 50, 276–297.

Moerke, E. L. (1983) *The Mother of Eve—as a First Language Teacher*. Norwood, NJ: Ablex.

Moerke, E. (1991) Positive evidence for negative evidence. *First Language*, 11, 219–251.

Mogford, K. (1988) Language development in twins. In D. Bishop & K. Mogford (Eds), *Language Acquisition in Exceptional Circumstances*. Edinburgh: Churchill Livingstone.

Mogford, K. & Gregory, S. (1982) The development of communication skills in young deaf children: Picture book reading with mother. Paper given to the Psycholinguistics and Language Pathology Colloquium, University of Newcastle, November 1982 (unpublished).

Morgan, J. L. (1986) *From Simple Imput to Complex Grammar*. Cambridge, MA: MIT Press.

Morgan, J. L. & Travis, L. L. (1989) Limits on negative information in language input. *J. Child Language*, 16, 531–552.

Moses, L. J. & Chandler, M. J. (in press) Traveler's guide to children's theories of mind. *Psychological Inquiry*.

Mowrer, O. H. (1960) *Learning Theory and the Symbolic Process*. New York: Wiley.

Mulford, R. C. (1987) First word of the blind child. In M. D. Smith & J. L. Locke (Eds), *The Emergent Lexicon: the Child's Development of a Linguistic Vocabulary*. London: Academic Press.

Mundy, P., Kasari, C. & Sigman, M. (1992) Nonverbal communication, affective sharing, and intersubjectivity. *Infant Behavior and Development*, 15, 377–381.

Mundy, P. & Sigman, S. (1989) The theoretical implications of joint-attention deficits in autism. *Development and Psychopathology*, 1, 173–183.

Murphy, C. M. (1978) Pointing in the context of a shared activity. *Child Development*, 49, 371–380.

Murphy, C. M. & Messer, D. J. (1977) Mothers, infants and pointing: A study of a gesture. In H. R. Schaffer (Ed.), *Studies in Mother–Infant Interaction*. London: Academic Press.

Murphy, G. L. & Medin D. L. (1985) The role of theories in conceptual coherence. *Psychological Review*, **92**, No. 3, 289–316.

Murphy, J. & Slorach, N. (1983) The language development of pre-preschool hearing children of deaf parents. *Brit. J. Disorders of Communication*, **18**, 119–126.

Murray, A. D., Johnson, J. & Peters, J. (1990) Fine-tuning of utterance length to preverbal infants: Effects on later language development. *J. Child Language*, **17**, 511–525.

Murray, L. & Stein, A. (1989) The effects of postnatal depression on the infant. *Bailliere's Clinical Obstetrics and Gynaecology*, **3**, 921–933.

Murray, L. & Trevarthen, C. (1985) Emotional regulation of interactions between two-month-olds and their mothers. In T. M. Field & N. A. Fox (Eds), *Social Perception in Infants*. New Jersey: Ablex.

Murray, L. & Trevarthen, C. (1986) The infant's role in mother–infant communication. *J. Child Language*, **13**, 15–29.

Musselman, C., Lindsay, P. & Wilson, A. (1988) An evaluation of trends in preschool programming for hearing impaired children. *J. Speech and Hearing Disorders*, **53**, 71–88.

Naigles, L. (1990) Children use syntax to learn verb meanings. *J. Child Language*, **17**, 3557–3574.

Nelson, K. (1973) Structure and strategy in learning to talk. *Monographs of the Society for Research in Child Development*, No. 38.

Nelson, K. (1974) Concept, word and sentence: Interrelations in acquisition and development. *Psychological Review*, **81**, 267–285.

Nelson, K. E. (1977) Facilitating children's syntax acquisition. *Developmental Psychology*, **13**, 101–107.

Nelson, K. (1979) Explorations in the development of a functional semantic system. In W. Collins (Ed.), *Children's Language and Communication, Child Psychology*, vol. 12 (pp. 47–81). Hillsdale, NJ: Erlbaum.

Nelson, K. (1985) *Making Sense: The Acquisition of Shared Meaning*. New York: Academic.

Nelson, K. (1987) What's in a name? Reply to Seidenberg and Petitto. *J. Experimental Psychology: General*, **116**, 293–296.

Nelson, K. (1988) Constraints on word learning? *Cognitive Development*, **3**, 221–246.

Nelson, K. (1990) Comment on Behrend's "Constraints and Development". *Cognitive Development*, **5**, 331–339.

Nelson K. E. & Bonvillian, J. D. (1978) Concepts and words in the 18-month-old: Acquiring concept names under controlled conditions. *Cognition*, **2** (4), 435–450.

Nelson, K. E., Carskaddon, G. & Bonvillian, J. D. (1973) Syntax acquisition: Impact of experimental variation in adult verbal interaction with the child. *Child Development*, **44**, 497–504.

Netsell, R. (1981) The acquisition of speech motor control: A perspective with directions for research. In R. E. Stark (Ed.), *Language Behaviour in Infancy and Early Childhood*. Amsterdam: Elsevier North-Holland.

Newport, E. L., Gleitman, H. & Gleitman, I. R. (1977) Mother, I'd rather do it myself: Some effects and non-effects of maternal speech style. In C. Snow & C. A. Ferguson (Eds), *Talking to Children*. Cambridge: Cambridge University Press.

Newson, J. (1989) The growth of shared understanding between infant and caregiver. In M. Bullowa (Ed.), *Before Speech*. Cambridge: Cambridge University Press.

Newson, M. (1990) Dependencies in the lexical setting of parameters: A solution to the undergeneralisation problem. In M. Roca (Ed.), *Logical Issues in Language Acquisition*. Dordrecht: Foris.

Nicholich, L. (1981) Toward symbolic functioning: Structure of early pretend games and potential parallels with language. *Child Development*, **52**, 785–797.

Ninio, A. (1992) The relation of children's single word utterances to single word utterances in the input. *J. Child Language*, **19**, 87–110.

Ninio, A. (1993) Is early speech situational? An examination of some current theories about the relation of early utterances to context. In D. Messer & G. Turner (Eds), *Critical Influences on Language Acquisition and Development*. London: Macmillan.

Ninio, A. & Bruner, J. S. (1978) The achievement and antecedents of labelling. *J. Child Language*, **5**, 1–15.

Norman, D. A., Rumelhart, D. E. & the LNR Research Group (1985) *Explorations in Cognition*. San Francisco: Freeman.

Ochs, E. & Schieffelin, B. B. (1984) Language acquisition and socialization. In R. A. Shweder & R. A. Levine (Eds), *Culture Theory*. Cambridge: Cambridge University Press.

Ogden, C. K. & Richards, I. A. (1923) *The Meaning of Meaning*. New York: Harcourt, Brace & World.

O'Grady, W., Peters, A. M. & Masterson, D. (1989) The transition from optional to required subjects. *J. Child Language*, **16**, 513–529.

Ogura, T., Notari, A. & Fewell, R. (1990) The relationship between language and play in Down's syndrome children. Poster presented at International Congress of Applied Psychology, Japan, July.

Olguin, R. & Tomasello, M. (in press) Twenty-five month old children do not have a grammatical category of verb. *Cognitive Development*.

Oller, D. K. (1980) The emergence of the sounds of speech in early infancy. In G. H. Yeni-Komshian, J. F. Kavanagh & C. A. Ferguson (Eds), *Child Phonology*, vol. 1. New York: Academic Press.

Oller, D. K. (1986) Metaphonology and infant vocalizations. In B. Limblom & R. Zetterstorm (Eds), *Precursors of Early Speech*. Wenner-Gren International Symposium Series, vol. 44 (pp. 93–112). Basingstoke: Macmillan.

Oller, D. K., Wieman, L. A., Doyle, W. J. & Ross, C. (1976) Infant babbling and speech. *J. Child Language*, **3**, 1–11.

Oster, H. (1978) Facial expression and affect development. In M. Lewis & L. A. Rosenblum (Eds), *The Development of Affect*. New York: Plenum Press.

Oviatt, S. L. (1980) The emerging ability to comprehend language: An experimental approach. *Child Development*, **51**, 97–106.

Pack, C. (1983) Interactional synchrony as an artifact of microanalysis. *Dissertation Abstracts International*, **43**, 3423A.

Panneton, R. K. & DeCasper, A. J. (1986, April) Newborns' postnatal preference for a prenatally experienced melody. Paper presented at the International Conference on Infant Studies, Los Angeles.

Papousek, H. & Papousek, M. (1977) Mothering and the cognitive headstart: Psychological considerations. In H. R. Schaffer (Ed), *Studies in Mother–Infant Interactions* (pp. 63–85). London: Academic Press.

Papousek, M. (1989) Determinants of responsiveness to infant vocal expression of emotional state. *Infant Behavior and Development*, **12**, 507–524.

Papousek, M., Bornstein, M. H., Nuzzo, C., Papousek, H. & Symmes, D. (1990) Infant responses to prototypical melodic contours in parental speech. *Infant Behavior and Development*, **13**, 539–545.

Papousek, M. & Papousek, H. (1989) Forms and functions of vocal matching in precanonical mother–infant interactions. *First Language*, **9** (Special Issue), 137–158.

Papousek, M., Papousek, H. & Haekel, M. (1987) Didactic adjustments in fathers' and mothers' speech to their three-month-old infants. *J. Psycholinguistic Research*, **16**, 491–516.

Papousek, M., Papousek, K. H. & Symmes, D. (1991) The meanings of melodies in mothers in tone and stress languages. *Infant Behavior and Development*, **14**, 415–440.

Pappas-Jones, C. & Adamson, L. B. (1987) Language use in Mother–child and mother–child–sibling interactions. *Child Development*, **58**, 356–366.

Paradise, J. L. (1981) Otitis media during early life: How hazardous to development? A critical review of the literature. *Pediatrics*, **68**, 869–873.

Parisi, D. (1993) Connectionism and language development. Invited lecture at VI International Congress for the Study of Child Language, Trieste.

Penner, S. G. (1987) Parental responses to grammatical and ungrammatical child utterances. *Child Development*, **58**, 376–384.

Perez-Pereira, M. (1989) The acquisition of morphemes: Some evidence from Spanish. *J. Psycholinguistic Research*, **18**, 289–312.

Perez-Pereira, M. & Castro, J. (1992) Pragmatic functions of blind and sighted children's language: A twin case study. *First Language*, **12**, 17–37.

Perez-Pereira, M. & Castro, J. (1993) Pronoun use by blind children. Paper presented at VIth International Congress for the Study for the Study of Child Language. Trieste.

Perner, J. (1991) *Understanding the Representational Mind*. Cambridge, MA: MIT Press.

Peters, A. M. (1983) *The Units of Language Acquisition*. Cambridge, MA: Cambridge University Press.

Peterson, G. A. & Sherrod, K. B. (1982) Relationship of maternal language to language development and language delay of children. *American J. Mental Deficiency*, **86**, 391–398.

Petitto, L. A. (1987) On the autonomy of language and gesture: Evidence from the acquisition of personal pronouns in American Sign Language. *Cognition*, **27**, 1–52.

Petitto, L. A. (1988) "Language" in the pre-linguistic child. In F. S. Kessel (Ed.), *The Development of Language and Language Researchers*. Hillsdale, NJ: Erlbaum.

Phillips, J. R. (1972) Syntax and vocabulary of mothers' speech to young children: Age and sex comparisons. *Child Development*, **44**, 182–185.

Piaget, J. (1932) *The Language and Thought of the Child*. London: Routledge & Kegan Paul.

Piaget, J. (1962) *Play, Dreams, and Imitation in Childhood*. New York: Norton.

Piattelli-Palmarini, M. (1980) *Language and Learning: The Debate between Jean Piaget and Noam Chomsky*. London: Routledge and Kegan Paul; Cambridge, MA: Harvard University Press.

Pine, J. M. (1992) The functional basis of referentiality: Evidence from children's spontaneous speech. *First Language*, **12**, 39–56.

Pine, J. M. & Lieven, E. O. M. (1990) Referential style at thirteen months: why age-defined cross-sectional measures are inappropriate for the study of strategy differences in early language development. *J. Child Language*, **17**, 625–631.

Pinker, S. (1982) A theory of the acquisition of lexical interpretive grammars. In J. Bresnan (Ed.), *The Mental Representation of Grammatical Relations*. Cambridge, MA: MIT Press.

Pinker, S. (1984) *Language Learnability and Language Development*. Cambridge, MA: Harvard University Press.

Pinker, S. (1987) The bootstrapping problem in language acquisition. In B. MacWhinney (Ed.), *Mechanisms of Language Acquisition*. Hillsdale, NJ: Erlbaum.

Pinker, S. (1989) *Learnability and Cognition: The Acquisition of Argument Structure*. Cambridge, MA: MIT Press.

Pinker, S. (1991) Rules of language. *Science*, **253**, 530–535.

Pinker, S. & Prince, A. (1988) On language and connectionism: Analysis of a parallel distributed processing model of language acquisition. *Cognition*, **28**, 73–193.

Plunkett, K. & Marchman, V. (1991) U-shaped learning and frequency effects in a multi-layered perception: Implications for child language acquisition. *Cognition*, **38**, 43–102.

Plunkett, K. & Sinha, C. (1992) Connectionism and developmental theory. *Brit. J. Developmental Psychology*, **10**, 209–254.

Porter, R. H., Balogh, R. D. & Makin, J. W. (1988) Olfactory influences on mother–infant interactions. In C. Rovee-Collier & L. P. Lipsitt (Eds), *Advances in Infancy Research*. Norwood, NJ: Ablex.

Porter, R. H., Cernoch, J. M. & Balogh, R. D. (1985) Odour signatures and kin recognition. *Physiology and Behavior*, **34**, 445–448.

Porter, R. H. & Moore, J. D. (1981) Human kin recognition by olfactory cues. *Physiology and Behavior*, **27**, 493–495.

Power, D. J., Wood, D. J. & Wood, H. A. (1990) Conversational strategies of teachers using three methods of communication with deaf children. *American Annals of the Deaf*, **135**, 9–13.

Premack, D. (1986) *Gavagia! or the Future History of the Animal Language Controversy*. Cambridge, MA: MIT Press.

Prinz, P. & Prinz, E. (1981) Acquisition of ASL and spoken English by a hearing child of a deaf mother and a hearing father: Phase 11. Early combinatorial patterns. *Sign Language Studies*, **30**, 78–88.

Pueschel, S. M., Gallagher, P. L., Zartler, A. S. & Pezzullo, J. C. (1987) Cognitive and learning processes in children with Down syndrome. *Research in Developmental Disabilities*, **8**, 21–37.

Putman, H. (1962) It Ain't Necessarily So. *J. Philosophy*, **LIX**, 658–671.

Putman, H. (1975) The meaning of meaning. Reprinted in *Mind, Language and Reality: Philosophical Papers*, vol. 1. Cambridge: Cambridge University Press.

Quigley, S. & Paul, P. (1987) Deafness and language development. In S. Rosenberg (Ed.), *Advances in Applied Psycholinguistics*, vol. 1: *Disorders of First Language Development*. Cambridge: Cambridge University Press.

Quine, W. V. O. (1960) *Word and Object*. Cambridge, MA: MIT Press.

Quine, W. V. O. (1969) *Ontological Relativity and other Essays*. New York: Columbia University Press.

Racette, K. & Fowler, A. (1993) Phonological bases of memory in normal preschoolers and young adults with Down syndrome. Paper presented at SRCD Conference, New Orleans.

Radford, A. (1990) *Syntactic Theory and the Acquisition of English Syntax: The Nature of Early Child Grammars in English*. Oxford: Blackwell.

Randall, J. H. (1992) The catapult hypothesis: An approach to unlearning. In J. Weissenborn, H. Goodluck & T. Roeper (Eds), *Theoretical Issues in Language Acquisition*. Hillsdale, NJ: Erlbaum.

Ratner, N. B. (1989) Atypical language development. In J. Berko-Gleason (Ed.), *The Development of Language*. Columbus, Ohio: Merill.

Ratner, N. B. & Pye, C. (1984) Higher pitch in BT is not universal: Acoustic evidence from Quiche Mayan. *J. Child Language*, **2**, 515–522.

Record, R. G., McKeown, T. & Edwards, J. H. (1970) An investigation of the difference in measured intelligence between twins and single births. *Annals of Human Genetics*, **34**, 11–20.

Reddy, V. (1991) Playing with others' expectations: Teasing and mucking about in the first year. In A. Whiten (Ed.), *Natural Theories of Mind: Evolution, Development and Simulation of Everyday Mindreading*. Oxford: Blackwell.

Reilly, J., Klima, E. S. & Bellugi, U. (1991) Once more with feeling: Affect and language in atypical populations. *Development and Psychopathology*, **2**, 367–391.

Remick, H. (1976) Material speech to children during language acquisition. In W. von Raffler-Engel & Y. Lebran (Eds), *Baby Talk and Infant Speech*. Amsterdam: Swets & Zeitlinger.

Rice, M. & Wexler, K. (1993) Types of agreement in SLI children. Paper presented at VIth International Congress for the Study of Child Language, Trieste.

Richards, M. M. (1979) Sorting out what's in word from what's not: Evaluation of Clark's Semantic Features Acquisition Theory. *J. Experimental Psychology*, **27**, 1–47.

Richards, M. P. M. (1974) First step in becoming social. In M. P. M. Richards (Ed), *The Integration of a Child into a Social World*. Cambridge: Cambridge University Press.

Ricks, D. M. & Wing, L. (1975) Language, communication, and the use of symbols in normal and autistic children. *J. Autism and Childhood Schizophrenia*, **5**, 191–221.

Roberts, J., Burchinal, M., Koch, M., Footo, M. & Henderson, F. (1988) Otitis media in early childhood and its relationship to later phonologic development. *J. Speech and Hearing Disorders*, **53**, 424–432.

Roberts, J., Sanyal, M., Burchinal, M., Collier, A., Ramey, C. & Henderson, F. (1986) Otitis media in early childhood and its relationship to later verbal and academic performance. *Pediatrics*, **78**, 423–430.

Robinson, E. J. & Mitchell, P. (in press) Children's interpretations of messages from a speaker with a false belief. *Child Development*.

Robson, K. S. (1967) The role of eye-to-eye contact in maternal–infant attachment. *J. Child Psychology and Psychiatry*, **8**, 13–25.

Rom, A. & Leonard, L. (1990) Interpreting deficits in grammatical morphology in specifically language impaired children: Preliminary evidence from Hebrew. *Clinical Linguistics and Phonetics*, **4**, 93–105.

Rondal, J. A. (1978) Developmental sentence scoring procedure and the delay-difference question in language development, of Down's syndrome children. *Mental Retardation*, **16**, 169–171.

Rondal, J. A. (1988) Down's syndrome. In D. Bishop & K. Mogford (Eds), *Language Development in Exceptional Circumstances*. Edinburgh: Churchill Livingstone.

Rosch, E. (1973) On the internal structure of perceptual and semantic categories. In T. E. Moore (Ed.), *Cognitive Development and the Acquisition of Language*. New York: Academic Press.

Rosch, E. (1978) Principles of categorization. In E. Rosch & B. B. Lloyd (Eds), *Cognition and Categorization*. Hillsdale, NJ: Erlbaum.

Rosch, E. & Mervis, C. B. (1975) Family resemblances: Studies in the internal structure of categories. *Cognitive Psychology*, **8**, 382–439.

Rosenfield, H. M. (1981) Whither interactional synchrony? In K. Bloom (Ed.), *Prospective Issues in Infancy Research*. Hillsdale, NJ: Erlbaum.

Ross, G. S. (1982) Language functioning and speech development of six children receiving tracheotomy in infancy. *J. Communication Disorders*, **15**, 95–111.

Ruben, R. J., Downs, M. P., Jerger, J., Fiellau-Nikolajsen, M., Paparella, M. M. & Ranney, J. B. (1985) Otitis media: Impact and sequelae. *Annals of Otology, Rhinology and Otolaryngology*, **94** (suppl. 16), 31–32.

Ruddy, M. G. & Bornstein, M. H. (1982) Cognitive correlates of infant attention and maternal stimulation over the first year of life. *Child Development*, **53**, 183–188.

Ruff, H. A. (1986) Components of attention during infants' manipulative exploration. *Child Development*, **57**, 105–114.

Rumbaugh, D. M. (1977) *Language Learning by a Chimpanzee*. New York: Academic Press.

Rumelhart, D. E. & McClelland, J. L. (1986) On learning the past tense of English verbs. In J. L. McClelland, D. E. Rumelhart and the PDP Research Group, *Parallel Distributed Processing: Exploration in the Micro Structure of Cognition*. Cambridge, MA: MIT Press.

Rumelhart, D. E. & Ortony, A. (1977) The representation of knowledge in memory. In R. C. Anderson, R. J. Spiro & W. E. Montague (Eds), *Schooling and the Acquisition of Knowledge*. Hillsdale, NJ: Erlbaum.

Russell, J., Mauthner, N., Sharpe, S. & Tidswell, T. (1991) The "windows task" as a measure of strategic deception in preschoolers and autistic subjects. *Brit. J. Developmental Psychology*, **9**, 331–349.

Russell, M. J., Mendelson, T. & Peeke, H. V. S. (1983) Mothers' identification of their infants' odour. *Ethology and Sociobiology*, **4**, 29–31.

Rutter, D. R. & Durkin, K. (1987) Turn-taking in mother–infant interaction: An examination of vocalizations and gaze. *Developmental Psychology*, **23**, 1, 54–61.

Ryan, M. (1978) Contour in context. In R. Campbell & P. Smith (Eds), *Recent Advances in the Psychology of Language*. New York: Plenum Press.

Ryther-Duncan, J., Scheuneman, D., Bradley, J., Jensen, M., Hansen D. & Kaplan, P. (1993) Infant- versus adult-directed speech as signals for faces. Poster presented at the Biennial Meeting of the SRCD, New Orleans.

Sachs, J. S. (1967) Recognition memory for syntactic and semantic aspects of connected discourse. *Perception and Psychophysics*, **73**, 437–442.

Sachs, J. & Johnson, M. L. (1976) Language development in a hearing child of deaf parents. In W. von Raffler-Enge & Y. Lebrun (Eds), *Baby Talk and Infant Speech*. Lisse, Netherlands: Swets & Zeitlinger.

Sak, R. J. & Ruben, R. J. (1981) Recurrent middle ear effusion in childhood. Implications of temporary auditory deprivation for language and learning. *Annals of Otology*, **90**, 546–551.

Savage-Rumbaugh, E. S. (1986) Giving, taking and sharing: The currency of symbolic exchange. *Ape Language: From Conditioned Responses to Symbols*. New York: Columbia University Press.

Savage-Rumbaugh, E. S. (1987) Communication, symbolic communication and language: Reply to Seidenberg and Petitto. *J. Experimental Psychology: General*, **116**, 288–292.

Savage-Rumbaugh, E. S. (1990) Language as a cause-effect communication system. *Philosophical Psychology*, **3**, No. 1.

Savage-Rumbaugh, E. S. (1991) Language learning in the Bonobo: How and why they learn. In N. Krasnegor, D. Rumbaugh, R. Schiefelbusch and M. Studdert-Kennedy (Eds), *Biological and Behavioural Determinants of Language Development*. Hillsdale, NJ: Erlbaum.

Savic, S. (1980) *How Twins Learn to Talk. A Study of the Speech Development of Twins*. London: Academic Press.

Scaife, M. & Bruner, J. S. (1975) The capacity for joint visual attention. *Nature*, **253**, 265–266.

Scarborough, H. & Wyckoff, J. (1986) Mother, I'd still rather do it myself: Some further non-effects of "motherese". *J. Child Language*, **13**, 431–438.

Schaal, B., Montagner, H., Hertling, E., Bolzoni, D., Moyse, A. & Quichon, R. (1980) Les stimulations olfactives dans les relations entre l'enfant et la mère. *Reproduction, Nutrition et Développement*, **20**, 843–858.

Schaffer, H. R. (1984) *The Child's Entry into a Social World*. London: Academic Press.

Schaffer, H. R., Collis, G. & Parsons, G. (1977) Vocal interchange and visual regard in verbal and pre-verbal children. In H. R. Schaffer (Ed.), *Studies in Mother–Infant Interaction*. London: Academic Press.

Schaffer, H. R. & Emerson, P. E. (1964) The development of social attachments in infancy. *Monographs of the Society for Research in Child Development*, No. 29 (3), Serial No. 94.

Schaffer, H. R. & Parry, M. H. (1969) Perceptual-motor behaviour in infancy as a function of age and stimulus familiarity. *Brit. J. Psychology*, **60**, 1–9.

Schank, R. C. & Abelson, R. P. (1977) *Scripts, Plans, Goals and Understanding*. Hillsdale, NJ: Erlbaum.

Schieffelin, B. B. (1979) Getting it together: An ethnographic approach to the study of the development of communicative competence. In E. Ochs & B. B. Schieffelin (Eds), *Developmental Pragmatics*. New York: Academic Press.

Schieffelin, B. B. (1990) *The Give and Take of Everyday Life: Language Socialization of Kaluli Children*. Cambridge: Cambridge University Press.

Schieffelin, B. B. & Ochs, E. (1983) Ethnographic orientation. In R. Golinkoff (Ed.), *The Transition from Prelinguistic to Linguistic Communication*. Hillsdale, NJ: Erlbaum.

Schiff, N. (1979) The influence of deviant maternal input on the development of language during the preschool years. *J. Speech and Hearing Research*, **22**, 581–603.

Schiff, N. & Ventry, I. M. (1976) Communication problems in hearing child of deaf parents. *J. Speech and Hearing Disorders*, **41**, 348–358.

Schiff-Myers, N. (1988) Hearing children of deaf parents. In D. Bishop & K. Mogford (Eds), *Language Acquisition in Exceptional Circumstances*. Edinburgh: Churchill Livingstone.

Schlesinger, H. S. & Meadow, K. P. (1972) *Sound and Sign: Childhood Deafness and Mental Health*. Berkeley: University of California Press.

Schwartz, R. & Camarata, S. (1985) Examining relationships between input and language development: Some statistical issues. *J. Child Language*, **12**, 1, 199–209.

Scollen, R. (1976) *Conversations with a One Year Old: A Case Study of the Developmental Foundation of Syntax*. Honolulu: University Press of Hawaii.

Searle, J. (1969) *Speech Acts*. Cambridge: Cambridge University Press.

Seidenberg, M. S. & Petitto, L. A. (1987) Communication, symbolic communication and language: Comment on Savage-Rumbaugh et al. *J. Experimental Psychology: General*, **116**, 276–287.

Seyfarth, R. M., Cheney, D. L. & Marler, P. (1980a) Monkey responses to three different alarm calls: Evidence for predator classification and semantic communication. *Science*, **210**, 801–803.

Seyfarth, R. M., Cheney, D. L. & Marler, P. (1980b) Vervet monkey alarm calls: Semantic communication in a free ranging primate. *Animal Behavior*, **28**, 1070–1094.

Share, J. B. (1975) Development progress in Down's syndrome. In R. Koch & F. de la Cruz (Eds), *Down's Syndrome: Research, Prevention and Management*. New York: Brunner/Mazel.

Shatz, M. (1983) On transition, continuity, and coupling: An alternative approach to communicative development. In R. M. Golinkoff (Ed.), *The Transition from Prelinguistic to Linguistic Communication* (pp. 337–55). Hillsdale, NJ: Erlbaum.

Shatz, M. & Gelman, R. (1973) The development of communication skills: Modification in the speech of young children as a function of the listener. *Monographs of the Society for Research in Child Development*, No. 38. SRCD: Chicago.

Sherman, B. (1927) Facial expressions in infants. *Journal of Psychology*, **6**, 151–72.

Sherrod, K. B., Friedman, S., Crawley, S., Drake, D. & Devieux, J. (1977) Material speech to prelinguistic infants. *Child Development*, **48**, 1662–1665.

Simon, B. M., Fowler, S. M. & Handler, S. D. (1983) Communication development in young children with long-term tracheotomies: Preliminary report. *Int. J. Pediatric Otorhinolaryngology*, **6**, 37–50.

Skinner, B. S. (1957) *Verbal Behavior*. New York: Appleton-Century-Crofts.

Slater, A., Cooper, R., Rose, D. & Morison, V. (1989) Prediction of cognitive performance from infancy to early childhood. *Human Development*, **32**, 137–147.

Slobin, D. I. (1966) Grammatical transformation in childhood and adulthood. *J. Verbal Learning and Verbal Behavior*, **5**, 219–227.

Slobin, D. (1973) Cognitive prerequisites for the development of grammar. In C. A. Fergusson and D. I. Slobin (Eds), *Studies of Child Language Development*. New York: Holt, Rinehart & Winston.

Slobin, D. I. (1985) *The Cross-Linguistic Study of Language Acquisition*, vol. 1: *The Data*. Hillsdale, NJ: Erlbaum.

Slobin, D. & Bever, T. G. (1982) Children use canonical sentence schemas: A crosslinguistic study of word order and inflections. *Cognition*, **12**, 229–265.

Sluckin, W., Herbert, M. & Sluckin, A. (1983) *Maternal Bonding*. Oxford: Blackwell.

Smith, B. (1977) Phonological development in Down's syndrome children. Paper presented at the 85th Annual Convention of the American Psychological Association, San Francisco.

Smith, N. V. (1989) *The Twitter Machine: Reflection on Language*. Oxford: Blackwell.

Smolak, L. & Weinraub, M. (1983) Maternal speed: Strategy or response? *J. Child Language*, **10**, 369–380.

Smolensky, P. (1988) On the proper treatment of connectionism. *Behavioural and Brain Sciences*, **11**, 1–74.

Snow, C. (1973) Mothers' speech to children learning language. *Child Development*, **43**, 549–565.

Snow, C. E. (1977) Mothers' speech research: From input to interaction. In C. E. Snow and C. A. Ferguson (Eds), *Talking to Children*. Cambridge: Cambridge University Press.

Snow, C. E. & Gilbreath, B. J. (1983) Discussion of the volume. Explaining transitions. In R. M. Golinkoff (Ed.), *The Transition from Prelinguistic to Linguistic Communication*. Hillsdale, NJ: Erlbaum.

Snow, C. S., Smith, N. & Hoefnagel-Hohle, M. (1980) The acquisition of some Dutch morphological rules. *J. Child Language*, **7**, 539–553.

Snyder, L., Bates, E. & Bretherton, I. (1981) Content and context in early lexical development. *J. Child Language*, **8**, 565–582.

Soja, N. N., Carey, S. & Spelke, E. S. (1990) Ontological categories guide young children's inductions of word meaning: Object terms and substance terms. *Cognition*, **38**, 179–211.

Soja, N. N., Carey, S. & Spelke, E. S. (1992) Discussion. Perception, ontology and word meaning. *Cognition*, **45**, 101–107.

Solan, L. (1983) *Pronominal Reference: Child Language, and the Theory of Grammar*. Dordrecht: Reidel.

Speidel, G. E. (1993) Phonological short-term memory and individual differences in learning to speak: a bilingual case study. *First Language*, **13**, 69–91.

Sperber, D. & Wilson, D. (1986) *Relevance: Foundations of Pragmatic Theory.* Cambridge: Cambridge University Press.

Stampe, D. (1969) The acquisition of phonemic representations. *Proceedings of Vth Regional Meeting of the Chicago Linguistic Society*, pp. 443–444.

Stark, R. E. (1980) Stages of speech development. In G. H. Yeni-Komshian, J. F. Kavanagh & C. A. Ferguson (Eds), *Child Phonology*, vol. 1: *Production.* New York: Academic Press.

Stark, R. E. (1989) Temporal patterning of cry and non-cry sounds in the first eight months of life. *First Language*, 9, 107–136.

Stemmer, N. (1987) The learning of syntax: An empiricist approach. *First Language*, 7, 97–120.

Stern, D. N. (1974) Mother and infant at play: The dyadic interaction involving facial, vocal and gaze behaviours. In M. Lewis & L. A. Rosenblum (Eds), *The Effect of the Infant on its Caregiver.* New York: Wiley.

Stern, D. N. (1977) *The First Relationship.* Cambridge: Harvard University Press.

Stern, D. N., Jaffe, J., Beebe, B. & Bennett, S. L. (1975) Vocalizing in unison and in alternation: two kinds of communication within the mother–infant dyad. *Annals of New York Academy of Sciences*, 263, 89–100.

Stern, D. N., Beebe, B., Jaffe, J. & Bennett, S. L. (1977) The infant's stimulus world during social interaction. In H. R. Schaffer (Ed.), *Studies in Mother–Infant Interaction.* London: Academic Press.

Stern, D. N., Spieker, S., Barnett, R. K. & MacKain, K. (1983) The prosody of maternal speech: Infant age and context related changes. *J. Child Language*, 10, 1–15.

Stern, D. N., Spieker, S. & MacKain, K. (1982) Intonation contours as signals in maternal speech to prelinguistic infants. *Developmental Psychology*, 18, 727–735.

Stevenson, R. J. (1987) *Models of Language Development.* Milton Keynes: Open University Press.

Stevenson, R. J. (1992) Maturation and learning: Linguistic knowledge and performance: A commentary on Clahsen and Felix. In J. Weissenborn, H. Goodluck & T. Roeper (Eds), *Theoretical Issues in Language Acquisition.* Hillsdale, NJ: Erlbaum.

Stewart, D. A. (1992) Initiating reform in total communication programs. *J. Special Education*, 26, No. 1, 68–84.

Stoel-Gammon, C. & Cooper, J. A. (1984) Patterns of early lexical and phonological development. *J. Child Language*, 11, 247–271.

Stoel-Gammon, C. & Otomo, K. (1986) Babbling development of hearing-impaired and normally hearing subjects. *J. Speech and Hearing Disorders*, 51, 33–40.

Stokoe, W. C. (1960) Sign language structure: An outline of the visual communicative system of the American deaf. *Studies in Linguistics*, Paper 8, University of Buffalo.

Strauss, M. S. (1979) Abstraction of prototypical information by adults and 10-month-old infants. *J. Experimental Psychology: Human Learning and Memory*, 5, 618–632.

Strawson, P. F. (1964) *Individuals: An Essay in Descriptive Metaphysics.* London: Methuen.

Streeter, L. (1976) Language perception of two month old infants shows effects of both innate mechanisms and experience. *Nature*, 259, 39–41.

Sugar, S. (1983) *Children's Early Thought: Development in Classification.* Cambridge: Cambridge University Press.

Sugarman, S. (1983) Empirical versus logical issues in the transition from prelinguistic to linguistic communication. In R. M. Golinkoff (Ed.), *The Transition from Prelinguistic to Linguistic Communication.* Hillsdale, NJ: Erlbaum.

Sylvester-Bradley, B. (1985) Failure to distinguish people and things in early infancy. *Brit. J. Developmental Psychology*, **3**, 281–292.

Tager-Flusberg, H. (1992) Autistic children's talk about psychological states: Deficits in the early acquisition of a theory of mind. *Child Development*, **63**, 161–172.

Tallal, P., Curtiss, S. & Allard, L. (1991) Otitis media in language impaired and normal children. *J. Speech, Language, Pathology and Audiology*, **15**, No. 4, 33–41.

Talmy, L. (1985) Lexicalization patterns: Semantic structure in lexical forms. In T. Shopen (Ed.), *Language Typology and Syntactic Description, vol. 3: Grammatical Categories and the Lexicon*. New York: Cambridge University Press.

Tannock, R. (1988) Mothers' directiveness in their interactions with their children with and without Down's syndrome. *American J. Mental Retardation*, **93**, 154–165.

Taylor, M. & Gelman, S. A. (1988) Adjectives and nouns: Children's strategies for learning new words. *Child Development*, **59**, 411–419.

Taylor, M. & Gelman, S. A. (1989) Incorporating new words into the lexicon: Preliminary evidence for language hierarchies in two-year-old children. *Child Development*, **60**, 625–636.

Teasdale, T. W. & Owen D. R. (1984) Heredity and familial environment in intelligence and educational level—a sibling study. *Nature*, **309**, 620–622.

Teele, D., Klein, J., Rosner, B. & The Greater Boston Otitis Media Study Group (1984) Otitis media with effusion during the first three years of life and development of speech and language. *Pediatrics*, **74**, 282–287.

Terrace, H. S., Petitto, R. J. & Bever, T. G. (1979) Can an ape create a sentence? *Science*, **206**, No. 4421, 891–902.

Thevenin, D., Eilers, R., Oller, D. K. & Lavoir, L. (1985) Where's the drift in babbling drift? A cross-linguistic study. *J. Applied Linguistics*, **6**, 3–15.

Thorpe, W. H. (1961) *Bird Song: The Biology of Vocal Communication and Expression in Birds*. Cambridge: Cambridge University Press.

Thorpe, W. H. (1963) *Learning and Instinct in Animals* (2nd edn). London: Methuen.

Tomasello, M. (1992) *First Verbs: A Case Study of Early Grammatical Development*. Cambridge: Cambridge University Press.

Tomasello, M. & Barton, M. (in press) Learning words in non-ostensive contexts. *Developmental Psychology*, revisions under review.

Tomasello, M. & Farrar, J. (1986) Joint attention and early language. *Child Development*, **57**, 1454–1463.

Tomasello, M. & Kruger, A. C. (1992) Joint attention on actions: Acquiring verbs in ostensive and non-ostensive contexts. *J. Child Language*, **19**, 311–333.

Tomasello, M., Mannle, S. & Kruger, A. C. (1986) Linguistic environment of 1- to 2-year-old twins. *Developmental Psychology*, **22**, 2, 169–176.

Tomasello, M. & Olguin, R. (in press) Twenty-three month old children have a grammatical category of noun. *Cognitive Development*.

Tomasello, M. & Todd, J. (1983) Joint attention and lexical acquisition style. *First Language*, **4**, 197–212.

Trevarthen, C. (1977) Descriptive analysis of infant communicative behaviour. In H. R. Schaffer (Ed.), *Studies of Mother–Infant Interaction*. London: Academic Press.

Trevarthen, C. (1979a) Communication and co-operation in early infancy: A description of primary intersubjectivity. In M. Bullowa (Ed.), *Before Speech*. Cambridge: Cambridge University Press.

Trevarthen, C. (1979b) Instincts from human understanding are for cultural co-operation: Their development in infancy. In M. Von Cranach, K. Foppa, W. Lepenies & D. Ploog (Eds), *Human Ethology* (pp. 530–571). Cambridge: Cambridge University Press.

Trevarthen, C. B. & Hubley, P. (1978) Secondary intersubjectivity: Confidence, confiding and acts of meaning in the first year. In A. J. Lock (Ed.), *Action, Gesture and Symbol: The Emergence of Language* (pp. 183–229). London: Academic Press.

Tronick, E. Z., Als, H. & Brazelton, T. B. (1977) Mutuality in mother–infant interaction. *J. Communication*, **27**, 74–79.

Trybus, R. & Karchmer, M. (1977) School achievement scores of hearing impaired children: National data on achievement status and growth patterns. *American Annals of the Deaf*, **122**, 62–69.

Ullman, M., Pinker, S., Hollander, M., Prince, A. & Roseen, T. L. (1989) Growth of regular and irregular vocabulary and the onset of overregularization, Paper presented at the 14th Annual Boston University Conference on Language Development, Boston, MA.

Ullman, S. (1979) *The Interpretation of Visual Motion*. Cambridge, MA: MIT Press.

Urwin, C. (1978) The development of communication between blind infants and their parents: Some ways into language. Doctoral dissertation, University of Cambridge.

Valian, V. (1990a) Syntactic subjects in the early speech of American and Italian children. Ms., Hunter College, New York.

Valian, V. (1990b) Null subjects: A problem for parameter-setting models of language acquisition. *Cognition*, **35**, 105–122.

Valian, V. (1993) Discussion: Parser failure and grammar change. *Cognition*, **46**, 195–202.

van der Lely, H. K. J. (in press) Canonical linking rules: Forward vs reverse linking in normally developing and specifically language impaired children. *Cognition*.

van der Lely, H. K. J. & Harris, M. (1990) Comprehension of reversible sentences in specifically language-impaired children. *J. Speech and Hearing Disorders*, **55**, 101–117.

van der Lely, H. K. J. & Howard, D. (1993) Children with specific language impairment: Linguistic impairment or short-term memory deficit? *American Speech-Language Hearing Association*, **36**.

van Valin, R. D. Jr (1991) Functionalist linguistic theory and language acquisition. *First Language*, **11**, 7–40.

Vargha-Khadem, F. & Passingham, R. (1990) Speech and language defects. *Nature*, **346**, 226.

Veneziano, E. & Georgakopoulos, J. (1993) Is early mother–child discourse really tied to the hic et nunc? Paper presented at the VI International Congress for the study of Child Language, Trieste, Italy.

Veneziano, E. & Sinclair, H. (1993) On the grammatical status of early prelexical vocalic segments: A case study. Paper presented at the VI International Congress for the study of Child Language, Trieste, Italy.

Veneziano, E., Sinclair, H. & Berthoud, I. (1990) From one word to two words: Repetition patterns on the way to structured speech. *J. Child Language*, **17**, 633–650.

Ventry, I. M. (1980) Effects of conductive hearing loss: Fact or fiction? *J. Speech and Hearing Disorders*, **45**, 143–156.

Vihman, M., Macken, M., Miller, R., Simmons, H. & Miller, J. (1985) From babbling to speech: A reassessment of the continuity issue. *Language*, **61**, 397–445.

Vinter, A. (1986) The role of movement in eliciting early imitation. *Child Development*, **57**, 66–71.

Volterra, V. (1983) Gestures, signs and words at 2 years. In J. Kyle & B. Wall (Eds), *Language in Sign*. London: Croom Helm.

Von Frisch, K. (1927) *Bees: Their Vision, Chemical Sense and Language*. Ithaca, NY: Cornell University Press.

Wallace, I. F., Gravel, J. S. & Ganon, E. C. (1991) Preschool language outcomes as a function of otitis media and parental linguistic styles. *Abstracts of the Fifth International Symposium on Recent Advances in Otitis Media* (Abstract No. 211).

Wallace, I. F., Gravel, J. S., McCarton, C. M. & Ruben, R. J. (1988) Otitis media and language development at 1 year of age. *J. Speech and Hearing Disorders*, **53**, 245–251.

Walton, G. E., Bower, N. J. A. & Bower, T. G. R. (1992) Recognition of familiar faces by newborns. *Infant Behavior and Development*, **15**, 265–269.

Wasz-Hockert, O., Lind, J., Vuorenkoski, V., Partanen, T. & Valanne, E. (1968) The infant cry: A spectrographic and auditory analysis. *Clinics in Developmental Medicine*, **29**. London: Spastics International Medicine Publications.

Weissenborn, J., Goodluck, H. & Roeper, T. (1992) Introduction: Old and new problems in the study of language acquisition. In J. Weissenborn, H. Goodluck & T. Roeper (Eds), *Theoretical Issues in Language Acquisition*. Hillsdale, NJ: Erlbaum.

Wellman, H. M. (1990) *The Child's Theory of Mind*. MIT Press, Cambridge, MA.

Wells, C. G. & Robinson, W. P. (1982) The role of adult speech in language development. In C. Fraser and K. Scherer (Eds), *The Social Psychology of Language*. Cambridge: Cambridge University Press.

Werker, J. F. & McLeod, P. J (1989) Infant preference for both male and female infant-directed-talk: A developmental study of attentional and affective responsiveness. *Canadian J. Psychology*, **43**, 230–246.

Werner, H. & Kaplan, B. (1963) *Symbol Formation: An Organismic- Developmental Approach to Language and the Expression of Thought*. New York: Wiley.

Wexler, K. & Culicover, P. (1980) *Formal Principles of Language Acquisition*. Cambridge, MA: MIT Press.

Wexler, K. & Manzini, M. R. (1987) Parameters and learnability. In T. Roeper & E. Williams (Eds), *Paramenter Setting*. Dordrecht: Reidel.

Whitehurst, G. J., Fischel, C. J., Lonigan, C. J., Valdez-Menchaca, M. C., DeBaryshe, B. D. & Caulfield, M. B. (1988) Verbal interaction in families of normal and expressive-language-delayed children. *Development Psychology*, **24**, No. 5, 690–699.

Whitehurst, G. J. & Valden-Menchaca, M. C. (1988) What is the role of reinforcement in early language acquisition? *Child Development*, **59**, 430–440.

Whitehurst, G. J. & Vasta, R. (1975) Is language acquired through imitation? *J. Psycholinguistic Research*, **4**, 1–12.

Wilbur, R. B. (1987) *American Sign Language: Linguistics and Applied Dimensions*. San Diego: College-Hill Press.

Williams, J. C. P., Barratt-Boyes, B. G. & Lowe, J. B. (1961) Supravalvular aortic stenosis. *Circulation*, **24**, 1311–1318.

Wilson, B. & Peters, A. M. (1988) What are you cookin' on a Hot? Movement constraints in the speech of a three-year-old child. *Language*, **64**, No. 2.

Wing, L. (1988) The autistic continuum. In L. Wing (Ed.), *Aspects of Autism: Biological Research*. London: Gaskell.

Wittgenstein, L. (1958) *Philosophical Investigations*, trans. G. E. M. Anscombe. London: Macmillan.

Wulff, S. B. (1985) The symbolic and object play of a child with autism: A review. *J. Autism and Development Disorders*, **15**, 139–148.

Yarrow, L. J. (1964) Separation from parents during early childhood. In M. L. Hoffman & L. W. Hoffman (Eds), *Review of Child Development Research*. New York: Russel Sage Foundation.

Younger, B. A. & Cohen L. B. (1983) Infant perception of correlations among attributes. *Child Development*, **54**, 858–867.

Zajonc, R. B., Murphy, S. T. & Inglehart, M. (1989) Feeling and facial efference: Implications of the vascular theory of emotion. *Psychological Review*, **96**, 395–416.

Zazzo, R. (1978) Genesis and peculiarities of the personality of twins. In W. E. Nance, G. Allen & P. Parisi (Eds), *Twin Research. Progress in Clinical and Biological Research: Psychology and Methodology*. New York: Liss.

Zukow, P. G. (1990) Socio-perceptual bases for the emergence of language: An alternative to innatist approaches. *Developmental Psychobiology*, **23**, 705–726.

AUTHOR INDEX

SUBJECT INDEX